362.76 / LYO

D0413706

This book is due for return on or before the last date shown below.

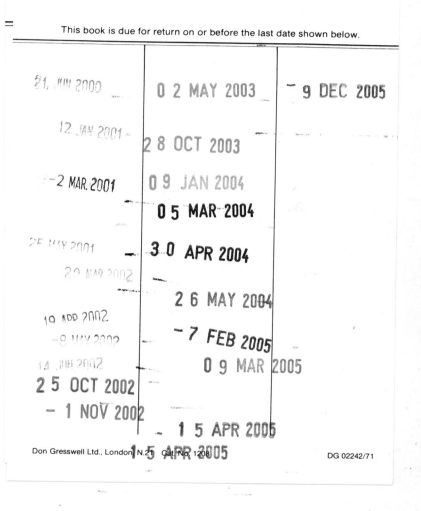

21. JUN 2000   0 2 MAY 2003   ‾9 DEC 2005

12 JAN 2001   2 8 OCT 2003

‾2 MAR. 2001   0 9 JAN 2004

                      0 5 MAR 2004

2E MAY 2001   ‾3 0 APR 2004

2 0 MAR 2002

                      2 6 MAY 2004

19 APR 2002

‾8 MAY 2002   ‾7 FEB 2005

14 JUN 2002   0 9 MAR 2005

2 5 OCT 2002

‾1 NOV 2002

                      ‾1 5 APR 2005

Don Gresswell Ltd., London, N.21   Cat. No. 1208   1 5 APR 2005   DG 02242/71

ALLT-YR-YN LIBRARY

CHILD ABUSE

Second edition

Christina Lyon LLB, Solicitor
Professor of Common Law
University of Liverpool

Peter de Cruz PhD
Lecturer in Law
University of Keele

ALLT-YR-YN LIBRARY

GWENT COLLEGE OF HIGHER EDUCATION LIBRARY

FAMILY LAW
1993

Published by Family Law
an imprint of Jordan Publishing Limited
21 St Thomas Street
Bristol BS1 6JS

© Jordan Publishing Limited 1993

All rights reserved. No part of this publication may be
reproduced, stored in a retrieval system, or transmitted in
any way or by any means, including photocopying or recording,
without the written permission of the copyright holder,
application for which should be addressed to the publisher.

This book is sold subject to the Standard Conditions of Sale
of Net Books and may not be resold in the UK below the net
price fixed by Jordans.

British Library Cataloguing-in-Publication Data

A catalogue record for this book is available
from the British Library

ISBN 0 85308 136 0

Typeset by Rowland Phototypesetting Limited, Bury St Edmunds, Suffolk
Printed in Great Britain by Henry Ling Limited, The Dorset Press, Dorchester

DEDICATION

This book is dedicated to Adrian and Lois, without whose support, love and encouragement it could not have been completed, and, of course, to our children, Sasha and David Lyon, and Stephen and David de Cruz.

ACKNOWLEDGMENTS

The authors would like to acknowledge the help of the following people for expressing views or giving information on matters contained in these pages: Guy Mitchell, Senior Guardian ad Litem, Boys and Girls Welfare Society, Cheadle, Cheshire and sometime lecturer on the Diploma in Child Care Law and Practice, Keele University; Jenny McEwan, Senior Lecturer in Law, Keele University; Margaret Leighton, Area Officer, Wirral Social Services; Judith Timms, Director, IRCHIN; Chief Inspector Frank Hope and Chief Superintendent Kenneth Hoskisson, Merseyside Police; Professor Robert Bluglass, Professor of Forensic Psychiatry at Reaside Clinic at the University of Birmingham; Anthony Townsend of the Conduct, Health and Standards Division of the General Medical Council; Ann Sommerville, secretary of the Medical Ethics Committee of the British Medical Association; Dr Susan Shepherd of the Department of Health; Adrian Lyon, Barrister at Law; and finally to the many students on the Keele University Diploma and MA courses in Child Care Law and Practice. We would also like to acknowledge the assistance of Miss Andrea Jackson who spent many hours on Lexis searching for cases before they were reported in any official series of law reports.

Most importantly of all, we acknowledge with extreme gratitude, the assistance provided by the secretarial staff at Keele University Law Department, namely Jackie Greatbatch, Freda Mainwaring, Margaret Hollins and June Poppleton.

FOREWORD

The present working of the Children Act is comprehensively reviewed in the second edition of *Child Abuse*. It sets out the legal framework of protection for children under the Act and discusses the judicial approach in the reported decisions, with comments, for instance, on what is seen as the retreat from *Gillick*. There is step by step advice on the intervention process in applying to the courts, with a section on judicial review, its place in child cases and its limitations. There is helpful advice on how to appeal, including the value to the appellate court of a chronology of principal events. Both the criminal and civil jurisdictions are referred to in detail, with useful discussion on the evidence of children in each venue.

The book is equally valuable in areas of the Act outside the courts. It gives a comprehensive insight into the duties of the local authorities set out in the Act and regulations, and explained in the multiplicity of DOH guidelines. In Chapters 4 and 5, the enormous importance of effective inter-agency co-operation is stressed and areas of conflict and likely barriers to communication between the agencies indicated. Chapter 6 sets out the rights and duties of guardians ad litem and comments upon the complaints procedures.

One feature of the book is the recognition throughout that the Act and the structure it created is intended to benefit children. It criticises failures in the system, such as access by a child to the complaints procedures revealed to be glaringly unavailable in recent children's homes inquiries.

This is a careful and thoughtful review of the present law and practice of protection of children from child abuse in its widest definition. It is an admirable book which ought to be required reading for judges, lawyers, guardians, social workers, the medical profession and all those who are involved in child care.

Dame Elizabeth Butler-Sloss DBE
August 1993

PREFACE

Child Abuse is making its appearance as a second edition, but both of us would like to take this opportunity to emphasise, as we are sure will be obvious to those familiar with the first edition, that we have undertaken a complete rewriting of the book. This has, of course, been necessitated by the complete reform of the civil law relating to children effected by the Children Act 1989 and the major reforms to the criminal justice system effected by the Criminal Justice Act 1991. In writing the book de novo as it were, we have, however, endeavoured to respond to a number of constructive criticisms and suggestions made by students, academic colleagues, and those in professional practice and various reviewers of the first edition. We have completely reorganised the structure of the book in order to make it both more coherent and comprehensible.

In the preface to the first edition, we noted that whilst the 1960s may have been the decade in which child abuse was discovered by the experts (see Kempe, Silverman, Steele, Droegemuller and Silver 'The Battered Child Syndrome' (1962) *Journal of American Medical Association* at pp 17 to 24), the following two decades seemed to produce a plethora of horrific child abuse cases. At the time of writing that preface, we were able to report that, including the report of the inquiry into events in Cleveland in 1987, there had been some 35 official inquiry reports into child abuse cases, the bulk of these occurring where children had died. Now, in 1993, one is forced to the depressing conclusion that the categories of child abuse never seem to close. Whilst Cleveland was unusual at the time of writing the first edition, in that it focused attention on failures by social services departments in the way in which they conducted child abuse investigations, subsequent inquiries, such as Pindown and the Orkney inquiry, have demonstrated that this was not an isolated incident. In addition, during the 1980s and early 1990s, increasing attention has focused on reports of child abuse occurring where children have been looked after by local authorities or in other establishments. Thus, the report on the Pindown regime (*The Pindown Experience and the Protection of Children: The Report of the Staffordshire Child Care Inquiry* (1991, Staffordshire Social Services) ('the *Pindown Report*')) identified a number of areas of potentially abusive treatment of children with challenging behaviour in our residential children's homes, and this was not an isolated example. Certainly, concerns about the care of children being looked after by local authorities had surfaced many times since *Kincora* (see the *Hughes Report, Report of the Inquiry into Kincora Boys Hostel* (1983, HMSO)). Thus, throughout the last decade there have been various reports into care provided at institutions run by different local authorities which have raised some serious doubts about the quality of that care. (See, for example: the *Report of the Inquiry into the conduct of Leeway's Children's Home* (1985, London Borough of Lewisham); the report of the then Department of Health and Social Security into the conduct of Melanie Klein House by Greenwich Social Services (1988, DHSS); and the NAYPIC's *Report on Violations of the basic human rights of young people in the care of the London Borough of Greenwich and Other Local Authorities*, (1990, London).) The *Pindown Report* seemed to open the floodgates further, and that report has been followed by the report of the Ty Mawr Community Home Inquiry conducted by Williams and McCreadie (1992, Gwent County Council) which considered complaints of abuse of children in the home run by Gwent Social Services. The *Pindown Report* also led to two reports published in early 1993 relating to the abuse of children in the care of Leicestershire Social Services by Frank Beck and other child care officers: the Kirkwood Inquiry *Management Responses to Complaints and Evidence of Abuse, Malpractice and other related matters in Leicestershire in the light of the trial of Frank Beck and other Child Care Officers for the period 1973–1976* (1993, Leicestershire County Council); and the Police Complaints Authority inquiry report *The Inquiry into Police Investigations of Complaints of Child and Sexual Abuse in Leicestershire Children's Homes* (1993), known as 'the *PCA Report*'. Even the Department of Health's own facilities have not escaped criticism. Thus, in 1991 an independent inquiry had to be set up to investigate complaints made by children at the St Charles Youth Treatment Centre in Essex (1991, DOH), the findings of which led to the suspension of the Centre's director, deputy-director and another staff member pending a disciplinary inquiry, wholesale management reorganisation and the appointment of a new advisory group to oversee children's rights both at St Charles and the other centre at Glenthorne in Birmingham. Other inquiries into the treatment of disabled children in establishments run by Lancashire social services and also the publication of the *Castle Hill Report* (1992), dealing with a residential school in Shropshire, make it clear that all children, even especially vulnerable children, are at risk wherever they are being looked after.

In the wake of a rising tide of allegations of maltreatment of children in residential establishments, and following the trial and conviction of Frank Beck, the Government announced, in January 1992, the establishment of a Committee of Inquiry under the chairmanship of Norman Warner. The terms of reference of that Committee were:

> 'to examine selection and recruitment methods and criteria for staff working in children's homes and recommend practicable improvements; to make such further examination as the Committee may consider justified of management and other issues relevant to the protection

of children and young people and to the support and guidance of staff in such homes; and to report with recommendations to the Secretary of State for Health'.

That report *Choosing with Care* (1992, HMSO) ('the *Warner Committee Report*') made a whole series of recommendations for the better development, management and running of residential children's homes and highlighted a number of issues upon which staff in such homes felt in need of further guidance. The report pointed out that staff wanted and needed advice on how to maintain good order when they had highly disturbed and violent children in a home. In Recommendation 76 of the *Warner Committee Report* (see **2.18.3** below) the Committee stated that 'The Government should issue *full* guidance for staff on the issues of control, restraint and physical contact with children in residential care; keep this up-to-date; and reinforce it by ensuring the provision of authoritative training material that allows staff to apply the guidance in real situations' (authors' emphasis added) (at pp 156 and 199). Even before the publication of the *Warner Committee Report*, the DOH had sent out a consultative draft document in August 1992, entitled *Guidance on Permissible Forms of Control in Children's Residential Care*, which was widely criticised for failing to offer enough positive advice about the control of volatile young people, and in early 1993 various members of the Government began to voice concerns about the behaviour and lack of real control over young offenders who are remanded to local authority accommodation. At this point, the Home Secretary announced that the guidance on the care and control of such troublesome children was being re-evaluated and it was issued in its substantially amended, final form on 28 April 1993 (see *Guidance on Permissible Forms of Control in Children's Residential Care* (1993, DOH and Local Authority Circular (93) 13)). This guidance is considered in Chapter 7. Reference can also be made to a further DOH guidance *Safe and Sound* (not yet published), which will deal with a range of management and practice issues, including control and discipline, which apply specifically to secure accommodation. Both volumes of guidance reflect increased concern felt by the Government and the wider public that legislation may have gone too far in stressing the rights of children at the expense of upholding the rights and responsibilities of parents and professionals in supervising them. Achieving the right balance so that we do not overstep the thin line between control and abuse is extremely difficult to achieve and the tortuous language of the guidance at times reflects the struggle to do so.

The various inquiry reports had further highlighted shortcomings in the legal system and its social work practice base which had been known about for a considerable number of years. It was hoped that the enactment of the Children Act 1989, together with the publication of the guidance issued by the DOH concerning the implementation of the Act and the good practice which should flow from it, *The Children Act 1989 Guidance and Regulations* (1991, HMSO), would go some way towards reducing the numbers of children at risk from abuse within our society generally. Whilst our problem with the first edition of this book was the complexity of the changes in child care law, different and no less difficult problems surfaced in the writing of this second edition. The publication of *The Children Act 1989 Guidance and Regulations* by the DOH has undoubtedly contributed to the development of the best possible practice in relation to working with children all round the country, so that any attempt to describe the legal framework of the Children Act 1989 must now take place in the context of such guidance. This has led to an increase in the number of pages in what was originally intended to be as succinct an analysis of the law and practice relating to the protection of children as was possible. We have had, therefore, not only to consider statutory provisions, but also *The Children Act 1989 Guidance and Regulations* and guidance issued by a range of other agencies, such as the General Medical Council, the British Medical Association, the Children Act Advisory Committee and other concerned professional bodies.

It is hoped that our analysis of the practice and procedure relating to child protection will inform practitioners not only of the role which they may play in particular proceedings, but also of the contributions which others may make before a decision is reached that a case must be taken to court. In this light, we have also had to devote considerable attention to DOH and other guidelines on inter-agency and multi-disciplinary co-operation, which is essential if children are to be protected and if we are to strive towards the goal of eradicating child abuse from our society. This may be somewhat of a Utopian dream, but both professional practice and the law in child abuse cases should operate to lead towards the fulfilment of that goal, not to impede it. As we indicate in our concluding chapter, we believe that the Children Act 1989, as a piece of legislation, goes a long way towards achieving that aim but early claims that such was the case may have proved premature. Thus, whilst the *Children Act Report 1992* (1993, DOH) shows a quite dramatic fall in the number of children on local authority child protection registers from 45,300 in 1991 to 38,600 in 1992, the *Children Act Advisory Committee Report 1991/92* (1992) sounds a note of caution in that the latter part of 1992 revealed a marked upturn in court activity in child protection cases. In addition, the number of children who were made the subject of care orders in 1992 was extrapolated from the first nine months to provide a figure of 36,000 compared with 41,638 such orders made in 1991. As all the reports have identified, however, there remains a problem with regard to resources which has yet to be seriously addressed by the Government or, indeed, by any political party (see, further, Chapter 10 below).

Finally, it should be made clear that responsibility for writing this book was divided more or less equally between us, with each commenting and revising drafts of each other's chapters. Nevertheless, Professor Lyon wrote the whole of the introduction, Chapters 3, 4, 6, 8, half of Chapter 9 and Chapter 10 and was responsible for all the diagrams and charts. Dr de Cruz wrote Chapters 1, 2, 5, **6.13** to **6.18** in Chapter 6, 7 and half of Chapter 9.

Our publishers, Jordans, have borne, with extreme fortitude and patience, our constant requests to defer submitting the manuscript until a number of reports and volumes of guidance had been issued and until various cases had been decided, but we suspect they felt that it would never be delivered. We had, perforce, finally to decide on a cut-off date and whilst it was possible to incorporate some late amendments with reference to new guidance, reports and to particular decisions in cases before the courts, we have endeavoured to state the law as it stands at 14 March 1993.

Professor Christina Lyon
Dr Peter de Cruz
March 1993

CONTENTS

TABLE OF CASES

TABLE OF STATUTES

TABLE OF STATUTORY INSTRUMENTS

LIST OF ABBREVIATIONS

1989 Act	Children Act 1989
1990 Order	Children (Admissibility of Hearsay Evidence) Order 1990, SI 1990/143
1991 Order	Children (Admissibility of Hearsay Evidence) Order 1991, SI 1991/1115
1993 Order	Children (Admissibility of Hearsay Evidence) Order 1993, SI 1993/621
ACPC	Area child protection committee
ASC	Advice and Advocacy Services for Children
The Board	Criminal Injuries Compensation Board
C(AP)O 1991	Children (Allocation of Proceedings) Order 1991, SI 1991/1667
CJA 1988	Criminal Justice Act 1988
CJA 1991	Criminal Justice Act 1991
CPR	Child Protection Register
CPS	Crown Prosecution Service
C(SA)R 1991	Children (Secure Accommodation) Regulations 1991, SI 1991/1501
C(SA)(A)R 1992	Children (Secure Accommodation) (Amendment) Regulations 1992, SI 1992/2117
CYPA 1933	Children and Young Persons Act 1933
CYPA 1963	Children and Young Persons Act 1963
CYPA 1969	Children and Young Persons Act 1969
DPP	Department of Public Prosecutions
EPO	Emergency protection order
FCBC	Family court business committee
FPC(CA 1989)R 1991	Family Proceedings Courts (Children Act 1989) Rules 1991, SI 1991/1395
FPR 1991	Family Proceedings Rules 1991, SI 1991/1247
MCA 1980	Magistrates' Courts Act 1980
MC(CYP)R 1992	Magistrates' Courts (Children and Young Persons) Rules 1992, SI 1992/207
MCR 1981	Magistrates' Courts Rules 1981, SI 1981/552
MoGP	*Memorandum of Good Practice on Videorecorded Interviews with Child Witnesses for Criminal Proceedings* (1992, DOH)
NCH	National Children's Home
NSPCC	National Society for the Prevention of Cruelty to Children
PACE Code	The Police and Criminal Evidence Code of Practice
PACEA 1984	Police and Criminal Evidence Act 1984
PCA	Police Complaints Authority
RAD	Reflex anal dilation
RP(C)R 1991	Representations Procedure (Children) Regulations 1991, SI 1991/894
RSSPCC	Royal Scottish Society for the Prevention of Cruelty to Children
The scheme	Criminal Injuries Compensation Scheme
SSI	Social Security Inspectorate

CHAPTER ONE

Forms of Child Abuse

1.1 Types of abuse

The phenomenon of 'child abuse' appears to have become increasingly common in modern society, provoking widespread public concern, and highlighting a conflict between the need to recognise parental rights and the rights of children to protection from harm or abuse. Yet the maltreatment of children has been considered reprehensible since at least the last half of the nineteenth century, when the National Association for the Prevention of Cruelty to Children ('NSPCC') was formed in 1866. There is no hard evidence that acts of child abuse have multiplied, only that public awareness of the problem has increased, closer monitoring of families and more effective reporting of incidents now occurs as well as greater professional recognition of its existence and a heightened social unwillingness to tolerate various forms of abuse.

In the last two decades or so, the focus tended to be on child abuse within the nuclear family, and not on acts of abuse perpetrated by strangers or professional carers. Many recent cases have involved alleged or proven cases of abuse by a parent or someone entrusted with a child's care. However, information has now come to light which suggests that abuse of children in children's homes and special schools has been taking place, in some cases, for at least 20 years (see *The Leicestershire Inquiry 1992 (The Kirkwood Report)* (1993, Leicestershire Social Services)) and in others, within the last decade (see *The Pindown Experience and the Protection of Children: The Report of the Staffordshire Child Care Inquiry* (1991) ('the *Pindown Report*') discussed in Chapter 2).

Child abuse is now widely recognised as encompassing physical harm and neglect, social harm, sexual abuse and emotional harm. Thus, the emphasis has now shifted to what constitutes unacceptable parental behaviour.

Other forms of child abuse which have recently attracted media attention have been ritual abuse, satanic abuse (not necessarily synonymous) and allied forms of 'organised abuse', for example by 'sex rings' or groups of people who orchestrate the carrying out of child abuse on several children in some way or other (see **1.3.1** below). In 1993, the NSPCC published two reports (Marchant and Page *Bridging the Gap* (1992); Westcott *Abuse of Children and*

with Disabilities (1992)) which suggest that a number of disabled chil-
.n are being sexually abused and that this is going undetected because the
public is unwilling to believe that anyone could mistreat a child unable to
walk or speak (see Chapter 2).

Another recent development which has spawned several public and private
inquiries has been 'abuse within the system' or abuse of children by care
staff which has taken place in residential children's homes (see Chapter 2).
This has led to immediate calls for reforms in the law relating to children's
residential care homes.

1.2 Definitional issues

As yet, there is still no universally agreed, all-encompassing definition of
child abuse which has been formulated by either researchers, Parliament or
the courts. Medical descriptions of physical injuries have steadily been
expanded to include a wide range of physically observable phenomena, social
work definitions, Department of Health ('DOH') guidelines (eg *Working
Together under the Children Act 1989* (1991, DOH) ('*Working Together*')),
statutory definitions (eg s 1 of the Children and Young Persons Act 1933)
and sociological and political definitions.

Despite the implementation of the Children Act 1989 in October 1991,
cases dealt with under the Act have continued to expose defects in the new
law and the difficulties faced in seeking to strike the right balance between
competing aims and objectives in social policy and child law. Statistics on
child abuse only give one aspect of the extent of the problem.

In the report compiled by the NSPCC on child abuse trends in England
and Wales (*Child Abuse Trends in England and Wales 1988–90* (1992,
NSPCC)), which covered the period 1973–90 and which included cases
reported to all child protection agencies, it appears that there was a marked
increase in the total number of registrations on the child protection registers
between 1984–86 and 1988–89, and the rate of registrations for sexual abuse
increased most between 1985–86 and reached a peak in 1987. In a 1992
report published by the National Children's Home ('NCH'), it was stated
that a third of people who sexually abuse children are under 18 (see *The
Report of the Committee of Enquiry into Children and Young People who Sexually
Abuse Other Children* (1992, NCH)). Numbers on the child protection registers in England increased from 41,200 in 1989 to 45,300 in 1991 (*Children
Act Report 1992* (1993, HMSO), at p 22), but figures for the period 14
October 1991 to 31 March 1992 show a fall of about 15 per cent in the
number of children on the child protection register, dropping from 45,300
to 38,600. There were originally 10 categories available under 'Reasons
for Registration': physical injury, sexual abuse, neglect, emotional abuse,
failure to thrive, grave concern and four other categories which gave various
permutations of neglect, physical and sexual abuse.

The deletion by the DOH of the use of the 'grave concern' category is now seen as an important element in accounting for the total number of registrations. This category was withdrawn in the 1991 version of the inter-agency guidance *Working Together*. In the 1988 version of *Working Together*, the 'grave concern' category constituted a fifth category of children whose situations did not fit into any of the four categories but were cases where 'social and medical assessments indicated that they were at significant risk of abuse'. The proportion of children newly registered in that category rose from 33 per cent in 1988 to 50 per cent in 1991, which amounted to 14,100 children out of a total of 28,300. With the implementation of the Children Act 1989 in 1991, the DOH amalgamated the 'grave concern' category with more specific categories of neglect and physical and sexual abuse. This means that, irrespective of whether a child has been abused or is merely thought likely to be at risk, he or she will show up under one or more of the same headings.

The DOH argues that different interpretations given to the category 'grave concern' was the reason for wide variations in the number of children on registers around the country, with some councils even recording three times more than the national average. The effects of removing this category will only properly emerge when statistics are available for the year from March 1992 to March 1993. The provisional statistics appear to indicate that certain children will ultimately disappear from the registers altogether and figures to the end of March 1992 show that the number of children in the 'grave concern' category fell from just over 21,000 in 1991 to 13,000. This approximates to the reduction of 6,700 in the total number of cases on the register.

It has been argued that 'socially defined phenomena cannot have boundaries which are necessarily fixed and permanent' (1976, NSPCC), and perhaps it is not desirable to have rigid definitions because it is a multi-faceted phenomenon. Case studies indicate a recognition that behaviour which can constitute child abuse can include not just purely the infliction of physical injuries, but also notions of social harm and sexual abuse of varying degrees. There is also a growing recognition of 'emotional' abuse. These concepts and forms of abuse are also recognised in the Children Act 1989 but, again, there are no statutory definitions of any of them (see, further, Chapter 2, on the incidence of abuse).

English child care law, therefore, consists of different pieces of legislation which lay down certain criteria whereby criminal or civil proceedings may be initiated, depending on the circumstances and severity of abuse. Non-legal definitions of abuse have ranged from 'serious physical injuries', to 'emotional maltreatment', to 'neglect'. Child abuse has been described as: 'harm to children that results from human action that is proscribed, proximate and preventable' (Finkelhor and Corbin 'Child Abuse as an International Issue' (1988) 12 *Child Abuse and Neglect* 40). A broad consensus about extreme or obvious cases may be found but marginal cases will continue to provide problems in interpretation. For example, since s 31(2) of the Children Act 1989 now establishes proof of 'significant harm' caused by a lack of reasonable parental care as the central criterion enabling various child protection court orders to be made under the Act, the question arises as to the circumstances in which harm may be said to be 'significant' (see Chapter 4).

The current DOH Guide for social workers, *Protecting Children: A Guide for Social Workers Undertaking Comprehensive Assessment* (1988, DOH) states: 'Judgment as to what constitutes abuse is . . . in part a matter of degree, opinion and values'. The definitional question is clearly not simply a matter of terminological neutrality since, as Richard Gelles puts it in 'A Profile of Violence Towards Children in the United States', presented at the Anneberg School of Communications Conference *Child Abuse Roots and Policy Options* in 1978 (at pp 1 to 2):

> 'The term "child abuse" is a political concept which is used to attract attention to a phenomenon which is considered undesirable or deviant. As a political issue, "child abuse" defies logical and precise scientific definition. Malnourishment, sexual abuse, failure to feed and clothe a child, beating a child, torturing a child, withholding medical care from a child, allowing a child to live in a "deprived or depraved" environment, and helping a child to stay out of school have all been defined at various times and in various laws as "child abuse". The definition of child abuse varies over time, across cultures, and between social and cultural groups.'

Among the many important definitions of abuse have been the Kempe, Silverman, Steele, Droegemuller and Silver notion of the 'battered child' syndrome (see 'The Battered Child Syndrome' (1962) *Journal of American Medical Association* at pp 17 to 24) and David Gil, in 'Unraveling Child Abuse' (1975) *American Journal of Orthopsychiatry* at pp 346 to 354:

> '. . . any act of commission or omission by individuals, institutions or society as a whole, and any conditions resulting from such acts or inaction, which deprive children of equal rights and liberties, and/or interfere with their optimal development, constitute by definition abusive or neglectful acts or conditions.'

Neuberger, in 'The Myth of the Battered Child Syndrome' (1973) 40 *Current Medical Dialog* at pp 327 to 330, has described child abuse as 'an illness with or without inflicted injury, stemming from situations in his home setting which threaten a child's survival'.

Although definitional debates may be regarded as reflective of ideological differences and thus intractable (eg CF Stoll 'Images of Man and Social Control' (1968) 47 *Social Forces* at p 119), a lack of definitional uniformity may reveal a 'primitive' theoretical level of child abuse research. Without a standardised definition, research findings and data are misleading because identical labels may be used to describe different phenomena. Policy makers [thus have] a problem whose 'magnitude, roots and solutions remain undefined' (Edward Zigler 'Controlling Child Abuse: Do we have the Knowledge and/or the Will?' in Gerbner, Ross and Zigler (eds) *Child Abuse: An Agenda for Action* (1980, OUP)). Hence, even the answer to the common question of how prevalent child abuse is, is largely dependent on the particular definition of the forms of child abuse that one is seeking to monitor and measure.

Dr Alan Gilmour, former Director of the NSPCC, concedes that the fact that there were so many definitions shows that none is adequate, but suggested a working definition: 'child abuse occurs when any avoidable act, or avoidable failure to act, adversely affects the physical, mental or emotional well-being of a child' (Gilmour *Innocent Victims: Questions of Child Abuse* (1988, M Joseph) at p 11).

Gilmour defines an 'avoidable act' as something that happened which need not have happened, but which need not have been deliberate, such as shaking a child in anger which causes a brain haemorrhage. The notion of avoidable harm is, of course, one which social workers and lawyers used to work with, under the former care grounds (contained in the Children and Young Persons Act 1969) which have since been repealed by the Children Act 1989 and replaced by the notion of 'significant harm' (see Chapters 3 and 4).

Four forms of child abuse are also listed by the NSPCC and the National Children's Home ('NCH'), namely: *'physical abuse'* ('when a child is physically hurt or injured'); *'emotional abuse'* ('when a child is deprived of love, attention and care and may be subject to verbal attacks and threats'); *'sexual abuse'* ('sexual contact between a child and adult for the purpose of the adult's sexual gratification'); and *'neglect'* ('where there is persistent failure to meet the physical, emotional and intellectual needs of the child').

1.3 *Working Together*: the inter-agency guidance

In *Working Together* there are no exhaustive definitions of child abuse, since the Children Act 1989 has now introduced the 'significant harm' criterion. However, guidance is given in the form of working definitions on the criteria to be considered when considering whether to place a child on the child protection register. It should be noted that Munchausen's syndrome by proxy has been included under 'physical injury', probably as a result of the publicity that was generated by the *Tameside* case (unreported) in 1987. This syndrome occurs where one parent, usually the mother, fabricates illness on behalf of her child by inducing physical signs of illness or by deliberately misleading the physician into believing the child is ill. The effect of this is that the child is abused by unnecessary admission to hospital, extensive medical investigation and unnecessary treatment (see Williams 'Munchausen Syndrome By Proxy: A Bizarre Form of Child Abuse' [1986] Fam Law 32). In some reported cases, the child has not only suffered as a consequence of this parental behaviour but has even died or suffered permanent disablement (see Meadow *Archives of Disease in Childhood* (1985) Vol 60 at pp 385 to 393). A particularly worrying feature of these cases is that the mothers involved appear to be quite normal and loving and coping well with the 'illness' of their child. Listening to minor exaggerations from a parent about a child's illnesses are part of a paediatrician's lot but it is when major falsifications occur that the syndrome arises by proxy. This is yet another phenomenon that will need to be detected, preferably in consultation with other professionals in the field.

The guidance given in *Working Together* which is reproduced in many local authority child protection procedures is to be found in Part 6 of that document.

'*6.40* The following categories should be used for the register and for statistical purposes. They are intended to provide definitions as a guide for those using the register . . . In some instances, more than one category of registration may be appropriate.

Neglect: The persistent or severe neglect of a child, or the failure to protect a child from exposure to any kind of danger, including cold or starvation, or extreme failure to carry out important aspects of care, resulting in the significant impairment of the child's health or development, including non-organic failure to thrive.

Physical injury: Actual or likely physical injury to a child, or failure to prevent physical injury (or suffering) to a child including deliberate poisoning, suffocation and Munchausen's syndrome by proxy.

Sexual abuse: Actual or likely sexual exploitation of a child or adolescent. The child may be dependent and/or developmentally immature.

Emotional abuse: Actual or likely severe adverse effect on the emotional and behavioural development of a child caused by persistent or severe emotional ill-treatment or rejection. All abuse involves some emotional ill-treatment. This category should be used where it is the main or sole form of abuse.

6.41 These categories for child protection register purposes do not tie in precisely with the definition of "significant harm" in section 31 of the Children Act which will be relevant if court proceedings are initiated. For example, with a case of neglect it will be necessary to consider whether it involves "ill-treatment" or "impairment of health or development" (in each case as defined by the Act). The Courts may well provide an interpretation of "sexual abuse" (which is not defined in the Act) which is different from that used in particular cases, in which case their definition should be used in relation to those cases.'

1.3.1 Organised abuse

Working Together also refers to *organised abuse*, which it describes as 'a generic term which covers abuse which may involve a number of abusers, a number of abused children and young people and often encompasses different forms of abuse. It involves, to a greater or lesser extent, an element of organisation' (at para 5.26.1). Paragraph 5.26.2 goes on to say that 'a wide range of activity is covered by this term, from small paedophile or pornographic rings, often but not always, organised for profit, with most participants knowing each other, to large networks of individual groups of families which may be spread widely and in which not all participants will be known to each other'. It then explains that 'some organised groups may use bizarre or ritualised behaviour, sometimes associated with particular "belief" systems'. Thus, forms of organised abuse may or may not involve the use of satanic rituals and it is incorrect to simply classify ritualistic and organised abuse as one and the same form of child abuse (see, further, Chapter 2). Paragraph 5.26.2 of the guide stresses that 'research suggests some caution in sharp distinctions between types of abuser'.

1.4 The Scottish approach

The Scottish Office document *Effective Intervention – Child Abuse – Guidance on Co-operation in Scotland* (1989) deals with definitions as follows.

'2.6 All local agreements or definitions should take account of existing guidance which set out the general categories of abuse. These are:

Physical Injury: ie an injury 'inflicted, or poisonous substance administered, or not knowingly prevented, by a person having charge of a child.

Physical Neglect: Where this has been persistent or severe.

Failure to Thrive: Where medical opinion confirms that this is due to neglect.

Children at Risk: ie a child at risk of abuse or in a household where an adult has abused a child or another child has been abused and is considered to be at risk.'

In addition, definitions should be developed of sexual abuse and emotional abuse, as several areas already have done.

'2.7 In agreeing definitions of Sexual Abuse and Emotional Abuse, Area Review Committees may find it helpful to note the following formulations:

Sexual Abuse: The involvement of dependent, developmentally immature children and adolescents in sexual activities they do not truly comprehend, to which they are unable to give informed consent, or that violate the social taboos of family roles.'

Two definitions are provided for emotional abuse, the first identical to the English *Working Together* model, first published in 1988, which the Scottish guidance acknowledges. The second appears to be derived from the Lothian Area Review Committee guidelines of April 1988 at p 11.

'Emotional Abuse: The severe adverse effect on the behaviour and emotional development of a child caused by persistent or severe emotional ill-treatment or rejection. All abuse involves some emotional ill-treatment; this category should be used where it is the main or sole form of abuse.

Emotional Abuse: The severe impairment of social and emotional development, it is the (eventual) consequences of repeated and persistent
   withholding of affection
   criticism
   verbal abuse
   scapegoating for all the family's problems
   rejection, or threat of rejection, to the child's distress
   lack of contact and interaction with the child in play
   lack of communication
   wilful destruction of a child's confidence in his/her own competence
   berating the child in front of others.
This may result in over-anxiety in the child; avoidance of contacts outside the home; low self-esteem; limited capacity for enjoyment; serious aggression; impulsive behaviour; retardation of physical development through deprivation.'

The definition used for sexual abuse is the well-known one used by Schechter and Roberge in 'Sexual Exploitation' in Helfer and Kempe (eds) *Child Abuse and Neglect: The Family and the Community* (1976, Ballinger) which was originally contained in the earlier version of *Working Together*, published by the DOH.

1.5 Physical abuse – non-accidental abuse

The first main category of abuse encompasses parental child-battering, institutional maltreatment of children, including child-battering, and child homicide. It covers a wide range of actions from spanking and other forms of 'justifiable chastisement' to grievous bodily harm, such as burning parts of the child with cigarettes, dipping the child into scalding hot water (see *R v Durkin* (1989) *The Times*, June 20, discussed at **7.23** below), punching, kicking, shaking, biting, beating a child until he is unconscious, breaking a child's limbs or, as in one case, putting a child into a washing machine.

The list of physically abusive acts continues to grow. A 1992 newspaper report described how a father beat and starved his four-year-old daughter to death and locked her in a stinking bedroom for many months and, in a case reported in February 1993, a mother who was suffering from a depressive illness, drowned her seven-week-old baby in a kitchen sink.

As far as parents are concerned, the punishment meted out to the child has to go beyond moderate and reasonable punishment before the parent can be held criminally liable for any injuries caused (*R v Hopley* (1860) 2 F & F 202). The power to discipline must be exercised reasonably. Reasonableness must be exercised in the light of all the circumstances of the case, with particular reference to the age, physical condition, intellectual understanding and emotional maturity of the child, and the reason for administering the punishment, for instance to protect him from immediate or imminent danger.

A parent may also be criminally liable for failing to fulfil his duty to protect the child from physical harm by failing to provide the necessities of life. This duty to protect arises at common law whenever anyone old enough to be held legally responsible assumes the care of someone who, because of immaturity or disability, is unable to look after himself. In response to the judiciary's reluctance to enforce this duty rigorously, Parliament passed the Children and Young Persons Act 1933 ('CYPA 1933') (see Chapter 7).

A person *in loco parentis* has the power to discipline and punish. The legal criterion to decide when a person stands *in loco parentis* is whether the care and control (or 'charge') of the child has been entrusted to the person by the parent, or where the parent is absent or there is no parent, care and control is assumed by that person (CYPA 1933, s 1 (see **7.2.1**)).

A debate on corporal punishment in schools was revived in early 1993 when the European Court confirmed that public schools could continue to administer limited corporal punishment such as 'slippering' (see *Costello-*

Roberts v The United Kingdom (1993) *The Independent*, March 26). This is discussed in greater detail in Chapter 7 on criminal proceedings in relation to the criminal infliction of punishment by teachers and parents.

1.5.1 Types of abuse reported to the NSPCC

According to NSPCC statistics, the types of abuse sustained during 1987 were: serious head injuries; long bone fractures; soft tissue fractures; and miscellaneous injuries, such as attempted strangulation, drowning, suffocation, ingestion, concussion and convulsions (see Gilmour *Innocent Victims: Questions of Child Abuse* (1988, M Joseph)).

In its sixth and final report, the NSPCC also gives an overview of the period 1973–90 and this study is the largest continuous survey of reported cases of child abuse ever conducted in the UK; the registers predate the introduction of official registers in 1976. Some of the findings are as follows.

'(i) There appears to have been a steady increase in the rate of recorded physical injury in the period 1979–1984 and a marked increase in 1984–5.

(ii) The average age of children registered for physical abuse almost doubled in the period 1976–1990 from 3.8 years to 7.1 years. Boys are more likely to be registered as physically abused, while girls are more likely to be registered as sexually abused. However, there is no correlation between gender and emotional abuse.'

It should be noted that while some injuries may be indisputably diagnosed as deliberately inflicted, others may not. In order to test one's suspicions, it would be necessary to ask further questions, such as whether the child shows other signs of abuse or whether there has been other reported abuse, for instance involving another child in the same household.

1.5.2 Neglect

Neglect includes cases where, rather than doing something wilfully cruel or vicious to a child, a child's caretaker fails to do something which is necessary for the child's well-being. Examples might be failure to provide food or drink or failure to seek medical attention for the child during serious illness. Other examples might be where there is a persistent failure to prevent a child from exposing himself or herself from danger or, as in the recent sensationalised case of the 'home alone mum', where a young child was apparently left alone at home by her mother who had gone to the Costa del Sol for a holiday. The mother claimed that she had in fact made childminding arrangements for the child and the Crown Prosecution Service ('CPS') has, in this case, decided not to prosecute the mother. Thus, the CPS and police will retain the discretion whether to proceed with a prosecution and there will doubtless be cases where sufficient evidence will be found for a prosecution to be initiated. The case of Heidi Koseda was one where her pitiful condition resulted from neglect and ill-treatment. Neglect is the form of abuse in which the mental element required by s 1 of the CYPA 1933 has been judicially considered (see Chapter 7).

1.5.3 Sexual abuse

The definition of child sexual abuse adopted by *Working Together*, to indicate one of the categories to be used for the child protection register, is:

> 'Actual or likely sexual exploitation of a child or adolescent. The child may be dependent and/or developmentally immature.'

Hence, on the face of it, the previous definition which derived from Schechter and Roberge in 'Sexual Exploitation', in Helfer and Kempe (eds) *Child Abuse and Neglect: The Family and the Community* (1976, Ballinger), is no longer being adopted. However, closer examination suggests that the new version is simply a more succinct definition. The former version mentioned sexual activities which the child 'did not truly comprehend', to which he or she was unable to give informed consent, or which 'violated the social taboos of family roles'. The use of the word 'exploitation' is arguably wide enough to cover these points.

In cases falling short of actual penetration or violence, it may be difficult to establish proof of harm to satisfy the Children Act 1989, s 31(2) criteria. Indeed, even where penetration or some form of violence has taken place, there are particular difficulties associated with proving sexual abuse of children (see, further, Chapter 2).

In a recent NSPCC report which deals with child protection of children with multiple disabilities, they suggest the following definition of sexual abuse:

> 'Any child below the age of consent may be deemed to have been sexually abused when a sexually mature person has, by design or by neglect of their usual societal or specific responsibilities in relation to the child, engaged or permitted the engagement of that child in any activity of a sexual nature which is intended to lead to the sexual gratification of the sexually mature person. This definition would apply whether or not this activity involves explicit coercion by any means, whether or not there is discernible harmful outcome in the short term.'

(See Marchant and Page *Bridging the Gap* (1992, NSPCC).)

1.5.4 Possible categories of sexual abuse

Ruth and Henry Kempe in *The Common Secret: Sexually Abused Children and Adolescents* (1984, WH Freeman) listed nine categories of sexual abuse.

(1) *Incest.* Any physical sexual activity between family members. The authors suggested 'family' should be interpreted as broadly as possible to include stepmothers and stepfathers, unrelated siblings connected through pre-

vious marriages who are living together as a unit, grandparents, and uncles and aunts who are living together permanently with the child. In English law, the legal definition of incest applies to acts of sexual inter- course between a man and a woman within the prohibited relationships which are: (a) a man and a woman who is his daughter, sister or half- sister, mother or granddaughter; and (b) a woman over 16 with a man who is her father, brother or half-brother, son or grandfather. Step- children are not covered by the law of incest but illegitimate children are. (See ss 10 to 11 of the Sexual Offences Act 1956 and s 54 of the Criminal Law Act 1977.)

(2) *Paedophilia.* The preference of an adult for pre-pubertal children as the means of achieving sexual excitement. The range of activity may include any of the forms of sexual abuse.

(3) *Exhibitionism (indecent exposure).* Involves the exposure of the genitals by an adult male to girls, boys and women. The exhibitionist seeks to experi- ence sexual excitement from the encounter (masturbation as well as exposure may take place).

(4) *Molestation.* Forms of indecent behaviour including touching, fondling, kissing the child, especially in the breast or genital areas, engaging in masturbation of the child, or urging the child to fondle or masturbate the adult. These activities may lead to mutual masturbation, or to oral-genital contact. Its limits are not clearly demarcated.

(5) *Sexual intercourse.* This can be with a child of either sex, including *fellatio* (oral-genital contact), sodomy (anal-genital contact), or penile-vaginal intercourse. As the Kempes emphasised, 'this may occur without physical violence through seduction, persuasion, bribes, use of authority or threats'.

(6) *Rape.* Sexual intercourse or attempted intercourse without the consent of the victim.

(7) *Sexual sadism.* Inflicting bodily injury on another as a means of obtaining sexual excitement.

(8) *Child pornography.* Arranging, photographing by still, video, or film pro- duction of any material involving minors in sexual acts, including other children, adults, or animals, regardless of consent given by the child's parent or guardian, and the distribution of such material in any form with or without profit, and the exhibition of such material, with or with- out profit. (See the Protection of Children Act 1978.)

(9) *Child prostitution.* Involving children in sex acts for profit and, generally, with frequently changing partners.

1.6 Emotional or psychological abuse

As *Working Together* acknowledges: 'All abuse involves some emotional ill-treatment' (at para 6.40); in other words, some element of emotional abuse. Indeed, Garbarino, Guttman and Seeley argue that 'Psychological maltreatment is the core issue in the broader picture of abuse and neglect. It provides the unifying theme and it is the critical aspect in the overwhelming majority of what appears as physical and sexual maltreatment cases' (*The Psychologically Battered Child: Strategies for Identification, Assessment and Intervention* (1986, Jossey Bass)).

Emotional or psychological abuse is, thus, gaining more widespread acceptance, although there continues to be some disagreement about its scope. Zigler argued that as a concept, it was difficult to comprehend, being in itself imprecise and having different meaning for different professionals (see Zigler *Child Abuse* in Gerbner, Ross and Zigler (eds) *An Agenda for Action* (1980, OUP)). No definition could cover every possible form of this type of abuse and the phrases used by professionals have included 'emotional neglect', 'mental injury', 'emotional deprivation', and 'psychological abuse' among others. Any number of acts or omissions might constitute a serious deprivation of love, care and attention that a child needs to such an extent that he or she suffers severe trauma and/or impairment of emotional and psychological development, such that there is a failure to thrive. One way to assess the emotional or psychological health of the child would be to consider whether the child's basic needs have been provided. These include: adequate physical care and protection; affection and encouragement; stimulation and instruction; proper discipline and control; and sufficient help to achieve independence (see Gilmour *Innocent Victims: Questions of Child Abuse* (1988, M Joseph), at Chapter 7). Another list of basic needs might include: the need for love and security; the need for new experiences; the need for praise and recognition; and the need for responsibility (Kellmer Pringle *The Needs of Children* (1974, Hutchinson: Unwin and Hyman)).

As far as the *Working Together* definition is concerned (see **1.3** above) Mitchell (in 'Towards a Definition of Psychological Maltreatment' (1993) *Liverpool Law Review* 1) argues that there are three elements that may be found in that definition:

> '(i) emotional abuse is recognizable in terms of actual or likely effects upon the child's emotional and behavioural development, which effects must be severe; (ii) a linking has to be established between these effects and their causes, which might number four: persistent emotional ill-treatment, severe emotional ill-treatment, persistent rejection, or severe rejection; (iii) there need be no attribution of culpability.'

He stresses that *Working Together* does not really offer any guidance as to what emotional ill-treatment is.

Wolkind, a leading child psychiatrist, has suggested that three things should be looked for to detect signs of emotional abuse: (1) parental behaviour that is deviant – but 'not in any way implying morally wrong but extremely unusual and which from research literature I know to have an adverse effect on a child'; (2) some form of child behaviour that is persistently and severely impairing the child's full attainment of mental health; and (3) whether appropriate treatment has been offered to, but rejected by, the parents. It would seem that while social workers, lawyers and the courts appear to concentrate on parental behaviour that falls below an 'acceptable' level, psychiatrists tend to look for evidence of emotional disturbance in a child (see Wolkind 'Emotional Signs of Child Abuse' (1988) JSWL 82).

Mitchell also finds this approach deficient and appears to be more sensitive to the position and difficulties of parents because: (1) Wolkind does not actually define what he calls emotional abuse; concepts like 'ill-treatment' and 'rejection' are not mentioned; (2) Wolkind's concept of deviance is statistical rather than moral, requiring harm to the child being shown but which must be predictable harm on the basis of research, but it may be unwitting; (3) Wolkind insists that treatment must have been offered and rejected before it is possible to speak about emotional abuse. Thus, although both Wolkind (and *Working Together*) focus on the actual *consequences* of the maltreatment, Mitchell finds that Wolkind's definition 'offers no help in operationalising the concept of psychological maltreatment [because] the notion of actual disturbance is at the heart of his thinking' (see Mitchell (above) at p 5).

Another definition is provided by Garbarino, Guttman and Seeley who define psychological maltreatment ((above) at pp 9 to 10) generally as:

'acts of omission or commission by a parent or guardian that are judged by a mixture of community values and professional expertise to be inappropriate and damaging.'

This general approach acknowledges that maltreatment is not purely a matter of science but has to do with community values and expertise, but does not depend upon demonstrable harm. Of course, Gabarino et al also state that 'in almost all cases, it is the psychological consequences of an act that defines that act as abusive' (Gabarino et al (above) at p 44). However, they also make it clear that the harm to children does not have to be actual but it can be predictable. The Children Act 1989, s 31(2), certainly allows for the 'likelihood' of harm, provided it is 'significant' and harm is defined broadly enough to include emotional harm (s 31(9)). Thus, 'predictable' harm is also envisaged under the Act but it is not enough to warrant legal intervention, since a deficiency in the child's carer to which that harm is attributable must also be shown (see s 31(2)).

Gabarino et al offer a more detailed definition of psychological maltreatment, namely a 'concerted attack on a child's development of self and social competence, a pattern of psychically destructive behaviour' which consists of five forms: (1) rejecting (the adult refusing to acknowledge the child's worth and the legitimacy of the child's needs); (2) isolating (cutting the child off from normal social experiences, preventing the child from forming friendships, and making the child believe that he or she is alone in the world); (3) terrorising the child (verbal assault, creating a climate of fear, bullying and frightening a child, making a child believe that the world is capricious and hostile); (4) ignoring (depriving the child of essential stimulation and responsiveness, stifling emotional growth and intellectual development); and (5) corrupting (stimulating the child to engage in anti-social behaviour, reinforcing that deviance, making that child unfit for normal social experience).

Mitchell (above) also offers what he calls a 'six-dimensional' definition of psychological maltreatment: (1) persistent hostility (which is closest to Gabarino's 'terrorising'); (2) persistent failure to respond to the physical, intellectual, emotional, social or behavioural needs of a child which may be (a) passive, (b) the result of poor parenting skills, and (c) intentional or unintentional, conscious or unwitting; (3) serious unrealistic expectations which could be manifested in (a) over-expectation of babies (eg to sleep all night, learn potty training very early in their lives) and young children's competence, and (b) having unrealistic expectations in that the child is 'under-expected' (resisting the child's growing independence, being over-protective, jealous of the child's relationships with other children or adults); (4) grossly inappropriate stimulation of a child's aggression or sexuality (this resembles Gabarino's 'corrupting' dimension); (5) serious exploitation of a child for the gratification of another's needs – not just sexual abuse but also 'driving' the child to achieve what the parent would like to have achieved, parents battling with each other through the child, or forcing the child to take risks which could result in criminal proceedings (the Fagin phenomenon); and (6) grossly inconsistent care (a child indulged and abused by turns).

Mitchell points out that the various categories may often be difficult to distinguish and that they would frequently overlap. However, he believes that recognition is more necessary than distinguishing between the various forms. He also fully acknowledges the objections that could be raised to these categories but makes no apology for them. For example, he argues that there are many value-laden words in his definition (persistent, seriously, grossly) but all judgments from all concerned professionals, including the courts, are 'judgments informed by values'. He also concedes that seeking to apply his definition would create formidable problems of proof but that such difficulties can be overestimated. On the other hand, he accepts Wolkind's third element as an answer to the obvious objection of potentially overloading the system beyond manageable levels: before legal intervention is sought, help should first be offered. Mitchell's main intention is to raise consciousness levels and to offer positive suggestions on how to 'operationalise' the concept of emotional abuse.

He also suggests that through 'meticulous observation, recording and assessment' social workers and lawyers will be able to 'stiffen up' their evidence and to stop leaving the responsibility for such assessment to doctors and clinical psychologists. It is submitted that while more rigorous observational skills could certainly be developed for social workers and lawyers in this particular context, the perception of judges and the entrenched professional hierarchical/class tradition in this country would certainly not generally prefer the views of a social worker or lawyer to those of a trained medical professional if a case came to court. Ironically, therefore, the assessment of value-laden terms such as 'persistent', 'seriously' and 'grossly', even if accepted as meriting legal intervention, would, in a case without any other physical or tangible evidence, be resolved on the basis of what a medically trained professional would say. At any rate, the comments of the various commentators suggest that the definition in *Working Together*, while limited, is at best a starting point, but the generality of the working definition certainly allows room for interpretation.

Before a child is placed on the child protection register, it would have to be shown that the child's emotional development had been severely affected by persistent neglect or rejection. Such a decision would have to be taken at a case conference which included social workers, doctors and other professionals. It should be remembered that emotional abuse is not a recognisable crime. However, under s 31(2) of the Children Act 1989 ('the 1989 Act'), a court will not make a care or supervision order unless it is satisfied that the child is suffering or is likely to suffer 'significant harm' and that the harm is attributable to a deficiency in the standard of parental care which the child is receiving. Harm is defined in s 31(9) to mean ill-treatment or the impairment of health or development. Ill-treatment is defined as including sexual abuse and forms of ill-treatment which are not physical; 'development' includes physical, intellectual, emotional, social, behavioural. The inclusion of emotional abuse gives effect to the decision in *F v Suffolk County Council* (1981) FLR 208. Under the 1989 Act, therefore, emotional abuse must be 'significant' and not merely moderate or trivial. The 1989 Act does not define 'significant', merely stating that the yardstick employed by the courts in considering whether the harm has been significant is to consider the development of a 'similar child'. There will, therefore, be considerable room for disagreement in marginal cases and, since proof of emotional abuse is mainly dependent upon opinion (expert) evidence, experts might, and frequently do, differ.

O'Regan argues that in the light of the many requirements imposed by the 1989 Act in order to establish significant harm, child protection in cases of emotional neglect will fall under the preventive provisions of s 17 of, and Sch 2 to, the 1989 Act. This is because of the need to provide services to safeguard and promote the welfare of children in need within their families (see O'Regan 'Emotional abuse within a changing legal framework' (1990) *The Journal of Child Law* 119). Under the Act, the local authority, in conjunction with the health service, has to be in a position to identify potentially emotionally abusive families, as well as emotionally damaged children, by speedy referral to child and family psychiatrists.

The problem will be in deciding whether the child's emotional state is the result of any flaw in its carer or because of some other totally uncontrollable or unavoidable reason, such as genetic inheritance. Fortunately (or unfortunately), emotional abuse is often one of the effects of other forms of abuse, such as physical maltreatment, physical neglect or sexual abuse. Hence, in many cases professionals and courts will be able to proceed on the basis of more clearly recognisable signs of abuse and the child's emotional needs may, thereby, also be addressed.

1.7 Concluding comments

We now have a working guide to the forms of child abuse currently recognised by various professionals working in the child care field. However, in order to further our understanding of child abuse and neglect, definitional issues must become 'an explicit methodological concern' (Besharov 'Towards Better Research on Child Abuse and Neglect' (1981) 5 *Child Abuse and Neglect* 383), so that there may be comparability of research findings, greater measurement reliability and greater clarity in delineating different groups of the population who possess different group dynamics (Besharov (above)). On a practical level, a more widely acceptable consensus among professionals on the scope of the forms of child abuse will also ensure a better basis for inter-agency co-operation, and guidance from the courts might help to ensure some consistency in the application of criteria in making important decisions about protecting children.

CHAPTER TWO

Issues in Child Abuse

2.1 Introduction

Over the years there have been several key issues that have troubled both the courts and child protection professionals in dealing with the problem of child abuse. Some of these have emerged in practice, others from public and private inquiries into child abuse cases and others from deficiencies in the law. The purpose of this chapter is to canvass the various issues which have arisen. We discuss their more general implications and impact and then examine salient points from influential child abuse inquiries and reports to see how some of these questions have been tackled and, in some cases, resolved. We also see how certain recommendations from child abuse inquiries have been given statutory recognition and become embodied in procedures as well as in the guidance to the various agencies which deal with child abuse, which have supplemented the implementation of the Children Act 1989. Finally, we examine the Rochdale cases of suspected ritual abuse of children, which raise other issues of investigation.

I CURRENT ISSUES

2.2 Legal responses to child abuse

In Chapter 3 we examine the new legal framework under the Children Act 1989 ('the 1989 Act'), which regulates the care and protection of children and explains the conditions which might necessitate courts granting orders under the 1989 Act when children are suffering or are at risk of suffering significant harm. We explain the working of child assessment orders, and emergency protection orders, which have replaced the former place of safety order, which appeared to fall into disrepute after the Cleveland controversy (see **2.9** below) as well as the new conditions for granting care and supervision orders.

The 1989 Act, which was implemented on 14 October 1991, has sought to introduce a radical reform of child law. One of its key philosophies is that for the most part, unless it can be proved otherwise, a child is best cared for in its own home by its own family, with (ideally) both parents playing a full part in the child's upbringing and without resort to legal proceedings. Hence, it must be proved to a court that it must be better for the court to make an order with regard to a child than not to make any order at all (s 1(5)). During the Cleveland controversy, it was alleged that social workers were responding to suspected cases of sexual abuse as if they were life-threatening situations and resorting to the removal of children sometimes, it was claimed, late at night or in the middle of the night. However, social workers were often acting in accordance with medical diagnoses of child sexual abuse, and the inquiry team which heard extensive evidence on the crisis concluded that the two key paediatricians involved in Cleveland were, albeit with the best of intentions, over-zealous in their efforts to contain what they perceived as a child abuse crisis of epidemic proportions. The new concurrent jurisdiction of courts which enables family proceedings cases, where certain conditions exist, to be transferred either horizontally or vertically so that they may be heard by trained judges and as expeditiously as possible, also has implications for the professions. These are discussed in Chapters 3, 4 and 5.

In the second part of this chapter, we discuss issues raised from the main findings and implications of several child abuse reports, including the *Report of the Inquiry into Child Abuse in Cleveland 1987* (1988, HMSO), Cm 412, ('the *Cleveland Report*'), residential care scandals investigated in reports such as *The Pindown Experience and the Protection of Children: The Report of the Staffordshire Child Care Inquiry* (1991, Staffordshire Social Services) ('the *Pindown Report*'); and the *Report of the Inquiry into the Removal of Children from Orkney in February 1991* (1992, HMSO) ('the *Orkney Report*'); *The Leicestershire Inquiry 1992* (1993, Leicestershire Social Services) ('the *Frank Beck* case'); *Accommodating Children* (1991); the *Castle Hill Report* (1992, Shropshire County Council); and *Choosing with Care* (1992, HMSO) ('the *Warner Committee Report*'). We also consider the issue of responding to allegations of ritual and organised abuse (*Rochdale Borough Council v A and Others* [1991] 1 FLR 192 ('the *Rochdale* case')).

The diagnosis and proof of child sexual abuse continues to present some of the most difficult evidentiary problems for child protection officers, health care professionals and the courts.

2.3 Detection and diagnosis of child abuse

Another fundamental question which has to be faced by courts, health care professionals and lawyers is the method of detection and diagnosis of child abuse. Jones, Pickett, Oates and Barbor, the authors of *Understanding Child Abuse* (1987, Macmillan), list six factors that constitute criteria for assessment.

(1) Parental history and personality.
(2) Marital history/parents' relationship.
(3) Vulnerability of child and siblings.

(4) Social circumstances.

(5) Nature of the precipitating incident.

(6) Resources available/community supports/lifelines.

Detection and diagnosis are examined in Chapter 4, while the current diagnostic techniques in the light of the evidential value placed on them by the courts are examined in Chapter 7. The child sexual abuse clinic at the Great Ormond Street Hospital for Sick Children has pioneered a technique which uses interviews utilising anatomically-correct dolls to encourage the child to demonstrate behaviour which he or she might be reluctant or unable to describe verbally.

2.4 Evidential value of child interviews

The major technological innovations which have been introduced into English courts have been: (1) the videotaped interview with a child witness in criminal proceedings to be presented instead of the examination-in-chief of the child in court, which is now admissible at all stages of the proceedings in trials on indictment and in youth courts for those sexual offences and offences of violence and cruelty to which the live-link provisions of s 32 of the Criminal Justice Act 1988 apply (see Chapter 7); and (2) the 'live' television link, which enables a child to give evidence via closed-circuit television from a room adjacent to the court (see Chapter 7). Two main legal problems arise in using videotaped interviews of children.

(1) The admissibility of such interviews as evidence.

(2) The reliability of such evidence.

The Home Office has now issued a guide to conducting videotaped interviews of child witnesses in criminal proceedings, the *Memorandum of Good Practice on Videorecorded Interviews with Child Witnesses for Criminal Proceedings* (1992, DOH) (the '*MoGP*'), which sets out a 'stepwise' approach to such interviews and this should go some way towards the standardisation of the conduct and quality of such interviews, with a view to their admissibility in criminal proceedings. Unfortunately, there are several problems that arise with the approach taken by the *MoGP*. These are discussed in detail in Chapters 6 and 7.

It should be noted that judges have exhibited a reluctance to accept a diagnostic interview as a means of proving the perpetration of sexual abuse (see, eg *C v C (Child Abuse: Evidence)* [1987] 1 FLR 321; cf *Re M (A Minor) (Child Abuse: Evidence) (Note)* [1987] 1 FLR 293). Hence, even if a videotaped interview is of good quality and sound, and the child appears to be reasonably coherent and articulate, so as to satisfy the general legal requirements of admissibility a judge still has the discretion to decide not to admit the video-tape in evidence (see Chapter 7).

If there are difficulties in obtaining sufficiently cogent evidence from a child through the use of these interviews, compliance with the *Cleveland Report* guidelines and the *MoGP* (see Chapter 7), which stress the unacceptability of an excessive amount of interviews, then becomes a major issue. To what extent should a child undergo the trauma of repeated questioning, albeit in the interests of his welfare, in order to satisfy the legal standards of proof in criminal proceedings?

2.5 Legal consequences of child abuse allegations

Allegations of child abuse have sometimes resulted in a local authority removing the child from its parent and this is still a possibility under the 1989 Act if the child is at risk of suffering significant harm (see, further, Chapter 4).

2.6 Legal issues in child abuse

Legal issues which frequently surface in child abuse cases arise in the following contexts.

(1) *Evaluation of evidence of abuse.* How was the diagnosis made? How was the evidence obtained? What explanations were tendered? Was a second medical opinion obtained? Would a court of law accept the evidence? (See Chapter 6.)

(2) *Emergency procedures.* Does the situation warrant an application for an emergency protection order? Would a court be satisfied that the child was suffering or was likely to suffer significant harm? (See Chapter 3.)

(3) *Legal procedures available.* Is there reasonable cause to suspect that a child is suffering significant harm? Is access to the child being denied? Is it a situation where a child assessment order would be appropriate? Or should an application be made for a care or supervision order? In any event, should an application for an interim order be made? (See Chapter 3.)

(4) *The child's evidence.* Should this be obtained and, if so, by what methods? Are there adequate technical facilities for a videotaped interview with the child to be carried out? Should an application be made for the court to transfer proceedings to a court that is equipped with the necessary technology? If an interview is carried out, what would be needed to ensure that it would comply with the requirements of the *Cleveland Report* and the *MoGP*? After the interview, what evidentiary value would a court place on that child's testimony? Is this a case where expert testimony should be called? Would another expert in the field possibly disagree with the first expert's opinion? (See Chapters 6 and 7.)

(5) *Longer-term remedies.* Is foster care or adoption best for the child? Can

the alleged abuser be persuaded to leave the home if the local authority can offer assistance with accommodation? (See Chapter 3.)

(6) *The legal dilemma in child abuse cases.* The legal dilemma which is often at the heart of child abuse cases is the conflict of two entrenched principles fundamental to a free society: (1) in cases where criminal proceedings are being considered – the need for a fair trial for the accused against the public interest in the protection of the child – (the standard of proof required in criminal prosecutions will be significant); (2) in cases where civil proceedings are being considered – the need to protect the child from abuse against the right to do justice to the alleged perpetrator – (can they promote the best interests of the child and still allow the suspected abuser to know the substance of the case against him?). On a balance of probabilities, is the evidence such that the protection of the child requires some form of civil proceedings? (See Chapter 3.) Another dilemma which might surface is the need to protect the child from abuse in the short term against the need to eventually reunite the family in the longer term.

Thus, cases of alleged child abuse are always exceptionally difficult since they involve a constant balancing of opposing principles. Certain cases have highlighted the problems that courts face in reconciling these principles when parents, who have been denied access to case conferences, claim that the rules of natural justice have been breached and that they are at least entitled to know the substance of any allegations made against them. They have also claimed the right to make representations at such case conferences and to be given a chance to refute any allegations. The 1991 version of the inter-agency Guidance *Working Together under the Children Act 1989* (1991, DOH) (*'Working Together'*), has not made parental attendance a right, merely subject to the child protection conference's chair's discretion, although parents are now expected to be invited to attend and their exclusion must be justified and will usually be considered exceptional.

Judicial review of decisions made by the local authority, such as to place a child on the child protection register, will still be possible, but continuing practical problems will be encountered in challenging a decision, the detailed basis of which will usually be unavailable to a parent or caretaker.

With the advent of the representations and complaints procedure under the 1989 Act (see Chapter 9), children in care now have a better opportunity of airing their grievances, although judicial review may be a more effective and speedy way of questioning the propriety of a local authority decision.

2.7 Other issues in child abuse

Faced with some of the legal issues, the social worker might then have to establish his or her case. In recent times, the standard of proof required to establish the guilt of an accused has come under scrutiny and, indeed, courts

have even stated that a higher standard of proof may be required if an allegation is made that a child has been abused by his or her parent (see, eg *Re G
(No 2) (A Minor) (Child Abuse: Evidence)* [1988] 1 FLR 314).

Further problems may be identified.

(1) What is the best way to co-ordinate and harmonise the work of the
    different agencies and professionals in their child protection work, bear-
    ing in mind the many differences that exist between agency and pro-
    fessional, ranging from their legal powers and duties to their traditional
    attitudes to their work and work styles? This is discussed in Chapter 5,
    in the course of reviewing the many guidances that were issues following
    the Cleveland controversy.

(2) How should a child protection professional respond to the need for par-
    ental involvement without compromising the well-being of the child? The
    case conference is an obvious example of a situation where, in the past,
    parents have complained that they have been kept 'in the dark' about
    allegations that have been made against them. There are many factors
    that the chairperson must bear in mind when making decisions about
    involvement or exclusion of parents, the latter course now generally
    requiring justification, and the implications of the 1989 Act on judicial
    review in the light of the complaints and representations procedures now
    available under that Act. Judicial review and the representations and
    complaints procedures are discussed in Chapter 9.

(3) Deciding what is in the best interests of the child in dealing with difficult
    and disruptive children in secure accommodation or in residential homes.
    The Pindown affair (see **2.18.2** below) exposed several problems peculiar
    to the running of residential children's homes. How should social workers
    working in such establishments deal with potentially dangerous situations
    without running the risk of being themselves accused of child abuse or
    having children abscond?

    In April 1993, the Department of Health issued a set of guidelines
    entitled *Guidance on Permissible Forms of Control in Children's Residential
    Care* (1993, DOH). This appears to be the first set of guidelines dealing
    with the control of children in residential care, which is to be followed
    by another, *Safe and Sound*, not published at time of writing, which will
    be confined to secure accommodation. An extremely difficult issue that
    residential care workers will have to face is determining the degree of
    force that will be legally permissible in exercising physical restraint on
    children in care, particularly if they are disruptive or have been convicted
    of serious crimes or have a history of absconding from institutions. Both
    criminal and civil actions could result from a flawed handling of tricky
    and emotionally sensitive situations which will doubtless arise in residen-
    tial care settings with 'difficult' children. A detailed analysis of this guid-
    ance is undertaken in Chapter 7.

(4) Deciding what weight to place on the statements of children either about themselves or about other children (as in Orkney and *Re E* (1990) *The Times*, April 2).

(5) Deciding how best to go about interviewing a suspected child abuse victim, in accordance with the *Cleveland Report* guidelines (para 12 thereof) and the latest Home Office guide to videotaped interviews with child witnesses for criminal proceedings, the *MoGP* (see Chapter 7 for a full analysis).

(6) Deciding what is in the best interests of a child who has revealed that he or she has been abused but insists that the person to whom this disclosure has been made keeps this information confidential.

(7) Dealing with possible ritual or satanic or organised abuse.

Within the last few years, the possibility of ritual abuse, satanic abuse and organised abuse (all three phenomena not necessarily synonymous) has been given prominence by the media. Two of the most widely publicised of these sorts of cases were the Rochdale affair and the Orkney Islands Affair. The difficulty here is again deciding if and when to act in response to what appear to be plausible allegations. The Rochdale and Orkney Islands cases are examined at **2.19.2** and **2.19.7** below.

Many of these issues have been highlighted in the child abuse inquiry reports which have been published over the years, and practitioners will find that a working knowledge of the key findings of these reports will provide a valuable window into insights and experience gained over many years by professionals dealing with the day-to-day problems of child protection.

II   THE CHILD ABUSE INQUIRY REPORTS

2.8 Child abuse inquiries

Between 1981 and 1992, there were approximately 40 child abuse inquiries held in Britain. Probably the most famous of these in recent times has been the Cleveland Inquiry of 1987. We wish to discuss, in some detail, the more salient features of a selection of these inquiries, their multifarious functions, and their significance to the law and to social work practice. In a book of this nature, it might be asked why there is any need to discuss or even consider those child abuse cases which prompted public and private inquiries. The answer is quite simply because it was these few cases and their inquiry reports which have had, and continue to have, an impact on day-to-day professional practice in child protection and which, in different ways, have influenced the development of the law relating to child protection, first in relation to the physical abuse and neglect of children and secondly by changes in the law relating to child sexual abuse prompted and guided by the Cleveland Inquiry and its *Report*.

The Maria Colwell case in the 1970s led to an inquiry which 'signalled the beginning of political, public and professional interest in child abuse' (Parton *Governing the Family* (1991, Macmillan) at p 52). In the mid-1980s, the Jasmine Beckford Inquiry (see **2.10.1** below) was influential in spotlighting *all* services which were involved in the case, the social services, health service, police and legal officers were all held responsible for the tragic death of the child concerned. It brought the problem of child abuse back into the public consciousness where both professional and non-professional interest had begun to wane. In the late 1980s, the Cleveland Inquiry shifted the focus to sexual abuse of children, whereas all previously publicised inquiries had dealt with physical abuse cases.

2.9 Functions of a child abuse inquiry

A child abuse inquiry may be said to have six objectives:

(1) to ascertain the true facts of the case (not usually within the remit of the inquiry);
(2) to outline critically the role/functions of relevant agencies, ie examining the nature and quality of their work and collaborative effort;
(3) to list recommendations for future legislation, governmental guidelines and professional action (*A Child in Trust: Jasmine Beckford* (1985, DHSS) ('the *Jasmine Beckford Report*'));
(4) to learn lessons for the future;
(5) to meet or placate public concern and restore public confidence;
(6) to establish who was responsible for actions and inaction; where responsibility should lie.

There are three main forms of inquiry: (1) an internal inquiry (case review) conducted by senior management; (2) the most common form – a locally commissioned external inquiry with an independent chairperson, sometimes with external members; and (3) an inquiry instituted by the Secretary of State for Social Services. The only statutory inquiry held in the 1980s was the Cleveland Inquiry.

2.9.1 Some common findings in child abuse inquiry reports

(1) There is no universally recognised list of factors which can predict child abuse.

(2) Collaboration between professionals is not always easy to obtain or sustain and should not perhaps even be assumed.

(3) Inter-professional and inter-agency communication need to be improved.

A breakdown in co-operation between the various agencies is consistently identified in the reports as one of the main causes of a particular tragedy or crisis.

(4) There is a need for health monitoring in child abuse cases.

(5) Racial differences and the implications of working cross-culturally need to be recognised and dealt with.

(6) Case conferences have not been used to maximum advantage.

(7) The extent of various authorities' involvement, co-operation and commitment to cases of non-accidental injury to children varies considerably.

2.9.2 Preliminary observations in child physical abuse reports

Two key preliminary points emerged from a study of various reports dealing with physical abuse and neglect.

(1) The need to monitor a child's progress.
(2) Inter-disciplinary communications.

2.9.3 The need to monitor a child's progress

The *Report of the Committee of Inquiry into the Care and Supervision Provided in Relation to Maria Colwell* (1974, DHSS) ('the *Maria Colwell Report*') drew attention to the importance of medical assessment as a baseline for monitoring the physical condition and progress of a child who has been fostered for several years and then returned home to live with his or her natural parent and step-parent. If Maria had continued to have regular medical examinations, the steady deterioration in her emotional and physical state would have been noticed and acted upon. The Committee suggested that an initial medical examination to coincide with the child's return home would provide vital baseline data which might help to prevent such tragedies (at p 234). (See also the *Report of a Panel Appointed by the Essex Area Review Committee* (1980, DHSS) ('the *Malcolm Page Report*') at s 2, paras 2.28 and 2.29, which discusses the importance of health monitoring in child abuse cases.) The *Maria Colwell Report* underlined the function of the psychiatrist and the paediatrician and highlighted the overlap of function between psychiatrist and social worker. It stressed that the social worker has to make the preliminary diagnosis of the needs of a particular child and consider whether those needs include a psychiatric referral, or any other specialist medical help. The social worker also needs to maintain contact with those people whom the child sees most often, such as the child's school teachers, in order to monitor the child's progress in these particular circumstances.

2.9.4 Inter-disciplinary communication and co-operation

The *Maria Colwell Report* was the first since the *Monkton Report* (1945, HMSO), Cmnd 6636, to achieve seminal and lasting importance. It stressed the need for inter-disciplinary training and communication. This theme recurs in most of the 18 reports covered by the DHSS study *Child Abuse: A Study of Inquiry Reports 1973–81* (1982, HMSO), yet deficiencies in this particular area once again marred efficient practice, for example in the case of Jasmine Beckford. Inter-disciplinary co-operation 'must not be assumed . . . is difficult to achieve, [and] requires active encouragement prior to involvement in an actual case of abuse' (Wendleken in *After Beckford?* (1987, Department of Social Policy and Social Science, University of London)).

A breakdown in inter-agency co-operation has been the fatal flaw mentioned in every child abuse inquiry report in the last decade, and the need for better inter-agency co-operation is echoed in a number of recent child abuse inquiry reports as well. (See also *Child Abuse: A Study of Inquiry Reports 1981–89* (1991, HMSO).)

2.9.5 The Maria Colwell story

Maria Colwell was killed by her stepfather in January 1972, 11 weeks before her eighth birthday. Although initially fostered by her paternal aunt and uncle for more than five years, while in the care of the local authority she had subsequently been taken back to live with her mother and stepfather whom she had been visiting regularly for some time before. Maria's mother sought the revocation of the care order and the local authority supported the application subject to the substitution of a supervision order. One of the criticisms highlighted in the *Report* was that there had been 'insufficient evidence' on which the local authority had decided to support her mother's application. The case revealed starkly the limitations of a supervision order which did not empower the supervisor to give legally effective directions about the upbringing or conduct of the child. In any event, the local authority was criticised, after her death, not only for failing to monitor the result of Maria's return home 'with sufficient care', but also for failing to react with due sense of urgency to the first sign of physical injury; and entirely failing to supervise Maria in the first six months prior to her death.

The case became the catalyst for a widespread public feeling that the role of social workers should be re-assessed, that there should not be 'private' social work and that social workers should be made accountable for their actions in sensitive areas of human behaviour.

2.9.6 Lessons from the Maria Colwell case

Certain principal facets of the child protection system have undergone significant changes since the *Colwell* case.

(1) Decision-making in relation to children in care has become more formalised. *Procedures* and *guidance* are distinguished: the former to be followed rigorously; the latter to be departed from only with good reasons which must be recorded.

(2) Risk-taking has been diminished considerably as compared to earlier practice and emphasis has been placed on social workers 'covering themselves', ie following all necessary procedures to the letter wherever possible.

(3) Policing and surveillance has become a critical area for further investigation, exploration and experience. The social worker is more conscious that he needs to be clear about the nature of his job.

The three most influential inquiries in the mid-1980s were the cases of Jasmine Beckford, Tyra Henry and Kimberley Carlile.

2.10 The Jasmine Beckford case

In July 1984, an extremely thin and emaciated child called Jasmine Beckford, aged four-and-a-half, died. There were multiple old scars on her body and evidence of many old fractures. There were numerous fresh injuries, such as abrasions, cuts and bruises consistent with the effects of a severe beating a day or so before her death. The fatal injury had been caused by a blow to her head. Her stepfather was subsequently convicted of her manslaughter and sentenced to 10 years' imprisonment. Her mother pleaded guilty to child neglect and was sentenced to 18 months' imprisonment. The most disturbing fact of this case, apart from its intrinsic horror, was that at the time of her death, Jasmine was in the care of a local authority.

The report (*A Child in Trust; Jasmine Beckford* (1985, DHSS) ('the *Jasmine Beckford Report*')) of the panel of inquiry concluded that both she and her sister, who had been under a care order, had been subject to daily or even hourly physical abuse. In September 1981, Jasmine had been boarded out with foster-parents, but in April 1982, she had been returned to her home and was physically in the care of her parents.

Almost every professional involved was criticised in the report – social workers, doctors, solicitors, police, health visitor, and magistrates all came in for censure.

The report stressed that Jasmine's death was both 'predictable . . . and preventable' (at p 287) and that:

'The blame must be shared by all those services. The making of a care order invests social services with pervasive parental powers. By such a judicial act society expects that a child at risk from abuse by its parents will be protected by social service personnel exercising parental powers effectively and authoritatively on behalf of society. Such a child is a child in trust.'

2.10.1 The Jasmine Beckford Report's recommendations

There were 13 recommendations of a general nature, including the following.

(1) The necessity for the local authority's relevant committee to meet immediately whenever a child dies or is seriously injured.
(2) The duty of a local authority to co-operate with a health authority should be made more specific, to include a duty to consult.
(3) The DHSS should consider issuing clearer guidelines to local authorities.
(4) All policy statements and guidelines should contain standard definitions.

Specific recommendations included improvements in child abuse procedures, with particular reference to social services, health services and schools.

2.10.2 Recommended legal changes in the Jasmine Beckford Report

The report recommended the following.

(1) That the law should state that a child in care is a child in trust. Legislation should also make it clear whether it is intended or not that preventive work is exhausted before care proceedings are initiated.
(2) A right of a parent or child to apply to a court for the setting aside of a place of safety order should be specifically stated in any future legislation.
(3) Any solicitor acting for children in care proceedings must see and, if possible, talk to or play with, those whose interests he is hired to protect and promote (at p 303).

2.10.3 Comment on the Jasmine Beckford Report

The report is a scathing criticism of the social work practice of the specific workers involved with Jasmine. Indeed, following Jasmine's death, social workers were strongly criticised for not paying enough attention to the group of factors that typically indicate risk; for instance:

(1) when parents themselves have been abused as children;
(2) when parents are of low intelligence;
(3) when parents are under 24;
(4) when parents are socially isolated, or abuse drugs or alcohol;
(5) when one parent is not the natural parent.

The point is that these factors are not, either in isolation or in any particular combination, a means of predicting abuse. Despite the report's castigation of social work practice in Jasmine's case, several questions remain unanswered.

(1) Are social workers now to be merely agents of the law and nothing else? Are their counselling and advisory functions no longer as important if similar circumstances arise?

(2) Are social workers supposed to investigate every piece of information which might possibly be untrue? For example, the report is highly critical of Jasmine's social worker for not finding out the identity of Jasmine's natural father. The report suggests that even though the social worker was presented with a birth certificate which confirmed what Jasmine's mother had said, relatives should have been questioned and health records should have been consulted.

Clearly, the report appeared to assume that the social worker was only working on one case at that time so that she could devote her full attention to its investigation. It also appeared to be relying on hindsight to frame its judgment. A rather different question arises as to whether there was any accurate perception by the panel of inquiry of the extent of a social worker's resources (such as a well-stocked office library), or indeed of the ongoing nature of a social worker's caseload. Louis Blom-Cooper is reported to have said in an interview subsequent to publication of the report that social workers should simply deal with a problem by taking a book from the shelves and finding an answer to the problem (Philpot 'Interview with Blom-Cooper' (1986) *Community Care* February 2). This certainly assumes the availability of resources to which most social workers do not have recourse, and in any event, which they would not have the time to consult in many cases, and also assumes that there is simply an 'answer' to most problems.

2.11 The Tyra Henry case

Tyra was murdered by her father Andrew Neill in September 1984 when she was aged only 22 months, while still legally in the care of Lambeth Council. The report of the public inquiry into Tyra's death (*Whose Child?* (1987, DHSS)) says that Lambeth Council's overriding responsibility as Tyra Henry's legal parent 'became lost in the tangle of administrative frustration and professional mismanagement which we have traced'.

The report (chaired by Stephen Sedley QC) concluded that Lambeth social workers largely overlooked Tyra, concentrating mainly on her mother 'who was incapable of taking responsibility for Tyra and let her get into the very hands [of her father] . . . which the care order had been designed to keep her out of'. The care order 'was not taken seriously enough, was not responsibly implemented and was finally all but shelved'.

The report recommended only one change in the law, namely that an authority seeking care should be obliged to place its proposals before the court in summary form when, if approved, the proposals would be annexed to the care order as part of it. The authority would have to go back to court for approval of any significant change. An emergency interim power to authorise a change would be given to a single magistrate or the director or chairperson of social services until the matter could be brought back before the court.

The report also suggested that a specialist legal adviser should be present at initial conferences considering legal measures to protect a child; if unavailable, such a specialist should be appointed subsequently and the conference reconvened if this is required by the advice given. There should also be compulsory training in chairing conferences for all social services staff before they may be allowed to chair reviews and non-accidental injury case conferences. The report considered it 'inexcusable' that neither Tyra's mother nor her grandmother were invited to case conferences about Tyra. It also made a request for a 'more considered' deployment of black social workers to work with black families but the report stressed that it was not thinking of 'racial matching or anything like it' (at p 109). They were simply concerned to ensure that where there is doubt about cultural aspects of behaviour or lifestyle, the input and evaluation of a social worker of a similar background would be present.

Its final recommendation was that future child abuse inquiries should be private, carried out by outside personnel, with witnesses having a right to be accompanied by a friend or adviser. Public inquiries should only be called if the case for them is 'overwhelming'.

2.11.1 Comment

The reason for the title of the report was that sight was lost of *whose* responsibility Tyra Henry was; she was passed from one carer to another (local authority, grandmother and mother) until she got into the hands of her father, which proved tragic and disastrous. Lambeth's social services department was found to have assisted in this process by concentrating its attention on Tyra's mother rather than on her grandmother, who needed all the help she could get, or on Tyra, whose safety was the object of the entire exercise. On the cross-cultural issue, it should be noted that this report at least made some mention of the need to face the question of possible cultural/racial stereotyping and misreading of cultural habits and attitudes. This was patently ignored in the *Jasmine Beckford Report* despite the fact that there the supervisor was American, the social worker Swedish, the health visitor Chinese, the family Afro-Caribbean and the foster-parent Anglo-Indian.

In addition, Tyra's grandmother was not given sufficient support because the social workers appeared to perceive her as a *type* rather than as an individual; a false perception in white British society of 'the Afro-Caribbean mother as endlessly resourceful, able to cope in great adversity, essentially unsinkable'; there was an 'unarticulated and unconscious sense that a woman like her would find a way of coping, no matter what' (*Whose Child?* (1987, DHSS) at pp 108 to 109).

2.12 The Kimberley Carlile case

Kimberley Carlile died, aged four-and-a-half, from a blow to her left temple, inflicted by her stepfather, Nigel Hall, who was later convicted of her murder. The post-mortem ascertained that she had multiple bruising and scarring on various parts of her body, some of them, according to the report 'obvious even to the most casual observer'; these wounds were consistent with repeated episodes of physical abuse. The report states that it was 'obvious that Kimberley had been tortured and starved for many weeks before her death'. Once again, having spent a happy 14 months with foster-parents, Kimberley was then returned by Wirral social services to her mother, her siblings and her stepfather, with whom she lived until her death some eight months later. Her mother's life had been very unsettled, and 'punctuated by bouts of marital violence'. Kimberley and her siblings had been in voluntary care on three occasions. She was killed while Greenwich social services were pressing to have her medically examined. Despite instantaneous arrests and damning admissions by Mrs Carlile, the period of time from death to trial was nearly a year. One of the report's recommendations was therefore to echo the *Jasmine Beckford Report* that in all child abuse prosecutions involving children in the care of a local authority, the criminal trial of the parents should usually take place within three to four months of the homicidal event.

The report of the Commission of Inquiry chaired by Louis Blom-Cooper into the death of Kimberley Carlile, *A Child in Mind; Protection of Children in a Responsible Society* (1987, DHSS) ('the *Kimberley Carlile Report*') pinpoints poor professional practice by the social worker and health visitor in contact with the family of Kimberley as bearing the largest responsibility for her death.

The inquiry found that the social worker in the case failed to assess the risk to Kimberley or have her medically examined and failed even to see her adequately himself. He failed to operate the existing child abuse system by not calling a case conference. The system itself, it acknowledged, permitted too much reliance to be placed on one person. This system was therefore 'inherently defective', was compounded by resource problems, reduced staffing, the disarray of community health services and a sudden increase in reported cases of children at risk. The system simply did not adequately support individual workers.

The health visitor was criticised for her failure to provide health surveillance, and the report indicated that her supervisor and the social worker's Area Manager should share responsibility. Four points of professional practice were made (at p 112):

(1) Those working in the field of child abuse must always be on their guard against the risk of seeing what they want to believe.
(2) At any meeting with the family it is vital to talk directly to the children

themselves (assuming that the children are capable of understanding).
(3) If child abuse is suspected, the parents must be confronted with that suspicion.
(4) Where the suspicion is denied, the parental explanation for the suspicion being unfounded must be put to the test.

The inquiry appeared to place practically equal blame for Kimberley's death on her mother. Yet her stepfather, Nigel Hall, was sentenced to life imprisonment for causing Kimberley's death, whereas Mrs Carlile received a sentence of 12 years' imprisonment for causing Kimberley grievous bodily harm. The report says 'A woman such as Mrs Carlile, fatally attracted to violent co-habitees, was highly vulnerable to the acuter problems of child-rearing' (at p 111). The report also criticised Wirral social services' handling of the case and wanted a fundamental review of the child protection service nationally. It also recommended that any legislative provision for co-operation between statutory and voluntary agencies in the investigation of harm, and protection of children at risk, should include a specific duty on a health authority to promote the welfare of children similar to that which had been contained in s 1 of the Child Care Act 1980. It proposed the following orders for investigation and intervention in cases of child abuse or suspected child abuse, in ascending order of interference with (parental) rights.

(1) A power to enter and inspect premises where a child is living and thought to be at risk, including a right to interview and examine the child.
(2) A 'child assessment order' for the production of a child at a clinic for medical examination.
(3) A warrant to search for or remove a re-enactment, with amendment, of s 40 of the Children and Young Persons Act 1933.
(4) An 'emergency protection order' as proposed in the White Paper (1987) to replace the place of safety order.
(5) A police officer's right of entry and search without warrant under s 17(1)(e) of the Police and Criminal Evidence Act 1984, to save life or limb.

2.12.1 Comment

Once again the criticism which dominates this report is that the social services did too little, and acted too late. In the Cleveland controversy (see **2.14** to **2.15** below) concerning cases of suspected child sexual abuse, however, the criticism levelled at the social services was that they did too much (eg by taking out place of safety orders), too soon. Of the various fresh recommendations made by the *Kimberley Carlile Report*, the 'child assessment' order is now contained in s 43 of the Children Act 1989 (see Chapter 3) as is the 'emergency protection' order (see Chapter 3), both of which have been implemented since 14 October 1991, and which replaced the former place of safety order. On a different point, a possible interpretation of the report's comments on Mrs Carlile regarding her 'fatal attraction' to Kimberley's stepfather, is that somehow 'women such as Mrs Carlile' might almost collude in any physical abuse of their children because of their particular feminine weakness, whereas the question of male violence (ie the stepfather, Hall's) is something which is almost taken for granted because of the particular circumstances of the case (see Parton and Parton 'Women, the Family and Child Protection' (1989) *Critical Social Policy* 38).

2.13 General comments on the physical abuse cases

The cases and reports on the physical abuse of children indicate that the main problem which social workers faced there was not acting and reacting quickly enough to the danger signals that were present. They were also criticised, with hindsight, for not monitoring the progress of the children involved, having too much faith in the rehabilitative powers of the fathers or stepfathers of the children, and not being sufficiently clear about where their responsibilities lay in the execution of their statutory duties. All these factors have now been addressed by the 1989 Act, but the question ultimately comes down to a question of professional judgment. In a case like Tyra Henry's, a hidden theme would appear to be questions of preconceived stereotyping, ethnicity and unconscious racism that have to be more openly recognised when dealing with deprived families, or simply families that are at risk to themselves and their most vulnerable members. Any changes in the status quo of such families must be monitored with follow-up procedures as now set up under the 1989 Act and its associated volumes of guidance.

Different sorts of problems present themselves when it comes to suspected child sexual abuse, as the *Cleveland Report* clearly illustrates.

2.14 Child sexual abuse

We are aware that the term 'child sexual abuse' has sometimes been criticised for its potential ambiguity – it could also refer to cases where the child has committed the abuse which, as Chapter 7 points out is, sadly, far too common a reality in the 1990s. However, we wish to make it clear that the present section deals with cases where it has been alleged that children have been sexually abused, usually by adults, although, as a recent report indicates, not necessarily (see *The Report of the Committee of Enquiry into Children and Young People who Sexually Abuse Other Children* (1992, NCH) ('the *NCH Report*')).

The most well-known inquiry report in this field is the *Cleveland Report*, which has been, and continues to be, cited and approved by the judiciary (see *Re E (Child Abuse: Evidence)* [1991] 1 FLR 420 and *Re C and L (Child Abuse: Evidence)* [1991] FCR 351) and, therefore, continues to wield an influence on the approach to investigations of suspected child sexual abuse.

The problem with child sexual abuse is that the assessment of evidence or tell-tale signs of it is particularly difficult to undertake because in many cases there would not be any physical signs of such abuse having taken place. Thus, only emotional or developmental impairment may be detectable. It would be possible to make an unequivocal diagnosis of sexual abuse only if there were tangible, physical signs of abuse such as traces of hair or semen, abrasions or similar damage to sensitive areas of the body. The *Cleveland Report* indicated that medical diagnosis which placed undue emphasis on any one physical sign was not to be elevated into an unequivocal diagnosis of sexual abuse. Before we examine the *Cleveland Report* it is important to bear in mind that even in proven child sexual abuse cases, unlike the four previous reports that we have just discussed, no deaths usually result from the abuse and the evidence of abuse is inevitably more contentious than in the physical abuse cases.

The Cleveland crisis did not involve an isolated case of individual abuse but concerned at least 121 children whom it was alleged had been abused. Place of safety orders were used as if these were life-threatening cases and both children and parents were, at some point in the crisis, alienated from each other and the professionals involved. Thus, the balance between the need to protect the child and the parents' right to be told the substance of the allegations was more strongly challenged than ever before. Although it was claimed that only 18 per cent of the cases in Cleveland used it, the controversial 'reflex anal dilatation' ('RAD') test took centre stage as the method of determining whether child sexual abuse had taken place.

2.15 The Cleveland crisis in the context of previous child abuse cases

Having examined the cases of Maria Colwell, Jasmine Beckford, Kimberley Carlile and Tyra Henry, it is clearly important to bear in mind that the last three cases had set the trend for media and professional criticism of social workers' failure to act effectively to protect or save the children involved from physical abuse and eventual death. Social work departments became extremely conscious of the need to act positively if there were indications that a child might be at risk. Unfortunately, the child abuse cases which started to develop in Cleveland were cases of child *sexual* abuse. Although the level of inter-professional co-operation between the various professional workers involved in child physical abuse appeared satisfactory, in terms of clear guidelines and personal relationships, it soon became apparent that these guidelines were inadequate and inappropriate in the context of child sexual abuse.

2.15.1 What went wrong in Cleveland?

The first inkling of the so-called Cleveland affair was given in June 1987 when a local newspaper in Cleveland began to publish stories concerning a large number of angry parents who claimed that their children had been taken from them by social workers on the basis of medical diagnosis by two paediatricians, Dr Marietta Higgs and Dr Geoffrey Wyatt. As the rate of referrals to hospitals of cases of suspected child sexual abuse continued to rise, conflicts of professional medical opinion made it extremely difficult, if not impossible, to update the existing child abuse procedures manual. Police surgeons disagreed with hospital paediatricians over diagnoses, opinions were polarised and a significant breakdown in working relationships resulted. Referrals continued to spiral, from GPs, school nurses, teachers and others to whom these children had apparently disclosed their abuse. Conflict of opinion also arose over which professional would be best to examine these children as well as the 'correct' method of examination. Allied to these problems were the following.

(1) The appropriate scope and nature of parental involvement. Should they be present at investigations? Should their permission be obtained before a medical examination was carried out?
(2) What would be the most suitable place for an examination?

Even more confusion ensued over the need to elicit a speedy response from the police surgeon so as to obtain vital forensic evidence before it faded away and the need to obtain a sufficient planning period which would allow appropriate plans to be made before confronting the parents with allegations of child sexual abuse. There were personality clashes, and joint working arrangements were ineffective in containing conflict between individuals. Some children were, therefore, subjected to three or four medical examinations and pressure mounted on social workers to obtain disclosures from the children about alleged abuse. Failure in effective inter-professional and inter-agency collaboration resulted in overloading of the system, exacerbated by increased referrals and placements in hospital and the notions that siblings might be involved and that medical conditions, such as failure to thrive or bowel malfunctions, might be caused by sexual abuse rather than any physical malfunction. There is general acceptance of Stuart Bell's description of the chaotic scenes in Ward 9 of Middlesbrough General Hospital, already full of sick children, being overrun by lively youngsters who had been brought there under referrals or place of safety orders (see Stuart Bell *When Salem Came to the Boro'* (1988, Pan Books) at p 352). Yet no instructions had been given to nurses about what to tell parents who were not being allowed to see their children. There was such a breakdown in communication and administrative direction that parents were generally not seen at all except to be confronted with suspicions of child abuse or simply being left in the dark.

Nobody seemed to have the power (or the presence of mind) to require or restore administrative control of the situation.

2.15.2 Lack of clear findings of abuse in the Cleveland Report

We have pointed out elsewhere (Lyon and de Cruz 'Child Sexual Abuse and the Cleveland Report' [1988] Fam Law 370) that one of the most worrying omissions in the *Cleveland Report* was the lack of a final decision by the inquiry about how many children were actually the subject of actual or suspected sexual abuse in Cleveland. In her introduction, Butler-Sloss LJ refers to the impossibility of arriving at any consensus from evidence available to the inquiry, or of obtaining any reliable figures of the general prevalence of sexual abuse in the country or Cleveland. Indeed, she urges caution to be exercised in accepting percentages as to the prevalence and incidence of sexual abuse. The report is inconsistent about the numbers of sexually abused children actually involved in the crisis: for example, para 64 mentions 125 cases, and para 9.3.22.1 mentions 121 cases, the figure most quoted by the media. The director of Cleveland social services has subsequently acknowledged that 12 of the families, involving 26 children, were wrongly accused, but, as we have said, there is no opinion expressed by the inquiry team as to the validity of the alleged abuse regarding the remaining 95 (?) children. Newspaper reports have suggested that 98 children were returned to their families and were living back at home by the end of the inquiry, although many of these remained wards of court or were subject to supervision orders which included medical examination.

2.15.3 No guidance on medical examination and contact in the Cleveland Report

The report did not provide any clear legal guidance on a host of problems attendant upon the consequences of a professional diagnosis of child abuse. These included problems arising from the need to obtain consent for medical examination of children under emergency orders, issues surrounding contact with children held under such orders, and rights of appeal against the making of such orders. These matters are now covered by the 1989 Act (see Chapters 3 and 4), but although the 1989 Act gives a '*Gillick*-competent' child (a child who has sufficient age and understanding) the right to refuse to submit to medical examinations, recent Court of Appeal decisions suggest that a child's refusal to consent to medical treatment may be overriden by someone who has parental rights and responsibilities or by the court (see *Re R (A Minor)* [1991] 4 All ER 177; *Re W (A Minor) (Consent to Medical Treatment)* [1993] 1 FLR 1). There is, therefore, some doubt about how far the *Gillick*-competent provisions in the 1989 Act now extend and in what circumstances they would be given full effect.

2.15.4 Rules of good practice not followed efficiently during crisis

Fundamental rules of good practice appear to have been ignored or simply not followed with any degree of efficiency during the crisis. There appeared to be a lamentable lack of understanding or proper use of the place of safety order; in effect, professionals reacted to the possibility of sexual abuse as they would to physical or life-threatening abuse. No information was given to parents concerning what was happening, or regarding their rights of access to their children. Concern about the potential impact and trauma of children being removed from home precipitately was overshadowed by professional zeal and the isolation of parents was insufficiently addressed. Parents, therefore, sought assistance from MPs, the clergy, and the media. Social workers were left trying to maintain the balance between parents' and children's needs and their actions were often the result of the medical diagnosis from the paediatricians involved in the crisis.

2.15.5 The doctors' role in the crisis

There is little doubt that the paediatricians involved in the crisis came to be perceived as the focal point of much of the controversy. The report clearly states that in the space of five months Doctors Higgs and Wyatt, the consultant paediatricians at Middlesbrough General Hospital, diagnosed 121 children out of the report's figure of 125 as having been sexually abused (para 5, at p 243). The majority were diagnoses by Dr Higgs, but 42 appeared to have been diagnosed by Dr Wyatt. These children were referred to them by a wide range of professionals in the field: social workers; family practitioners; health visitors; community medical officers; junior medical staff; and nurses. However, it was not the diversity of reporting agents nor the scale of the purported abuse that was eventually seen to be at the heart of the crisis but the paediatricians' unswerving belief in particular physical signs to be the basis of their diagnosis of sexual abuse and their response to the findings as if there was an imminent threat to life or limb.

This appeared to be one of the crucial findings of the report, which states:

'By reaching a firm conclusion on the basis of physical signs and acting as they would for non-accidental injury or physical abuse; by separating children from their parents and by admitting most of the children to hospital, they compromised the work of social workers and the police. The medical diagnosis assumed a central and determining role in the management of the child and the family.'

Thus, although the report conceded that it was perfectly proper for the paediatricians to play a part in the identification of abuse in children referred to them, they 'also had a responsibility to examine their own actions, to consider whether their practice was correct and whether it was in the best interests of the children, their patients'. This, the report concludes, 'the doctors manifestly failed to do'. Higgs and Wyatt were therefore criticised for:

> 'their certainty and over-confidence with which they pursued the detection of child sexual abuse in children referred to them. They were not solely nor . . . principally responsible for the subsequent management of the children concerned [but] the certainty of their findings . . . posed particular problems for the police and social services.'

2.15.6 Abuse neither proved nor disproved by the reflex anal dilatation test

A key physical sign of sexual abuse used by Drs Higgs and Wyatt was the controversial reflex anal dilatation ('RAD') test. However, having heard and carefully considered the views of several medical practitioners of different specialities on the possible significance of the RAD test, the inquiry team concluded that 'from the evidence . . . the consensus is that . . . anal dilatation is abnormal and suspicious and requires further investigation. It is not in itself evidence of anal abuse'. The researchers (Wynne and Hobbs) on whom Dr Higgs had relied, had in fact stressed in their seminal paper that RAD should be considered in combination with other factors relating to the child and the family. An ironic effect of Cleveland is that it focused attention on the fact that just as physical abnormalities may have an innocent explanation, sexual abuse of children may occur *without* ano-genital contact (see (1987) *The Lancet*, October 10, at p 832).

2.15.7 Recommendations of the Cleveland Report

The *Cleveland Report* concluded with 10 pages of recommendations, including a flow-chart model for inter-agency response to child sexual abuse. The report found that child sexual abuse cannot be conveniently categorised as a medical, social work or legal issue. Most of the recommendations are addressed to the professionals concerned, reiterating the need for training, collaboration and procedures, but stressing that 'neither parents' nor children's needs and rights can be adequately met or protected unless agencies agree a framework for their inter-action'. They also recommended the 'development of inter-agency co-operation which acknowledges that no single agency has the pre-eminent responsibility in the assessment of child sexual abuse'.

Other key recommendations include:

(1) local authorities setting up specialist assessment teams;
(2) devising codes of practice on the administration of emergency court orders;
(3) exhorting the professionals to listen to the child;
(4) abandoning of repeated or confrontational 'disclosure' interviews;

(5) giving parents the right of access to their children generally, notification in writing of access arrangements should be given by the social services;

(6) keeping parents informed and advised of their rights and treating them with courtesy;

(7) allowing parents the right to attend case conferences unless, in the chairman's view, their presence will preclude a full and proper consideration of the child's interests;

(8) reminding social workers that irrespective of whether parents attend case conferences, social workers have a primary responsibility to ensure that the conference has information both of the family background and parents' views on the relevant issues;

(9) the police developing inter-agency working arrangements including joint planning and interviewing.

2.15.8 Cleveland Report recommendations to the medical profession

The following recommendations were also made by the *Cleveland Report* to the medical profession (at p 247) which we have summarised as follows.

(1) They should agree a consistent vocabulary to describe physical signs associated with child sexual abuse.

(2) They should investigate the natural history and significance of signs and symptoms associated with child sexual abuse.

(3) There should be further consideration given to the significance of RAD.

(4) They should make full and accurate records (a 'full medical history') which should provide the necessary information for protective agencies and, wherever necessary, the courts.

(5) Repeated forensic medical examinations of the child should not be carried out purely for evidential purposes. In every case, the medical profession should seek the informed consent of parents for examinations unconnected with immediate treatment.

2.15.9 Effects of the Cleveland controversy and Report

The immediate and tangible effect of the Cleveland controversy and *Cleveland Report* was the publication of a range of advisory booklets aimed at all professionals working in the field of child abuse in general and child sexual abuse in particular. The main features and guidelines of these booklets are discussed in Chapters 4 and 5 of this book. They have been used by all health care professionals including doctors, midwives and nurses, teachers and social workers. Various recommendations from the *Cleveland Report* have found their way into legislation (eg in relation to contact with the child (see Chapter 8)) and incorporated into various guides such as *Working Together* which was updated in 1991 to take account of more recent developments such as organised abuse (see Chapter 5) and cases dealing with parental involvement in case conferences (see Chapter 9). These are just a few examples of a number of reforms and improvements that are directly traceable if not in origin, then certainly in impetus, to the *Cleveland Report*'s recommendations. There are now special child abuse officers, joint training for police and social workers, as well as special child abuse teachers in many schools throughout the country. Medical sources inform us that the use of second opinions has now gained widespread acceptance.

The Cleveland crisis was, of course, responsible for both focusing attention on medical opinions and doctors' roles in child abuse investigations, and also for diminishing doctors' hitherto central importance in cases where there was no other *unequivocal* evidence of sexual abuse. At the height of the controversy, it became commonplace to read about differences of opinion between medical 'experts' in different branches of the profession: the police surgeon tended to disagree quite sharply with the views of Higgs and Wyatt and could support her views by referring to her superior experience in investigating ano-genital abuse over 20 years. Thus, the status of the medical diagnosis was undoubtedly put into a lower category of child abuse indicia than before and no longer seen as conclusive unless there was other corroborating evidence.

The practice of interviewing children, as carried out by police and social workers, has also undergone changes, partly attributable to the 'Cleveland factor': the admissibility of videotaped interviews to replace the examination-in-chief of a child witness, and the Home Office guide to such videotaping for children who might become witnesses in subsequent criminal proceedings, the *Memorandum of Good Practice* ('*MoGP*') (see Chapter 6 and, especially, Chapter 7). The *MoGP* takes up where Cleveland and *Working Together* left off, but it is not a mandatory code. The Cleveland guidelines on interviewing child witnesses are now seen as complementary to the *MoGP* and have been judicially approved. Parliamentary passage of the 1989 Act was hastened by the Cleveland crisis and it undoubtedly spelt the demise of the place of safety order, a reform which had already been suggested in documents such as the 1987 Government White Paper *The Law on Child Care and Family Services* (1987) Cm 62.

In 1991, the Royal College of Physicians issued their guidelines on detection of sexual abuse of children, *Physical signs of sexual abuse in children* (1991, Royal College of Physicians of London) which confirmed the importance of RAD but reiterated the importance of a 'multi-disciplinary investigation with full inter-agency co-operation' (at para 6.3) before making a diagnosis of child sexual abuse. It states unequivocally that 'The single most important feature is a statement by the child' (at p 46). One doubts whether such a statement would have been made before Cleveland occurred and its repercussions are clearly being felt across all child protection agencies (see, further, Chapter 5). The Cleveland crisis also shifted the focus of child protection agencies, at least in the public perception, from physical to sexual abuse. In a sense, it provided a foil to the earlier criticisms of social workers not acting early enough to their acting too soon and over-zealously. By discrediting an all-encompassing medical test, however, it actually restored the balance of professional status to other non-medical agencies. No one agency's opinion should now be seen as determinative or predominant but their various opinions must now be seen as complementary to the others' diagnoses. The Cleveland crisis and *Cleveland Report* succeeded in making inter-agency co-operation the main method of approaching cases of suspected child abuse.

2.16 The compilation of child abuse inquiry reports

The compilation of child abuse inquiry reports (which reviews 19 child abuse inquiries but excludes Cleveland) (*Child Abuse: A Study of Inquiry Reports 1980–89* (1991, HMSO) ('the *Compilation Report*')) highlights several important points.

The reports seem to suggest that there is a 'fragmentation/isolation of child protection services from the rest of child care'. The compilation authors stress that the inquiries are the 'most extreme form of special arrangements, legal and administrative, for scrutinising for child protection services as distinct from the rest of the services which children in need should receive'. This, they argue, has a direct bearing on the way in which the professions advise and assist the local authority.

> 'The inquiries represent in an extreme form the polarisation of points of view, and of people, in a framework that is supposed to bring people into working together. This is . . . reflected in the adversarial nature of the inquiries . . . [and] in the stance of the media in those major public events and in the polarisation of the children's interests versus the parents' interests versus public interests versus professional interests.'
> 'The inquiries struggle both with defining their standards of judgment – usually "what could reasonably be expected on the basis of what was known at the time" – and defining standards of professional practice.'
> 'The inquiries make a number of interesting comments about training and yet the reader is left with no clear view about what kind of training is most needed.'

We would suggest that management training should have a high priority since it is deficiencies in management decisions that have frequently been exposed in the reports.

> 'The single most important outcome from inquiries of the 80s has been the establishment of a set of principles for professional relationships to parents and children, in the Cleveland Report. Yet if this is to be more than a convention of good manners strategies for turning policy into practice and sharing best practice, nationally, need to be developed.'

The inquiries are, in the view of the *Compilation Report*, limited in their usefulness since their focus has tended to be on presenting a view of what happened and who was to blame (although not within the specific remit) but not why, except to the extent of administrative or procedural mistakes. The *Compilation Report* points out, further, that a key issue is 'the relationship between policies, procedures and practices of individual agencies in relation to child protection [and] how they relate to the law and the statutory duties of the local authority and the most effective way the agencies can work together'.

2.17 Effects of child abuse inquiries on social work practice

It appears that whereas the earlier physical abuse cases prompted the increased use of place of safety orders (between 1985 and 1987), the publication of the *Cleveland Report* has certainly led to a re-thinking within the social work profession about how best to respond to referrals from other agencies and information that they might receive themselves. The NSPCC and DOH figures giving an estimate of the national incidence, in the aftermath of Cleveland, for the period 1988 to 1990 in terms of children registered for sexual abuse shows a six per cent increase between 1988 and 1989 and a fall of 20 per cent between 1989 and 1990 (see *Child Abuse Trends in England and Wales 1988–90* (1992, NSPCC)). It is impossible to say what direct effect might have been played by the 'Cleveland factor' but there is no doubt that for many agencies, it constitutes a reminder that although every professional concerned must continue to be vigilant against child abuse, the words of Butler-Sloss must continue to be the watchword: 'The child is a person and not an object of concern'.

As far as the current situation under the 1989 Act is concerned, we discuss the latest trends in the final chapter of this book.

2.18 The residential homes inquiries

2.18.1 General survey

Residential care may be defined as:

'continuous residence in permanently staffed accommodation for more than three children, which provides or enables access to the care and services normally available to children and such additional measures of care, control and treatment as resident children require' (*Children in the Public Care* (1991, HMSO), ('the *Utting Report*') at para 2.1).

There have been many reports and inquiries into aspects of residential care for children, some of which date from the 1950s. Inquiries into serious misconduct were the *Report of the Inquiry into the Conduct of Leeway's Children's Home* (1985, London Borough of Lewisham), *The Pindown Experience and the Protection of Children: The Report of the Staffordshire Child Care Inquiry* (1991, Staffordshire Social Services) ('the *Pindown Report*') and the *Ty Mawr Community Home Inquiry* (1992, Gwent County Council) as well as various general reports reviewing the state of children's homes, such as the *Utting Report* (above) and *Choosing with Care* (1992, HMSO) ('the *Warner Committee Report*').

There has also been an investigation into misconduct with children at a special school, which led to a guide being produced for professionals who may need to deal with these sorts of problems (see the *Castle Hill Report* (1992, Shropshire County Council)). We provide an overview of some of the main features of these and other reports in order to highlight recurrent themes and issues.

(1) The *Leeway's Report* concerned an officer in charge of a children's home who was convicted of various offences involving indecent photography of young children. The report's main findings indicated that for about six years this officer's superiors were aware of his unacceptable behaviour which had sexual implications but failed to tackle him about their concerns. The report found that 'at almost every point at which collectively or individually the people involved had to choose between making the welfare of the child the first consideration, and some conflicting loyalty or priority, they chose the latter'. Accountability for people in managerial positions and allocation of clearer job descriptions were recommended by the report.

(2) The *Hughes Report* (1985) on the Kincora 'scandals' involved homosexual acts and prostitution in nine boys' homes and hostels in Northern Ireland. It dealt with serious and politically controversial issues including allegations of an official cover-up and linkage with loyalist para-military organisations. It made 56 recommendations including the maintenance of training profiles for staff and managers, introduction of a staff appraisal scheme, regular staff meetings as an integral part of homes' management and a statement of aims and objectives for each home. Independent and unannounced visits to homes as well as more regular monitoring of homes by off-site managers were also recommended. Another suggestion was the strengthening of complaints procedures with police being brought in at an early stage where there were criminal allegations.

(3) The *Pindown Report* in 1991 revealed unacceptable practices in a local authority's children's homes for exercising control over children by means of a regime of isolation and deprivation of liberty. Staff were found to lack qualifications and experience and various recommendations were again made on specialist training in residential care. This report is discussed in greater detail below (see **2.18.2**).

(4) *Accommodating Children* (1992, Social Services Inspectorate, Wales and Social Information Systems), the 1991 Review of Homes in Wales, identified three striking features in current management of, and practice in, children's homes therein: (a) the functions they are expected to perform are ill-defined and their locus within local child care strategies is marginal

and unspecific; (b) a great deal of good and some excellent work is being done which is largely unrecognised by the managing and purchasing departments; consequently, it is greatly under-exploited; (c) their principal explicit function, managing and treating seriously challenging behaviour, is poorly achieved for a number of reasons; most notable among these is the incompatibility of that function with the other demands upon them.

The report places great store on the design and location of buildings and not forcing children in residential care to share rooms. The report's major recommendation is that there should be two types of children's homes: (a) those for children who are displaying seriously challenging behaviour which cannot be contained in a family, a home or in foster care; and (b) those children in residential care as a matter of choice or as a result of circumstances rather than behaviour.

(5) The report of the Williams Inquiry on Ty Mawr Community Home (the *Ty Mawr Community Home Inquiry* (1992)) in Gwent reviewed a number of incidents of suicide and self-harm and concluded that the home should close as soon as possible. There was, in this case, an 'inappropriate mix of residents cared for in large measure by unqualified staff'. Senior management was criticised as well as the actions of elected members in appointing staff. A recommendation was made that 'the local authority should care for its own employees'.

(6) The *Castle Hill Report* (1992) was issued by Shropshire County Council as a practice guide, but it also reviews briefly the development of child protection in Great Britain, in particular child sexual abuse and the sexual and physical abuse perpetrated by the founder of the school, who had established a power structure in the school of sinecures and bullying. Several of the boys, aged between 12 and 16, who resided at the school, were physically and sexually abused by Morris, the founder of the school, over a period of four years. Morris was sentenced to 12 years' imprisonment on 16 counts of offences against young people in his care, ranging from physical assault to indecent assault and buggery. Among the recommendations made by the report were the confirmation and validation of staff qualifications and backgrounds (Morris had fabricated some of his qualifications), and an effective method of monitoring pupil numbers by checking registers and by making unannounced visits to the establishment.

2.18.2 The Pindown affair

(a) The Pindown regime

The Pindown affair involved the regimentation of 132 children in four children's homes in Staffordshire which set up a system of deprivation of liberty and solitary confinement to punish teenagers. These children were sometimes left in a room containing only a table and chair for weeks at a time with only their nightclothes, when undergoing the 'Pindown' regime. Children were sometimes forced to bunny-hop outside in their underwear and bare feet, around a social worker with a cane in his hand (see the *Pindown Report* at para 4.45). All these measures grew out of what Tony Latham (who had said 'we must pin down the problem'), the chief architect and prime practitioner of Pindown, called 'behaviour modification'. This consisted of removal of clothes and personal possessions on admission; baths; wearing of night wear, underwear and dressing gown and 'no footwear of any description'; meals in the room; knocking on the door for permission to impart information or to go to the bathroom (one of the children told of how she often had to wait a considerable time for anyone to respond to these knocks when she needed to go to the toilet); no communication with residents; no television, music, magazines, cigarettes or telephone calls; requirements to do physical exercise outdoors in their underwear; and rising at 7am and going to bed at 7pm after having a bath. Latham himself described the regime as 'the isolation of a young person to a room away from the main care of the building, where loss of privileges are asserted'. The actual use of Pindown, as used in four residential establishments in Staffordshire, went far beyond its basic philosophy. Four main features were identified by the report as characteristic of the Pindown regime: (1) isolation for part of the time in a section of a children's home cordoned off as a 'special' or Pindown unit; (2) removal of ordinary clothing for part of the time and the enforced wearing of shorts or night clothes; (3) being told of having to earn privileges; and (4) being allowed to attend school or a 'school room' in the unit and changing back into shorts or night clothes after returning from school.

Among the traumatic effects on the children were feelings of isolation, humiliation of having to wear night clothes, intense frustration, boredom and lack of recreation. The children were already extremely difficult, had a history of violence and were frequently disturbed and unwanted. Eighty-one boys and 51 girls were subjected to the regime.

Eventually, one of the girls, aged 15, who had been placed in the home, jumped 20 feet out of a window in an attempt to escape, sprained her ankle and went a considerable distance before being returned by the police. The girl managed to contact a local solicitor, Kevin Williams, who telephoned the deputy director of Staffordshire County Council's social services department expressing his concern about the girl, for whom he was acting in care proceedings. The following day, after various consultations, the then Director of Social Services terminated the Pindown regime. Subsequently, the girl and a boy, also 15, were made wards of court by Williams and the High Court later granted injunctions prohibiting the use of Pindown by social services.

Over the next few months considerable concern was expressed and the media became interested in the Pindown regime. On 29 June 1990, Levy and Kahan were appointed by Staffordshire County Council to conduct an independent inquiry into the whole matter.

The Pindown Experience and the Protection of Children: The Report of the Staffordshire Child Care Inquiry ('the *Pindown Report*') published in 1991 categorically condemned Pindown, saying that it fell outside anything that could be considered as good child care practice.

(b) Recommendations

The *Pindown Report* made 39 recommendations but among the more significant are the following:

(1) Regular scrutiny of measures of control used in residential establishments.

(2) Close liaison between those monitoring measures of control and the legal department.

(3) Completion of log books in such a way that:
   (a) they disclose who is on duty on the day on which entries are made;
   (b) all entries are written in appropriate and clear language;
   (c) all entries are signed with the name of the signatory clearly identified; and
   (d) all entries are clearly dated.

(4) Forms used by statutory visits to residential care establishments to highlight the question of 'control' and direct the visitor to make specific comments regarding measures of control.

(5) Prior circulation of previous visitors' completed forms to the next statutory visitor.

(6) Visitors' reports to go unaltered to the appropriate committee.

(7) No advance notice be given of statutory visits.

(8) Amendment of law relating to 'control and discipline' of children in residential homes. *The Children Act 1989 Guidance and Regulations Vol 4 Residential Care* (1991, HMSO) has now been issued, which prohibits various disciplinary measures explicitly. In addition, the DOH has issued its *Guidance on Permissible Forms of Control in Children's Residential Care* (1993, DOH), and a further document specifically dealing with secure accommodation is promised. The problems which arise in the interpretation of the DOH guidance are discussed in detail in Chapter 7. It should be noted that under this guidance, children in residential homes may be restrained, if suspected of trying to abscond, but usually only where there are sufficient staff at hand to ensure that it can be achieved safely. Under no circumstances must a child (of whatever age or competence) be locked into his or her bedroom at night. Physical

restraint is permissible, if necessary, to prevent injury to any person, or serious damage to property, but physical restraint should always be used as an act of control not punishment. Children in care may be prohibited from going out as a punishment but the child must not be prevented from leaving by being locked in or physically restrained, and Children's Homes Regulations 1991 (SI 1991/1506), reg 8(2)(c) is observed. The acceptable limits to the restriction of liberty will depend on 'circumstances including the space available to the child within which he is restricted, his age, competence and physical and emotional well-being' (see para 4.5 of the *Pindown Report*).

(9) A named person at senior management level to have responsibility (a) for ensuring that care and attention has been given to the education, career development and working life of children in care and (b) for the consideration of any policy or practice issues.

(10) The named person to provide an annual report on the matters for which he has responsibility.

(11) Social services departments to issue written guidance to staff dealing with the topic of the protection of children in residential establishments and, in particular, covering the regulation and vetting of general visitors to such establishments.

(12) The Home Office and DOH to clarify or extend the present arrangement concerning the disclosure of the criminal background of those with access to children, so that a local authority may make appropriate police checks, if necessary.

(13) A member of the social services department to be made specifically responsible for liaison with the legal department in order to review jointly, on a regular basis, matters which may require specific consideration and advice from the legal department. (The legal department for Staffordshire social services was never consulted on the legality of the Pindown measures.)

(14) Complaints procedure to be established for staff, foster parents and children.

(15) The social services department to implement a system of supervision as a matter of urgency.

Supervision of staff was minimal and even described as 'the blind leading the blind'. The *Pindown Report* describes a form of supervision which would combine an independent appraisal with clear objectives.

(16) Strategy of training for the next five years to be developed as a matter of urgency.

(17) An urgent review of the social services department's staffing policy to
be undertaken.

The *Pindown Report* listed Staffordshire Social Services' many deficiencies
as: restrictive advertising; inadequate staff selection procedures; low staffing
ratios; dependence on untrained staff; over-reliance on volunteers and casual
staff; lack of training; lack of supervision; absence of career structures for
residential staff; and inadequate budget support.

Since the publication of the *Pindown Report*, a number of compensation
claims have been made against the county council, in the High Court. Something in the order of nearly 140 children who endured the Pindown regime
have received cash payments in a 1.7 million pound compensation settlement,
with claims ranging from £500 to £41,000. The last action of the current
batch of claimants was heard in March 1993 in the High Court.

In June 1992, it was reported that a Social Services Inspectorate report
(see (1992) *The Times*, June 11), criticised Staffordshire County Council for
making only slow progress in reforming the way that it runs its children's
homes. The report makes it clear that there was no evidence akin to Pindown
and that most of the homes offer a warm, caring environment and that virtually all the young residents and their parents had praised the staff and the
quality of care. However, there were still failings at strategic and operational
levels. The authority still had no overall policy for children's services and was
in breach of regulations in not having statements of purpose. Staffordshire
responded that 24 of the recommendations had been implemented and that
there had been serious staff shortages and inadequate government funding.

2.18.3 The Leicester Inquiry: the Frank Beck case

(a) The background

In 1991, another child sex abuse residential care scandal emerged which
involved Frank Beck, a senior social worker, who had apparently terrorised
and abused children and young people in his care for 13 years. Beck had been
employed by Leicestershire's social services department between 1973 and 1986,
during which time a number of complaints about the treatment of children in
his care were made, both to the social services department and to the police.

Frank Beck, a former Royal Marines sergeant, had been appointed officer
in charge of a children's home in Leicestershire having just qualified in social
work, on the basis of a reference from a lecturer in social work and another
reference, which was riddled with spelling mistakes, from a former officer
in charge. At his interview, Beck made it clear he intended to establish a
'therapeutic community' at the home using 'regression therapy'.

It later transpired that regression therapy, as practised by Beck and his
care staff, involved the bizarre use of the paraphernalia of babyhood in the
treatment of adolescent boys and girls. It was under the guise of regression

therapy that much of the physical abuse of children took place and ultimately led to the sexual abuse of children. Beck was a dominant personality and was willing to accept the most difficult children in the country. He appeared to have a high level of success which impressed his senior managers. Beck eventually even managed to establish himself as an expert in child care.

In 1989, Mrs Outhwaite who, as a young woman had been in residential care at one of the three homes that Beck ran, told her family's social worker of her experiences while in Beck's charge. This involved physical abuse of herself and other children. Police were informed and a thorough and wide-spread police investigation was precipitated in the course of which almost 600 potential witnesses were identified and traced and witness statements were taken from 383 of them. In May 1990 the police arrested four men who had been employed in children's homes in Leicestershire, including Frank Beck. It was thought that Beck may have abused up to 200 children.

Beck was convicted on 17 counts involving sexual and physical assault, and was sentenced to five life sentences, in total 33 years' imprisonment. Following the conclusion of the 11-week trial, which had been the longest sex abuse trial in Great Britain, the Secretary of State for Health announced the setting up of two inquiries, one examining the selection and appointment methods and criteria for staff working in children's homes (see *Choosing with Care* (1992, HMSO) ('the *Warner Committee Report*')); and the other (the Kirkwood Inquiry) to report on management responses to complaints and evidence of abuse, malpractice and other related matters in Leicestershire in the light of the trial of Frank Beck and other child care officers for the period 1973–86 ('the *Kirkwood Report*') (see below). The Police Complaints Authority also conducted an inquiry and published its findings on the same day as the Kirkwood Inquiry.

(b) The Leicestershire Reports

Two reports were published in early 1993, *The Leicestershire Inquiry 1992 (The Kirkwood Report)* (1993, Leicestershire Social Services) ('the *Kirkwood Report*') and the police complaints inquiry report, *Inquiry into Police Investigation of Complaints of Child and Sexual Abuse in Leicestershire Children's Homes* (1993, Police Complaints Authority) (the '*PCA Report*').

Both reports condemn Leicestershire County Council and the police for a combination of blunders that failed to stop Beck's reign until 1989.

The *Kirkwood Report* notes that the ease with which Beck was able to abuse the children in his care was due, in large part, to the 'management vacuum' in Leicestershire social services department which, therefore, created the environment for the abuse and ill-treatment to flourish (see para 50.19 of the report). It names 10 managers who held managerial responsibility for the circumstances that arose. Furthermore, Management Officers knew that specialist treatment resources out of the county were extremely expensive.

Their naivety in believing that Mr Beck had established a local specialist resource (at para 50.13):

> ' "on the cheap" and without meeting any of the necessary criteria is astonishing, but is part and parcel of Care Branch (sic) [the department responsible for dealing with children's homes] as a whole. Mr. Beck's treatment methods, the product of untutored and ill-digested study of therapeutic theories, were the antithesis of good child care and were fundamentally abusive.'

The tightly knit staff who worked for Beck were 'caught up in their own misguided enthusiasm' for his methods. Further, the absence of a policy framework for child care managers based upon principles of openness and good child care left them without a bench mark against which the style of the home and child care practices within it could be tested. A host of other criticisms were made of the relevant office managers, ranging from a failure to perceive the likelihood that a complaint might well raise child care and management issues that needed to be addressed, to Beck's indispensability, since he was willing to take on even the most difficult children. Managers were consequently afraid to challenge Beck. Whilst aware of allegations about specific sexual and physical assaults, as well as numerous complaints, other officers in charge adopted an 'out of sight, out of mind attitude'. Management simply failed to formulate any sort of guidance or framework for the investigation of complaints. Worst of all, the report mentions a 'general disposition not to believe children. There was an assumption that children either had an ulterior motive for complaint or would be likely, for whatever reason, to fabricate' (at para 50.23).

The *PCA Report* looked at 29 cases where complaints were made about Beck and concluded that Beck's activities could have been exposed by investigations into his conduct in 1977, 1985 and 1986. Ironically, 'the substance of these complaints was greater than that of the complaint in 1989 which led to Beck's ultimate conviction'. In nearly every case, a complaint arose because a child had absconded from a children's home but officers failed to follow up and establish why the children had run away. Indeed, they openly disbelieved children's complaints, exhibiting hostility to the children. In every case the police returned the child to the home and the social worker accused of abuse was allowed to remain at work throughout the course of the investigation. Although police interviewed the children either at the home where they were abused or, often, in front of the abuser, or in a police station, they failed to record or investigate complaints and did not question key witnesses. Moreover, where there was evidence of physical injury, it was often not taken seriously and treated by some officers as 'summary justice'.

The *PCA Report* calls for a review of the law in respect of information disclosure, so that Chief Police Officers may be given discretion to alert employers to suspicions about their staff even when investigation of alleged child abuse leads to no charges being brought. It also recommends special training for officers dealing with abuse cases and better liaison between police and social services departments.

2.18.4 Comment on the Leicestershire Reports

No one involved with the Beck case appears to have emerged with their credibility or reputation intact. There were clearly serious flaws in the system in Leicestershire, and the *Kirkwood Report* is the ninth in the last eight years. Even allowing for the fact that Beck was obviously a dominant figure, forceful, manipulative and petulant, the absence of adequate checks on his activities, the appalling management vacuum, and the lack of a formalised framework of independent supervision and regular monitoring of children's homes all contributed to the abuse being allowed to carry on for so many years. There is now an independent inspection procedure and a complaints procedure under the 1989 Act. But apart from quality control, it is really the residential care worker who needs to be better trained and, therefore, better able to cope with the particular pressures of residential care work. The *PCA Report*'s recommendations should also be considered seriously. Local authority control of children's homes is clearly facing great pressures and tensions. Perhaps it is time for a reappraisal of how, and who best, to run children's homes, including the possibility of having representatives from the police, councillors and respected lay people.

2.18.5 General comments

It only remains to highlight some of the main concerns which have been identified in all these reports.

(1) The reports illustrate the far-reaching consequences of a less than rigorous recruitment policy for residential care workers.
(2) They emphasise the need for specialised training for those intending to work in children's homes.
(3) They suggest that managers need to receive specialised training over and above any other training which they already have undergone.
(4) The pay and career structures of residential care workers must be enhanced so that the image of such workers can be upgraded and incentives provided which will attract persons of integrity and high morals.
(5) The reports demonstrate the need for 'spot-checks' by independent auditors, so that 'one-man shows' such as those run by Morris, Latham and Beck are unable to operate within such wide measures of managerial freedom which allows abuse to flourish.
(6) There is still a need for greater inter-agency co-operation.
(7) Attitudes towards children who have been in trouble must be changed so that when children disclose abuse, they are taken seriously and have

their complaints properly investigated and are not treated as 'problem children' who are not to be believed in any event. However, an open mind rather than one with preconceptions is required, so that a child protection officer is prepared to investigate complaints but is also prepared for the investigation not to lead to anything.

(8) On a more radical note, perhaps, different types of residential children's homes are required, to cater for different types of children in need.

Whatever is finally decided upon, however, the aims, objectives and needs of the child must be considered carefully in every case, so that expediency is never allowed to override the welfare of the child.

2.19 Other cases of suspected child abuse

2.19.1 Satanic abuse and ritual abuse

Satanic or ritual abuse appears to cover a wide range of abusing activities involving groups of adults and extends from 'sexual abuse committed in a ritualistic context to psychological abuse in the context of bizarre rituals which are horrifying experiences for the children' (see Latham, 'Satanic and Ritual Abuse' [1991] FCR 693). Latham suggests that the current understanding of ritual abuse falls broadly into four categories: (1) sexual abuse committed by a group of adults in bogus circumstances (see *Re C and L (Child Abuse: Evidence)* [1991] FCR 351 ('the *Manchester* case'); (2) ritual sexual abuse, usually involving the administration of hallucinogenic drugs; (3) satanic abuse, involving bizarre and horrifying ritual and psychological and sexual abuse; and (4) involvement in rituals without a sexual component arising from strong or fanatical religious beliefs, involving abuse which amounts to cruelty.

Judgments were given in open court in two cases which were tried in Manchester which were allegedly satanic/ritual abuse cases. These were *Rochdale Borough Council v A and Others* [1991] 2 FLR 192 ('the *Rochdale* case') and *Re C and L* (above) ('the *Manchester* case') which are discussed below.

As far as satanic abuse is concerned, in the course of giving evidence at the *Rochdale* case, Mrs Valerie Mellor, Consultant Clinical Psychologist, testifying as an expert witness, said that:

'satanic abuse refers to practices which take place within the framework of a belief system, namely belief in witchcraft or the occult. In such a situation children would be used as instruments of the people holding such a belief in order to (a) indoctrinate the children and cause them to become disciples of the belief and (b) in order for them to carry out particular ceremonies which would call for the use of children. The term "ritual abuse" has been used within the last two years to describe the use of children in bizarre activities or in pseudo satanic abuse. This would involve the use of children by adults mainly or wholly to satisfy the needs of adults. The use of the rituals would be to fulfil three functions: (i) to gain the co-operation of the children by fear; (ii) to discourage any adults who wish to change their minds about the situation; and (iii) to disinform any persons making inquiries about the children and to ensure that should the children talk inadvertently, they would not be believed. Whether abuse is satanic in origin or is pseudo or ritual abuse, the effect on the children is very similar; that is, any children involved in either practice would be very seriously damaged and would require long-term treatment to aid some kind of recovery. However, it must be borne in mind that sexual abuse of children, particularly if sadistic elements are incorporated, can cover a very wide range of behaviours including many of those described in the American literature as only being present in satanic abuse: eg bondage, knives, urination and defecation onto others, drinking of urine, eating of faeces, insertion of sticks or other objects into the vagina or anus, use of drugs or alcohol, and use of photography. The effect of sadistic sexual abuse on children can be equally as devastating as that of so-called satanic or ritual practices.'

It should be remembered that being a witch or satanist is not, in itself, a crime. However, some of their associated practices most clearly could be, if proven. Proof of buggery of children by objects or insects, rape, and indecent assault, would render the perpetrators liable to criminal charges. However, the only two widely reported cases of suspected organised abuse, which were also allegedly ritual or satanic in character, were cases in Nottingham and Kent.

In the *Nottingham* case there were allegations of abuse against 23 children; 10 adults were charged and jailed in February 1989 for incest, indecent assault and cruelty against the children. The police had, in the course of their inquiries, discounted the allegations and serious flaws in the investigative process were uncovered. An inquiry team reported that there was no evidence of satanic or ritual abuse. Yet, it has only been in Nottingham that any sort of ritualistic abuse has been believed.

In the *Kent* case, there were nine separate trials involving 75 children and 17 defendants; it was discovered that a sex ring had been operating with children being routinely shared as sex tools within a circle of family members. Convictions followed.

In 1990, the NSPCC apparently had seven of its 66 child protection teams working with victims of ritualistic abuse, which, as well as sexual and physical abuse, 'involved calling on supernatural powers, the use of masks, animal sacrifices, the drinking of blood and urine and smearing of faeces on the victims'. (see Renvoize *Innocence Destroyed* (1993, Routledge) at p 120). Considerable uncertainties remain with regard to all these cases, since 'normal' child sexual abuse might well account for the terror and trauma exhibited by some of these abuse victims. Despite the recognition of organised abuse in *Working Together* (1991), however, the fact remains that there is a serious lack of positive evidence of satanic and ritual abuse. Courts and the general public remain sceptical and, perhaps, the best that professionals can do is to keep an open mind and ensure that, as in every child abuse investigation, the main priority is to safeguard the well-being and emotional stability of the child.

2.19.2 The Rochdale case

Rochdale Borough Council v A and Others ('the *Rochdale* case') [1991] 2 FLR
192, involved allegations made by the local authority that 20 children from
six families were involved in satanic or ritual abuse. There did not seem to
be any allegation of sexual abuse as such. This is the first reported case where
the nature of such abuse is considered and described in the judgment.

The facts of the case were as follows. Teachers at a school in Greater
Manchester reported to their social services department that a boy aged 6
was severely disturbed and talked to them about ghosts and a ghost family
that were part of his life. This started a sequence of events which led to 20
children in six families being made wards of court, the majority being
removed from their homes, as a result of allegations by the local authority
that they had been subjected to, or were at risk of, satanic or ritual abuse
by adults, either involving the parents or with the parents' co-operation or
complicity. Two social workers interviewed two of the children who talked
of ghosts in the house who took the boy from his home, of being given drinks
that made him fly and of the killing of babies. Place of safety orders were
obtained for all four children of the family. The children were interviewed
again on a number of occasions. Most of the interviews were not videotaped
or, if they were, the machine was often faulty. In the following months, social
workers became convinced that the children and probably most of the family
had been given hallucinogenic drugs and subjected to organised ritual abuse.
Wardship orders were then obtained on another five families. The children
were subsequently sent to foster homes. By that time, all the children had
been medically examined and no evidence of sexual abuse had been found,
with the possible exception of one child in family 2. Six of the children had
mentioned ghosts in interviews. In a consolidated wardship hearing, the local
authority proposed that the majority of the children concerned should be
permanently removed from their parents. By the end of the 47-day hearing,
the final decision of the local authority was: (i) that satanic or ritual abuse
had taken place, on the balance of probabilities, in the case of two children
in family 1 who had been interviewed; (ii) that it was possible that three of
those children interviewed in family 2 had been involved; (iii) that there was
insufficient evidence of satanic abuse in families 4 and 6. Of the remaining
families, two of the children had remained with their mother throughout and
the remaining child had already been allowed to go home.

2.19.3 The judgment

The court (per Douglas Brown J) held as follows:

(1) On the evidence, the only conclusion was that the children's statements
    about flying, killing babies and similar statements 'were most likely not

to have been induced by drugs. It was obvious that the children had not been describing real events when they talked of flying and killing babies but were fantasising'.

(2) The case turned on what the children themselves had said. Consequently, it had to be shown that the children's evidence had been obtained in a reliable form and that it had been correctly and accurately analysed. As to reliability, the manner of questioning the children and the method of recording the interviews were unsatisfactory. The judge found the video recordings flawed in several respects – the figures were distant and indistinct so that facial expressions were not observable, the sound was muffled, and although the children were often inaudible, the interviewers' questions were plainly heard which had the effect of throwing the interview technique into high relief. There were also instances where interviews were not videotaped and some of these were crucial.

(3) Before removing children precipitately from their homes, the social services should have sought the advice of a consultant child psychiatrist or child psychologist as a matter of urgency. A key statement which was made by Douglas Brown J in the *Rochdale* case was thus: 'Where social workers suspect satanic or ritual abuse and the evidence consists of children's behaviour and statements, they should not remove children from their family before they have taken the advice of an experienced child psychiatrist or child psychotherapist . . . The court, on an *ex parte* application, should be slow to act in a ritual abuse case in the absence of such an expert overview'.

Other illuminating comments were made:

(1) 'If children have to be removed it is potentially harmful to them to be removed early in the morning when, as here, they were aroused from sleep in many cases and . . . they were needlessly traumatised. If, as is almost certainly the case, it is the police who insist on such timing, the social worker should be prepared to act independently of the police and remove the children later in the day, for example, at the end of the school day.'

(2) There were so many breaches of the *Cleveland Report* guidelines that the information received from the children was valueless and unreliable. Indeed, 'over-interviewing led to exaggeration and fabrication by the child'.

(3) Anatomically correct dolls which had been utilised were referred to in the judgment. Douglas Brown J declared that these had been used recklessly, encouraging sexual non-directed play. (See also Chapter 7 on judicial attitudes to these dolls.)

(4) A multi-disciplinary approach was emphasised.

Accordingly, although there was no evidence to involve any of the families with satanic or ritual abuse: (1) the children in family 1 would not be returned to their parents, but an assessment of the parents would be ordered and the matter would be reviewed later in the year; (2) the children in family 2 would remain wards of court but would be returned to the care and control of their parents forthwith; (3) the only child in family 3 who had remained with her mother would be dewarded; (4) for family 4, the local authority had conceded there was no evidence of satanic or ritual abuse involving the family. One of the children had already returned home to her father and the remaining child would be returned forthwith to her father's care and control. Wardship would continue; (5) all the children in family 5 had been returned home and been dewarded by consent on the first day of the hearing; (6) the children of family 6 would remain wards but would also be returned immediately to their parents.

2.19.4 *General comment*

This case again revealed errors in judgment by the social workers involved, but with the added element of the possibility of ritual or satanic abuse – terms which are by no means synonymous. Children behaving strangely and talking about ghosts must, of course, be seen and talked to and, if necessary, counselling and therapy must be considered, apart from an investigation of the family circumstances. Abuse was certainly a possibility worth exploring but, in the cases themselves, there was no medical evidence of sexual or other abuse, with the exception of one child. In that child's case, it was clear that the possible abuse was not connected with any alleged satanic or ritual abuse. There was also no sign of sexualised behaviour in any of the children. To compound what was already rather inconclusive evidence, the interviews of the children were either carried out improperly or excessively and when videotaped, frequently with poor quality on-screen and in-sound reproduction. It is not surprising, therefore, that having heard the experts in the case, having considered the medical evidence and having watched the defective videos, the court came to the conclusion that the children were simply fantasising when they talked about ghosts, flying and killing babies. There was of course, no evidence of missing or dead babies. The children's physical demeanour was also not consonant with persons who had been administered hallucinogenic drugs, which are not widely available, and which require highly specialist knowledge to administer the proper dosage to produce just the right effect of apparent normality and compliance in the children.

The court called for 'proper and intensive training for those engaged in interviewing children whether ritual abuse or sexual abuse is suspected'. That training should be carried out by those skilled and experienced in the task such as child psychologists, but other professionals could also undertake the training. At the very least, the court stressed, the whole of the *Cleveland Report* should be read by social workers engaged in this sort of task.

2.19.5 The Manchester case

In the earlier case of *Re C and L (Child Abuse: Evidence)* [1991] FCR 351 ('the *Manchester* case'), an allegation had been made of sexual abuse in circumstances involving ritual abuse.

The facts of the case were that there were five applications in wardship in respect of 13 children who were all members of the same extended family. Suspicions of sexual abuse were first aroused in respect of two sisters (aged 8 and 6). Medical examinations showed they had been sexually abused. They were taken into care and fostered. They were also subjected to numerous and prolonged interviews. Based on what these children said, 10 other children were eventually taken into care and made wards of court. Based on what these 10 children had said, the social workers were convinced that there was a ring of abusers and that abuse had been carried out within a ritual or ceremonial setting and possibly in connection with satanic rites. The thirteenth child, who had been made a ward of court, was not the subject of allegations of sexual abuse, and was allowed to stay in the care of her parents.

All the other children were subjected to numerous interviews, at which notes were taken. Medical evidence confirmed that sexual abuse appeared to have been perpetrated on 12 of the warded children.

The hearing lasted 11 weeks, after which eight of the children were returned to their parents and five remained in care. Hollings J remarked that the social workers involved in this case were obsessed with the belief that they were investigating group satanic ritual abuse. He ruled that 'in almost every respect' the *Cleveland Report* guidelines (para 12.34) had been breached. Consequently, 'the value of the so-called disclosures' was much more limited than it might otherwise have been. The breaches included the use of untrained and inexperienced interviewers, the use of leading questions rather than open-ended ones, and excessive interviewing (an 8-year-old boy had apparently been interviewed 27 times). The judge also noted that there had been 'a great deal of fantasy and misleading replies to leading questions'. He held that as far as some of the children were concerned:

'there was probably abuse of a sadistic nature of the children in bogus ritual circumstances . . . sometimes of a ritual or ceremonial nature, and probably by more than one adult, but there is no reliable evidence of anything more, that is satanic or ritual abuse on a larger scale or abuse involving the use of video or for commercial purposes.'

He further ruled that early morning removals of children from their homes (as had happened with some of these children) 'should only be effected where it was essential to protect the children from significant harm or vital evidence was only obtainable by such means'.

2.19.6 Comment

The *Manchester* case (as with the subsequent *Rochdale* case) also stressed the necessity of conducting credible interviews, which should be carried out by trained and experienced interviewers. Medical evidence supported the suspicion that the children had been sexually abused but the court clearly drew a distinction between sadistic abuse carried out in ritual or ceremonial circumstances and satanic abuse. The problems of proving satanic or ritual abuse will doubtless remain for child protection officers seeking to establish the existence of such phenomena, but if abused children are rescued from *any* sexual abuse, irrespective of the circumstances, this must be a worthy objective in itself.

2.19.7 The Orkney Islands affair

(a) The events in Orkney

The most widely publicised child abuse case since Cleveland occurred in February 1991, when nine Orkney children, aged 8 to 15, were removed from their parents, on the basis of allegations of their having suffered ritual abuse. The removal of the Orkney children was sparked off by the reaction of social workers to allegations made by the children of another Orkney family, the W family, and which initiated the detention of the nine children. The father of the W family had been sentenced to seven years' imprisonment after having pleaded guilty to various offences of sexual abuse involving certain children of the family. Three of the W family apparently made allegations of what was interpreted as organised sexual abuse involving the children and parents of other families and a local minister. The minister's church was searched for five hours and his funeral robes removed as well as a broken cross. An assortment of books, a written quotation in Latin and French and a statuette were removed from the children's homes, supposedly items associated with ritual abuse.

Some of the nine children's families had corresponded with the W family and had supported Mrs W. Place of safety orders were obtained from a sheriff, following which the Orkney social services department took steps to remove the nine children at around 7 am carrying out a so-called 'dawn raid' with the aid of police.

The children were flown to placements in the Highland and Strathclyde Regions and were, for the most part, not allowed to take personal possessions with them. The children's placements were also split, with five of the children being placed with foster carers in the Highland Region, two sisters in Strathclyde placed together with one foster carer, their brother with another foster carer and one boy placed in a residential school. Access between the children was refused as was access by their other relatives. Social workers were later reported as saying that this was to prevent messages (either of intimidation or of ritualistic content) passing from relatives to the children and that 'there was the fear not only that one child might discourage another from disclosing but also that evidence might be contaminated with other members of the family' (see para 8.13 of the *Report of the Inquiry into the Removal of Children from Orkney in February 1991* (1992, HMSO) ('the *Orkney Report*')). As the report states: 'little attention was given to the possibility that the situation regarding the nine children might be different' (at para 8.13).

During the weeks following their removal, the children were interviewed by the police and RSSPCC staff and for some of the children the number of interviews was excessive (see para 14.98 of the *Orkney Report*). The parents were denied the grounds for referral, contrary to Scots law, and a hearing was eventually arranged before the sheriff. At the outset, an attack was made on the competency of the proceedings. Sheriff Kelbie dismissed the case on 4 April 1991, saying that the earlier children's hearings had been 'fatally flawed' and that the sooner the children were returned to their parents the better. The evidence was never heard. After the sheriff's decision, and on the same day, the children were returned to their parents in Orkney.

Television coverage, as well as photographs and eye-witness accounts at Orkney, suggested there were scenes of great rejoicings between parents and children and joyous celebrations at the reunion. Some of the parents had earlier stormed into the offices of the Director of Social Services in Orkney, demanding an apology when the verdict on the case had been handed down.

The Acting Reporter subsequently appealed to the Court of Session against the sheriff's decision but although he won the appeal he had already announced that whatever the outcome of the appeal he would not proceed with the case because of the 'incalculable media publicity' which had become so prejudicial and had damaged any prospects of the case ever having an objective hearing.

The parents of the children involved have declared their intentions to sue for 'substantial damages' but it has not been disclosed against whom the actions will be taken.

(b) The *Orkney Report*

The *Orkney Report* is a thorough and comprehensive 363-page document, which records certain findings derived from an eight-month inquiry which heard evidence from 69 witnesses called to testify on the allegations that the children had been subjected to sexual rituals in a disused quarry in South Ronaldsay. It is important to note, however, that the remit of the inquiry did not include establishing the truth or falsity of the allegations. The inquiry was set up only to consider the procedures used by the social work department and the police and the effect of the attendant publicity in relation to (a) the decision to remove the nine children from their homes and to detain them in a place of safety and (b) the decision not to continue proceedings before the sheriff for a finding on the evidence.

2.19.8 The Orkney Report's criticisms

The *Orkney Report* made 135 criticisms of the way the case was handled and declared that the social work department had not made a detailed enough study of the problem relating to the original family, had failed to keep an open mind on the allegations and had allowed their thinking to be 'coloured by undefined suspicions which they failed to explore' (at para 13.3).

Among the main criticisms were the following.

(1) The social work department had viewed the case as an extension of the earlier case of the W children. They had, therefore, failed to consider the position of each of the nine children or to assess the degree of risk to which they were exposed.

(2) Police and social workers failed to distinguish adequately between taking the children's allegations seriously and believing them.

(3) The social work department had failed to give sufficient thought to the question of whether it was necessary to remove the children, they therefore acted too precipitately and failed to take time to pause and think.

(4) There was failure by the RSSPCC, the social work department and the police to appreciate the significance of the fact that the allegations did not come from the allegedly abused children.

(5) There was insufficient detailed analysis by the same agencies of the information in the allegations.

(6) Greater regard should have been given to the particular source from which the particular allegations had come.

(7) The timing of the removal of the children was beyond serious criticism but the children should have been allowed to discuss the allegations during the course of their removal.

(8) The older children should have been given a full explanation of their rights and the procedure during the removal.

(9) The prohibition on personal possessions was inappropriate.

(10) Inadequate consideration was given by the social workers to the support of the parents and they failed to support or visit the parents after the removal of the children.

(11) Further and fuller information should have been given to the parents. They should have been invited to the case conference held in March 1991 and they should have been given information about the whereabouts of their children.

(12) Some access between siblings and by the parents and other relatives should have been allowed and the matter of access should have been kept under more active review.

(13) There was no detailed consideration of the purpose of the interviews of the nine children and no detailed planning of them.

(14) The interviewers failed to plan adequately how to deal with a child's denial or allegations and how to introduce explicit information and they over-stressed their belief in the truth of the allegations.

(15) The police interviewers were inadequately trained and they were inadequately supervised (this was a reference to relatively inexperienced officers carrying out the interviews without proper supervision).

(16) There was some deficiency in the experience and skill of the RSSPCC interviewers, inadequate control of their practice and no clear system for supervision and support.

(17) The interviewers made inappropriate use of the technique of re-introducing earlier drawings, of leading questions and in one case, of personal material.

(18) The parents should have been asked to sign written consent forms for the medical examinations carried out on the children during their period of removal.

2.19.9 The report's key recommendations

The report makes 194 recommendations, many of which follow on from the criticism but some of the most instructive are as follows.

(1) Those most involved in investigating allegations of child sexual abuse must keep an open mind and not fall into the trap of confusing taking what a child says seriously with believing what a child has said.

(2) Where allegations are made by a child regarding sexual abuse those allegations should be treated seriously, should not be accepted as true but should be examined and tested by whatever means are available before they are used as the basis for action.

(3) In cases of child sexual abuse neither a referral nor the removal of a child should be undertaken unless an objective assessment of the situation has been made and, in addition, meticulous planning, so as to balance the risk inherent in intervention against the success of the legal process.

(4) There should be greater recognition by agencies, training colleges, central Government departments and the public of the complexity of the task of interviewing children where allegations of sexual abuse arise.

(5) The purpose, techniques and course of any interviews should be planned at the outset as well as the need to make an overall assessment of the child.

(6) The consent of parents and of children, where of a maturity to give consent, should be sought prior to investigative interviews being undertaken.

(7)   No more than two investigative interviews should be undertaken and
       the interviewers' workloads should be regularly monitored.
(8)   In general, a maximum of two investigative interviews per child per
       week should be appropriate and the frequency of interviews is a matter
       for regular review.
(9)   An initial series of investigative interviews should usually not exceed
       four.
(10)   Any departure from the purpose or number of interviews should only
       be made after a full review of the situation and the agreement of all
       agencies.
(11)   Restrictions on access should only be imposed if there are compelling
       reasons justifying such restrictions in the interests of the child. Access
       should be kept under constant review while a child is in a place of
       safety.

In English law, of course, there are several statutory provisions dealing
with access to a child in care, or contact as it is now called (see Chapter 8),
and the new child protection orders which are of shorter duration than the
former place of safety orders (which have now been repealed) ensure that
there should not be an unnecessarily long period of separation between child
and parent, where the child is removed on the basis of significant harm.
Removal itself under a court order is an issue that has to be considered
carefully, since the 1989 Act has also placed the onus on the applicant for
removal to satisfy the court that removal would be better for the child than
no order at all. The 1989 Act also requires a planned response to be made
in any child abuse investigation (s 47) and, although the inclusion of parents
in case conferences is not mandatory, it is at least encouraged wherever
appropriate.

2.19.10 General comment

The Orkney affair indicates that, Cleveland notwithstanding, social workers
in Scotland felt compelled to take drastic measures to deal with what was
perceived to be ritual abuse of children. A key diagnostic difficulty was trying
to decide how much credibility to place on the allegations of abuse made by
a child when that child was not himself claiming to be a victim of that abuse.
The other situation they appear to have let themselves get into was 'guilt by
association'. The fact that the parents and families of the nine children had
been in contact with the W family and had supported Mrs W, whose husband
was convicted of various charges of abusing children, appeared to be a factor
that lent credence to the W children's allegations. However, the flawed interviewing procedures and, indeed, excessive interviewing which the children
themselves spoke about in newspaper interviews given after they had been
allowed to go home, suggest that the lessons of Cleveland have not sufficiently
been learnt north of the border.

The current suspension of Orkney's Director of Social Services in the light of an internal council's report and the calls for more suspensions and sackings of others in the department as well as the pending legal actions by the parents, further suggest that sadly, in Orkney, although the children have been returned to their homes, the saga continues.

2.20 Concluding comments

Despite a wealth of experience in child protection investigations and a series of child abuse inquiries stretching from 1973 to 1992, it would appear that the complexity, ambiguity and open-ended nature of indicators of child abuse makes a number of the shortcomings exposed by the child abuse reports depressingly inevitable in many cases.

It is submitted that the inquiry reports tell us a great deal about the key issues in child protection and have several lessons which can be learnt: (1) to be aware that there may be more than one explanation for a child's injuries or for a child's allegation of abuse if it does not relate to the child personally; (2) to bear in mind that the removal of a child from his or her home has to be justified by the evidence and a decision to do so should usually be an inter-agency one. No amount of law or volumes of guidance and regulations will prevent social workers, doctors or judges making mistakes in the future. On the other hand, the existence of such guidelines and their proper application might prevent professionals from making mistakes quite so frequently; (3) more specialised training, particularly in interview techniques, will also help to avoid carrying out or recording poor interviews which might fail to satisfy legal evidentiary requirements and constitute a needless trauma for both child and interviewer. Specialist training for residential care workers appears to be an urgent priority. Given a set of circumstances, a professional has to respond accordingly. But these reports, their stories and their recommendations, should provide child protection agencies with an instructive store of knowledge and experience to complement their training, to illuminate their perceptions of the problems associated with child abuse and to be better able to recognise certain danger signals when dealing with a variety of suspected child abuse cases.

CHAPTER THREE

The Legal Framework

3.1 Introduction

It is proposed in this chapter to examine the broad legal framework within which the protection of actually or potentially abused children may be sought. Attention will be focused upon those provisions which give social workers, NSPCC officers and, on occasions, police officers, the powers to react to information concerning possible child abuse, to conduct investigations, to consider initiating emergency procedures, to proceed in conjunction with other agencies in pursuing proceedings, whether these be criminal or civil proceedings and, briefly, to set out the position with regard to appeals. As such, this chapter will constitute an outline overview of the remainder of the book, but it is also intended to describe the courts in which, if it is decided to proceed with formal legal action, such actions may be pursued. Finally, the position of the child who is made the subject of a care order is considered, since it is important to understand the local authorities' statutory responsibilities towards children in their care. This is also of vital importance when one may be asked to consider the position of children abused while in the care of the authority. (See *The Pindown Experience and the Protection of Children: The Report of the Staffordshire Child Care Inquiry* ('the *Pindown Report*') (1991, Staffordshire Social Services) and Utting *Children in the Public Care* (1991, DOH/HMSO).)

3.2 The identification and support of children at risk of abuse

Local authority social services departments are placed under a very wide duty, by s 17 of the Children Act 1989 ('the 1989 Act'), to safeguard and promote the welfare of children within their area who are in need; and, so far as is consistent with that duty, to promote the upbringing of such children by their families by providing a range and level of services appropriate to those children's needs. Pursuant to that, s 17(2) of the 1989 Act goes on to provide that for the purpose of facilitating the discharge of their general duty under s 17, local authorities must have specific regard to their duties and powers set out in Sch 2, Pt I to the 1989 Act.

Under Sch 2, para 1 to the 1989 Act, a duty is imposed upon local authorities to take reasonable steps to identify the extent to which there are children in need within their area, and it is further provided that local authorities must publish information about services provided by them and by voluntary organisations, pursuant to their duties under Part III of the 1989 Act and must take such steps as are reasonably practicable to ensure that those who might benefit from the services receive the information relevant to them. Local authority social services departments all over the country have now published information leaflets setting out details of those children whom they regard as being in need and what services are available to support the families of those children in need. In many of these leaflets a high profile is given to the local authority's duty to safeguard children and it is made clear that children in need of protection will be given high priority for the provision of services. (See the *Children Act Report 1992* (1993, DOH), at Ch 2). In order to reinforce this approach the 1989 Act goes on further to provide, in para 4 of Sch 2, that local authorities must take reasonable steps, through the provision of services under Part III of the 1989 Act, to prevent children within their area suffering ill-treatment or neglect. Further reinforcement of the local authority's duty to safeguard is provided by Sch 2, para 7, which requires local authorities to take reasonable steps designed to reduce the need to bring care or supervision order proceedings with respect to children in their area. As if to emphasise the point that children who abuse are, potentially, equally to be viewed as children in need as those children who are abused, the local authority is also required to take reasonable steps designed to reduce the need to bring criminal proceedings against children within its area and to take reasonable steps designed to encourage children within its area not to commit criminal offences (Sch 2, para 7(a) and (b)). The methods by which local authorities establish which children require safeguarding services will depend upon the measures for inter-agency collaboration in the identification process laid down by local Area Child Protection Committees pursuant to the guidance provided in *Working Together under the Children Act 1989* (1991, DOH) (*'Working Together'*) at Ch 2. As *Working Together* points out 'co-operation at the individual case level needs to be supported by joint agency and management policies for child protection, consistent with their policies and plans for related service provision' (at Ch 2.4).

A coherent prevention policy and plan is therefore necessary if local authorities are to take seriously their duty to safeguard the welfare of children in need within their area. Other prevention measures can also be identified within the provisions of the 1989 Act. These include the provision in s 17(3) that any service provided by an authority in the exercise of its functions may be provided for the family of a particular child in need or *for any member of his family*, if it is provided with a view to safeguarding or promoting the child's welfare. It is important to realise, therefore, that where an abused child is suffering at the hands of a family member, whether this is a parent, an older sibling or some other relative living in the family, it may be the case that the local authority will seek to provide services to those family members in order to attempt to safeguard the child who has been abused. Where it is felt desirable that an abusing member of the family should move out of the family home, the provision of Sch 2, para 5 to the 1989 Act could be used to encourage the perpetrator to move out of the premises and to provide accommodation for him or her. This, of course, will demand the co-operation of the perpetrator and where one is considering the case of child perpetrators, who may well have been abused themselves, it may be more appropriate to consider the provision of the service of accommodation under s 20 of the 1989 Act, together with other necessary services such as psychiatric, psychological or social work assessment. The use of both the service of accommodation under s 20 and other support services for such children will, of course, depend upon the level of co-operative partnership achieved between parents and workers. (See *The Care of Children – Principles and Practice in Regulations and Guidance – The Children Act 1989* (1989, HMSO).) In those situations where police action has resulted in the removal of either an adult or child perpetrator the necessity for the local authority to use the provisions of s 20 or Sch 2, para 5 will have been removed, possibly by the imposition of bail conditions in respect of an adult perpetrator, or in a remand to local authority accommodation in the case of a child perpetrator.

Given that the overriding philosophy in the 1989 Act is that children are best brought up by their families, the provision of services under s 17 and Sch 2, in order to prevent children suffering from or perpetrating abuse, is clearly the most desirable policy. The duty to safeguard, and the powers and duties provided pursuant to it, are examined in greater detail in Chapter 4 and are generally referred to as 'preventive statutory measures'. The main problem with regard to the achievement of the goal of prevention is that it depends upon available resources which, following the implementation of the 1989 Act, are felt to be in very short supply. (See, generally, *Children Act Report 1992* (1993, DOH).) The whole idea behind the preventive measures contained in the Act and highlighted in the *Guidance*, whether these result in services being provided by local authority social services, health, education or voluntary organisations, is to improve the lot of families under stress so that the potential for child abuse is diminished, if not totally eroded. Since it is now clearly recognised that even in the most severe examples of child abuse one is dealing with a continuum of abuse which may be becoming more and more serious rather than with single isolated incidents, even limited resource input by social services and the other agencies may achieve the prevention of a situation turning into a case of serious child abuse. Local authorities in particular must, therefore, devote far more attention to prioritising resources in the direction of preventive services, since, in the words of the old adage, 'prevention is better than cure'.

3.3 The identification and investigation of suspected child abuse

By s 47 of the 1989 Act, a local authority in particular is under a duty to investigate whenever it is provided with information which may suggest that a child living or found within its area is suffering or is likely to suffer significant harm, or where it is informed that such a child is the subject of an emergency protection order or is in police protection. Where information is passed to the NSPCC, a local authority also may undertake appropriate enquiries and investigations (see, eg s 44(1)(c) and s 31(1) and (9)). To undertake such investigations the local authority, in particular, is required to consult with a range of other agencies to enable it to decide what action it should take to safeguard or promote the child's welfare. The local authority social services may also request other agencies to assist them in such enquiries and investigations. These processes are described in further detail in Chapters 4 and 5.

3.4 Consideration of legal action

At the child protection conference (see, further, Chapter 4) a number of options may be considered, many of which are provided for by the law. The investigations may have revealed that the family is under stress and needs the provision of some sort of respite care in respect of some or all of the children. In this situation, as was pointed out earlier (see **3.2** above) consideration may be given to providing the service of accommodation under the provisions of s 20 of the 1989 Act. Those present at the child protection conference would, however, have to be satisfied that, in making such a recommendation to social services, appropriate protection was being offered to the child who had been abused or who was at risk of abuse.

In the period leading up to implementation of the 1989 Act and in the year following implementation, concern has been expressed that the principles underpinning the 1989 Act, concerned with working in partnership with parents, were encouraging local authorities to move away from the consideration of court proceedings and that this move was putting children at greater risk. In the first six to nine months of the operation of the 1989 Act a considerable amount of judicial concern was expressed (see the foreword to *Children Act Advisory Committee's First Annual Report* (1992, Lord Chancellor's Department)) that the remarkable downturn in court activity since implementation might indicate that more children were being left at risk of serious abuse because of the widespread view of local authorities that in order to be able to succeed in court proceedings a breakdown in partnership or the exhaustion of service provision would have to be proved.

Arising from this concern, the Department of Health ('DOH') commissioned a Social Services Inspectorate ('SSI') study to examine the decision-making processes in four local authorities with regard to children at risk. It appeared as a result of this study (*A Study of Local Authority Decision-making about Public Law Court Applications* SSI: Court Orders Study (December 1992)) and departmental discussions with a number of local authorities, that there was a belief that the 'no order' principle requires authorities to demonstrate that working in partnership has broken down or been exhausted before an order would be made. The DOH, in its first *Children Act Report* in 1992 (1993, HMSO) has stated clearly that this was not the intention of the legislation. The report states (at para 2.2(1)) that:

> 'where a local authority determines that control of the child's circumstances is necessary to promote his welfare then compulsory intervention, as part of a carefully planned process will always be the appropriate remedy. Local Authorities should not feel inhibited by the working in partnership provisions of the CA 1989 from seeking appropriate court orders. Equally, the existence of a court order should not of itself impede a local authority from continuing its efforts at working in partnership with the families of children in need. The two processes are not mutually exclusive. Each has a role to play, often simultaneously in the case management of a child at risk.'

Nevertheless, the reluctance which might have been felt under the former law to use the provision of voluntary care because this was felt to lessen the local authority's ability to argue for the need for a care order, is not replicated in respect of the new law. Thus, it is perfectly possible for local authorities to offer the service of accommodation in partnership with parents, and in those situations where such an arrangement does not work, or parents seek to remove children pre-emptively, local authorities know that under the widely drawn provisions of s 31 it will be possible for them to seek a care order or an emergency protection order (s 44 of the 1989 Act).

As will be seen in Chapter 4, the case conference may further have recommended that it is more appropriate to engage informal social worker involvement with the family, and the provision of additional services on top of this from a range of other agencies. (See *Working Together* at paras 4.2 and 4.3.) The provision of such services is again made possible by s 17 of the 1989 Act and if services from other agencies are to be provided, this may require the invoking of s 27 of the 1989 Act. Under s 27, a local authority may request the help of one or more other agencies including health, education and housing in performing its duties to provide services under Part III of the 1989 Act and those agencies must comply with such requests unless they can prove it is not compatible with their own statutory or other duties or it unduly prejudices the discharge of any of their functions. The recommendation to provide services and monitoring of the provision of such services in terms of the effects on the family does, of course, leave open the option of taking more formal legal action if and when this might be required.

It should be noted that the case conference's only decision-making power is to place a child on the local Child Protection Register and, if registration is agreed, to allocate the key worker. The key worker must be a social worker, from either the social services department or the NSPCC (see *Working Together* at para 5.15.4). Upon registration of a child, consideration will be given to the provision of a written child protection plan which will be dependent upon a full assessment of the child and family having been undertaken. (See *Working Together* at paras 5.16 and 5.17 and *Protecting Children – A Guide for Social Workers undertaking a Comprehensive Assessment* (1988, DOH) and see, for more detail, Chapter 4.) The production of the child protection plan must include consideration of the wishes of the child and the parents, local resources, the suitability of specialist facilities, their availability for addressing the particular needs of the child and his or her family. *Working Together* points out that 'special attention will need to be given to ensuring the services provided under the plan are co-ordinated, structured and ethnically and culturally appropriate for the child and the family, with built-in mechanisms for programme review and crisis management'. The decision to register a child and formulate a child protection plan is a formal process, but, in the same way as with more informal social worker involvement and provision of services where things go wrong or emergencies intervene, consideration will have to be given to more formal legal action.

In certain cases, however, the recommendation of the case conference may be that more formal court action is immediately required.

3.4.1 Criminal proceedings

Where a child has been abused, the police, who will have been involved at every stage of the investigation, assessment and case conference process, may wish to consider bringing criminal proceedings in the criminal courts. The suspected abuser will have to have been charged, consideration given to bail or to remand in custody or local authority accommodation in the case of a child perpetrator, and the case handed over to the Crown Prosecution Service ('CPS'). The onus will be on the CPS to determine whether or not there is sufficient evidence to take the case forward and whether it is in the public interest to do so.

In addition, it must be remembered that the CPS will wish to satisfy themselves that there is evidence sufficient to suggest that a jury is likely to be satisfied, beyond reasonable doubt, that the person charged has committed the offence. In order to satisfy themselves that evidence of sufficient quality is available to go before a jury in any particular case, the CPS will wish to look at the video recordings of the testimony of child witnesses compiled in accordance with the new provisions inserted into the Criminal Justice Act 1988 ('CJA 1988') by the Criminal Justice Act 1991 ('CJA 1991'), the *Memorandum of Good Practice* and the new *Crown Court Rules*. (See CJA 1991, ss 54(2) and 55; the *Memorandum of Good Practice on Videorecorded Interviews with Child Witnesses for Criminal Proceedings* ('the *MoGP*') (1992, DOH); and the Crown Court (Amendment) Rules 1992.) Where a child is to give evidence instead by means of participation in the proceedings through a live television link (s 32 of the CJA 1988), the CPS may wish to determine whether the child is likely to be able to withstand cross-examination in such difficult cases. Pilot programmes are now under way for the development of a preparation programme for child witnesses and these may clearly play a key part in the future in prompting the CPS to feel more confident that the child will be able to endure the court process and be able to give evidence without breaking down. (See Aldridge and Freshwater 'The Preparation of Child Witnesses' (1993) *Child Law* at pp 25 to 27.)

The CPS, as a result of viewing the video recording, or of considering the nature of the evidence to be given by the child, may have very considerable concerns about proceeding with the case. It is for this reason that there may be occasions (which might be frustrating to individual police officers) where the CPS decide that, while the evidence gathered may be sufficient to justify the taking of civil care proceedings in respect of the child (where a lesser burden of proof has to be satisfied), it is nevertheless insufficient to justify the continuation of criminal proceedings. It should be noted that the reason that it may be possible to pursue civil proceedings is that the conditions precedent for the taking of care proceedings do not look to the guilt of any one particular named individual, but rather to the fact that abuse has occurred and that this is due to the inadequacy of the care or control offered to the child in whichever setting the abuse has occurred. Care proceedings, therefore, are not in that sense focused upon the 'guilt' of particular individuals.

In addition, the CPS must also have regard to the status of the witnesses. Thus, if the only evidence available is that of a small child, uncorroborated by any other material evidence or witness, then, despite the fact that there is a good quality video recording of the child's testimony which could be put before the court, the CPS may, nevertheless, be reluctant to recommend that a criminal case should be taken any further. (This is further examined in Chapter 7.) Thus, even where someone has originally been charged with a criminal offence, whether it is a child or an adult, that charge ultimately may not be proceeded with on the direction of the CPS. Indeed, it may even have been the case that it was the police who were initially involved in the case, with an incident attracting police attention, resulting in the removal of the child victim temporarily to a police station under police powers of protection provided by s 46 of the 1989 Act. The police would then notify the social services (provided they are available for contact) that they were holding the child with regard to the likelihood of an offence having been committed against the child and that the child was to be examined by a police surgeon. (This is considered in more detail in Chapter 4.)

The position with regard to criminal proceedings is examined in more detail in Chapter 7, together with the role of the child as a witness in such proceedings. Also considered is the somewhat rarer situation where the child is himself a perpetrator of abuse and is over the age of 10. In addition, guidelines on sentencing will be examined in some detail.

3.4.2 Civil proceedings

The 1989 Act effected a radical overhaul of the range of legal provisions under which it had previously been possible to take children into care as a result of actual or potential abuse. The complexity engendered by there being more than 17 routes into local authority care had attracted a huge body of criticism over the years. The repeal of all those provisions, together with the introduction of just one route into care, using s 31 of the 1989 Act, has been amongst the most important of the reforms achieved by that Act. The Act further provided, through the repeal of s 7 of the Family Law Reform Act 1969, that wardship, which through the 1970s and 1980s had been used extensively by local authorities to have children committed into their care, cannot be used as a back door route into care any more.

The 1989 Act (s 31(9)) further gives local authorities and authorised persons (currently only the NSPCC) power to intervene at an early stage where there are merely suspicions that a child is being ill-treated or is failing to develop properly (s 43), extended powers to remove children from their homes if certain criteria are satisfied (s 44), and gives the police the right to exercise new powers of police protection (s 46). In addition, a new recovery order is provided to protect children who may have been abducted or run away from any place where they were being looked after while subject to a care or emergency protection order, or in police protection (s 50). Moreover, provision is made for refuges for children at risk of harm (s 51) and a system of certification exempting those who run such a refuge from liability to prosecution for certain offences (s 51(1) and (2)). Members of the public concerned about the actuality or potentiality of abuse to children with whom they are involved in some way, have the ability (which they had under the old law) to invoke the provisions dealing with emergency protection (s 44(1)(a)), although most will be happier to inform relevant agencies such as the police, social services or the NSPCC and to see them take the appropriate action.

The opportunity presented by the reform of the substantive law was also used to reform the jurisdictions of the courts in children's cases (1989 Act, s 92 and Sch 11; and see *Fig 1*), the law on evidence in civil cases involving children (s 96) and the law governing procedure in all civil cases involving children (s 93 (as amended by the Courts and Legal Services Act 1990, s 116, Sch 16, para 22), s 95 and s 100).

Where, therefore (and this will be considered in much more detail in Chapter 4), there is reasonable cause to believe that the child is likely to suffer significant harm if either the child is not removed to accommodation provided by or on behalf of the applicant, or does not remain in the place in which he is then being accommodated, any person may make an application

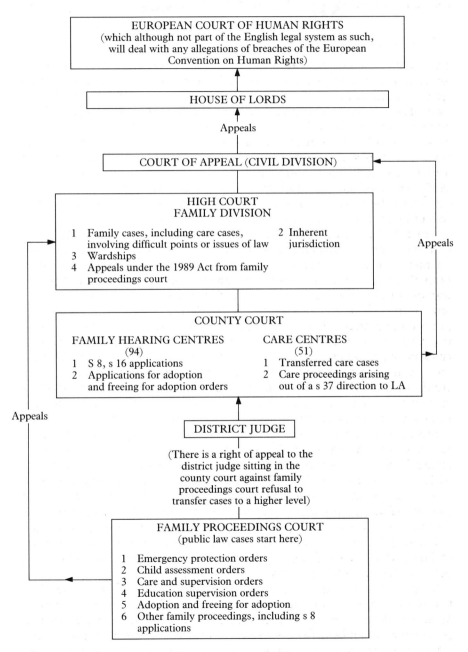

Fig 1: Court Structure Diagram

for an emergency protection order. Such an application is made pursuant to s 44(1)(a) of the 1989 Act, and may be made *ex parte* (ie without other parties being present) to a single magistrate (Sch 11, para 3(1)(a) to the 1989 Act). Such *ex parte* applications for emergency protection orders may also be made by any of the relevant child protection agencies using the provisions of s 44(1)(a). Local authority social services and the NSPCC are given additional rights to apply for orders under s 44 in cases of emergencies. Thus, in the case of an application made by a local authority, s 44(1)(b) provides that, where enquiries are being made with respect to the child in pursuance of an investigation, and those enquiries are being frustrated by access to the child being unreasonably refused to a person authorised to seek access, and the applicant social worker has reasonable cause to believe that access to the child is required as a matter of urgency, the court may make an emergency protection order authorising the removal of the child to accommodation provided by social services or the child's detention in the place in which he is being accommodated. Almost identical provision is made with respect to officers employed by the NSPCC (s 44(1)(c)).

In response to criticisms made in the *Cleveland Report* in respect of the duration, nature and powers granted under the old place of safety orders (see *Report of the Inquiry into Child Abuse in Cleveland 1987* (1988, HMSO) at para 16.15), the new law provides that: emergency orders should last for only eight days (s 45(1)), with a provision for an extension in exceptional circumstances of seven days (s 45(5)); that there should be a right of challenge after 72 hours (s 45(8) and (9)) for parents and children and others who were providing care immediately before removal; that, if contact is to be anything other than what may be presumed to be reasonable (s 44(13)), specific court directions should be sought (s 44(6)(a)); and, finally, that where it is proposed that the child be subject to medical, psychiatric or other assessment, specific directions of the court must be sought (s 44(6)(b)).

As already indicated, such applications in respect of emergency protection orders will be made out-of-hours to a single magistrate, possibly at his home, but may, of course, be made during court time to a full bench of magistrates sitting in the family proceedings court (in which all family proceedings take place at magistrates' courts level). Under the relevant orders issued by the Lord Chancellor, public law applications must generally be commenced in the family proceedings court (see Children (Allocation of Proceedings) Order 1991, SI 1991/1677, art 2) but, provided the relevant criteria are satisfied such cases, may, once they are beyond the emergency order stage, be transferred, upon application to a district judge, to a county court care centre, or even to the High Court (art 18(3)). Even where an application is made *ex parte* to a single magistrate at home out of court hours, provision is made, under s 41(6) of the 1989 Act, for the court to appoint a guardian ad litem at this early stage and, where the court believes the child should have a solicitor, the court can appoint one (s 41(3)).

Where there are merely concerns or suspicions that a child is suffering or likely to suffer significant harm, the local authority or the NSPCC may now seek an order usually from the family proceedings court, known as a child assessment order (s 43 of the 1989 Act). Before granting such an order the court must be satisfied that the applicant has reasonable cause to suspect that: (1) the child is suffering or is likely to suffer significant harm; (2) an assessment of the state of the child's health or development or of the way in which he has been treated is required to enable the applicant to determine whether or not the child is suffering or is likely to suffer significant harm; and (3) it is unlikely that such an assessment will be made, or be satisfactory in the absence of a child assessment order. Since an application for such an order is likely to be a planned response to concerns, court rules provide that the application must be made on notice and this underlines the fact that the order should not be made in emergencies. (See Family Proceedings Courts (Children Act 1989) Rules 1991, SI 1991/1395, r 4(1).) The child assessment order must specify the date by which the assessment is to begin, and it has effect for such a period, not exceeding seven days, beginning with that date as may be specified in the order (s 43(5)).

It should be noted that in relation to proceedings for a child assessment order, the court is required, by s 41 of the 1989 Act, to appoint a guardian ad litem for the child unless satisfied that it is not necessary to do so in order to safeguard the child's interests. Figures available from the *Children Act Advisory Committee's First Annual Report* (1992, Lord Chancellor's Department), appear to indicate that guardians ad litem are appointed for children in 47 per cent of public law proceedings in the magistrates' courts, 32 per cent in the county court and 13 per cent in the High Court (at p 41). Whilst there is no breakdown as between the different types of public law applications which these figures represent, so that applications for contact, and unopposed applications for discharge of care or supervision orders would be included, the picture would appear to be a rather disturbing one when set against estimates available in relation to the former law (see Murch *Separate Representation for Parents and Children* (1984, Family Law Research Unit, University of Bristol); Masson and Shaw 'The Work of Guardians ad Litem' (1988) JSWL 164; and *In the Interests of the Child – A Report of the Inspection of the Guardian ad Litem and Reporting Officers Service* (1990, Social Services Inspectorate)). The conclusions of these reports were that guardians ad litem were appointed for children in at least 50 per cent of cases and that in some areas this rose as high as 80 per cent of all cases which came before the court under the old law. Certainly, the Social Services Inspectorate Report in 1990 stated that an appointment rate of 66 per cent in care proceedings was a reasonable starting point for future planning on a national level. Despite planning for such a rate of appointment under the new law, the actual appointments made reveal that under the new law the appointment rate has yet to reach the first 50 per cent.

A small-scale survey was, however, conducted by one of the authors with a West Midlands family proceedings court to test out the analysis of the forms distributed by the Home Office in 1992. This had revealed that on a crude numerical count this particular court had an appointment rate for guardians ad litem of 59 per cent, well above the national average. The magistrates and court clerks were not happy with this result as they knew that their appointment rate for guardians ad litem was 100 per cent. A more careful reading and analysis of the forms produced a figure of 99 per cent but the court clerk felt that if the court's administrative officers had done the count in simple numerical terms without considering whether cases were ongoing, or whether a guardian had already been appointed at emergency protection order (EPO) stage, this would have distorted the return to give a reading of 59 per cent for the Home Office official statistics which had then been forwarded to the Lord Chancellor's Department for use in the *Children Act Advisory Committee's Annual Report* (1992, Lord Chancellor's Department).

It should, of course, be pointed out that where evidence of abuse arises in certain situations the local authority may have the power simply to remove the child rather than being required to go to court to obtain an order to do so. This will be the case where the child is being 'looked after' pursuant to s 20 of the 1989 Act or pursuant to a care order made under s 31 of that Act, and concerns about the child have developed as a result of care in a particular children's home or other residential placement, or where the child is being cared for by foster-parents.

Concerns about child abuse may also surface in the course of any family proceedings brought in the family proceedings court, the county court or the High Court. In such family proceedings, a court welfare officer may have been requested to investigate the children's circumstances and returned to court indicating that there was a degree of concern about the possibility of the children having suffered or being likely to suffer significant harm. In such circumstances, s 37 of the 1989 Act provides the court with the power to direct the local authority to undertake an investigation of the child's circumstances where it appears to the court that it may be appropriate for a care or supervision order to be made. Where the court gives a direction under this section, the local authority is required, when undertaking the investigation, to consider whether it should apply for a care order or a supervision order with respect to the child (s 37(2)). Where the local authority decides that there are grounds for the institution of care or supervision order proceedings, those proceedings may be commenced in the same level of court as the original family proceedings. It should be noted that whilst all magistrates' courts are of equal standing under the 1989 Act, the county court's jurisdiction has been classified according to the nature of the case being brought. Thus, county courts have been classified into divorce county courts, family hearing centres and care centres by the Children (Allocation of Proceedings) Order 1991, SI 1991/1677, art 2. The judges who can hear proceedings in the designated trial centres, and the types of proceedings to which they are restricted, are provided in the Family Proceedings (Allocation to Judiciary) Directions 1991. Where an application for a care or supervision order or any associated orders arises from a direction to conduct an investigation made by the High Court or county court under s 37 of the 1989 Act, then, provided that court is a county court care centre, the application can be made there (SI 1991/1677, art 3(2)(a)), or in such care centre as the court which directed the investigation may order (SI 1991/1677, art 3(2)(b)). Where a s 37 direction is made by the High Court, it has jurisdiction to proceed to hear the application for the care or supervision order made by the local authority.

Where concern over actual or potential abuse has not escalated suddenly, consideration may be given instead to initiating care proceedings by way of issuing an application for a care or supervision order in the family proceedings court. Such action may also be taken following on from an emergency protection order, the exercise of police powers of protection, the result of a s 37 investigation or the obtaining of evidence pursuant to an assessment done under the provisions of a child assessment order. An application is made by filling in the relevant form (see Form CHA 19) but since it is unlikely that everybody will be ready to proceed to a full hearing on the first occasion, an order is actually issued in the form of an interim care or interim supervision order for such period as is determined by the court under the provisions of s 38 (see Form CHA 27). It should be remembered that care proceedings are civil proceedings and the standard of proof required will be proof on the balance of probabilities. Thus, under the terms of s 31 of the 1989 Act the applicant will be required to 'prove on the balance of probabilities' that the particular child concerned is suffering, or is likely to suffer significant harm and that the harm or likelihood of the harm is attributable to:

(1) the care given to the child or likely to be given to him if the order were not made, not being what it would be reasonable to expect a parent to give to him; or
(2) the child being beyond parental control.

It should be noted that the new grounds provide for a care or supervision order to be made, not only where it can be established that abuse has actually taken place, but where there is also a fear that abuse may occur in the future. In considering whether or not to make an order the court can look not only at the care actually being given to the child but look to the care which is likely to be given to the child if the order was not made and set that against a standard of care which it would be reasonable to expect a parent to give to the child. In *Re A (A Minor) (Care Proceedings)* [1993] 1 FCR 824, it was emphasised that where the issue before the court was 'whether the child is likely to suffer significant harm', this was not to be decided on the basis that the court must be satisfied that it was more probable than not that the child would suffer significant harm. Thorpe J stressed that the words of the statute were not to be construed unduly restrictively and a care order could be made where the evidence clearly indicated its necessity. The new grounds in the 1989 Act do not, of course, mention the word abuse but instead look to whether the child is suffering or is likely to suffer *significant harm*. Harm is further defined in s 31(9) and (10) of the 1989 Act and this will be considered, in detail, in Chapters 4 and 6. The new grounds for the taking of care or supervision order proceedings are couched in such wide terms because it was recognised that the specific detailed grounds of the Children and Young Persons Act 1969 did not adequately cater for risk, and also in recognition of the fact that local authorities were no longer to be allowed to use wardship as a back-door route into care.

In addition to satisfying the grounds laid down in s 31(2) of the 1989 Act, the court is required when making such orders or an interim order under s 38, to be satisfied that making an order is better for the child than making no order at all (s 1(5)). It may also be of the view, perhaps as a result of the guardian ad litem's report, that the making of a care or supervision order would actually be the wrong order to make. The provision of s 1(4) enables the court to decide whether to make one of a range of orders which are available under the 1989 Act, including the making, where relevant, of any of the s 8 orders which could be made in conjunction with a supervision order. Thus, the local authority may have applied for a care order in respect of a child and the guardian ad litem's report may recommend the making of a residence order in favour of grandparents or other relatives and the making of other s 8 orders in respect of the parents, such as a contact order in favour of the mother and a prohibited steps order in respect of the father, thus preventing the father from having contact with the child. Where the local authority or the court consider that contact should be supervised in any way, this should be done by means of using a s 16 family assistance order (see the comments of Booth J in *Leeds City Council v C* [1993] 1 FLR 269).

The requirement in s 1(5) that the court be satisfied 'that making an order is better for the child than making no order at all', has been characterised as the 'no order principle'. Given the confusion which this shorthand nomenclature has caused (see *Children Act Report 1992* (1993, DOH) at para 2(2) and *S v R (Minors) (No Order Principle)* [1993] Fam Law 42), the authors prefer the use of the term 'the positive advantage principle'. In order to prove to the court's satisfaction that there is to be some positive advantage derived from the making of a care or supervision order, the local authority is now expected to submit its plan for the care or supervision of the child before the court will proceed to the making of either the care or supervision order. Where the court is proposing to make a care order, the local authority should, under the provisions of s 34(11), further submit to the court the arrangements which are being proposed for the child to have contact with members of his or her family. Where the court is proposing that there should be no contact, or the family or child do not agree with the arrangements being proposed, an application will have to be made to the court to determine issues of contact under the provisions of s 34. This will be considered in much greater detail in Chapter 8.

Both in proceedings for care and supervision orders, or in any contact proceedings, the child is a party to the proceedings under the relevant rules of court and the court is required to appoint a guardian ad litem for the child where one has not earlier been appointed. This may have occurred, for example, in emergency protection order or child assessment order proceedings and, where the proceedings are being continued, either the guardian ad litem or the court must further consider whether an appointment of a solicitor for the child should also be made (s 41). This unique system of the dual representation of the child by a solicitor representing what the child wants (where he is capable of giving such instructions) and of the guardian ad litem representing what is in the child's best interests, has, despite fears when the Children Bill was first introduced, nevertheless been strengthened by the provisions in the 1989 Act and the relevant rules of court. (See s 41 of the 1989 Act; the Family Proceedings Rules 1991, SI 1991/1247; and the Family Proceedings Courts (Children Act 1989) Rules 1991, SI 1991/1395, rr 10, 11 and 12.)

Whereas in most situations the making of a care or supervision order will be sufficient to guarantee the protection of the child suffering, or at risk of suffering, significant harm, there may be situations in which the local authority will need additional protection for the child, or specific guidance in relation to some aspect of the care of the child. Where this is necessary and where it is not possible by any other means, including the use of the provisions of the 1989 Act, to acquire such protection, the local authority may have to use the inherent jurisdiction of the High Court to obtain the relevant orders. Since a local authority which has a child in its care is unable to use the provisions of s 8 to obtain a prohibited steps order or a specific issues order (see s 9(1) of the 1989 Act) (although the court can grant such orders of its own motion under s 10(c)), the local authority will have to apply to the High Court to be given leave to make an application for an order providing relevant protection under s 100. The High Court may only grant leave where it is satisfied that the result which the authority wishes to achieve could not be achieved through the making of any other order under the provisions of the 1989 Act and there is reasonable cause to believe that if the court's inherent jurisdiction is not exercised with respect to the child, the child is likely to suffer significant harm (s 100(4)). The sorts of situations in which it is envisaged that the High Court's inherent jurisdiction may have to be invoked by the local authority include those situations where an injunction is required to prevent an abusing parent or child from going near or having contact with the child in need of protection or, where some operative procedure is required in respect of the child, the child's parents are refusing to give consent and the relevant authority is concerned about accepting the consent to operative treatment provided by the local authority holding a care order. (See, further, Chapter 9 below.)

3.5 Appeals

A brief reference is made here to the appeals possible in respect of the proceedings which will be described in detail further on in this book (see Chapters 6 and 7). Where criminal proceedings have been taken against an individual then, depending upon the court in which the proceedings were eventually determined, a decision can be made regarding an appeal. Where an offence has been tried in the magistrates' court, or in the youth court, there can be an appeal to the Crown Court either against conviction or sentence. Where a person is convicted in the Crown Court, there can be an appeal, under very strictly defined conditions, to the Court of Appeal, Criminal Division, against either conviction or sentence and this is considered in detail in Chapter 7.

In care and contact order proceedings, an appeal lies by the child or by the parents or by any other persons who have been made parties to the proceedings from the magistrates' court to the Family Division of the High Court against the magistrates' decision to make or refuse to make any order (s 94(1)), except in the following situations, where there is no right of appeal.

(1) Against the making or refusal to make an emergency protection order, the granting of an extension of or refusal to extend the effective period of the emergency protection order, the discharge of or refusal to discharge the emergency protection order, or the giving or refusal to give any directions in connection with the order (s 45(10) as substituted by the Courts and Legal Services Act 1990, s 116 and Sch 16, para 19).
(2) Where the magistrates' court has exercised its powers to decline jurisdiction because it considers that the case can more conveniently be dealt with by another court (s 94(2)).
(3) Against decisions taken by courts on questions arising in connection with the transfer or proposed transfer of proceedings, except as provided for by orders made by the Lord Chancellor (under s 94(10) and (11)).

On hearing the appeal the High Court (Family Division) can make such orders as may be necessary (s 94(4)), including such incidental or consequential provision as appears to be just (s 94(5)), in order to give effect to its determination of the appeal. Any order of the High Court made on appeal, other than one directing a rehearing by the magistrates shall, for the purposes of the enforcement, variation, revival or discharge of the order, be treated as if it were an order of the magistrates' court from which the appeal was brought and not an order of the High Court (s 94(9)). The role and powers of the appellate courts in civil proceedings will be considered in more detail in Chapter 6.

An appeal from the decision of a judge in a county court centre or in the High Court is made direct to the Court of Appeal and there are no special rules relating to such appeals. These will be considered in more detail in Chapter 6.

3.6 Exercise of parental responsibilities and children's rights where a child is in care

Where a care order is made with respect to a child it is the duty of the local authority, designated by the care order, to receive the child into its care and to keep him in its care while the order remains in force (s 33(1)). As far as the exercise of parental responsibility in respect of the child is concerned, it is provided that whilst the care order is in force the local authority shall have parental responsibility for the child, and shall have the power, subject to certain exceptions, to determine the extent to which a parent or guardian of the child may meet his responsibility for him (s 33(3)). It is further provided that the local authority may not exercise its powers to limit parental exercise of responsibility unless it is satisfied that it is necessary to do so in order to safeguard or promote the child's welfare (s 33(4)). Where such a decision is made and the parents disagree with it, or, indeed, in relation to any of the other statutory duties which local authorities have in respect of the care or upbringing of children, if the local authority fails to observe its duty or if the local authority can be shown to have acted unreasonably in any decision reached with regard to a child, or to have acted in bad faith, then an application may be made for judicial review (see Chapter 9 for further details).

The provisions of the 1989 Act also make it clear that whilst a care order is in force with respect to a child the local authority cannot change the child's religion nor does it have the right to consent to, or refuse to consent to, the making of an adoption order or an order freeing the child for adoption, nor does it have the right to appoint a guardian for the child (s 33(6)). Furthermore, whilst a care order is in force with respect to the child, no person may cause the child to be known by a new surname or remove him from the UK without either the written consent of every person who has parental responsibility for the child or the leave of the court.

Where an abused child finds his way into the care of the local authority by virtue of a care order made under s 31 of the 1989 Act, the local authority is under a duty to safeguard and promote the child's welfare and to make use of such services available for children cared for by their own parents as appears to the local authority to be reasonable in the child's case (s 22(3)). Before making any decision with respect to a child it is looking after, or proposing to look after, the local authority must, so far as is practicable, ascertain the wishes and feelings of the child, his parents (including unmarried fathers), anyone else with parental responsibility and any other relevant person, which includes all the relevant statutory agencies who might have been involved with the child, and the local authority may contact the child's school or GP (see *The Children Act 1989 Guidance and Regulations, Vol 3 Family Placements* (1991, HMSO) at para 2.51). Where the child has a guardian ad litem, he or she must also be consulted (see *R v North Yorkshire County Council, ex parte M* [1989] 1 All ER 143, and see further, *The Children Act 1989 Guidance and Regulations, Vol 4 Residential Care* (1991, HMSO) at para 2.51) and the guardian ad litem may be of considerable use to the local authority in helping to ascertain the child's wishes and feelings. In making any such decision, a local authority is required to give due consideration: (1) to such wishes and feelings of the child as it has been able to ascertain and having regard to his age and understanding; (2) to such wishes and feelings of any parent or person with parental responsibility or other relevant persons; and (3) to the child's religious persuasion, racial origin and cultural and linguistic background (s 22(5)). Where it appears to the local authority that it is necessary for the purpose of protecting members of the public from serious injury, to exercise its powers with respect to the child whom it is looking after in a manner which may not be consistent with its duties to the child, it may do so.

When a local authority is trying to determine where a child, who is being accommodated by it or who is in its care, is to live, then the local authority may provide accommodation and maintenance for any child by placing the child in one of a wide range of living situations (s 23(2)). Thus, a local authority can provide accommodation and maintenance for any child whom it is looking after by: (1) placing him with a family, a relative of his or any other suitable person on such terms as to payment by the authority and otherwise as the authority may determine; (2) maintaining him in a community home, voluntary home or registered children's home; (3) maintaining him in a home provided in accordance with arrangements made by the Secretary of State; and (4) making such other arrangements as appear appropriate to the authority and to comply with any regulations made by the Secretary of State (s 23(2)), as amended by the Courts and Legal Services Act 1990, s 116, Sch 16, para 12(1). There is, thus, an extremely wide range of provisions which can be made to cater for a child, while the child is being looked after by the local authority. In addition, it should be pointed out that a child, while he is being looked after by the local authority may, in certain circumstances, be placed in accommodation provided for the purpose of restricting his liberty (s 25(1)). Where the child or person is being kept in secure accommodation for more than 72 hours in any 28-day period, an application must be made to a court for an order to keep the child in secure accommodation (s 25(2)); Children (Secure Accommodation) Regulations 1991, SI 1991/1505, regs 10 to 12, as amended by the Children (Secure Accommodation) (Amendments) Regulations 1992, SI 1992/2117).

In order to cater for a large number of difficult situations with regard to the standard of care exercised in respect of children being looked after by a local authority, the 1989 Act provides for a system of reviews of cases to enable the child complainant's voice to be heard (s 26(1) and (2)). Where a child is complaining about abuse occurring in either a residential home provided by the local authority, a home provided by a voluntary organisation or in a foster home, then *Working Together* (at paras 15.19.1 to 15.20.10) advises that social services must take such complaints seriously and investigate in the same way as they would for abuse occurring within the family setting. *Working Together* states that 'children in accommodation provided for them are entitled to the same level and standard of protection from harm as is provided for children in their own homes'. It goes on to point out that:

> 'it must be clear that whether the child is placed with a foster parent or living in a residential home or school, the agency's actions must take place within the agreed child protection procedures even though other procedures, such as an agency's internal disciplinary procedures or wider considerations about the future of an establishment may need to be pursued in parallel.'

Both the system of reviews and the new representations procedure (established by local authorities under s 26(3) of the 1989 Act) are intended to ensure that children's complaints are brought to the surface particularly in the wake of residential child care scandals such as *Beck, Ty Mawr, Castle Hill, St Charles, Melanie Klein* and *Kincora*. Where a child or young person does wish to make a complaint about the treatment he is receiving in any accommodation provided by or on behalf of a local authority, he will have to obtain information about the local authority, voluntary organisation or registered children's homes complaints procedure. Such a procedure is required to be established for considering any representations and the procedure is a two-stage process. This complaints procedure is considered in more detail in Chapter 9.

CHAPTER FOUR

Identification, Investigation and Initiation of Proceedings

4.1 Introduction

Article 19 of the United Nations Convention on the Rights of the Child (UN 1989), which imposes, in clause 1, an obligation on States Parties to take measures to protect children from abuse, continues, in clause 2, to state that:

'such protective measures should, as appropriate, include effective procedures for the establishment of social programmes to provide necessary support for the child and for those who have the care of the child, as well as for other forms of prevention and for identification, reporting, referral, investigation, treatment, and follow up of instances of child maltreatment described heretofore, and, as appropriate, for judicial involvement.'

Few would assert that the Children Act 1989 ('the 1989 Act') could be said to have included *effective procedures* for the establishment of social programmes to provide necessary support for the child and for those who have the care of the child. This is due to the fact that compliance with many of the provisions which could be combined to forge such a social programme, for example s 17, Sch 2, Pt I, and s 27, is largely discretionary, empowering of local authorities rather than duty imposing. The combination of the 1989 Act and various volumes of Department of Health guidance (including, most importantly, *Working Together under the Children Act 1989* (1991, DOH) '*Working Together*'), have, nevertheless, contributed towards the construction of a more effective framework for the identification, reporting, referral, investigation, treatment and follow-up of child abuse cases. Arguments may continue to rage about whether the new grounds for care proceedings have raised or lowered the threshold of state intervention in the lives of children and their families, but most would acknowledge that the 1989 Act's provisions for judicial intervention represent a potentially very responsive and effective framework when such intervention is necessary.

As *Working Together* indicates (at Ch 4), a very wide range of agencies or individual professionals may be called upon at different stages in situations where child abuse is suspected and individual professionals or members of the community may also be involved by reason of their initial voicing of concern about a child. Those often described as being in the front line in

cases of child abuse include social workers, workers in day care or child
minding situations, teachers, psychologists, residential care staff and all types
of health workers, such as health visitors, community nurses, general practitioners, psychiatrists, paediatricians and staff in accident and emergency
units. In whichever way agencies or individuals are involved, they are
unlikely to view the law as any sort of universal panacea for dealing with the
problem of child abuse but rather as 'one *possible* resource for dealing with
social troubles' (Dingwall et al *Protecting Children, Controlling Parents: State
Intervention in Family Law* (1983, Basil Blackwell)) (emphasis added).

Since one of the most difficult tensions inherent in the 1989 Act is that of
the balance to be struck between children's needs and families' rights, which
is a tension at the heart of all child protection work, it is not surprising that
official guidance recognises the risks of law-based intervention. Thus, in *The
Care of Children – Principles and Practice in Regulations and Guidance* (1989,
DOH) it is stated that 'measures which antagonise, alienate, undermine or
marginalise parents are *counter-productive*, for example taking compulsory
powers over children can *all too easily* have this effect though such action
may be *necessary* in order to provide protection' (at para 2.7, emphasis added).

The building of a partnership relationship between the child's family and
the various concerned agencies may have been a continuing one, involving
a prolonged period of contact with, and service provision into, the child's
family. Regrettably, however, most cases of child abuse triggering intervention through the court will come from those families with whom the
relevant agencies have an existing contact (see Dale et al *Dangerous Families*
(1986, Tavistock) at Ch 2, generally), rather than from families with which
there has been little or no pre-existing contact. As Morrison points out,
'whatever efforts and measures are directed towards voluntary partnership
with parents, there will always be a significant proportion of abused children
for whom a level of intervention involving court orders will be necessary'
(see T Morrison 'Change, Control and the Legal Framework' in Adcock,
White and Hollows (eds) *Significant Harm*, (1991, Significant Publications)).
What, perhaps, is also different about the new law is that the positive advantage principle contained in s 1(5) of the 1989 Act requires local authority
social services to demonstrate that the rights given them by court orders will
assist in the process of actually improving the child's situation and possibly
changing the child's family conditions.

4.2 Prevention

The principle of prevention has been elevated by the 1989 Act to a position
of central importance in the work of all agencies concerned with the protection
of children and the positive promotion of their health and welfare. It was no
accident that Part III of the 1989 Act, coming immediately as it does after
those parts dealing essentially with the private law relating to children in

their families, begins with the heading 'Local Authority Support for Children and Families'. What has emerged in the 1989 Act, therefore, is a recognition of the point made by the interdepartmental *Review of Child Care Law* (1985, DHSS) ('the *Review*'), that prevention 'was an inadequate term to describe the purpose of local authority provision for families with children'. The *Review* indicated that there were two main aims of such a provision: 'to provide family support to help parents bring up their children; and to seek to prevent admission to care or court proceedings except where this is in the best interests of the child'. The *Review* working party recommended that revised legislation should include 'a broad power to provide services to promote the care and upbringing of children within their families' as well as 'the specific preventive duty to seek to diminish the need for children to be received into care or brought before a juvenile court'. This recommendation was enacted in s 17 of the 1989 Act, which places a general duty on local authorities to safeguard and promote the welfare of children in their area who are in need and, subject to that duty, to promote the upbringing of such children by their families. This is further reinforced by the provisions in Sch 2, Part I of the 1989 Act, which impose upon local authorities the duties of identification of children in need and provision of information to them about services provided by the local authority and voluntary organisations (Sch 2, Pt I, para 1); to take reasonable steps through the provision of such services to prevent children within their area suffering ill-treatment or neglect (Sch 2, Pt I, para 4); to take responsible steps designed to reduce the need to bring care proceedings, criminal proceedings or any other sort of proceedings in respect of children (Sch 2, Pt I, para 7); and it provides local authorities with the power to provide services to help to maintain the family home in which the child is living (Sch 2, Pt I, paras 8, 9 and 10). It can be seen that support for families with children is linked to the issue of whether the child is assessed to be a child in need. A child is taken to be in need if:

- the child is unlikely to achieve or maintain or to have the opportunity of achieving or maintaining a reasonable standard of health or development without the provision for him/her of services by a local authority;

- the child's health or development is likely to be significantly impaired or further impaired without the provision for him of such services; or

- the child is disabled (s 17(10)).

The definition of a child in need is further expanded by reference to the concept of health, development and disability in s 17(11)). Thus, 'development' means physical, intellectual, emotional, social or behavioural development; 'health' means physical or mental health; and a child is described as 'disabled' where he is blind, deaf or dumb or suffers from a mental disorder of any kind or is substantially and permanently handicapped by illness, injury or congenital deformity or such other disability as may be prescribed.

In many parts of the country, local authorities have expanded upon the definition of 'child in need' provided in the 1989 Act and have produced their own 'Children in Need' documents which also contain information about types of services which are available for children in need within those areas. Professionals working within the area of child protection should, therefore, be aware of the contents of those 'Children in Need' and service information documents in order to be able to identify which of the various services a family with a child in need of protection actually requires. The need for the sort of support services provided pursuant to Part III of the 1989 Act may, thus, be identified by anyone involved with the family or indeed by the family themselves. In addition to the more general duties described in Sch 2, Pt I of the 1989 Act, Part III of the Act goes on to identify a variety of other services to meet the needs of families for support and assistance in caring for children. Thus, the local authority is under a duty to provide such day care for children in need within their area who are aged five or under and not yet attending schools as is appropriate. This is, of course, a discretionary power and it would be virtually impossible to argue that any local authority is under an absolute duty to make wide ranging provision for day care places. The 1989 Act does go on to provide, in s 18(5), that local authorities must also provide the children in need within their area who are attending school, such care or supervised activities as are appropriate outside school hours or during school holidays. As to the range of other services which could be provided by local authorities under the provisions of the 1989 Act to support the families of children in need, these include: advice, guidance and counselling (Sch 2, Pt I, para 8(a)); occupational, social, cultural or recreational activities (para 8(b)); home help, including laundry services (para 8(c)); facilities for, or assistance with, travelling to and from home for the purpose of taking advantage of any other service provided under the 1989 Act (para 8(d)); assistance to enable the child concerned and his family to have a holiday (para 8(e)); and family centres (para 9).

The role of family centres in promoting preventive work in the area of child abuse has long been recognised. Family centres are certainly not new inventions, since Family Advice Centres were being set up in the 1960s (A Leissner *Family Advice Centres* (1967, Longmans), and some have even traced the new Family Centres back to the Victorian settlements (EM Goldberg and I Sinclair *Family Support Exercise* (1986, National Institute for Social Work)), but with the new centres there appears to be a greater emphasis on mutual help, user participation and local control. It has been suggested (J Gibbons, S Thorpe and P Wilkinson *Family Support and Prevention: Studies in Local Areas* (1990, HMSO)), that a distinction must be made between family centres which are part of the array of personal social services delivered by local authorities themselves, and projects and centres which are either outside statutory services altogether or occupy a boundary position. Thus, whilst many local authorities provide their own family centres, the Church of England Children's Society (later the Children's Society) has played a crucial part in the development of family centre provision and other large voluntary children's charities have followed on in providing their own centres (D Birchall *Family Centres* (1982, National Children's Bureau)). De'Ath, in her research in 1985, identified some 250 centres in England and Wales which shared certain common features which could be seen as promoting their greater use and acceptance by families under stress (E De'Ath *Self Help and Family Centres: A Current Initiative in Helping the Community* (1985, National Children's Bureau)). Holman *Putting Families First: Prevention and Child Care: A Study of Prevention by Statutory and Voluntary Agencies* (1988, Macmillan), in a study of 10 voluntary family centres, considered that they were particularly active in five forms of preventive activity: preventing the reception of children into care or custody; preventing neglect and abuse; preventing children from experiencing poor parenting; and preventing them from experiencing severe social disadvantages both in the home and in the community. Further support of the value of family centres in performing the local authorities' preventive role can be derived from the DOH guidance on the 1989 Act (see *The Children Act 1989 Guidance and Regulations, Vol 2 Family Support, Day Care, and Educational Provision for Young Children* (1991, HMSO) at paras 3.18 to 3.24). Indeed, the *Children Act Report 1992* (1993, DOH) para 3.16 and Table 3.2 revealed a particularly strong showing on the provision of family centres with 50 out of 60 local authorities already providing centres, and 27 local authorities intending to introduce or develop further the provision of such centres.

Provisions of the 1989 Act and the DOH guidance (above) further recognise the positive duties placed upon local authorities to provide services for children with disabilities within their area so as to minimise the effect of their disabilities and to give such children the opportunity to lead lives which are as normal as possible (1989 Act, Sch 2, para 6). The range of services previously described should all be available for families with disabled children and respite care, which, formerly, was always thought of as a particular service to meet the needs of families with disabled children, should now also be seen in a much wider context as being available to serve all families with children in need. The provision of such temporary accommodation is, of course, governed by the provisions of s 20 of the 1989 Act, and respite care is, thus, controlled by the protective provisions relating to the placement of children in accommodation provided by the local authority. (See, generally, *The Children Act 1989 Guidance and Regulations, Vol 3 Family Placements*) (1991, HMSO).

Whilst preventive work was certainly important under the previous law, current provisions in the 1989 Act have elevated the principle of prevention to the top of local authorities' child protection agendas. As a result of the new duties and powers comprised in the 1989 Act, prevention could be seen as being practised at two levels or in two stages. Parker's analysis in

RA Parker (ed) *Caring for separated children: Planned procedures and priorities* (1980, Macmillan), of primary and secondary prevention, probably now most closely reflects the approaches taken by many local authorities to the provision of services under Part III of the 1989 Act. Thus, Parker stated that 'primary prevention is thought of as comprising those services which provide general support to families and reduce the general levels of poverty, stress, insecurity, ill-health and bad housing'. He went on to argue that secondary prevention represents the next stage: 'once problems have actually arisen help of various kinds may supply a remedy or at least forestall something worse' (at p 45). At this stage, services are liable to be restricted to those who are assumed to be at special 'risk' or whose circumstances warrant special priority.

Whilst it might appear that an undue burden is placed on local authorities, and particularly on social services, to provide the various services under Part III of the 1989 Act, it should be noted that s 27 provides social services departments of a local authority with the ability to request help from a range of other authorities within the local area, such as local housing authorities, local education authorities, health authorities, and health service trusts. Such a request of help made by social services or the particular local authority must be complied with by the other authority, provided that it is compatible with its statutory functions and does not unduly prejudice the discharge of those functions. As the DOH guidance states, social services will, on occasion, turn to the education authority for assistance in meeting the duties placed on social services departments in respect of family support (*The Children Act 1989 Guidance and Regulations, Vol 2 Family Support, Day Care and Educational Provision for Young Children* (at para 1.13)). The type of service envisaged here might include the services of an educational psychologist or speech therapist where efforts are being made to mitigate the effects of possible child abuse or neglect. The guidance goes on to state that the local authority carries the principal responsibility for co-ordinating and providing services for children in need, although in some cases its services will be supportive of other key agencies. Local authorities and other relevant agencies remain responsible for decisions about their own service provision or legal and administrative issues assigned to them. They should, however, seek out and have available the best relevant help from other agencies. Similarly, they must 'be available and prepared to contribute to the work of other key agencies in meeting the legitimate needs of children and their families' (at para 1.14).

Thus, it can be seen that the elevation of the prevention principle represented in the enactment of Part III of the 1989 Act will mean that the provision of day nursery places, playgroup places, child-minding facilities, family aids, family centres, respite care, short holidays and access to various educational and health facilities, will all have been considered and some will have been used before resort will be made to legal action through such means as care proceedings. The task of all professionals working within the child protection arena should, therefore, be to provide services to help to maintain the child in the family, provided always that to do so is consistent with the child's welfare. The legislative support for the principles of prevention represented by the enactment of Part III of the 1989 Act serves only to reinforce the good practice carried on by a range of professionals prior to the enactment of the 1989 Act. Where families are known to any one of the various agencies dealing with children, and children have been identified as being in need, there is no doubt that considerable effort will have been expended on keeping the family out of the court framework and the ambit of proceedings involving possible compulsory removal of the child from his family.

The basic aim of all documents of guidance produced for social workers and other professionals in the context of child abuse is to stress that, wherever it is possible to promote and protect the welfare of the child by leaving him in his family, this approach is to be preferred to damaging and possibly unnecessary removal. (See *Protecting Children: A Guide for Social Workers undertaking a Comprehensive Assessment* (1988, DOH); *The Care of Children – Principles and Practice in Regulations and Guidance* (1989, HMSO), at Ch 2, paras 5, 6 and 7 and 8; *Working Together*, at para 1.4.) Even where social services or other professional agencies have had some continuing contact with the family, one particular incident may spark off a need for an investigation leading to a full child protection conference or, alternatively, in situations where families have previously been unknown to any agencies, a report of suspected abuse or concerns over a child may come through from another professional having contact with the child (eg a teacher), or from neighbours, relatives or friends of the family.

4.3 Reporting

Unlike 47 of the States of the USA, the law in England does not provide for the compulsory reporting of child abuse. The idea of a reporting law was discussed by the DHSS in *Review of Child Care Law* (1985, DHSS) but the working party decided against such a proposal (at para 12(4)). There is, therefore, no legal duty laid upon members of the public to report suspicions or knowledge of incidents of child abuse. Nevertheless, every encouragement is given to the public to ensure that if they provide such information their anonymity will be protected. As Lord Diplock pointed out in *D v NSPCC* [1977] 1 All ER 589, HL, the private promise of confidentiality must yield to the general public interest that in the administration of justice truth will out, unless by reason of the character of the information or the relationship of the recipient to the informant, a more important public interest is served by protecting the information or the identity of the informant from disclosure in a court of law. Their Lordships concluded in this case that the public interest of ensuring the protection of children was greater than the public interest in ensuring that the whole truth be told, and it thus refused to allow the disclosure of any details relating to the original informant in the particular case.

It also has to be said, however, that the different professional groups working with children, whilst not subjected to any mandatory reporting law as such may, nevertheless, find their own professional association's guidance seeks very strongly to encourage them to do so. For example, the standards committee of the British Medical Council has produced new guidelines for doctors which were approved by the Council in May 1993. These guidelines do appear to recognise implicitly that the notion of the *Gillick*-competence of children may demand a different approach in cases of child abuse involving older children but that in the case of younger children they cannot be deemed to be competent in giving or withholding consent to disclosure. The new guidelines state that:

> 'deciding whether or not to disclose information is particularly difficult in cases where a patient cannot be judged capable of giving or withholding consent to disclosure. One such situation may arise where a doctor believes that a patient may be the victim of abuse or neglect. In such circumstances the patient's interests are paramount and will usually require the doctor to disclose information to an appropriate, responsible person or an officer of a statutory agency.'

Apparently, the Council also agreed to amend the guidance which deals with disclosures in the public interest, to state explicitly that information about a patient may be released to protect a particular individual (eg an abused child) as well as unknown members of the public. The new guidance reads as follows:

> **'Disclosures to Third Parties**
> Rarely, cases may arise in which disclosure in the public interest, or in the interests of an individual, may be justified, for example, a situation in which the failure to disclose appropriate information would expose the patient, or someone else, to risk of death or serious harm.'
> (*Disclosures in the Clinical Management of the Patient – Guidelines approved by the General Medical Council, May 1993* (Conduct, Health and Standards Division))

The British Medical Association's Ethics Committee has also been considering the issue of the dilemmas posed by the duty to protect children and the need to respect their views. In advance of the publication of its document *Medicine Today – Its Practice and Philosophy* containing a section entitled 'Dilemmas in Confidentiality and Consent' (BMA, July 1993), the Secretary of the Medical Ethics Committee indicated that the committee's broad view was that in the case of young children caught up in abuse there was an *ethical imperative* upon the doctor to inform the relevant statutory agencies where the child had made disclosures or the doctor had observed any form of abuse. In the case of older children, the BMA's view would appear to be that the doctor should, wherever possible, seek to encourage the child to agree to disclosure but that this might occur after a referral to expert counsellors, very much following the model adopted in Holland in these sorts of cases.

The Secretary and other members of the BMA Ethics Committee have also worked closely with Dr Susan Shepherd at the Department of Health in producing *Guidelines on Medical Confidentiality in Child Protection*, which is expected to be published in September 1993. These *Guidelines* are intended to act as a supplement to *Working Together* and will make it clear that whilst the local authority social services, the police and the NSPCC have statutory *duties* to investigate where they believe a child is, or is at risk of, suffering significant harm, when the person providing them with information is a doctor, he or she must be clear about the position with regard to confidentiality. If doctors are to fulfil their full and proper participatory role in inter-disciplinary procedures in child protection cases they should appreciate that their normal duty to maintain doctor/patient confidentiality is *overriden* in cases of child abuse by the public interest in protecting children. The *Guidelines* will go on to emphasise that the difficult area in child protection is the process of determining whether or not a child is, or is at risk of, suffering significant harm and this process demands the full exchange of information between concerned professionals. The approach of the *Guidelines* would appear to be very much one of encouraging people to joint agreement as to how to handle such sensitive information. It would appear that the *Guidelines* will, like the General Medical Council Guidance, be sympathetic to a difference of approach by doctors dealing with older children. In the case of young children there would seem to be general acceptance of the view that the doctor should regard it as imperative to pass on the relevant information immediately to the statutory agencies in order to guarantee the child's protection, but that in the case of disclosures by older children there should be an attempt to talk through the issues surrounding disclosure and its possible consequences in order to pave the way to disclosure to third parties such as the statutory agencies. In such circumstances, it may be that there is a considerable risk of danger to the child or young person disclosing, as well as to siblings or other members of the family, and such fears must be worked through and may require specialist counselling.

It should also be pointed out at this stage that doctors may receive information suggesting concerns about child abuse from patients who are not the abused children. Such disclosures may come from the abusing or non-abusing parent and it should be clear to doctors that the same considerations as above must apply. Thus, where the doctors receive information indicating possible child abuse they must take steps to inform the relevant statutory agencies and should clearly take steps to ensure that appropriate advice, counselling and support is available if such disclosures will attract risks to the person giving the original information.

Clearly the GMC, the BMA and the Department of Health have put a considerable amount of work into producing their new revised Guidelines and it would appear that they have made a serious attempt to address the difficult issues arising from disclosures made by older children. Similar guidance also exists for senior nurses, health visitors and midwives (see *Child Protection – Guidance for Senior Nurses, Health Visitors and Midwives* (1992, HMSO)) and, although the 1992 guidance does not make a duty to disclose explicit, it is, nevertheless, implicit throughout the document wherever it discusses the relevant actions of nurses, health visitors and midwives in responding to suspicions about child abuse. That document makes reference, at para 13.2, to the United Kingdom Central Council's 'Code of Professional Conduct for the Nurse, Midwife and Health Visitor' and to the advisory paper of confidentiality published in April 1987. There the advice is rather more explicit in that it states:

> 'in all cases where the practitioner deliberately discloses or withholds information in what he thinks is the public interest, he must be able to justify the decision. These situations can be particularly stressful, especially where vulnerable groups are concerned, as disclosure may mean the involvement of a third party as in the case of children or the mentally handicapped. Practitioners should always take the opportunity to discuss the matter fully with other practitioners (not only or, necessarily, fellow nurses, midwives and health visitors) and, if appropriate, to consult with a professional organisation before making a decision. There will often be ramifications and these are best explored before a final decision as to whether to withhold or disclose information is made.'

It will be noted that such advice falls some way short of the ethical imperative in respect of young children suffering or at risk of suffering significant harm advised in the guidance for doctors.

Given their key involvement, it is even more surprising to find a very cautious stance adopted by the British Association of Social Workers in 1986, in their *Code of Ethics for Social Work* (1986, BASW). This states, as a principle of practice, that social workers will:

> 'recognise that information clearly entrusted for one purpose should not be used for another purpose without sanction. They will respect the privacy of clients and others with whom they come into contact and confidential information gained in their relationships with them. They will divulge such information only with the consent of the client (or informant) except where there is clear evidence of serious danger to the client, worker, other persons or the community or in other circumstances judged exceptional on the basis of professional consideration and consultation.'

The current DOH guidance on the other hand, which is specifically aimed at social services, is rather more direct in its approach. Thus, guidance on the issue of confidentiality is to be found in a DOH circular to local authority social services departments (LAC (88) 17) headed 'Personal Social Services: Confidentiality of Personal Information'. The approach in that document is admirably summed up at para 3.15 of *Working Together*. It states there that:

> 'in child protection work the degree of confidentiality will be governed by the need to protect the child. Social workers and others working with the child and family must make clear to those providing information that confidentiality *may not* be maintained if the withholding of the information will prejudice the welfare of a child.'

Other staff, particularly in the education service, may also be deemed to be in the front line as far as initial identification and referral processes in child abuse cases are concerned. Local education authorities all over the country have, in compliance with local Area Child Protection Committee guidelines, issued education staff with an explanation of the new law and the new procedures which may flow from the referral of a case of suspected child abuse. Whilst local education authorities (LEAs) are responsible for staff in the education service, such as teachers, education welfare officers, educational psychologists and youth workers, they have no responsibility for the private sector. This, instead, falls on social services departments, who should ensure that educational establishments, not maintained by the LEA, are aware of the local inter-agency procedures, and the governing bodies/proprietors of these establishments should ensure that appropriate procedures are in place, seeking advice, as necessary, from social services. It is obviously advisable that for all educational establishments, procedures should also cover circumstances where a member of staff is accused of suspected abuse. As *Working Together* states (at para 4.37):

'the key element essential to ensuring that proper procedures are followed in each educational establishment, is that the head teacher or another senior member of staff should be designated as having responsibility for liaising with social services and other relevant agencies in cases of child abuse. Furthermore for establishments maintained by them, LEAs should keep up to date lists of designated staff and ensure that these staff receive appropriate training and support.'

It is, perhaps, unfortunate that in the period leading up to the implementation of the 1989 Act and, indeed, following implementation up to the present time, few education authorities in England and Wales had actually engaged in training upon the implications of the 1989 Act, either generally or particularly in relation to child protection work. Staff in educational establishments often feel extremely vulnerable because of their ignorance on what they rightly deem to be a very important subject. Whilst the materials for the national curriculum now include modules within each of the key stages relevant to children keeping themselves safe and having relevant education in matters of personal relationships and development, many teachers feel that they are engaged in teaching such areas of the curriculum without themselves having the necessary background knowledge to act in cases where there may be a need to refer concerns about possible child abuse to a relevant agency. These criticisms have all been raised, in addition, by staff in day nurseries and nursery schools and, further, by registered child minders.

Probation officers may also have concerns about possible child abuse in cases in which they become involved, either as a result of their responsibility for the supervision of offenders, including those convicted of offences against children or, even more likely, in the performance of their role as court welfare officers in proceedings involving family relationship breakdown (s 7 of the

1989 Act). Through their work in preparing reports for courts, they may turn up concerns about whether a child is suffering or likely to suffer significant harm. In non-urgent cases they may refer their concerns back to court and the court is then able, under s 37 of the 1989 Act, to direct a local authority to conduct an investigation into the child's circumstances to see whether or not it is necessary to take proceedings for a care or supervision order. In urgent cases, the probation service must notify social services of their concerns, and social services will then be under a duty to make enquiries and to take such action as may be necessary. Of relevance also to this issue of reporting is the fact that arrangements exist to ensure that when offenders convicted of offences against children are discharged from prison, probation services inform the local authority in the area in which the discharged prisoner plans to reside. This allows the social services department to make enquiries and to take action where it is believed that there may be a danger to children residing at the same address. In many parts of the country, it is now the case that pre-release case conferences will be held involving probation and social services, where the prisoner is believed to constitute a danger to children living in a particular family. This should provide the forum in which appropriate arrangements can be agreed in order to safeguard and protect the relevant children. Where prisoners are being released from psychiatric units it may be appropriate to hold such a case conference at the psychiatric unit and to involve not only staff from the unit but those who may be involved in community psychiatric support.

As far as police reporting of concerns about child abuse is concerned, this stems from their primary duty to protect members of the community and to bring offenders to justice. As will be seen in the following paragraphs, the police have special powers to take action in emergencies but, where they have concerns about the possibility of child abuse which is of a non-urgent nature, they would be expected to notify such concerns to social services.

It should be noted that what has been said about the duties of the different agencies in respect of reporting concerns about particular children applies with equal force to later stages in the child protection process, such as investigation and assessment (see **4.5** and **4.10** below).

Finally, whilst reporting of concerns about child abuse may come from any of the professionals in any agencies already discussed, and may come through to a social services department, the police or the NSPCC, referrals may also come from members of the public, or those working with children and families who are not accustomed to dealing with child protection matters. *Working Together* points out (at para 5.11.1) that:

> 'all referrals whatever their origin, must be taken seriously and must be considered with an open mind which does not prejudice the situation. The statutory agencies must ensure that people know how to refer to them, and they must facilitate the making of referrals and the prompt and appropriate action in response to expressions of concern. It is important in all

these cases that the public and professionals are free to refer to the child protection agencies without fear that this will lead to uncoordinated and/or premature action.'

As events in Cleveland, Rochdale and the Orkneys have demonstrated, a balance needs to be struck between taking action designed to protect the child from abuse and protecting that child and the family from the harm caused by unnecessary intervention.

4.4 Stages of work in individual cases

To provide the appropriate responses to concerns about child abuse in individual cases, there must be a very high level of co-operation between the agencies providing protection for children. The moves to produce a 'Working Together' document, which appeared in its first draft in April 1987 (see *Working Together, a draft* (April 1987, DHSS)), were undoubtedly influenced by the findings of *A Child in Trust: The Report of the Panel of Inquiry investigating the circumstances surrounding the death of Jasmine Beckford*, (1985, London Borough of Brent) and given added impetus by the findings of the *Report of Inquiry into Child Abuse in Cleveland 1987* (1988, HMSO), Cm 412 ('the *Cleveland Report*') at p 248). The first *Working Together* document in 1988 was published in the wake of the *Cleveland Report* and followed very closely its recommendations as to inter-agency working. The current *Working Together* document, 1991, states clearly that 'to be effective, co-operation between agencies providing protection to children must be underpinned by a shared agreement about the handling of individual cases' (at para 5.10). The document goes on to identify the various stages of work in individual cases of child abuse and it would seem appropriate to set these out here. These stages are:

(1) referral and recognition;
(2) immediate protection and planning the investigation;
(3) investigation and initial assessment;
(4) child protection conference and decision making about the need for registration;
(5) comprehensive assessment of planning;
(6) implementation, review and, where appropriate, de-registration.

The document goes on to point out that these stages do not necessarily stand alone nor are they clearly divided in time and there is likely to be some overlap. It is suggested, however, that the sequence should assist professionals to see more clearly the focus of work at each stage. (See, for further detail, Chapter 5 on Inter-agency Co-operation.)

4.5 Investigation

By s 47 of the 1989 Act, where a local authority receives information that there is a child in its area who is subject to an emergency protection order, or in police protection, or it has reasonable cause to suspect that a child in its area is suffering or is likely to suffer *significant harm*, the authority must make or cause to be made such enquiries as it considers necessary (s 47(1)(a) and (b)). The purpose of such enquiries is to enable the local authority social services department to determine whether it should take any action to safeguard or promote the child's welfare. It should also be remembered that a local authority may receive information about the possibility of a child suffering or being likely to suffer significant harm, via a court welfare officer engaged in providing a report to the court in family proceedings, under the 1989 Act, or the local authority may receive a direction from the court itself to conduct an investigation into whether there is a need to institute care or supervision proceedings under s 37 of the 1989 Act.

4.5.1 The meaning of 'significant harm'

The concept of *significant harm* will be discussed in greater detail in Chapter 6, but it is worth examining briefly here since it is the trigger for much of what follows in the way of investigation, and is also the ground to which the concerned agencies and courts must look when deciding whether to apply for orders, to exercise any special powers or, in the case of the courts, to make orders. Harm is defined by s 31(9) of the 1989 Act as meaning 'ill-treatment or the impairment of health or development'; development is defined as meaning 'physical, intellectual, emotional, social or behavioural development'; health is defined to include 'physical or mental health' and, finally, ill-treatment is defined as including 'sexual abuse and forms of ill-treatment which are not physical'. When looking to satisfy the criterion of harm, it would appear to be the case that the court may be satisfied that the child is suffering from harm if any one of the three types of harm envisaged in s 31(9) is present. This is indeed the guidance offered by the DOH in *The Children Act 1989 Guidance and Regulations, Vol 1 Court Orders* (1991, HMSO), where it states that these three types of harm are 'alternatives' and that 'only one of these conditions needs to be satisfied but that the proceedings may refer to all three' (at para 3.19). The new grounds for intervention could thus be seen to be very wide and, indeed, the Court of Appeal in *Newham London Borough Council v AG* [1993] 1 FLR 281 at p 289, has emphasised that the words of the Act must be considered but were not meant to be unduly restrictive when the evidence clearly indicated that a certain course of action should be taken in order to protect a child, a point reiterated by Thorpe J in *Re A (A Minor) (Care Proceedings)* [1993] 1 FCR 824. The condition as to *significant harm* is drawn with reference to the child concerned, and so those conducting the investigations and the courts who may be called upon to make orders, must look at the position, characteristics and needs of each particular child. The new criteria which may trigger off an investigation and subsequent making of orders are intended to cover both situations where the child is suffering or is *likely to suffer* significant harm. The use of the term 'is suffering' is intended to concentrate attention on present or continuing conditions where problems have been temporarily ameliorated since the involvement of the investigating agency, but where the problems could, nevertheless, still give rise to legitimate concerns and justify considerable exploration. Clearly, an investigation relating solely to past events is unlikely to proceed much further unless it is being linked in some way to the present evidence by some harm continuing, or being likely to continue. (See *Northamptonshire County Council v S* [1992] 3 WLR 1010.) As to looking at the likelihood of the future possibility of harm as indicated by the words 'likely to suffer significant harm', the investigating agency in consultation with other professionals concerned with the child must seek to establish that there would be a greater risk to the child in leaving him in his current situation than by seeking to provide services to ameliorate the situation or, in the worst cases, by seeking the child's removal through an application for court orders.

Some concern has been expressed with regard to the fact that emotional abuse was not specifically mentioned in the 1989 Act but, since ill-treatment can include forms of ill-treatment which are not physical, and the impairment of emotional development can constitute 'harm' under the 1989 Act, such fears may appear to be unfounded. It was a matter of considerable concern, however, that the view had been expressed that in cases of 'emotional' or 'psychological' harm, the approach which would be taken under any reform of the law would be such as to prevent unwarranted intervention. (See *Review of Child Care Law* (1985, DHSS) at para 15.18.) Although few cases have thus far emerged which deal specifically with issues of emotional development, Scott Baker J in *Re H (A Minor) (Section 37 Direction)* [1993] 2 FLR 541), emphasised that 'the likelihood of harm is not confined to present or near future but applies to the ability of a parent or carer to meet the *emotional* needs of a child in years ahead'.

The harm suffered or apprehended must be 'significant' and, where this turns on the child's health or development, his health or development shall be compared with that which could be expected of a similar child (s 31(10)). As far as the word 'significant' is concerned, the DHSS *Review of Child Care Law* (1985, DHSS), stated that minor shortcomings in the health care provided, or minor deficits in physical, psychological or social development, should not give rise to compulsory intervention unless they are having, or are likely to have, serious and lasting effects upon the child (at para 15.15). The Lord Chancellor has also stated that 'unless there is evidence that a child is being, or is likely to be, positively harmed because of failure in the family, the State, whether in the guise of a local authority or a court, should not interfere' (see Lord Mackay in the Joseph Jackson Memorial Lecture (139) NLJ 505 at p 508). The comparison to be made with a similar child is not without problems, however, since one is required to compare this subjective child with that hypothetically similar child. This issue came up for consideration by the court in the case of *Re O (A Minor) (Care Order: Education: Procedure)* [1992] 2 FLR 7, where Ewbank J took a very robust view of what constituted a similar child. In this particular case he was dealing with a young girl who had been truanting from school and the issue was whether she had suffered harm compared with a similar child. In Ewbank J's view a similar child in this case meant 'a child of equivalent intellectual and social development, who has gone to school and not merely an average child who may or may not be at school' (at p 12). Clearly, if the child is disabled in some way, and that has affected his health and development, the investigating agency must ask itself what state of health or development could be expected of a child with a similar disability. As to whether 'similar' connotes any consideration being given to the child's background, this is doubtful since, according to the Lord Chancellor, 'the care that a parent gives to his child must be related to the circumstances attributable to that child in the sense of physical, mental and emotional characteristics' (*Hansard*, Deb Committee, Vol 503, col 355). Whilst the child protection agencies, when investigating issues of significant harm, will have to be sensitive to racial, cultural and religious issues (see further on this, A Lau 'Cultural and Ethnic Perspectives on Significant Harm: Its Assessment and Treatment' in Adcock, White and Hollows (eds) *Significant Harm* (1991, Significant Publications)) nevertheless, what the Lord Chancellor was clearly indicating is that the agency must focus on the needs of the particular child.

4.5.2 Location of the abuse and identity of the perpetrator

The duty placed upon the local authority to investigate in cases of suspected child abuse is the same, no matter where that abuse has occurred or by whom it has been perpetrated. Thus, whilst *additional* special procedures may be invoked where children are abused in residential settings, outside the family home, in foster placements or in schools, the first duty upon the local authority is to engage in an investigation under s 47, which may well include taking steps to involve the police (see *Working Together* at paras 5.19 to 5.24.5).

4.5.3 Processing the investigation

The provisions in s 47 of the 1989 Act, which go on to deal with processing the investigation by social services, provide that enquiries must, in particular, be directed towards establishing whether they should make any application to the court or exercise any other of their powers under the 1989 Act, which could include using any of the measures described in **4.2** above. Where the local authority is carrying out an investigation in respect of a child with respect to whom an emergency protection order has been made, and who is not in accommodation provided by or on behalf of the local authority, the local authority must further decide whether it would be in the child's best interests for him to be in such accommodation (s 47(3)). The local authority is not apparently in a position to be able to insist on taking over the child's accommodation but in most cases the other agencies concerned will deem it appropriate to transfer care of the child to the local authority. The local authority is also under a duty to consider whether, in the case of a child in police protection, it would be in the child's best interests for the local authority to request that an application be made by the designated officer (see **4.6**) for an emergency protection order on behalf of the local authority (s 47(3)(c) and s 46(7)).

4.5.4 Obtaining access to the child

In the course of pursuing its investigation under s 47 of the 1989 Act, the local authority must take such steps as are reasonably practicable to obtain access to the child, or to ensure that access is obtained on its behalf by a 'person authorised' by it for this purpose, unless it is satisfied that it already has sufficient information with respect to the child (s 47(4)). Such enquiries must be conducted with a view to enabling the authority to determine what action, if any, to take with respect to the child. As to who might be authorised by the authority to assist it in the making of such enquiries, it is made clear by s 47(9) to (11), that it is the duty of any person employed by the local authority, any local education authority, any housing authority or any health authority or health service trust, to assist in the making of such enquiries unless it would be unreasonable in all the circumstances of the case. As we saw with the provisions on prevention contained in the 1989 Act, Part III (see **4.2** above), s 27 contains a statutory enactment of the principles of *Working Together*. The provisions of s 47(11) also go on to indicate that the local authority could call upon any person authorised by the Secretary of State for the purposes of this section to assist it in making its enquiries. Thus far, no persons have been authorised under this provision, although presumably the local authority would be able to call in aid the services of the NSPCC, using the NSPCC powers of investigation provided under ss 31 and 44. It should be noted that the list of those who can be called upon to assist the local authority does not include the police, but it was stated by the Minister concerned with piloting the bill through the House of Commons, David Mellor, that 'police refusal to co-operate on any matter would be indefensible' (see *Hansard*, Deb Standing Committee B, col 317). The probation service are also not specifically included under these provisions but the Minister further stated that 'probation officers are officers of the court and are already under a duty to assist in these matters'. It would make more sense to have included probation officers and the police in the list provided in s 47 and guidance issued to the police in *Working Together* (at paras 4.14 to 4.15) emphasises their abilities to act in cases of dire emergency, which would include a specific request from social services. The guidance goes on to state that information which the police hold may be highly relevant to a decision about a child who may need protection from abuse, and should, therefore, where appropriate, be shared with other agencies. Despite previous difficulties with the police, most police forces up and down the country have now fostered extremely good relations with social services through the establishment of their own specialist child protection teams and the clear import of the guidance offered in *Working Together* suggests that there should be no problems in requesting the assistance of the police to further investigations under s 47.

Where, pursuant to s 47(4), the local authority social services do consider that they need the assistance of any of the other agencies in trying to gain access to a child, it may well be that consideration is given to who might best seek such access. It is well known that in families where there are young children in particular, health visitors may find it relatively easy to obtain access to the child. It would not, therefore, be unreasonable for social services to make such a request of the health visiting service, although clearly, where there are concerns about the safety of any person seeking to gain such access, a refusal by the health visitor, in such circumstances, would be deemed to be reasonable within the provisions of s 47(10).

In addition to engaging the assistance of other agencies in accordance with s 47(9) and (11), the local authority is required to consult the relevant local education authority where, as a result of any such enquiries, it appears to the authority that there are matters connected with the child's education which should be investigated. In those cases, therefore, where the concern is primarily focused on issues connected with the child's intellectual development, this should allow the local authority service and the local education authority to determine whether it would be more appropriate for the education services to deal with the child's case. This might then involve the services of an educational psychologist or counsellor and, in cases of non-attendance, might prompt the education authority to consider proceedings for an education supervision order (s 36).

Where the local authority's investigation under s 47 has been frustrated by an unreasonable refusal of access to the child, it should be noted that such refusal may constitute grounds for the local authority to seek an emergency protection order under s 44(1)(b) (see **4.6.1** below). In any event, under the provisions of s 47, where the local authority or person authorised by it has been refused access or denied information as to the child's whereabouts in the course of an investigation, the local authority is bound to apply for an emergency protection order, child assessment order, care order or supervision order 'unless they are satisfied that the child's welfare can be satisfactorily safeguarded without their doing so' (s 47(6)). These provisions, taken together, clarify the procedure to be followed by social workers when access to the child is being denied and addresses the problems raised by *A Child in*

Mind; Protection of Children in a Responsible Society (1987, London Borough of Greenwich) ('the *Kimberley Carlile Report*'), which criticised the social workers for failing to be aware of, and to use, powers under the old law to gain access to Kimberley Carlile, which, had they been invoked, might have prevented her death (see the old law contained in the Children and Young Persons Act 1933, s 40, which is further retained in the current law by virtue of s 48(9) of the 1989 Act).

In addition to the duties imposed on local authorities, the NSPCC is also empowered under s 44(1)(c) of the 1989 Act to take action to protect a child in situations where it has been unable to gain access or, more generally, to institute proceedings under s 31 of the 1989 Act, and the police also have special powers under the provisions of s 46. The first and paramount concern of the social services, NSPCC or the police is to ensure that the child is protected. Where an allegation has been made or the suspicions of the police, social services or NSPCC officers have been aroused, as many details as possible relating to the child should be gathered, including the child's name, address, names of parents, names of others in the household, name of the family's GP, details of any nursery or school which the child attends, and details of the family's or child's social worker, if there is one. The next step will be to check with the Child Protection Register.

4.5.5 Checking the Child Protection Register

The purpose of the Register is to provide a record of all children in the area who are currently the subject of an inter-agency child protection plan and to ensure that the plans are formally reviewed every six months at least. All social services departments normally maintain such registers at their headquarters, although if the situation arises out of office hours, the Register can normally be checked by a call to the social services emergency duty team, where these are operative. Key information to be held on the Child Protection Register is detailed in Appendix 4 of *Working Together*, but includes information in four sections. The first section deals with identification of the child, including information as to the child's personal details and location, the names and addresses of members of the child's family and other regular visitors to the household and details on other children in the household; the second section deals with the nature of the abuse which may have been perpetrated against the child; the third section includes information on the key worker and the core group of representatives of service providers included in the child protection plan; and, finally, the fourth section deals with the detail of the child protection plan, including a programme of reviews and a record of all enquiries to the Register. Appendix 4 goes on to advise, very crucially, that 'all staff involved with the child of the family should notify changes in the information to the key worker so that the Register may be kept up to date'. It is, of course, particularly important (if child protection registers are going to be used as a means of speedily checking whether a child has been noted as giving cause for concern) that such records are as up to date as possible and, in the investigative stages, it may be particularly relevant to note recent enquiries to the Child Protection Register contained in the fourth section.

4.5.6 Involvement of the various agencies in emergencies

Social services or the NSPCC are the agencies most likely to be involved during daytime hours in the week, whilst the police are more likely to be involved in emergency situations arising out of other incidents within the family (eg domestic violence primarily directed against the spouse which has peripherally involved children), or out of hours (eg at night, over weekends or over Bank Holidays, when social services may find it difficult to provide emergency duty cover).

4.5.7 Checking with other agencies

Whenever there is time, as well as checking the Child Protection Register, the agency involved may also check with the health visitor, school, education welfare department, the probation service, the family GP, the police and the NSPCC. All such checks provide essential information, but it might be that speed is of the essence and, therefore, action is required without being able to make all the desired enquiries. Discussions within a child protection conference setting (see *Fig 3* below) may, therefore, have to be postponed until after the taking of emergency action. In a non-emergency situation where there is felt to be a risk of abuse which has not yet materialised, there may be on-going work with the family which has identified a looming, potential crisis. In such circumstances, it may be possible to convene a child protection conference with all the relevant personnel (see *Fig 3* below); an opportunity is thus provided for giving measured consideration to take further legal steps, such as obtaining a child assessment order (see s 43 of the 1989 Act) or the institution of proceedings for a care or supervision order (see s 31 of the 1989 Act).

In an emergency situation, however, it may (as has been indicated) be impossible to hold a case conference, and the social workers, NSPCC officer or police officer may have to take action on their own initiative, perhaps without the time for consultation with a senior. As *Working Together* (at para 5.12.1) points out:

'where there is risk to the life of the child or likelihood of serious injury, the agencies with the statutory child protection powers need to secure the immediate safety of the child. A decision must be taken urgently as to whether the child should be removed to some other place, either on a voluntary basis or by obtaining an Emergency Protection Order.'

It must be remembered, however, that even in an emergency it is essential to adhere to the principles underpinning the 1989 Act and, in particular, that of partnership with parents. The *Cleveland Report* had, as one of its major criticisms, the failure to involve parents at an early stage when considering protective action, and this has been highlighted, subsequently, in the *Report of the Inquiry into the Removal of Children from Orkney in February 1991* (1992, HMSO), at para 18.31. *Working Together* further emphasises the importance of partnership, where it advises that 'the urgency of the situation should not detract from every effort being made to ensure that those with parental responsibility are given appropriate opportunities to participate throughout the process' (at para 5.12.2).

4.5.8 Involvement of the police in investigations

If, at any point in the early stages of the investigation by social services or the NSPCC, it becomes apparent that there is a possibility of a criminal offence having been committed against the child, the police should be notified. It may be the case, of course, that the police have been involved in some way either in the initial referral or in the early stages of investigation following referral, but it is essential that there is an early strategy discussion between police and social services in order to plan the investigation properly, and, in particular, the role of each agency and the extent of joint investigations. (See *Fig 2* below, and for the background of such strategy discussions see N Parton 'Coordination Management and Assessment' in *Governing the Family* (1991, Macmillan) Ch 5, especially at pp 127 to 129.) It is the responsibility of the agency receiving the referral to initiate this and, throughout the early stages of the investigation, both police and social services must keep in mind that it may be necessary to invoke civil child protection proceedings or criminal proceedings, or both, against the perpetrator. Interviewing the child victim or the child or adult perpetrator must be conducted in accordance with established codes of practice and current case-law and this is considered in detail in Chapter 6 (in relation to civil proceedings) and Chapter 7 (in relation to criminal proceedings).

4.6 Application for an emergency protection order

4.6.1 Making the application

Any person may apply to the court, usually a single justice in the magistrates' court, for an order authorising a child's removal to accommodation provided by or on behalf of the applicant, or authorising the child to remain in the place in which he has been accommodated, provided that the court is satisfied (on the balance of probabilities) that there is reasonable cause to believe that to do otherwise would mean that the child would be likely to suffer significant

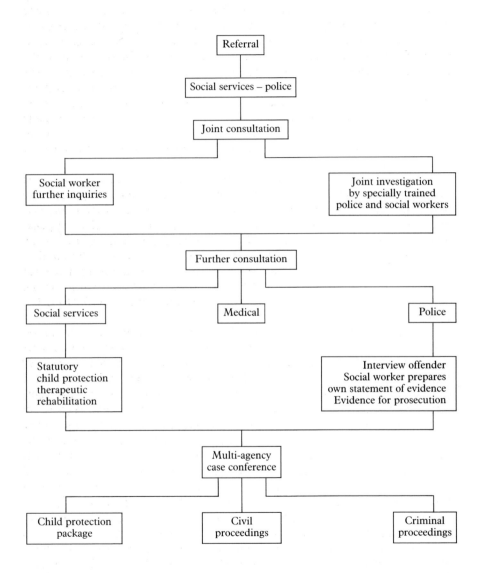

*Fig 2: A working model demonstrating police and social services involvement in a child
abuse case*

harm (s 44(1)(a)). (For a discussion of the meaning of 'significant harm', see **4.5.1** above and Chapter 6.) The order is to be referred to as 'an emergency protection order' (s 44(4)) and the fact that such orders are only to be made in real emergencies appears to have been understood by all the relevant agencies in England and Wales in the wake of the events of Cleveland, Rochdale and the Orkneys. Thus, in the first year of the operation of the 1989 Act, a very considerable decrease has been reported in relation to the use of emergency protection orders when compared to the numbers of place of safety orders taken out under the old law. The *Children Act Report 1992* (1993, DOH) reports that 2,300 emergency protection orders were made compared to approximately 5,000 children who were removed to a place of safety on the instructions of a magistrate in the year ending 31 March 1991 (at para 2.15).

An emergency protection order application can be made either *ex parte* (without the other parties being present) or on notice. Given the urgent nature of the grounds for making an order and the nature of the order itself, it is understood that most magistrates' clerks are giving leave for such an application to be made *ex parte* (under the Family Proceedings Court (Children Act 1989) Rules 1991, SI 1991/1395 (FPC(CA 1989)R 1991), r 4(4)). An application for an emergency protection order is made by filing the appropriate form (Form CHA 34) (and there should be one in respect of each child), at the time the application is made or as directed by the justices' clerk (FPC(CA 1989)R 1991, r 4(1)(a)).

The fact that *any person* can apply for an emergency protection order under s 44(1)(a) of the 1989 Act means that the protective net could potentially be thrown very wide, but for the most part the first year's operation of the 1989 Act has tended to show that in child protection cases the applications come almost exclusively from child protection agencies. Those cases where emergency protection orders were used by private individuals tended to be in cases very early on under the 1989 Act, where attempts were made to use orders to prevent child abduction. It should be noted that *The Children Act 1989 Guidance and Regulations, Vol 1 Court Orders* (1991, HMSO) states that 'in dire circumstances a neighbour or a relative or school teacher may need to protect a child at risk by using the procedure for the application of an Emergency Protection Order' (at para 4.32). The police may also apply for an emergency protection order but they also have available to them the procedure under s 46 (see **4.8** below). It should further be noted that rules of court necessitate the applicant notifying the local authority, as well as others, of the fact that an order has been made (FPC(CA 1989)R 1991, r 21(8)(b)(iii)). Once the local authority has received such notification of an order having been made, it will be required to carry out an investigation under the provisions of s 47 (see **4.5** above). Where an order has been made, the Emergency Protection Order (Transfer of Responsibilities) Regulations 1991, SI 1991/2003, commit the authority to take over the order itself and attendant powers and responsibilities where it considers that it would be in the child's best interests to do so (reg 2(c)). In reaching a decision as to whether to take over an order, the local authority is required to consult the applicant and also to have regard to the ascertainable wishes and feelings of the child, the child's needs, the likely effect of any change in the child's circumstances, the child's age, sex and background, the circumstances which gave rise to the application, any directions of court and any other orders, the relationship, if any, of the applicant to the child and any plans the applicant may have in respect of the child. This list mirrors, in broad terms, the s 1(3) checklist to which courts are required to have regard before they make any orders other than those relating to the protection of the child contained in Part V of the 1989 Act (which includes emergency protection orders, child assessment orders and recovery orders). The NSPCC is also covered by these regulations.

A local authority, in addition to being able to rely on the more general grounds, can apply for an emergency protection order where enquiries are being made in the course of a local authority investigation under s 47 (see **4.5** above) and those enquiries are being frustrated by access to the child being unreasonably refused and the applicant has reasonable cause to believe that access to the child is required as a matter of urgency (s 44(1)(b)). A similar power is vested in any authorised person under the 1989 Act, which at the moment only extends to the NSPCC (s 44(1)(c) and see s 31(9)).

4.6.2 Applying for directions to be included in emergency protection orders

The form which is used to make an application for an emergency protection order is eight pages long and requires the applicant to give as many details as he can about the child, the child's family, any other applications or orders which might affect the child and the grounds upon which the order is being sought. In response to criticisms made in the *Cleveland Report*, the emergency protection order gives the applicant the power to seek directions from the court with respect to the contact which is to be allowed between the named person and the child (s 44(6)(a)); or as to the medical or psychiatric examination or other assessment of the child (s 44(6)(b)). It should be noted that there is no reason why a direction under the latter provision may not be a direction for no, or no further, medical or psychiatric examination or other assessment. Where either direction is sought (or, indeed, further additional powers, see **4.7** below) the applicant must be prepared to give reasons to the magistrate for seeking such directions from the court, although reasons as such are not required on the form itself. Where the court makes an order then the order will be set out as in Form CHA 35.

4.6.3 The management of emergency protection order applications

Emergency duty teams in social services departments or, where relevant, the NSPCC, will have available lists of magistrates providing cover at weekends and during the evening, which are usually drawn up by the local magistrates' clerks. Indeed, following on from Cleveland and now with the implementation of the 1989 Act, many magistrates' clerks have made provision for emergency duty cover not only by magistrates but also by the clerks themselves. Thus, in some areas, contact will be made initially with the emergency cover clerk, who will then arrange for a magistrate to be available and will be with him when an emergency protection order is granted. Because of the emphasis on the emergency nature of the provision, it would appear, from the first year's working of the 1989 Act, that applications have only been sought where it was a real emergency. Even despite the presence of a clerk, it is difficult for justices to refuse to grant such orders, bearing in mind that they have to be satisfied (on a balance of probabilities – the civil standard of proof) that there is reasonable cause to believe that a child is likely to suffer significant harm if an order is not made. Where a social worker or NSPCC officer states the circumstances giving rise to his or her belief, many magistrates would find it extremely hard to question the sincerity of that belief by denying the protection which would be afforded by an emergency protection order. The only provision which might allow the magistrate some opportunity in an emergency situation of questioning the decisions of social services or the NSPCC would be by the appointment of a guardian ad litem. This can be done at this much earlier stage of the emergency protection order by reason of s 41(6)(g). In order to cope with this provision, many guardian ad litem panel managers sought to set up special arrangements to provide emergency guardians who could be summoned by the magistrates' clerk to meet at the magistrate's house in out-of-hours applications, and in some areas of the country special emergency duty teams of guardians ad litem were available. Although there was much concern, early on, amongst those working as guardians ad litem that the service would not be able to cope with the demands of the 1989 Act, this does not actually seem to have been borne out in practice and where guardians have been required to be present on emergency protection order applications, it has generally been possible to arrange for one to be there. (For a more detailed consideration of the work of guardians ad litem, see Chapter 6.) It should be noted here, however, that guardians ad litem are appointed to provide an *independent* social work perspective on what might be argued to be in the child's best interests. Despite changes in court rules the guardian will not generally be appointed from the social services department which is the applicant in the proceedings, since one aspect of their role in this early stage in the proceedings is to advise the court on the appropriateness of the social services department's or the NSPCC's application. Where the court, through the clerk, has ordered the appearance of the guardian ad litem in the emergency protection order proceedings, then an order for the guardian's appointment should be made on Form CHA 4. Once appointed in the emergency protection order stage, the guardian will generally stay involved in the case until the termination of proceedings involving the child, and may also go on to appoint a solicitor for the child, who will act as the child's representative and advocate for what the child wants out of the proceedings.

4.6.4 Effects of an emergency protection order

The emergency protection order requires any person who is in a position to produce the child to the applicant to do so and then provides that the child may either be removed to accommodation provided by or on behalf of the applicant or that the child may not be removed from premises on which he is then being accommodated (s 44(4)(a) and (b)). The order also operates to give the applicant parental responsibility for the child. The parental responsibility which the applicant acquires pursuant to these provisions is exercisable *only* so far as it is necessary to safeguard the welfare of the child and *does not permit* (in response to the criticisms of Cleveland) the denial of contact between the child, his parents, and other members of his family as it might be appropriate for him to see. Such contact between the child and these persons is presumed to be at a *reasonable* level and, where the local authority or NSPCC feels that contact should not be allowed, it will have to seek a direction to this effect under s 44(6)(a). Again, in response to Cleveland, such parental responsibility as is given *does not* extend to allowing the medical or psychiatric examination or other assessment of the child to take place without a specific direction to this effect from the court (s 44(6)(b)). Directions as to contact may impose conditions, and directions as to medical, psychiatric or other examinations or assessments may be to the effect that there are to be no medical, psychiatric or other examinations or assessments, or no such examination or assessment unless the court otherwise directs. It should also be noted that where, in the heat of the moment and under pressure, the applicant has forgotten to apply for such directions, s 44(9) makes it clear that such directions may be given any time during the period of the emergency protection order, and that, similarly, where parents or children disagree with any such directions, they or the local authority may apply for such directions to be varied at any time.

4.6.5 Duration of emergency protection orders

It is provided that an emergency protection order should have effect for such period not exceeding eight days as may be specified in the order (s 45(1)). The relatively short duration of the emergency protection order is a further response to concerns voiced at the height of the Cleveland crisis and represents the enactment of recommendations made originally in the government White Paper entitled *The Law on Child Care and Family Services* published in January 1987. However, where it appears to the applicant that since the granting of an order it has become safe for the child to be returned to a place from which the child had been removed, or it appears to the applicant that it is safe for the child to be removed from the place in which he was being detained, the applicant should either return him or (as the case may be) allow him to be removed (s 44(10)). The 1989 Act requires the return of the child to the care of the person from whose care he was removed or, if that is not reasonably practicable, to return the child to the care of any parent, person with parental responsibility or such other person as the applicant (with the agreement of the court) considers appropriate (s 44(11)). The 1989 Act does, however, envisage situations in which the child may have been returned pursuant to these provisions, but, within the duration of the emergency protection order, it becomes necessary, once again, to remove the child. This can be done within the terms of the original order for such period that remains unexpired of that order (s 44(12)).

4.6.6 *Extending the duration of emergency protection orders*

Whilst the initial duration of an emergency protection order is eight days, except where the last of those eight days is a public holiday, in which case the court may specify a period which ends at noon on the first later date which is not such a holiday, there is provision under the 1989 Act for application to be made to have the period of the emergency protection order extended for up to seven days (s 45(4) and (5)). Once such an application is made the court may only make such an order if it has reasonable cause to believe that the child concerned is likely to suffer significant harm if the order is not extended (s 44(5)). Such an extension may only be granted on one occasion (s 44(6)). Interestingly, in the first nine months of the operation of the 1989 Act the statistics show that emergency protection order extensions were made in 240 cases and were refused only in 10 cases. This would appear to suggest that extensions may be granted rather more easily than those using emergency protection orders might have expected.

4.6.7 *Applications to discharge emergency protection orders*

If no such move to return the child is made then, again, directly in response to Cleveland, provision is made for the child, any parent, person with parental responsibility or any person with whom the child was living immediately before the making of the order, to apply to the court for the discharge of the order. Such an application for discharge, however, may only be made after the expiry of a period of 72 hours, beginning with the making of the order. Statistics so far gathered (see *Children Act Advisory Committee Annual Report 1991/1992* (1992, Lord Chancellor's Department) and the *Children Act Report 1992* (1993, DOH)) do not reveal the numbers of applications for discharge of emergency protection orders made in the first year of the operation of the 1989 Act. Other than this provision for the making of an application for discharge of an emergency protection order, the Act makes it clear that no appeal may be made against the making of, or refusal to make, an emergency protection order, or against any direction given by the court in connection with such an order. The possible concerns to which this provision might give rise where an application by social services is turned down by the magistrates, were highlighted in *Essex County Council v F* [1993] 1 FLR 847. In this case a seven-month-old baby had been in and out of hospital with problems relating to her immune system and feeding. The evidence of the social workers was that when the baby was with the mother she was not given proper medication nor proper feeding. In the four-month period prior to the application for an emergency protection order, the baby had spent 14 days with her mother and had been returned to hospital on three occasions. The mother was living apart from the father and at the point when she proposed to resume care of the child she had no baby food or nappies. The mother appeared at the application but the magistrates declined to deal with the matter on the basis that the mother had not been given due notice under the rules. They refused to order short service and adjourned the application for four days and further refused to deal with the application on an *ex parte* basis. Counsel for the local authority and guardian ad litem argued that the refusal to make an order meant a refusal after hearing the application on its merits, which the magistrates had not done. On appeal, however, Douglas Brown J reluctantly reached the conclusion that the words of the 1989 Act compelled him to find that refusal meant any refusal and the local authority had no right of appeal even though the case 'cried out for the intervention of the court'. In such a situation it would, of course, be possible to apply afresh to a different bench of magistrates although this would be subject to the co-operation of the clerk, or given Douglas Brown J's reaction, it might have been appropriate instead to apply to the High Court to exercise its inherent jurisdiction to make an order for the child to stay in hospital or with other relatives since such an order would not be caught by the rules excluding orders in favour of local authorities provided by s 100 (see, further, Chapter 9).

4.6.8 Evidential issues

Where an applicant for the emergency protection order seeks to rely not just upon their own evidence but also upon evidence contained in reports made to the court, the rules of hearsay do not apply and the courts may take account of any material given in evidence or in writing which is relevant to the application (s 45(7)).

4.6.9 Supplementary powers

Finally, a court making an emergency protection order may direct that the applicant may, whilst exercising any powers under that order, be accompanied by a registered medical practitioner, district nurse or registered health visitor, if the applicant so chooses. This mirrors similar provisions made under the old law relating to place of safety orders and no statistics are available to indicate its level of use. It would appear to be rare that such powers are exercised except where they relate to orders where additional powers have been sought under the provisions of s 48 (see **4.7** below).

4.7 Further additional powers

Special provision is made under the 1989 Act to enable the court to require a person with information about a child's whereabouts to disclose that information when this is not available to the applicant (s 48(1)). The possibility of self-incrimination or the incrimination of a spouse does not excuse a person from compliance but, perhaps to the frustration of some police officers, any statements or admissions made in compliance are not admissible in evidence against that person in proceedings for any criminal offence other than perjury. It should be noted that this is an extension of the general principle contained in s 98, that statements or admissions made in actual proceedings are not admissible in evidence against the person making them or his spouse in proceedings for criminal offences. The interesting point to note about s 48(2) is that, of course, such statements will not generally be made in *the course of any proceedings*. The failure to comply with the court order to provide information, is contempt of court and may amount to an offence under s 44(15).

The court is also able to authorise entry to premises to search for the child (s 48(3)) or any other child on the premises (s 48(4)). Interestingly, the section on the application form for an emergency protection order does not require that a separate application be made in respect of possible other children. If, however, on searching the premises a second child is found and the applicant believes there are sufficient grounds for making an emergency protection order, the order authorising the search for the second child can be treated as an emergency protection order (s 48(5)). Where any person intentionally obstructs anyone exercising the powers for entry and search granted pursuant to s 48(3)(4), that person will be guilty of a criminal offence.

Where it is anticipated that the applicant will meet opposition to entry on the premises to execute an emergency protection order or to execute any additional powers under s 48, an application can be made for a warrant authorising a constable to assist the authorised person in entering and searching the named premises (s 48(9)). *The Children Act 1989 Guidance and Regulations, Vol 1 Court Orders* recommends that whenever an application is being made for an emergency protection order the applicant should consider whether, at the same time, he needs to apply for a warrant for a police officer to accompany him where he is requesting authorisation to enter and search premises (at para 4.57). The guidance goes on to state that 'if any difficulties in gaining entry are foreseen, or if the applicant believes that he is likely to be threatened, intimidated or physically prevented from carrying out this part of the order, the possibility of simultaneously obtaining a warrant should always be considered'. Where a warrant is issued it must be addressed to, and executed by, a police constable who can be accompanied by the applicant where that person desires and provided the court does not direct otherwise (s 48(10)). In addition to granting the issuing of a warrant, the court is further empowered to direct that a police constable may, in executing the warrant, be accompanied by a registered medical practitioner, registered nurse or registered health visitor where the police constable so chooses. The guidance also states that it would always be good practice to request such a direction (at para 4.56).

Where a warrant is issued, it provides that the constable may use such reasonable force as is necessary in order to assist the applicant in the exercise of his or her powers to enter and search the premises for the child (s 48(9)). Where the applicant has omitted to obtain a warrant at the same time as requesting authorisation to search and gain entry to premises, *Working Together* points out that where speed is essential to protect a child and a warrant would take too long to obtain, the police can act without a warrant to enter premises in order to save life and limb under s 17(1)(e) of the Police and Criminal Evidence Act 1984. That Act goes on further to provide, under s 25(3)(e), that police officers may arrest any persons without warrant where this is necessary to achieve the protection of a child (*Working Together*, at para 4.15).

4.8 Police powers of protection

In some situations it may be that the police are the first to discover that a child is suffering or is likely to suffer significant harm, and the 1989 Act provides the police with powers of protection to remove a child or to authorise the child remaining in a particular place such as a hospital (s 46(1) and (6)). This power can be exercised by the police for up to 72 hours but, where the police believe this period should be extended, they should either contact social services with a view to the local authority applying for an emergency protection order under s 44 or an interim care order (under s 38), or apply for and obtain an emergency protection order on behalf of the local authority (s 46(7)). While the police are exercising their powers of protection, they must notify parents and those with parental responsibility or with whom the child has been living of what is happening (s 46(4)), and afford such people reasonable contact with the child unless that would not be in the child's interest (s 46(10)).

It should be noted that, where the police or the local authority apply for an emergency protection order, the period of police protection and the emergency protection order together cannot exceed eight days (s 45(3)). Since the period to be spent in police protection is relatively short, as contrasted with the maximum period of an emergency protection order, the fact that the police do not acquire parental responsibility (s 46(9)(a)) but must nevertheless do what is reasonable in all the circumstances to safeguard or promote the child's welfare, may give rise to some confusion as to their particular powers in a case involving child protection. It is thought that whilst the police would be able to give consent to any required emergency medical treatment, it is unlikely that they could give consent to treatment which was not urgently required or to any form of medical examination, psychiatric or other assessment. Where such an examination or assessment is required, this will necessitate an application for an emergency protection order and the request for directions from the court as to the conduct of such an examination or treatment.

Police powers under the 1989 Act can, thus, be seen to be quite wide and attention should also be given to the provision in s 102 of the 1989 Act which allows an application to be made by any person (including a police constable) for a warrant to be issued by the court when that person has attempted to exercise powers under different parts of the 1989 Act and has been prevented from exercising such powers. The provisions giving such persons the right to exercise a right of access to premises include ss 62, 64, 67, 76, 80, 86 and 87, Sch III, paras 8(1)(b),(2)(b) and the Adoption Act 1976, s 33. The primary power for the exercise of the right to enter premises falls chiefly upon social services but, as *Working Together* points out, the police can obtain a warrant under s 102 to enter the premises and search for children (*Working Together*, at para 4.15).

In the first year of the operation of the 1989 Act there had been some speculation that reduced court activity might have increased instances where children had been looked after under police protection. The *Children Act Report 1992* (1993, DOH) reveals that in the first six months of the operation of the 1989 Act there were approximately 400 occasions where a child was looked after by a local authority under police protection provisions, or about half the number of instances where a child was looked after under an emergency protection order. The report points out that 'although the incidence of police protection is low, the balance between the two categories is not very different compared to the balance of activity under the previous legislation'.

4.9 Action during the emergency protection order

(a) Medical examination, psychiatric or other assessment of the child

Unless such a direction has been sought from the court it will be virtually impossible for social services to determine whether to press forward with further legal proceedings. Whether the child has been known to social services or any of the other agencies previously, or whether it is a completely new referral, considerable attention will have to be given to the process of engaging in a detailed assessment of the child as provided for in *Protecting Children* –

A Guide for Social Workers Undertaking a Comprehensive Assessment (1988, DOH). In addition to this guidance, many social services departments, as well as the NSPCC, produce their own guidelines, generally referred to as a child protection manual, in which detailed guidance is laid down to assist social workers and others in understanding the process of assessment in child protection work. In addition, area child protection committees may supplement this further, although, generally, guidance issued by these committees will tend to concentrate more on inter-agency working.

As far as social work assessment is concerned, Part II of *Protecting Children* (above) describes a comprehensive assessment with eight components. Each component begins with explanatory paragraphs, followed by a series of basic questions for exploration with parents, the child(ren) and other family members involved in the assessment. The guidance does, however, make it clear that social workers should not use the questions merely as a checklist and in a prescribed and mechanistic fashion, but that they are expected to use them in ways which will reflect their own training, experience and style and that the more experienced may wish to modify and experiment with the format provided in the guidance.

At the same time that social workers are undertaking their own assessment procedures, a psychiatrist may also be involved in seeing the child for the purposes of a psychiatric assessment ordered by the court. It should be noted that where a request for such a direction has been made in the application for an emergency protection order, the request can be specific as to the person whom the applicant would like to carry out the psychiatric assessment.

A direction as to the medical examination of the child will be sought early on in any period after the granting of an order and, again, specific requests can be made as to the sex of the doctor who carries out the medical examination and, even more specifically, a request can be made for a *particular* doctor to conduct the examination.

No matter what the nature of the assessment or examination is to be, it should be noted at this point that the child might *appear* to have the *right* to overrule the court's direction where he is deemed to be of sufficient understanding to make an informed decision (s 44(7)). This is one of the so-called *Gillick* provisions of the Act where not only are the child's wishes and feelings considered and taken into account but where it is apparent that the legislature intended that they should be determinative of the issue. As has been pointed out in the preface, however, it would appear that the courts are not prepared to accept the child's autonomy interest (see Chapter 10) in being able to make mistakes where acknowledgment of such an interest might lead to the child suffering harm. This is most starkly pointed up by the decision of Douglas Brown J in *South Glamorgan County Council v W and B* [1993] 1 FLR 574, dealing with the corresponding consent provision in s 38(6) of the Act (see below and Chapter 10). In that case Douglas Brown J stated that the Children Act 1989 could not be taken to have abrogated the power of the High Court in the exercise of its inherent jurisdiction to override in a *proper* case the wishes of a child and give consent for medical assessment even where the child was of sufficient understanding and had refused such assessment. As Douglas Brown J put it, 'where other remedies within the Children Act 1989 have been used and exhausted and found not to bring about the desired result [the court] can resort to other remedies'. The question which must be asked is 'the result desired by who?' and the clear answer is the result desired by the courts. Thus, the apparent rights given by the provisions such as s 44(7), s 38(6) and s 43(8) are not *rights* at all but perhaps only a *power to express a preference* which can then be outweighed by a heavy injection of judicial paternalism no doubt informed by relevant professional opinion. The role of the guardian ad litem is then seen to have become crucial in flagging up for the court's attention immediately the likelihood of the child refusing to consent to the court-ordered direction for assessment and possible treatment. Where a guardian ad litem has been appointed and in the event of an application having been filed on notice, thus allowing the guardian time to see the child, the guardian ad litem may be able to advise the court on whether the child is both of sufficient understanding and likely to refuse to give consent to relevant medical, psychiatric or other assessments ordered by the court to proceed. Where the child does refuse to comply with such court-ordered directions, consideration will have to be given in the wake of such court decisions as *South Glamorgan County Council v W and B* (above) and *Re W (A Minor) (Consent to Medical Treatment)* [1993] 1 FLR 1 (and see the discussion in the preface and Chapter 9) as to whether the applicant or the guardian should return the matter to court for the magistrates or judge to determine whether the case be immediately transferred to the High Court so that an order under s 100 might be made dispensing with the child's refusal (see, further, Chapter 9).

(b) Liaison with other agencies

In cases concerning child abuse a mention has already been made of the vital importance of close liaison between police and social services who may be involved with pressing ahead with investigations regarding the possibility of a criminal offence having been committed. Both *Working Together* and the *MoGP*, if viewed pursuant to the Criminal Justice Act 1991 (see, further, Chapter 7) stress that joint investigation is to be conducted by both police and social workers who have been specially trained. Similar advice is given with regard to those handling the interviewing of children. (See, further, *Fig 2 above, – A working model demonstrating police and social services involvement in a child abuse case.*)

Where a child has been removed to a hospital or is being detained in a hospital, care should be taken by the key worker involved to explain fully to all hospital personnel the fact that an emergency protection order has been obtained and its legal and practical effects. Failure to do so may have disastrous consequences (see the *Report of the Inquiry into the Death of Simon Peacock* (1978, DHSS)). These days it may, therefore, be appropriate to ensure, pursuant to the principles laid down in *Working Together*, that a member of the nursing staff in the hospital concerned with the care of the child is not only notified as to the effects of an emergency protection order but is also invited to attend any child protection conference which may be held. *Working Together* also makes it clear that practitioners will need time to de-brief, record and plan after each session and that the family will need to be advised well in advance who is to attend each session, where it is to be held and what general issues are to be covered. *Working Together* is essential reading for all professionals who may be involved in dealing with cases of child abuse whether or not they themselves are actually engaged in the assessment process.

Part III of *Working Together* describes the use to which the assessment may be put as a basis for planning. It also reviews the factors which may influence key decisions about future care of the child and, thus, contains vital advice for those who may participate in any child protection conference. It is only where such an evaluation is thoroughly carried out that a reasoned decision can be reached to determine the future course of action.

4.10 Convening a child protection conference

Working Together states that the child protection conference is central to child protection procedures, although it goes on to emphasise that it is not a forum for a formal decision that a person has abused a child as that is a matter for the courts. The purpose of the child protection conference is to bring together the families and the professionals concerned with child protection to provide them with the opportunity to exchange information and plan together. *Working Together* goes on to state that the conference symbolises the inter-agency nature of assessment, treatment and the management of child protection. Throughout the child protection process, the work is conducted on an inter-agency basis and the conference is a prime forum for sharing information and concerns, analysing risks and recommending responsibility for action.

Where emergency action has been required and a case conference is held *after* the granting of an emergency protection order, a considerable amount of investigation and inter-agency contact will be necessary in order to gather together the necessary information for the case conference. Where the case conference is itself going to be charged with the task of making a recommendation for further action, including the possibility of applications for child assessment orders, emergency protection orders, or the initiation of proceedings for care or supervision orders, it is obvious that the conference has a major task in evaluating the data which will be presented to it by representatives of all the various agencies invited. Whether the child has been known to social services or any of the other agencies previously, or whether it is a completely new referral, attempts will have been made during any investigation or, perhaps, pursuant to directions given on an emergency protection order, to engage in a detailed assessment of the child. As far as social services are concerned, guidance in undertaking such a comprehensive detailed assessment of the child in the family is given in *Protecting Children* (1988, DOH) (and see **4.9** above), although where abuse has occurred in other settings such as residential homes, residential schools or foster placements then consideration must be given to the guidance contained within *The Children Act 1989 Guidance and Regulations*, particularly Volumes 3 and 4, and to guidance on such issues given in *Working Together* at paras 5.19 to 5.24. Where such comprehensive assessment is not possible owing to the timetable of the particular case, the issue of conducting such an assessment will actually be discussed at the child protection conference and the plan may include a comprehensive assessment as part of its structure. Whether assessment is carried out before a child protection conference, as a result of a conference recommendation or while legal proceedings are under way, it must be remembered that assessment and reassessment are continuing activities throughout the child protection process.

Both *Working Together* and *Protecting Children* (above) provide considerable guidance on the range of personnel who could be called upon to be present at case conferences, and this is shown in *Fig 3* below. Careful note should be made of the fact that the professionals who should be present at the case conference are those who have a *contribution* to make to the discussion. *Working Together* (at para 6.24) points out that an initial child protection conference which is unnecessarily large will inhibit discussion and does not use valuable resources to the best advantage. It also points out that large numbers of professionals, some of whom make no apparent contribution, are particularly inhibiting to parents and children who will, in any event, probably find the conference a difficult occasion. Nevertheless, the guidance which *Working Together* then gives as to who should be present, constitutes quite a large group. It is recommended that all those who are invited should be informed that the child, the parents and other carers have also been invited. *Working Together* acknowledges that the initial child protection conference may be a large gathering in the early stages where a number of agencies could be contributing to an investigation or an assessment for planning but, once a long-term plan has been formulated, and a group led by the key worker has been identified to work with the family, the number attending future child protection reviews will usually be reduced. It is important to remember that it is the responsibility of the chair to ensure that the appropriate people are invited to the initial child protection conference. *Working Together* states that the chairperson must be able to call on advice from a lawyer from the local authority's legal section, particularly when court action is under consideration and on other specialist advice when necessary, for example the advice of a

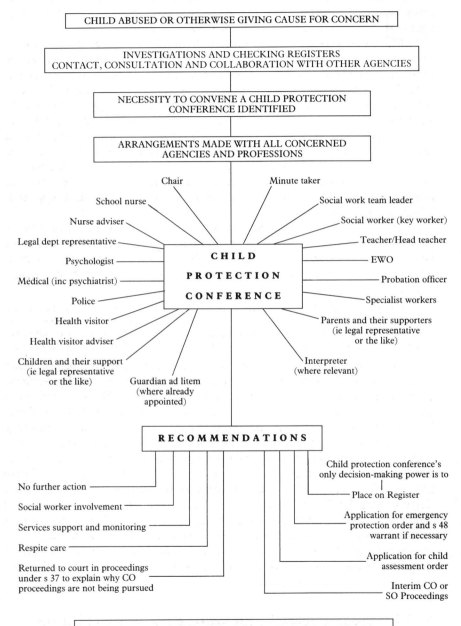

Fig 3: Steps leading to child protection conference and the making of recommendations for further action in child abuse cases

psychiatrist, a psychologist or workers and interpreters with special knowledge either of working with people with a disability or of working with people from a particular race or culture (see *Fig 3*).

If the case conference is to have available to it legal advice, it must also be recognised that parents may also feel more confident in attending if they are encouraged to bring a friend or supporter. The parent may wish to be accompanied by a lawyer and, if this is the case, lawyers should be aware of the fact that local legal aid boards have been willing to sanction the grant of legal aid to allow for coverage of the costs of having lawyers present at the case conference. Legal aid boards have been able to justify this approach on the basis that if the presence of the lawyer at the case conference diminishes the need to proceed to a care or supervision order the legal aid fund will have been saved the costs not only of representing the child but also of representing the parents. It is, of course, an individual decision in each particular case but the general approach of the Legal Aid Board is to be welcomed.

Finally, it is clear that sound administrative arrangements should be in place to support the child protection conference process, and this is a matter which is now generally addressed either through area child protection committees ('ACPCs') or local child protection procedures. *Working Together* states:

> 'a system should be established which ensures that the appropriate people are invited to each conference and that they are given as much warning as possible of when and where it will be held. It should be held in a place and at a time which will ensure the maximum attendance possible, and particularly the attendance of the relevant people working with the family.'

Guidance which is given through ACPC guidelines or local child protection procedures should emphasise that there will be an expectation that all those attending a conference will be properly prepared for it. Wherever possible it would be anticipated that those conducting investigations and key workers, in particular, should have prepared thoroughly for the conference and they would normally be expected to provide written reports summarising both past and present incidence of abuse, information about the family circumstances, details of work undertaken and possible proposals for the future. Where notification is being sent out to other professional workers such as teachers, the police or health workers, they should be encouraged to bring to the conference other written reports to which they may need to refer, such as school reports, police statements, medical reports and growth charts. Where parents and/or children are to attend, it is crucial that they too should be properly prepared for the conference so that they can play their full and proper part in its deliberations.

4.11 Procedure at the initial child protection conference

Working Together stresses that the initial child protection conference should have distinct and clearly defined functions and tasks, and that ACPC procedures should detail these functions and address issues of membership and process in relation to both initial child protection conferences and child protection reviews. The procedure followed at case conferences, therefore, varies considerably from one local authority to another. Nevertheless, child protection conferences should have a clearly defined purpose, be task centred and should not be seen, by the professionals involved, as an end in themselves. As has been noted earlier, if protection conferences are too large, wrongly timed, have no clear purpose, involve the wrong people or are poorly conducted, they may not only fail to facilitate good practice, but may also bring inter-agency working into disrepute.

Child protection conferences should provide a forum (as stated above) for the exchange of information between professionals involved with the child and the family and allow for inter-agency multi-disciplinary discussion of, amongst other things, allegations or suspicions of abuse, the outcome of investigations, an action plan for protecting the child and helping the family, and provision for child protection reviews. The only decision-making power of the case conference is a determination that the child should be placed on the Child Protection Register, but other results of the discussions of the case conference will take the form of recommendations to individual agencies for action. While the decision to implement the recommendations must rest with the individual agency concerned, any deviation from them should not be made, except in an emergency, without informing the other agencies through the key worker.

As has already been stated, the number of people present at child protection conferences should, wherever possible, be kept low and confined to those with a need to know, or who have a contribution to make to the task involved. Whenever anyone, including a parent or child, is unable to attend, the key worker should ensure that their contribution is made through a written submission to the chairperson. The role of the chairperson is particularly crucial to the effectiveness of the inter-agency child protection conference. The main tasks of the chairperson are to ensure that:

(1) conferences focus on the child as the primary client whose interests must transcend those of the parents or other carers when there is any conflict;
(2) the purpose of the particular conference is made clear;
(3) the people present are the ones required for fulfilment of that purpose;
(4) all those present contribute, and full consideration is given to their contribution;
(5) the waiting arrangements for parents and children who may not be able to remain throughout the conference are properly organised;
(6) the confidential nature of the occasion and of the reports and any information shared is understood;
(7) where an ongoing involvement is identified as being necessary, the key worker and core group are identified;

(8)   a plan, based on assessment and clearly understood by all concerned, is developed and agreed for recommendation to the agencies, and any reservations or dissenting views recorded;

(9)   arrangements for review of the plan and the date of the first child protection review are agreed;

(10) where appropriate, parents or carers and, where relevant, the child are informed of the plan for inter-agency cooperation and, where a decision has been made to place the child on the Child Protection Register, are informed of the purpose of the Register;

(11) a written note is made of the case conference which records those participating, absentees, the essential facts, the decisions and the recommendations and the inter-agency child protection plan. Also that an account is made of the discussion on which the decisions and recommendations were based and the list of those to whom it should be circulated must be agreed.

It is by no means the case that all of those tasks will be relevant to every child protection conference and, whilst it has been indicated that appropriate administrative support for case conferences should include the provision of someone to take the minutes, the chairperson should, nevertheless, be responsible for checking the accuracy of the minutes. Where appropriate administrative support in the form of secretarial assistance in taking minutes is not provided, the chairperson should make clear that key workers are not responsible for taking notes at the meeting, as this will detract from their ability to make a major contribution to the child protection conference.

4.12 Involvement of parents and children in conferences

Wherever possible it should be made clear that at every stage of the investigation or intervention leading up to a child protection case conference, parents and/or carers and children (where they are of sufficient age and understanding) must be kept informed of what is happening. Over recent years there has been a great deal of criticism of the failure to involve parents in child protection processes at an appropriately early stage. In *R v The United Kingdom* [1988] 2 FLR 445, the European Court of Human Rights found that the UK Government was in breach of Articles 6 and 8 of the European Convention on Human Rights in failing to involve parents in decision-making with regard to children in care. See also the criticisms for similar failure in the *Cleveland Report, Rochdale Borough Council v A and Others* ('the *Rochdale* case'), and the *Report of the Inquiry into the Removal of Children from Orkney in February 1991* (1992, HMSO) ('the *Orkney Report*'). It is now acknowledged that parents need to know the reasons for professional concern, the statutory powers, duties and roles of the agencies involved, their own legal rights and responsibilities and the changes in the family's situation which the agencies may consider necessary or desirable in the interests of the child.

The 1989 Act is built upon the principle of working in partnership with parents. Openness and honesty and the ability of professional staff to use their authority appropriately are an essential basis on which to build a foundation of understanding between parents and professionals, so parents should be informed or consulted wherever possible at every stage of investigation. It is further stated that their views should be sought on the issues to be raised prior to a case conference, to afford them the opportunity to seek advice and prepare their representations. It is at this point that parents may seek the advice of a solicitor which, as has already been indicated, may be paid for through the legal aid fund. The solicitor should, of course, be aware of local practice and procedure in such matters.

Working Together bases such advice as it gives with regard to the presence of parents at child protection conferences on the premise that their presence at such conferences should be the norm. Thus, *Working Together* states (at para 6.15) that:

> 'while there may be exceptional occasions when it will not be right to invite one or other parent to attend a case conference in whole or in part, exclusion should be kept to a minimum and needs to be *especially justified*. The procedure should lay down criteria for this, including the evidence required.'

Working Together goes on to suggest that examples of grounds for excluding the parents might be the strong risk of violence by the parents towards either the professionals or the child, or evidence that the conference might be likely to be disrupted. *Working Together* does, however, point out that the mere possibility that one of the parents may be prosecuted for an offence against the child does not *in itself* justify exclusion.

Whenever children have sufficient understanding and are able to express their wishes and feelings and to participate in the process of investigation, assessment, planning and review, they should be given the opportunity to indicate whether they wish to attend the child protection conference. They should be advised that if they wish to have a friend or supporter present they may do so. If the child does not wish to attend, or his age or understanding make this inappropriate, the conference should be provided with a clear and up-to-date account of the child's views by the professionals who are working with the child. In most situations it would be anticipated that the key worker would be able to inform the conference about the views of a child who is not attending.

It should be noted, however, that neither the recommendations of the *Cleveland Report* nor the guidelines laid down in *Working Together* provide parents or children with an absolute right to attend such conferences (see, further, N Parton *Governing the Family* (1991, Macmillan) ch 4). It is left to the chairperson to determine whether or not the parents' or the child's presence would preclude a full and proper consideration of the child's interests.

It is, nevertheless, the case that where a decision is taken to exclude a parent, carer or child from a conference the chairperson should record his or her decision based upon the exclusion criteria in the local child protection procedures. The decision to exclude a child, parents or carers and the reasons for so doing should be recorded on the child's file. It should also be remembered that adults who wish to make their views known at the child protection conference may not wish to speak up in front of other adult carers. There will also be situations when the wish of the child to attend and the desire of the parent to do so are in conflict and the chairperson will need to make the necessary arrangements to allow both to be present at different times. Such issues will probably be covered in broad terms in local child protection procedures, but a decision will have to be made by the chairperson in each case.

Where parents are excluded for the whole or for part of any child protection conference, they should receive, at the minimum, written confirmation of the main findings of the conference, a note of who attended and who was absent and confirmation of the decisions and the recommended plan of action. Where the child does not attend the conference, he should be kept informed of the progress of the meeting and both parents and children should be clear about the expectations professionals have of them and the expectations they are to have of the professionals as a result of the recommendations made at the conference.

4.13 Child protection conference recommendations

It is not intended here to set out an exhaustive list of recommendations of any particular case conference, but merely to set out some of the recommendations which may be made. (See also *Fig 3* above.)

4.13.1 Provision of services

The child protection conference may recommend that the key worker should involve himself more with the family in the provision of such services as day care, child minding, family centres, family aids, respite care and after-school child care. The DOH guidance *The Children Act 1989 Guidance and Regulations, Vol 2 Family Support, Day Care, and Educational Provision for Young Children* (1991, HMSO) points out (at para 2.10) that where a local authority has to allocate resources to a range of services – for example, a family aid for the family or a day nursery place for the child – the plan must identify how long the service may be required, what the objective of the service should be and what else others are expected to do. Again, so as to emphasise the nature of partnership and allocations of responsibility between parents and the local authority and in order to be effective, this plan should form the basis of an agreement with the parent or other carer and be reviewed at appropriate intervals. The guidance requires that the arrangements are reviewed once within the first four weeks of operation, a second review within the following 12 weeks and thereafter once in every six-month period (para 2.10) (see the Review of Children's Cases Regulations 1991, SI 1991/895, reg 3).

4.13.2 Informal social worker involvement

It may well be that the family has recognised the need to have informal social work support and is prepared to accept a high level of assistance in order to ensure that the child does not need more extensive protection. As to how this might be achieved and be made effective in local authority areas where preventive resources are scarce and personnel are already unable to cope with casework demands is a vexed issue (see, further, N Parton 'The Children Act 1989: Reconstructing the Consensus' in *Governing the Family* (1991, Macmillan) at ch 6).

4.13.3 Further investigation and re-convention

Where the child protection conference has followed on very soon after the obtaining of an emergency protection order arising from a new referral, it may be necessary to set an early date for a child protection review. The purpose of the child protection review is to review the arrangements for the protection of the child, examine the current level of risk and ensure that the child continues to be adequately protected. The child protection review should further consider whether the inter-agency co-ordination is functioning effectively and should also review the protection plan. Where a recommendation has been made in the child protection conference to place a child on the Child Protection Register, the child protection review should consider whether registration should be continued or ended. It may be necessary to have an early child protection review where assessments by specialists, such as paediatricians, psychiatrists and psychologists, have yet to be provided, and it may, of course, be necessary to reconvene a full child protection conference where the results of such assessments are felt to be necessary before a proper plan can be devised.

4.13.4 Placement on the Child Protection Register

The only decision-making power of the child protection conference is the decision to place the child's name on the Child Protection Register and to formalise inter-agency co-operation. *Working Together* (at paras 6.36 to 6.37 and 6.49 to 6.50) describes the provision and purpose of such registers as follows:

'In each area covered by a social services department, a central register must be maintained which lists all the children in the area who are considered to be suffering from, or likely to suffer from, significant harm and for whom there is a child protection plan. This is not a register of children who have been abused but of children for whom there are currently unresolved child protection issues and for whom there is an inter-agency protection plan. The register should include children who are recognised to be at risk and who are placed in the local authority's area by another local authority or agency. Registration does not of itself provide any protection and it must lead to an inter-agency protection plan. Registration should not be used to obtain resources which might otherwise not be available for the family.

The purpose of the register is to provide a record of all children in the area for whom there are unresolved child protection issues and who are currently the subject of an inter-agency protection plan and to ensure that the plans are formally reviewed every six months. The register will provide a central point of speedy enquiry for professional staff who are worried about a child and want to know whether the child is the subject of an inter-agency protection plan. The register will also provide useful information for the individual Child Protection Agencies and for the ACPC in its policy development work and strategic planning.

It is recommended that the register is established and maintained by the social services department or the NSPCC on its behalf. The register should be held separately from agency records in conditions safeguarding confidentiality. It should be managed by an experienced social worker with knowledge and skills in child abuse work to be known as the register "custodian".'

Information about how to contact the Register should be available to all agencies concerned. *Working Together* continues:

'Some registers are now computerised and this can lead to uncontrolled access to information if appropriate steps are not taken to prevent unauthorised access. This undermines the confidentiality of the register. This and other issues related to computerised registers should be covered in ACPC procedures. A record should be kept of any children not on the register about whom enquiries are made, and of the advice given. If the child's name is on the register when an enquiry is made the name of the key worker should be given to the enquirer. If a child's name is not on the register when an enquiry is made but there is another child on the register at the same address the custodian should see that this is followed up.'

The entry of a child's name on the Register should normally only occur following discussion at a child protection conference when significant harm or the risk of significant harm has been confirmed and a child protection plan has been agreed between relevant agencies who will then work co-operatively to protect the child. Before entering a child's name on the Register, the conference must be satisfied that there has been one or more identifiable incidents which can be described as having adversely affected the child and these may include acts of omission. Such acts can be either physical, sexual, emotional or neglectful, and it is important to identify a specific occasion or occasions when any incidents may have occurred or behaviour which indicates a process of abuse over time, particularly important in cases of emotional maltreatment. The professional judgment of those present at the child protection conference should also be that further incidents or such behaviour are likely. Alternatively, the child protection conference must be satisfied that significant harm is expected to occur on the basis of the professional judgment of the findings of the investigation in the individual child's case or based upon research evidence. The child protection conference will need to establish, so far as it can, a cause of harm or the likelihood of harm. This cause might also be of relevance when considering siblings or other children living in the same household and the conference may wish to go on to register them.

Working Together lists four categories of abuse, which should be used for the purposes of registration and for statistical purposes, and which are intended to provide definitions as a guide for those using the Register. (These are discussed in detail in Chapter 1.) In some instances, more than one category of registration may be appropriate and this issue must be discussed in the protection plan – but multiple abuse registration should not be used simply to cover all possible eventualities. It should again be noted that the four categories of abuse (neglect, physical injury, sexual abuse and emotional abuse) do not coincide with the definition of 'significant harm' provided by s 31 of the 1989 Act, which will be the relevant test where any court proceedings follow the protection conference.

Working Together advises that local authorities and other agencies may find it helpful, for general social work and child protection purposes, to maintain a list of all offenders in the area who have been convicted of offences listed in Sch I of the Children and Young Persons Act 1933. It points out, however, that such a list has its limitations because it is difficult to keep it up to date and, although the prison service, through the probation service, may notify local authority social service departments of the discharge of Sch I offenders, such people are often highly mobile. Appendix 4 of *Working Together* goes on to advise that child protection registers should include information on relevant offences committed by members of, and regular visitors to, the household. Who constitutes a 'regular visitor' will be a matter of judgment in relation to the circumstances of the case and it is suggested that this would normally be identified in the course of a comprehensive assessment of the family. A 'relevant offence' will be an offence established by a criminal conviction, which is relevant to the reasons for which the child is thought to be at risk and the child's name entered on the Register. Information about such offences will normally emerge from the assessment of the family or at the initial child protection conference but should also be considered during child protection reviews, particularly where the family's composition has changed.

Working Together reverses the previous practice in relation to the names of adults posing a *possible* threat to children (that care should be taken with records containing information about adults suspected, but not convicted, of offences against children) and states that 'a list of such people should not be held' (at para 6.54). Clearly, such records possessed by social services or other agencies, such as doctors and psychiatrists, should be kept confidential and should not be shared except for child protection purposes. Any publicity given to such records could lead the agency into areas of legal challenge although, again, where such action is taken purely on the basis of protecting individual children the local authority would expect to be able to mount a reasonable defence to any action taken by an aggrieved party (see *R v Devon County Council ex parte L* [1991] 2 FLR 541). In that case a man (L) had been suspected of sexual abuse of his step-daughter whose name had been placed on the child abuse register and a social worker appointed to her case. L had been arrested and later interviewed by the police but denied the allegations and no criminal proceedings were ever instituted against him. The man then moved out of his first partner's home and moved in with another woman, who already had a son, and who later gave birth to L's child. However, by this stage, L had left the second partner's home as a result of a visit by the social worker responsible for his step-daughter. The social worker, on that occasion, had told the second partner that L was alleged to have sexually assaulted a girl aged four, that he had not been prosecuted because there was not enough evidence, that she (the social worker) and her department had no doubt that L was responsible for sexual misconduct in respect of the young girl and that if he continued to live under the second partner's roof, consideration would have to be given to placing her son and her unborn child on the 'at risk' register. L then moved on through a further two families and in each case the families were warned by social services that the applicant was a serious threat to children. L then contacted solicitors and the solicitors asked that the county council should give an assurance that they would instruct all their employees to stop disseminating their beliefs about L. The department maintained that it had been justified in its actions with a view to their concerns for the protection of children generally and that the action they had taken did not amount to a decision capable of being judicially reviewed. The court stated that social workers, in the discharge of the local authority statutory obligation to protect the welfare of the children in this case, were under a duty to inform the two mothers and the grandmother that they believed that the applicant was an abuser, if they honestly believed, on reasonable grounds, that he was an abuser. In the circumstances of the case there were sufficient grounds for reasonably and honestly believing the step-daughter's original allegations to be true. The court also found that the applicant, as a result of the intervention by social workers, had undoubtedly suffered prejudice, in the sense that he had been forced to leave his home on several occasions. However, adopting the words of Butler-Sloss LJ in *R v Harrow London Borough ex parte D* [1990] 1 FLR 79 at p 84:

> 'in balancing adequate protection for the child and fairness to an adult, the interests of an adult may have to be placed second to the needs of the child. All concerned in this difficult and delicate area should be allowed to perform their tasks without looking over their shoulder all the time for the possible intervention of the court.'

Where local authorities intend to use such information which they have to enter an adult's name in a separate part of the Child Protection Register, the adult must be informed and told of the possibility of questioning the details or making representations about the entry, either in a separate forum or before any conference which is held to discuss the matter (see *R v Norfolk County Council ex parte M* [1989] 3 WLR 502; and *R v*

Harrow London Borough ex parte D (above), which are examined in detail in Chapter 9).

4.13.5 Applying for a child assessment order

In circumstances where the child protection conference comes to the conclusion that there are a number of serious suspicions about whether or not a child is suffering or likely to suffer significant harm, it may recommend that the social services or the NSPCC seek an order, under s 43(1) of the 1989 Act, usually from the family proceedings court, known as a child assessment order. Before granting a child assessment order the court must be satisfied that the applicant has reasonable cause to suspect (1) that the child is suffering or is likely to suffer significant harm, (2) that an assessment of the state of the child's health or development or of the way in which he has been treated is required to enable the applicant to determine whether or not the child is suffering, or is likely to suffer significant harm, and (3) that it is unlikely that such an assessment will be made, or be satisfactory in the absence of a child assessment order (s 43(1)).

An application for a child assessment order must be made by filing an application in respect of each child in the appropriate form and providing sufficient copies for service on each respondent (FPC(CA 1989)R 1991, r 4(1) and see Form CHA 33). The period of notice which must be given in respect of a child assessment order application is seven days (see FPC(CA 1989)R 1991, Sch 2, col (ii)) and this underlines the fact that the order should not be used in emergencies. It should be seen, instead, as a planned response to concerns voiced in the initial child protection conference about a child's health or development. Action to apply for a child assessment order could, of course, also be taken without the necessity to have convened a child protection conference.

Where it is intended to restrict contact with a child or to provide for medical examination, psychiatric or other assessment of the child, the application should include a request for such directions from the court (s 43(9)) and such directions requests can include a request that a particular doctor, or a doctor of a particular sex, should conduct a medical examination. It should be noted that whilst the court may give a direction that a medical examination, psychiatric or other assessment should take place, the 1989 Act provides, in the same way as was discussed for emergency protection orders, that where the child is of sufficient understanding to make an informed decision he may refuse to submit to such examination or assessment (s 43(8)). The comments which were made in relation to the court's possible ability to override the child's refusal (in relation to emergency protection orders) would apply equally here. It should be noted that a guardian ad litem could be appointed to be present at the hearing under the provisions of s 41(6)(g) and this may be particularly useful when there is concern about the child who refuses a medical examination, or psychiatric or other assessment.

The child assessment order must specify the date by which the assessment is to begin and it will have effect for such period not exceeding seven days, beginning with the date specified in the order (s 43(5)). In some courts this is being interpreted to allow assessment to take place on one day a week for up to seven weeks, which clearly makes sense where a prolonged assessment is required, although whether it is strictly within the words of the section is debatable. The child assessment order can provide that the child lives away from home for a period or periods not, in total, exceeding seven days (s 43(5) and (9)). There is no provision for extending a child assessment order, although the child, his parents and anyone with parental responsibility, and any person with whom the child was living immediately before the making of the order, may apply for the discharge of the order (s 43(11) and (12)) and provisions on contact may be challenged by these people and anyone in whose favour the courts had previously made a contact order under s 8 or s 34 and which is still in force (FPC(CA 1989)R 1991, Sch 2, col (iii)).

As was noted earlier, as soon as is practicable after the commencement of proceedings for a child assessment order, the court is required, by s 41(1), to appoint a guardian ad litem for the child concerned unless it is satisfied that this is not necessary to safeguard the child's interests. The court (or the guardian if one has already been appointed) may further appoint a solicitor under s 41(3) to represent the child where it is of the view that the child has sufficient understanding to instruct a solicitor and wishes to do so, or it appears to the court to be in the child's best interests for him to be represented by a solicitor, or no guardian ad litem has, in fact, been appointed.

Whilst the powers given by a child assessment order would no doubt be extremely useful in cases where parents persist in a refusal to co-operate with all the various agencies, the very fact that the order exists seems to have resulted in its non-use. Thus, in the first year of the operation of the 1989 Act only 80 orders were actually made. There may be a variety of reasons for this but the most likely is that if the social workers are able to say to the parents that either they give their consent to the child being properly assessed or the social workers will go to court to get an order to this effect, then the parents realise the futility of a refusal. In addition, of course, there is also the risk that whilst the social workers may approach the court for a child assessment order, the court is able instead, under the provisions of s 43(3)), to treat the application as an application for an emergency protection order where it feels this would be more appropriate. If, therefore, parents are warned that non-compliance may mean not only the possible making of an assessment order but could lead to the children being removed from them upon the making of an emergency protection order, opposition to an agreed assessment is likely to evaporate. (See, further, J Dickens 'Applications for Child Assessment Orders' [1993] JSWFL 89; and see *Children Act Advisory*

Committee Annual Report 1991/92 (1992, Lord Chancellor's Department) at
Table 2.)

4.13.6 Applying for an emergency protection order

Considerable attention has already been focused (see **4.6** above) on the abilities of any interested person, social services, the NSPCC or the police to
obtain emergency protection orders and also to the responsibility of the holder
of such an order in respect of issues such as the medical examination of the
child, contact with the child whilst subject to the order, and the right of
application for discharge of the order.

4.13.7 The issuing of care or supervision order proceedings and the obtaining of interim orders

Where it has not been thought appropriate to use an emergency protection
order, but where the results of an assessment carried out under a child
assessment order demonstrate that full care or supervision order proceedings
should be instituted, consideration must be given by the local authority or
the NSPCC to making an application to the court for a care or supervision
order where it is believed that the criteria for making such an order are met.
It should also be remembered that where a court in family proceedings has
directed the local authority to undertake an investigation as to whether care
or supervision proceedings should be instituted (see s 37(1)), the local authority may be returning to court pursuant to such an investigation and may
be pressing ahead with an application for a care or supervision order. In any
of these situations it is now likely to be the case that a directions appointment
will be held to consider a range of matters such as the possible appointment
of a guardian ad litem and a solicitor for the child, the timetable of the case
and any other relevant matters, such as directions for further or additional
assessments.

   Care or supervision order proceedings must generally be commenced in
the family proceedings court for the area in which the child ordinarily resides
(s 32(8)) or for the area in which the incident occurred if a child is visiting
(s 31(8)). Where an order is eventually made, it must be made in favour of
the authority in whose area the child ordinarily resides, unless the child is
from outside the jurisdiction, in which case the order must be made to the
local authority in whose area the incidents or neglect occurred (s 31(8)(a)
and (b)).

   Where any party to proceedings is not happy for the application to proceed
in the family proceedings court, or where the clerk and/or magistrates believe
that the case should be transferred, the position will be considered by the
court, according to specified criteria (under the Children (Allocation of Proceedings) Order 1991, SI 1991/1677, art 7) and the case may then be allocated

to a higher court. If the family proceedings court refuses to transfer the case, an application can be made to a district judge in the relevant care centre (*ibid*, art 9) to determine whether the case merits a transfer under the transfer criteria and, if so, to which court the case should be transferred (*ibid*, art 9(2) and (3)). The Children (Allocation of Proceedings) Order 1991, SI 1991/ 1677 also provides for the transfer down to a family proceedings court or county court where the higher court deems it appropriate under the terms of the order (*ibid*, arts 11, 12 and 13).

As indicated, an application for a care or supervision order may have been preceded by the granting of a child assessment order, an emergency protection order, the exercise of police powers of protection or as a result of a court-directed investigation under s 37. Equally, the applicant may be applying to court for an order where no previous action has been taken in respect of the child, but whatever has been the previous course of the action an applicant proposing to bring proceedings for a care or supervision order must file an application in respect of each child, in the appropriate form laid down in the rules, together with sufficient copies for one to be served on each respondent and anyone else to whom notice must be given (see FPC(CA 1989)R 1991, r 4(1)(a)).

The notice for service which is part of the form must notify each respondent, and anyone else to whom notice is required to be given, of the date, time and place fixed for the hearing and give three full days' notice of the hearing (FPC(CA 1989)R 1991, Sch 2, col (ii)). Those persons who are respondents are the child and anyone else with parental responsibility for the child and the local authority if it is not the applicant, and the persons to whom notice must be given are persons caring for the child at the time proceedings were commenced, every person whom the applicant believes to be a parent without parental responsibility, a refuge provider if the child is staying in a refuge and every person whom the applicant believes to be a party to pending relevant proceedings in respect of the same child (*ibid*, Sch 2, col (iv)).

As indicated earlier, upon receipt of the application, the justices' clerk in the family proceedings court or the clerk in a higher court will fix a date, time and place for a directions hearing if there has been no prior hearing or for a first hearing when matters, which might have been sorted out at the directions hearing, have already been dealt with.

There is no provision in the case of an application for a care or supervision order for the respondents to the application to file an answer.

(a) Interim orders

The court has power, under s 38 of the 1989 Act, to make either an interim care order or an interim supervision order (s 38(1)) and see Form CHA 27 and also the comments of Hollings J in *Croydon London Borough Council v A*

(No 1) [1992] 2 FLR 341. Interim orders can be made on the adjournment of proceedings for a care or supervision order (s 38(1)(a)), or in family proceedings in which the court has given a direction that a local authority should investigate a child's circumstances with a view to considering whether or not it should commence proceedings for a care or supervision order (s 37(2) and see Form CHA 19). Where, in any proceedings for a care or supervision order, the court exercises its discretion to choose from the range of orders available (s 1(3)(g)), and makes a residence order, it must also make an interim supervision order with respect to the child, unless the child's welfare would be satisfactorily safeguarded without an interim supervision order being made (s 38(3) and see Form CHA 27). It should be noted that it is not possible to make an interim residence order, although an order can be made for a short time with liberty to come back and seek the discharge of, or addition of conditions to, the residence order (ss 8 and 11). This course of action was actually adopted in *C v Solihull Metropolitan Borough Council* [1993] 1 FLR 290, when, on appeal, Ward J substituted a residence order in favour of the child's parents, subject to conditions, together with an interim supervision order, subject to conditions.

The court cannot make an interim care or supervision order unless it is satisfied that there are reasonable grounds for believing that the criteria set out in s 31(2) of the 1989 Act are satisfied (see *Re B (A Minor) (Care Order: Criteria)* [1993] 1 FLR 815 and note also *Northamptonshire County Council v S* [1992] 3 WLR 1010), and that the welfare principles in s 1 are adhered to. In particular, making an order must be better for the child than making no order at all. In *Humberside County Council v B* [1993] 1 FLR 257, the local authority had placed a baby, born to two schizophrenic parents, on the Child Protection Register. At the age of three months the baby had been left on her own in the parents' flat, had been left with relatives for overnight stays and, on one occasion, an aunt had observed bruising to the baby's arms and thighs. The local authority applied for an interim care order and the hearing was adjourned for four days. Early in that four-day period the authority decided that it might be appropriate to consider an interim supervision order instead, but further evidence emerged and the local authority reverted back to an application for an interim care order. The local authority obtained the interim care order and the baby, through the guardian ad litem, appealed. Booth J, allowing the appeal, stated that on the evidence before the justices, there were certainly reasonable grounds for believing that the baby would be likely to suffer significant harm attributable to the care of the parents if she were returned to them. Thus, the threshold conditions in s 31(2) were satisfied. But the court was then required to have regard to the welfare of the child, which must be the court's paramount consideration, and to the matters set out in s 1 of the 1989 Act. In particular, there had been no consideration of the range of orders that were available to the court as required in s 1(3)(g). The justices had confused the welfare consideration under s 1, with their findings relating to the likelihood of significant harm, which was a matter of factual proof. The justices had failed to apply the s 1 principles to the issue of whether or not to make an order and, if so, what type of order should be made. On the interpretation of s 1(5), Booth J went for a wider approach, thus focusing on benefits arising from the order, and suggested that the degree of intervention entailed by different orders should be taken into consideration. Booth J allowed the appeal and remitted the case back to the justices to consider in the light of s 1. She further made a prohibited steps order preventing the child's residence being altered until the rehearing and an order for contact between the child and her parents. On this interpretation the justices had failed to consider whether the child's need could be satisfied without removing parental responsibility.

Since, at a first hearing, it is most unlikely that all the evidence which a local authority might ultimately wish to rely on will be available, the proceedings in which a first interim order is made will not be as lengthy as for a full order but may, nevertheless, be hotly contested.

It is already apparent that first hearings are taking considerably longer to deal with than was the case under the old law, because of the requirements to satisfy the care conditions and to convince the court that the particular order sought is the best one in the circumstances and better for the child than making no order at all. Even where the making of a first interim order is unopposed, the court is still bound by the positive advantage principle and must, therefore, consider all the alternatives. In such circumstances, the guardian ad litem should be able to advise whether any such alternatives are viable and what options have already been examined and to what effect. The magistrate, or other court, hearing an application for an interim care order, has a mandatory duty to comply with the Rules of Court which require him to read any documents filed before the commencement of the hearing.

Since a number of problems have arisen in practice in relation to hearings for interim orders, Cazalet J took the opportunity in *Hampshire County Council v S* [1993] 1 FLR 559 to lay down a number of guidelines for courts hearing applications for interim care or supervision orders.

(1) An interim care order is a holding order but the court should, nevertheless, consider all relevant risks pending the substantive hearing and should ensure, perhaps by giving directions, that the final hearing takes place at the earliest possible date.
(2) If there is insufficient court time in that court the case should be transferred laterally.
(3) In an interim order hearing the court should only rarely make findings on disputed facts.
(4) Courts should be cautious about changing a child's residence on an interim order.
(5) Where an interim care order would lead to a substantial change in the

child's position the court should permit the hearing of limited evidence but must ensure there is not a dress rehearsal of the full hearing.

(6) The court should ensure that it has the written advice of the guardian ad litem and that any party opposed to the guardian's recommendations should be given an opportunity to put questions to the guardian.

(7) Justices hearing a case must comply with the mandatory requirements of the Rules.

(8) When granting interim relief, justices should state their findings and reasons concisely and summarise briefly the essential factual issues between the parties. The justices will not, however, be able to make findings on disputed facts since they will not have heard the evidence in full.

Where the court makes a first interim care or supervision order it may last up to eight weeks from the date on which it was made (s 38(4) and see Form CHA 27), although the DOH has issued guidance that this should not become the standard duration of a first order (see *The Children Act 1989 Guidance and Regulations, Vol 1 Court Orders* (1991, HMSO) at para 3.44). A second or subsequent order may last up to four weeks beginning with the date on which it was made (s 38(4)(b) and (5)(a) and see Form CHA 27), or, where the first order was for less than four weeks, the second or later order may last for more than four weeks but cannot expire more than eight weeks from the beginning of the first order. Thus, in many cases the sequence of orders may be a first order for eight weeks, followed by a subsequent order for four weeks and, perhaps, one further order for a period of four weeks, bearing in mind the findings of the Children Act Advisory Committee's first annual report looking at the time span of proceedings (*Children Act Advisory Committee Annual Report* 1991/92 (1992, Lord Chancellor's Department), at Table 9).

In some cases the first order may only be for two weeks, in which case a second care order could last for up to six weeks, providing that the total period does not exceed eight weeks from the making of the first order (s 38(4)(b) and (5)(b)). In that situation, third and subsequent orders could be made for up to four weeks at a time. There is no limit to the number of interim orders which may be made but, again, special attention must focus on the requirements of s 32 and s 1(1) and (2). As the DOH points out:

> 'although there is no limit to the number of interim orders which can be made under the Act a balance will have to be struck between allowing sufficient time for enquiries, reports and statements and risking allowing the child to continue in interim care or supervision for so long that the balance of advantage is distorted in favour of continued intervention.' (*The Children Act 1989 Guidance and Regulations, Vol 1 Court Orders*, at para 3.46 (1991, HMSO)).

Pursuant to the court's power to be able to give directions as to the medical or psychiatric examination or other assessment of a child in proceedings for child assessment orders or emergency protection orders, similar power is given to the courts on the making of an interim care order or an interim supervision order (s 38(6) and see Form CHA 27). The court must consider whether it should grant any request for such directions but, even where such directions are issued, if the child is of sufficient understanding to make an informed decision he may refuse to submit to the examination or assessment under the provisions of the section (s 38(6)). Nevertheless, as was pointed out earlier in the discussion relating to a similar *Gillick*-type provision pertaining to child assessment orders (see **4.9**(*a*)), action can be taken to overrule the child's refusal in such circumstances. Indeed, the case of *South Glamorgan County Council v W and B* [1993] 1 FLR 574 concerned an application by the local authority to invoke the inherent jurisdiction of the High Court to direct medical and psychiatric assessment of a 15-year-old child who had refused to comply with such a direction made under s 38(6). The local authority's application was successful with Douglas Brown J holding that there was inherent power under the parens patriae jurisdiction to override the refusal of a minor, whether over the age of 16 or not, to submit to assessment and medical examination and treatment, if it was in her best interests, and notwithstanding that she was of sufficient understanding to make an informed decision about medical examination or psychiatric examination or other assessment (at pp 583 to 584).

It should be noted that if the local authority does not seek specific directions, decisions as to such examinations and assessments will be the local authority's responsibility (s 31(11) and s 33(3)(a)), and if any person with parental responsibility objects he should seek a direction that no such examination or assessment should take place (s 38(7)). It should be noted, however, that, following the decision of Rattee J in *Re O (Minors) (Medical Examination)* [1993] 1 FLR 860, where the court gives a direction for medical tests to be carried out, the effect of such a direction is mandatory and does not merely give the local authority a discretion as to whether or not the tests should be performed. In the case of *Re O* (above) the magistrates had made an interim care order as it was known that both parents were HIV positive. The magistrates had given a direction that tests should be carried out on the children to determine whether or not they were HIV positive. The local authority appealed, querying first whether they ever had the power to appeal a decision to make directions under the section, because DOH guidelines indicated that such directions were unappealable (see *The Children Act 1989 Guidance and Regulations, Vol 1 Court Orders*, at para 3.47). The local authority further contended that the power to give such directions was permissive only, and did not include a power to direct a local authority to subject a child to an examination or assessment if the local authority did not choose to have it carried out. The local authority also stated that the results of an HIV test were not relevant to the court's consideration of the local authority's application for a care order and that the magistrates had not allowed the local authority to call expert evidence as to the desirability of such tests. Rattee J held that directions as to medical, psychiatric or other assessments were appealable to the High Court and the statement in the DOH guidance that such a direction was unappealable was wrong. Directions once given in the form of an order were, however, mandatory and not discretionary, and so a local authority was bound to comply with the directions. He went on to hold that the court's function was not limited to determining whether the threshold criteria were met. Once the court was satisfied that the criteria had been met, its function extended to considering whether, having regard to the welfare of the child concerned and, in particular, to the matters set out in the welfare checklist, it was appropriate to make a care order. In this case, said the judge, the question of whether these children were or were not HIV positive might have a real bearing on the particular choice of placement for their long-term future.

Unlike the position with regard to emergency protection orders and child assessment orders, there is no power simply to give directions on contact where an interim care order is made, since, for these purposes, the making of an interim care order is treated like the making of a full order (s 31(11)). Before making a care order the 1989 Act requires the court to consider any proposed contact arrangements and to invite the parties to the proceedings to comment upon them (s 34(11)). Where any party is dissatisfied with the proposed contact arrangements under an interim order they can seek a contact order under s 34 of the 1989 Act, as can the child if he is unhappy about contact proposals. The guardian ad litem would further be expected to advise the court in such situations, and, if necessary, to make a report.

It should further be noted that the making of a residence order, at any stage in the proceedings, discharges an interim care order.

When considering an appeal against the making of an interim order the appellate court will have to consider the decision-making process of the lower court. In *W v Hertfordshire County Council* [1993] 1 FLR 118, the local authority, having obtained emergency protection orders in respect of two boys and having arranged that a third, the youngest boy, should stay with a great-aunt, sought interim care orders in respect of all three children. The local authority sought the order in respect of the youngest boy to ensure that the mother did not attempt to remove him from the great-aunt. Relatively little time was allowed for the applications, and counsel for the local authority was not permitted enough time for cross-examination of witnesses. The magistrates made an interim care order in respect of the middle boy, refused to make interim care orders in respect of the other two boys and made a prohibited steps order prohibiting the mother from allowing the man, whom she had accused of causing the middle boy's injury, into her house. The magistrates gave no reasons for their decision and, when asked to give reasons, were told by the clerk that it was not necessary for them to do so as the court was only making interim orders. Booth J, in allowing the appeal, emphasised that the relevant rules of court spelled out the decision-making process (see FPC(CA 1989)R 1991, r 21(5) and (6)). Thus, before the court makes an order or refuses an application or request, the justices' clerk must make a written record of the reasons for the court's decision and any findings of fact. At the time of making an order or refusing an application, the court must state any findings of fact and the reasons for its decision. Those provisions were mandatory and applied to an *interim* decision, as well as to a final decision. In ruling that the document purporting to be the magistrates' reasons, which had been prepared two weeks after the hearing, was factually flawed and could not be admitted on appeal, Booth J followed the earlier case of *Hillingdon London Borough Council v H* [1992] 2 FLR 372. She further stated that as the magistrates had failed to comply with the court rules, their decisions were unsafe and could not be relied upon. It appeared that by interrupting the advocate for the local authority in his cross-examination of the mother, the magistrates had deprived themselves of material information upon which to base their decision. Booth J directed that the matter should be transferred to the county court and remitted for rehearing.

(b) Concurrency of criminal proceedings

Any delay is unacceptable, even where criminal proceedings are pending at the same time against one or both of the child's parents or other parties. It is not tenable to argue that the care proceedings should be adjourned pending the outcome of criminal proceedings save in wholly exceptional circumstances. This has been stressed in a whole series of cases which, it has been stated, are still of relevance under the 1989 Act (*R v Exeter Juvenile Court ex parte H and H* [1988] 2 FLR 214; *R v Waltham Forest Juvenile Court ex parte B* [1988] 2 FLR 214; *R v The Inner London Juvenile Court ex parte G* [1988] 2 FLR 58; and *Re S (Child Abuse: Cases Management)* [1992] 1 FCR 31). In a hearing of the first two cases the President of the Family Division, Sir Stephen Brown, stated that the guiding principle in care proceedings is the paramountcy of the child's welfare and, thus, delays should, wherever possible, be avoided. Where it is felt that continuing the proceedings may cause problems for the relevant court, and an adjournment is being requested pending the outcome of criminal proceedings, the court should give serious consideration as to what could possibly be the justification for such a request. It should be noted that in the case of *Re S*, Thorpe J has emphasised that in relation to the 1989 Act care cases should only *exceptionally* be held up to await the outcome of any criminal proceedings, since the welfare principle and the 'no delay principle' would militate naturally against such postponement. Reference was also made in that case to a Home Office Circular, 84/1982, which sought to encourage the resolution of care proceedings without awaiting the outcome of criminal proceedings.

(c) Attendance of the child

It should further be noted that in any proceedings in which a court is hearing an application for a care or supervision order, an interim care or supervision order or any of the orders contained in Part V of the 1989 Act, or is considering whether to make such an order, the court may order the child concerned to attend such a stage or stages of the proceedings as may be specified (s 95). It should be noted that this is a power to require the attendance of the child and, in the vast majority of cases, it would appear that the child's presence in court has not been required under the 1989 Act. This marks a change from the old law but signifies a recognition by the legislature that the child's views can be put to the court through the child's solicitor and the views about what is in the child's best interests may be presented to the court by the guardian ad litem. The view has clearly been taken, therefore, that the child's position before the court is adequately safeguarded by this system of dual representation but, where a child states a desire to be present, the guardian ad litem should put this matter before the court in order to obtain a court direction. The court would clearly wish to be guided by the advice of the guardian ad litem on whether the child is really of sufficient age and understanding to be present in court for the whole or part of any of the proceedings. Such was the situation in *Re C (A Minor) (Care: Child's Wishes)* [1993] 1 FLR 832 where the guardian ad litem had advised the family proceedings court that the 13-year-old girl wished to be present throughout the care proceedings. The guardian felt this to be in her best interests and the magistrates had exercised their discretion under s 95(1) of the 1989 Act to allow the child to be present during the hearing. None of the other parties had raised any objection at that stage, nor on the appeal. Notwithstanding this, Waite J ruled that 'the pressure of children should not be encouraged to develop into settled practice'. He further directed that guardians ad litem who arranged for children to be present at hearings should consider their reasons for doing so carefully and should be prepared to give them in court if wished. Given that the philosophy which underpinned the 1989 Act was that of according increasing recognition and respect for the ascertainable wishes and feelings of children, this seems quite an extraordinary direction. In advising the court that the child should be present, the guardian will have to have concluded that it was in the paramount interests of the child, and so the direction would seem to suggest that it is the judges rather than the child who find the child's presence during court proceedings uncomfortable. To exclude the child in such circumstances is also in breach of Article 12 of the UN Convention on the Rights of the Child.

4.13.8 Challenging recommendations and decisions to take proceedings

The child protection conference can only make a recommendation to initiate care proceedings because the actual decision to initiate proceedings lies with the social services or the NSPCC alone. Parents and their legal advisors wishing to discuss or challenge a decision of this kind would have to take issue with the agency concerned; it is not a matter for the protection conference which is, in the main, a consultative, advisory body, and not a body with executive powers. Where the child or parents have complaints about the conduct of the child protection conference they may consider using the complaints procedures which each ACPC must establish in compliance with *Working Together* (see Chapter 4). Similarly, parents who have a complaint about a particular agency service should take it up with the agency concerned. In the case of social services or other local authority provision this might be via the representation procedure (see, further, Chapter 8) and, where there is a complaint about the NHS, by using the National Health Service Complaints Procedure.

Other agencies are also currently establishing clear procedures to enable parents, children and other carers to pursue complaints against them, and agencies should, furthermore, ensure that all those involved in a child protection conference are provided with information about their complaints procedures.

4.13.9 No further action

Occasionally, it will be found, after detailed investigations and assessments, that allegations or suspicions about a particular family have not, in fact, been substantiated. *Working Together* makes it clear that in these cases it is essential that this is made clear to parents and that any distress or inconvenience to them is acknowledged (see, however, the problems caused after the Cleveland controversy (1988), Rochdale (1990) and the Orkneys (1990)). In some cases the family may benefit from some supportive counselling as a follow-up measure to what has occurred, in which case the child protection conference should consider making an offer of counselling. It should also consider who should be expected to provide such a service, given the hostility which the initiation of investigation, assessment or even of an emergency protection order or child assessment order may have engendered. Parents will obviously react very bitterly in such situations, but the professionals involved need to be able to acknowledge and work with such reactions without, at the same time, becoming defensive about the proper exercise of their professional responsibilities. Their task will be made much easier if they manage to work in partnership with parents and convince parents that they have been acting only in order to safeguard and protect the child's interests.

4.14 Pre-birth child protection conferences

There will, in some situations, be considerable concern about the future risk to an unborn child such as to require the implementation of child protection procedures and the calling of a child protection conference to consider the need for registration and the need for a child protection plan. Such pre-birth child protection conferences must, according to *Working Together*, have the same status and be conducted in the same manner as an initial child protection conference. Thus, those people who would normally be invited to attend an initial child protection conference should be invited to the pre-birth conference. Again, working in partnership with parents will be a crucial issue and, thus, parents or carers should be invited in the same way that they would be to other child protection conferences and be fully involved in plans for the unborn child's future. Once a decision is made that the child's name needs to be placed on the Child Protection Register as soon as it is born, the main cause for concern should then be determining the criteria for registration.

4.15 Conclusion

Whatever the recommendation of the child protection conference it will almost certainly demand a considerable degree of co-operation at various levels between different agencies and a commitment to working in partnership with the parents. This is, therefore, examined in much greater detail in Chapter 5. As a result of further investigation and assessment, a decision may be made by social services to press ahead with civil proceedings for a care or supervision order, and this is examined in Chapter 6. Where the police feel that criminal proceedings should be instituted as a result of the investigation and assessment, this will generally take place after consultations with social services and the decision whether to prosecute will be determined by the Crown Prosecution Service. The factors which will dictate whether a prosecution will be proceeded with, and the possible course of such proceedings, are considered in depth in Chapter 7.

CHAPTER FIVE

Inter-agency Co-operation

'No single agency – health, social services, police or voluntary organisation has the pre-eminent responsibility in the assessment of child abuse generally and child sexual abuse specifically. Each agency has a prime responsibility for a particular aspect of the problem. Neither children's nor parents' needs can be adequately met or protected unless agencies agree a framework for their inter-action.' (*Report of the Inquiry Into Child Abuse in Cleveland 1987* (1988, HMSO), Cm 412 ('the *Cleveland Report*')).

5.1 Agencies and professionals responsible for child protection

Part 4 of the governmental inter-agency guide *Working Together under the Children Act 1989* (1991, DOH) ('*Working Together*') deals with the roles of agencies and groups working in the public sector as well as voluntary agencies such as the NSPCC, in contributing to inter-agency co-operation for the protection of children. It reiterates that 'the responsibility for protecting children should not fall entirely to one agency: awareness and appreciation of another's agency role will contribute greatly to collaborative practices' (at para 4.1). Thus, the roles of the social services, the police, health services, the probation service, the education service and the NSPCC are clearly set out in Part 4, with every opportunity being taken to emphasise the need for every agency to collaborate wherever possible and to be aware of each other's complementary duties and responsibilities.

Among the voluntary agencies are the NSPCC and the Royal Scottish Society for the Prevention of Cruelty to Children ('RSSPCC'). The NSPCC have certain statutory responsibilities relating to preventive work which are: investigating suspicions about children's safety and welfare; monitoring families whose children appear to be experiencing problems with their health or well-being; counselling and responding to the needs of families whose children have been found to be ill-treated or neglected; and rehabilitation of children and their families after abuse has been identified or risk of abuse is strongly indicated and recognised. NSPCC officers frequently work together with the social services, police and health service in child abuse investigations.

However, as we shall see, effective and integrated inter-agency co-operation is far easier to formulate than it is to implement, for a variety of reasons.

5.2 The need for inter-disciplinary collaboration

When the Children Act 1989 ('the 1989 Act') came into force on 14 October 1991, its statutory changes were in part based on the philosophy that there should be closer co-operation between all professionals and agencies involved in child protection (see also Chapter 4). The changes introduced by the 1989 Act have numerous implications for social services, police, health professionals, education authorities, lawyers and voluntary organisations. Apart from the new approach to court work, the 1989 Act's new orders, such as the child assessment order and the emergency protection order, require the collaboration of the health care and social work professions. The recent Home Office guidance, the *Memorandum of Good Practice on Videorecorded Interviews with Child Witnesses for Criminal Proceedings* (1992, DOH) ('the *MoGP*') presupposes close co-operation between the police and social workers in interviewing children suspected of having been abused and the application of mutually agreed procedures on interviewing suspected child abuse victims (see Chapters 6 and 7 for an analysis of the *MoGP*). The guidance issued to accompany the 1989 Act has also reiterated the need for inter-agency co-operation, where appropriate, so that there is no doubt about its role in the child protection field. In addition, the concurrent jurisdiction created by the 1989 Act (a lateral and vertical court transfer scheme) also requires co-operation between judges (and court clerks) presiding at different levels and in different courts. New or revised guidance has also been issued to medical staff since the first edition of this book was published (eg *Child Protection* (1992, DOH); *The Children Act: An Introductory Guide for the NHS* (1992, DOH); *What every nurse, health visitor and midwife needs to know about the Children Act* (1992, DOH); *Physical Signs of Sexual Abuse in Children* (1991, Royal College of Physicians); all discussed below), which also stresses the inter-agency element.

A system of child abuse management dealing with non-accidental injury began to be formalised on a national basis in 1974, when a DHSS circular was issued soon after the Maria Colwell inquiry. This had been preceded by two earlier guidances issued in 1970 and 1972 which only dealt specifically with battered babies. The need for greater co-operation and teamwork was highlighted, as well as the need to establish case conferences, area review committees and registers. (For further details see N Parton *Governing the Family* (1991, Macmillan) at pp 118 to 121.) The current general guidelines for inter-agency collaboration are contained in *Working Together* issued jointly by the Department of Health, the Home Office, the Department of Education and Science, and the Welsh Office. This document is a revised version of an earlier booklet, published in 1988, which was itself issued in response to various child abuse scandals and inquiries (see Chapter 4). One of its main objectives was to strengthen inter-agency co-operation, declaring itself to be a 'guide to arrangements for inter-agency co-operation for the protection of children from abuse'. Yet it did not deal with a number of issues and, instead, concentrated on how agencies should respond to suspected child abuse cases. It was the *Cleveland Report* which highlighted a breakdown in inter-agency and inter-disciplinary co-operation as a major cause of a child abuse crisis. The lack of professional understanding and co-operation was nothing new to professionals working in the field and, as was pointed out in Chapter 2, is a dominant theme that runs through over a decade of child abuse inquiry reports. Yet child abuse procedures and joint working arrangements have been developing since the mid-1970s, in response to various child abuse inquiries and, in the late 1980s, the issues relating to child sexual abuse have been regarded as an area, the detection of which requires particularly close co-operation between child protection professionals. Ironically, just before the Cleveland controversy erupted in a blaze of publicity, health care professionals and social workers had felt that there were sufficiently clear guidelines and procedures to cope with any emergency or crisis. Cleveland shattered that illusion, not least because of the scale of referral, and highlighted the need to spell out, with far greater precision, the procedures which should be adopted in the course of child abuse investigations. It further emphasised that no professionals could be left to their own devices to decide which procedures to implement unless a clearer framework was devised within which to operate. Nevertheless, a positive result of the controversy has been the publication of new or revised guidelines and circulars on inter-agency co-operation for child protection and welfare agencies engaged in child abuse work, the main implications of which are the concern of this chapter.

The *Cleveland Report* also emphasised that both the diagnosis and management of child abuse must be seen as the responsibility of several agencies and professionals. Experience over nearly two decades has shown that it is fundamental to the good management of child abuse that professionals concerned are able to co-operate and communicate with each other. Since the death of Maria Colwell there have been nearly 40 inquiries into the deaths of abused children, some set up by central government and others by local authorities. Given the vast range of agencies involved in child protection, it is axiomatic that co-operation and collaboration among the agencies is essential in order to keep the welfare of the child in the forefront of everyone's mind.

5.3 Working together under the 1989 Act

Despite its history, or perhaps because of it, inter-agency co-operation is by no means easy to co-ordinate or implement in the day-to-day management of child protection. As Williams puts it:

'Each statutory agency has its own procedures, terminology, priorities, resources, infrastructure and legal duties. These are not always designed to dovetail with those of other agencies but rather are intended to operate within each agency's own "culture". Individual agencies are dealing with legislation and practice based upon a *multi*-agency approach rather than an integrated *inter*-agency approach' (Williams 'Working Together II' (1992) *Journal of Child Law* 68).

The reality, therefore, is that the various agencies are still working as they always have done, which is within their own terms of reference and are continuing to contribute individually rather than really 'working together' as an integrated team.

The 1988 version of *Working Together* clearly needed revising in the light of the 1989 Act. The introduction to the 1991 version, therefore, emphasises the need to work in partnership with families and the role of the area child protection committees ('ACPCs'), which will provide the forum within which child protection policies will be developed, and should be monitored and reviewed (see 'Key Areas in *Working Together*' at **5.3.1** below).

The 1989 Act requires a corporate local authority policy which will cover all issues connected with investigation of child abuse and neglect. Under s 47 of the 1989 Act, there is now a planned response which should be followed whenever local authorities investigate cases where they have reasonable cause to suspect that a child is suffering or is likely to suffer significant harm. Although responsibility is placed primarily on the social services committee and its officers, the 1989 Act addresses the local authority as a whole. Further, under s 47(9), when conducting enquiries a local authority may request any other local authority, education authority, housing authority or health authority to assist, particularly by supplying relevant information. As has been pointed out earlier (see Chapter 4) the police are not included in this list even though they play a vital part in joint investigation and their role has been highlighted by the *MoGP* (and see Chapter 7, generally).

The police are, however, expressly mentioned in the context of exchanging relevant information in case conferences and in the course of making arrangements for the protection of children from abuse (see **5.3.5** below).

Apart from co-operation between the police and social services with regard to the orders under the 1989 Act, two other types of situations requiring close co-operation are (1) cases where the police use the child protection order under s 46 and (2) where access to a child is sought. The exchange of information between police and social services is an area where co-operation usually takes place at case conferences and there is explicit guidance in *Working Together* on the role of the police in sharing information they hold with other agencies (*Working Together*, at para 4.14).

Part III of the 1989 Act deals with the provision of services for children in need and their families and reinforces the need to prevent abuse and neglect (see Chapter 3 for a full discussion of prevention strategies). Social services, education services, housing and health services must co-operate in relation to children with special educational needs. Such children may, of course, also suffer child abuse as may children with multiple disabilities (see Chapter 7 which includes a brief discussion of interviews with such children).

A successful implementation of the inter-agency ethos under the 1989 Act will, therefore, require a high degree of co-ordination between and within agencies.

5.3.1 Key areas in Working Together

Working Together has expanded on a number of key areas in inter-agency co-operation, which include: (1) the responsibilities of the ACPC; (2) legal and ethical considerations; (3) preventive measures; (4) exchange of information between agencies; (5) the child protection conference; and (6) organised abuse.

5.3.2 The responsibilities of the area child protection committee

The area child protection committee ('ACPC') is designated as the forum for inter-agency and inter-disciplinary work. In order to be fully effective, para 2.5 of *Working Together* states that 'a joint forum should have a clearly recognised relationship to the responsible agencies'. Thus, one ACPC should cover one local authority and all the police or district health authorities or parts of them within that local authority boundary. The pivotal role undertaken by ACPCs is underlined by the recommendation that all agencies should appoint senior officers to it 'with sufficient authority to speak on their agencies' behalf and to make decisions to an agreed level without referral to the appointees' agencies' (at para 2.5). In other words, such officers should have sufficient authority and autonomy to act in the course of a child protection investigation. It has to be said that this is not always possible because senior and experienced personnel tend to have several other responsibilities and, as a result, less senior workers may be appointed. Each agency is supposed to be responsible for monitoring the performance of its own representative and must have procedures for considering reports from that representative in order to identify appropriate action within that agency (see para 2.11). *Working Together* also states that 'decisions which have implications for policy, planning and resources need to be reported on and discussed at appropriate levels within agencies'. This presupposes the existence of an efficient and effective communication and referral system within agencies and, while this might well be the case, the sheer volume of paper work and case-loads may sometimes cause a delay in communicating information from one level to another. The other, more serious difficulty is that it may not be possible at an early stage of investigation to know if the particular case is one which will require consultation with colleagues or superiors. Hence, delays can occur while the case is developing.

The main tasks of the ACPC are spelt out in *Working Together*, at para 2.12. These are:

(1) to establish, maintain and review local inter-agency guidelines on procedures to be followed in individual cases;

(2) to monitor the implementation of legal procedures;

(3) to identify significant issues arising from the handling of cases and reports from inquiries;

(4) to scrutinise arrangements to provide treatment, expert advice and inter-agency liaison and make recommendations to the responsible agencies;

(5) to scrutinise progress on work to prevent child abuse and make recommendations to responsible agencies;

(6) to scrutinise work related to inter-agency training and make recommendations to the responsible agencies;

(7) to conduct reviews required under Part 8 of the guide (ie incidents leading to the death of a child where child abuse is suspected, or where a child protection issue is likely to be of major public concern); and

(8) to publish an annual report about local child protection matters.

Williams points out that while the main tasks of the ACPC deal with inter-agency work, its composition is rooted in a multi-agency approach, since *Working Together* appears to treat ACPC members as accountable to the individual agencies which they represent (J Williams 'Working Together II' (1992) *Journal of Child Law* 69). He believes it is difficult to see how a representative body of this nature is capable of developing policies and procedures which transcend individual agency perspectives.

It is submitted that this is certainly true in terms of developing an inter-agency policy which is 'agency-neutral', but it is equally difficult to see how, without imposing a national procedure which would still have to take account of an individual agency's perspective and local conditions, anything further could be done at this stage.

5.3.3 *Legal and ethical considerations*

An outline of the legal framework of the child care and protection field is set out in Appendix 2 to *Working Together*, but it stresses that it will be necessary to obtain legal advice in relation to every case since this is not a complete statement of all relevant legal provisions (see, further, Chapter 3). Part V of the 1989 Act and the proforma for applications for emergency protection orders and child assessment orders are reproduced in this Appendix 2 to *Working Together*. Part 3 of *Working Together* discusses some of the legal issues raised in the area of child protection and needs to be read with Appendix 2 and the volumes of guidance and regulations on the 1989 Act. Several central issues have already been discussed (see Chapters 3 and 4 above) but it needs to be noted that the inter-agency perspective is emphasised, particularly in terms of procedure. Appendix 3 also discusses preventive work (see Chapter 3 above). On the question of removal of children from home, for example, *Working Together* states that this gives rise to:

'public and professional concern, causes great distress if not handled sensitively, and can be damaging both for the child and for the rest of the family. Therefore, *except where a child is in acute danger it is essential that the timing of the removal of the children from their homes should be agreed following consultation with all appropriate professionals.'*

Various legislative provisions are then considered which have implications for child protection work, including: the Criminal Justice Act 1988 (see Chapter 7 below); the Police and Criminal Evidence Act 1984; the Prohibition of Female Circumcision Act 1985 (see Chapter 7); the Access to Personal Files Act 1978; and the Access to Health Records Act 1990.

5.3.4 Preventive measures

The 1988 *Working Together* placed great emphasis on inter-agency work involving child protection and the 1991 version has supplemented this by reference to the duty imposed in Part III of the 1989 Act, namely, to provide for children in need, which is defined in s 17(10) in terms far broader than the child at risk of abuse or neglect. Under s 27 of the 1989 Act, 'where it appears to a local authority that any authority (such as an education, housing, or health authority) . . . could, by taking any specified action, help in the exercise of their functions under Part III, they may request the help of that other authority' (see Chapter 3 for a full discussion of these measures). Again, as in s 47(9) (see **5.3** above), the police are not included in the list of agencies whose help may be requested, although it is extremely unlikely that they will decline to help, unless there is a serious problem of resources at the time when assistance is required (see, further, Chapters 3 and 4). *Working Together* says very little else with regard to preventive work, since it is, after all, intended to be a guide to inter-agency working in cases where abuse has occurred or is suspected. The development of appropriate preventive strategies is a task for local authorities pursuant to their duties under Part III of the 1989 Act.

5.3.5 Exchange of information between agencies

As far as the exchange of information between agencies is concerned, para 3.10 of *Working Together* states:

'Arrangements for the protection of children from abuse, and in particular child protection conferences, can only be successful if the professional staff concerned do all they can to work in partnership and share and exchange information, in particular with social services departments (or the NSPCC) and the police. Those in receipt of information from professional colleagues in this context must treat it as having been given in confidence. They must not disclose such information for any other purpose without consulting the person who provided it.'

The issue of confidentiality has been discussed in the previous chapter (see **4.3**).

Para 4.14 of *Working Together* is noteworthy. It states:

'In investigating an allegation of child abuse the police will normally collect a considerable amount of information. Irrespective of their decision whether or not to institute criminal proceedings, the information they hold may be highly relevant to a decision about a child who may need protection from abuse, and should, where appropriate, be shared with other agencies.'

The exchange of information is, therefore, seen as vital to the proper conduct of investigation of child abuse allegations.

Working Together proceeds to say (at para 3.11) that:

'ethical and statutory codes concerned with confidentiality and data protection are not intended to prevent the exchange of information between different professional staff who have a responsibility for ensuring the protection of children.'

It then reproduces extracts from medical, nursing and social work guidances on the issue of confidentiality. It concludes by stating (at para 3.15) that:

'the degree of confidentiality in child protection work will be governed by the need to protect the child. Thus social workers and others working with a child and family must make it clear to those providing information that confidentiality may not be maintained if the withholding of the information will prejudice the welfare of a child.'

However, this does not resolve the difficult issues that bedevil confidentiality in individual cases and different professional contexts.

Apart from the issues referred to in Chapter 4 on this point, the following considerations may also be mooted. First, although the General Medical Council, the British Medical Association and the Department of Health have now drawn a distinction between disclosures made by 'older' and 'younger' children, the problem remains in deciding where one draws the line between these two types of children, apart from obvious cases where the child is clearly incapable of making any sort of informed decision or understanding its consequences. The question arises in the case of 'older' '*Gillick*-competent' children (see *Gillick v West Norfolk and Wisbech Area Health Authority* [1986] 1 AC 112) as to whether they would retain the right to insist on confidentiality. Recent case-law suggests they might not have such a right once their disclosure was communicated to someone who subsequently assumed parental responsibility for the child (such as a local authority) or if the matter came to court (see *Re W (A Minor) (Consent to Medical Treatment)* [1993] 1 FLR 1) on the analogy with the right to refuse medical examination or treatment in certain circumstances.

Secondly, in the case of older children, the latest guidelines (see **4.3** above) indicate that doctors presumably retain some discretion as to whether or not to disclose information they receive regarding abuse of children, in the light of an evaluation of possible risks to the child or young person disclosing as well as to siblings or other members of the family, In such cases, the long-term and short-term consequences of revealing such confidential information must be fully and carefully considered and discussed with the older child.

Thirdly, social workers continue to have to reconcile their conflict of roles which, depending on the particular situation, require them to be counsellor, witness and investigator. Well-coordinated inter-agency co-operation appears to be the only way forward.

Since we have already discussed the procedures involved in convening a child protection conference and the procedure at the initial conference in detail in the previous chapter (see **4.10** and **4.11** above), we shall proceed to the phenomenon of organised abuse.

5.3.6 *Organised abuse*

Working Together considers organised abuse for the first time, in the wake of cases which indicate that it does occur. (For a discussion of these cases see Chapter 2.) Organised abuse is described as 'a generic term which covers abuse which may involve a number of abusers, a number of abused children and young people and often encompasses different forms of abuse. It involves, to a greater or lesser extent, an element of organisation' (at para 5.26.1). This is discussed in Chapters 1 and 2. It need only be said here that it must not be necessarily equated with ritual abuse, which itself may or may not involve satanic worship (see further Chapter 2). As para 5.26.4 of *Working Together* aptly puts it, 'Investigations which come within the category of organised abuse will put inter-agency procedures to the test'. Clearly, the timing of the intervention will be significant, since the risk to child victims may be exacerbated if the operation is only partially successful or unsuccessful. Hence, in some cases, professionals involved will have to weigh the risk of delaying intervention for an individual child against the benefits of collecting evidence which might eventually assist in protecting a wider group of children.

Further demands on agencies are also mentioned: (1) the involvement of senior management will be essential to ensure a sufficiently 'high level' operation which will function speedily yet without neglecting the welfare issues; (2) agencies will need to co-operate in assessing what is best for the child in any individual case on questions such as: should the child be called as a witness? What are his or her immediate needs?; (3) senior managers will need to consider the resource implications in the handling of organised abuse; (4) co-operation across geographical boundaries will need to take place and links with neighbouring authorities will have to be established; and (5) regular strategy meetings will have to be arranged with a view to 'review activity frequently to ensure that it complies with agreed child protection practice and procedures and continues to engage the active co-operation of all agencies'.

The question which arises is whether all these objectives and ideals are really realisable in the current climate of economic stringency, cost-effectiveness and accountability in terms of economic productivity. Further, do we have the necessary atmosphere, resources and professional environment within the various agencies to achieve a successful and effective inter-agency approach to child protection?

5.3.7 Recommended content of local procedural handbooks

Appendix 6 of *Working Together* contains a recommended standard content and format of local procedural handbooks concerned with the handling of inter-agency issues. This has been revised to include the sections of the 1989 Act dealing with investigation, assessment and matters relating to implementation, review and de-registration.

The sections which are suggested in the Appendix are: (1) *Law and Definitions*; (2) *Who is Involved?* (ie dealing with the role of the personnel involved); (3) *Referral and Recognition* (ie dealing with how members of the public and staff locally should refer concerns which they have about individual children; the role of the local authority social services department, the NSPCC and police in investigating suspected child abuse); (4) *Immediate Protection and Planning the Investigation* (the mechanisms of inter-agency co-operation in developing an agreed plan of action; the role of the key worker; and how parents should be involved in the investigation; (5) *Investigation and Initial Assessment*; (6) *Child Protection and Decision-making about the Need for Registration*; (7) *Comprehensive Child Protection Planning*; (8) *Implementation, Review and Registration*; (9) a miscellaneous section, which *Working Together* suggests could be entitled 'Other', which could provide advice pertaining to special circumstances, eg children of Service families, organised abuse, abuse by professionals or cases where it is known or suspected that a child may be subjected to female genital mutilation; and (10) local agency procedures.

Working Together finally recommends a loose-leaf form of handbook to aid regular review and revision of the material, with full indexes, a summary page showing important telephone contacts and addresses, concisely worded, short paragraphs and good typography to highlight important paragraphs.

5.3.8 Comments on the suggested procedural format

If implemented into any local authority's procedural guidelines, Section (4) (above) must be carefully worded and the advice in *Working Together* on parental involvement must be noted: parents would *normally* be invited to participate in partnership with professionals in child protection conferences but not where there is a conflict between parents and between parents and children (see para 6.12). The chairperson of the child protection conference may exclude a parent, although this 'needs to be specially justified' (see para 6.15). (See Chapters 4 and 9 for a full discussion of the issues involved in parental involvement and non-involvement in child protection conferences.)

Section (5) contains a misprint, since it should refer to *Part 5* rather than para 5. It also refers the reader to para 5.14, which is the correct cross-reference. Paragraph 5.14.9 suggests that it may be useful for ACPCs to consider the use of videotaped interviews with the child, in readiness for the implementation of the Criminal Justice Act 1991 and the forthcoming 'Code of Practice'. The 1989 Act is now in force and under it a videorecording of an interview with a child may be used as the child's main evidence in criminal proceedings, subject to certain conditions (see Chapter 7 below). It should also be emphasised that the quality of the recording should also be of a standard which is good enough to withstand judicial and legal scrutiny and to refer to the *MoGP* (see Chapter 6 and especially Chapter 7 below). The *MoGP* is the Home Office 'Code of Practice' to which para 5.14.9 of *Working Together* refers. However, it was not, after all, called a code, since it does not have statutory force and is not mandatory.

5.3.9 Guidance for doctors

According to para 4.1 of the DHSS guidance *Diagnosis of Child Sexual Abuse* (1988) 'no one body, group, organisation or individual can be held solely responsible for the identification of cases of child sexual abuse and the administrative and management procedures which follow such identification'. This guidance was issued in the wake of the Cleveland controversy and the publication of the *Cleveland Report* (see Chapter 2) and echoes Butler-Sloss LJ's view that there was insufficiently cogent medical evidence to warrant removing the child from its home in at least some of the suspected child abuse cases, since they were not matters of life and death.

In a subsequent guidance issued by the Royal College of Physicians in April 1991, *Physical Signs of Sexual Abuse in Children*, it is emphasised that the interpretation of physical findings is only one aspect of the diagnostic process in detecting child abuse. Among the more salient points on child sexual abuse are: (1) a substantial proportion of sexually abused children show no abnormal physical findings (at para 4.12); (2) physical findings are influenced by the examination techniques employed; (3) very few signs are diagnostic of abuse in the absence of reasonable alternative explanation; (4) pregnancy in a child or young person under 16 years of age should raise the question of abuse; (5) there is a clear overlap between abused and non-abused populations with regard to physical signs which are consistent with, and even suggestive of, abuse. This is particularly so in the case of anal findings and reflex anal dilation (see para 6.38); (6) the diagnosis of child sexual abuse is confirmed *following a multi-disciplinary investigation with full inter-agency co-operation* (at para 6.3) (emphasis added); (7) physical findings – including normality – are consistent with abuse and it is, therefore, important to document carefully even minor ano-genital signs as well as negative findings. The single most important feature is a statement by the child; (8) physical signs alone are on rare occasions sufficient to make the diagnosis. The interpretation of physical findings is a matter for a doctor with experience in this field (see para 2.3); (9) a multi-disciplinary investigation with full agency co-operation is necessary whenever there is concern that child sexual

abuse is concerned. This guidance is again a direct response to the findings
of the Cleveland inquiry, with its special reference to the sexual abuse of
children. It has, in fact, been referred to and quoted in cases dealing with
suspected child sexual abuse.

5.3.10 Guidance for nurses, midwives and health visitors

The nurses' guidance, *Child Protection*, has been revised and a second edition
was published by the DOH in 1992. It also states (at para 17.3) that 'child
sexual abuse is difficult to diagnose and it is generally accepted that no one
professional can be responsible for making the diagnosis. It is a multi-
disciplinary process'. It emphasises that the senior nurse should develop a
communication system and establish links at the appropriate level with social
services departments and managers of other agencies, such as a family health
services authority, local education authorities, housing departments and the
police about current concerns, as well as particular cases. He or she must
ensure effective liaison between his or her staff and those of other agencies.
It goes on to say that the senior nurse must also given professional advice
and information to other professionals and agencies about the specific role of
the particular nurse in child abuse cases (eg school nurse, health visitor) and
emphasise the importance of his or her role in prevention and detection.

It also contains a new section on organised abuse (Section 18) and suggests
that advice on dealing with such abuse should be sought through the social
services child protection specialist adviser or specialist member of the police
force.

Another booklet was also published by the DOH, *The Children Act 1989
– What every nurse, health visitor and midwife needs to know* (1992, DOH),
which is a condensed version of *The Children Act 1989 – An Introductory
Guide for the NHS and Child Protection* (1992, DOH). Apart from giving a
summary of the main principles of the 1989 Act, it lists the implications of
the 1989 Act for district health authorities, NHS Trusts and family health
services authorities. These authorities are, inter alia, asked (at pp 2 and 4)
to:

– review and revise the existing policies and procedure for handling child
  protection cases at all levels against the guidance outlined in *Working
  Together*;
– contribute to the local ACPC's review of its procedures;
– identify a senior doctor, a senior nurse with a health visiting qualification
  and a senior midwife (designated senior professional) as the co-ordinators
  of all aspects of child protection work within their district. This will include
  the provision of advice to social service departments and to health professionals; and
– appoint a named person to co-ordinate child protection.

It also stresses that any nurses who come into contact with children may be the first people to alert others, in particular paediatric nurses, nurses working in accident and emergency departments, psychiatric nurses, mental handicap nurses and practice nurses, who will need to have an agreed practice protocol.

Apart from reiterating the main orders under the 1989 Act, it once again emphasises that although health visitors and school nurses may identify children in need of care or emergency protection, the local authority has prime responsibility. Full inter-agency co-operation is essential in the decision-making process.

5.3.11 *Guidance for social workers: Protecting Children*

Protecting Children: A Guide for Social Workers Undertaking a Comprehensive Assessment (1988, DOH) ('the *Orange Book*'), contains several pertinent sections on inter-agency co-operation. It is worth noting that the guide does not deal with assessment as part of an initial investigation but addresses comprehensive assessment for long-term planning in child protection cases. As Parton puts it: 'It was an attempt to ensure that the rationalisation of the inter-agency procedures was matched by attempts to develop the required practice skills' (N Parton *Governing the Family* (1991, Macmillan) at p 139).

The guide also bases its approach on the concept of 'dangerousness', discussed in the work of Peter Dale et al *Dangerous Families* (1986, Tavistock), who quote a definition from Hamilton that dangerousness referred to the potential to cause physical and psychological harm to others. It moves from this to 'inter-agency dangerousness' (on which see **5.4.1** below). It also stresses the different roles of each profession and agency, their differing values and philosophies, styles, structures, management systems, and their levels of decision-making and professional autonomy. It makes it clear that the child's social worker has a central responsibility in relation to the assessment task 'but there will be a need for other skills and participation from within the multi-agency network'.

In other words, there was no attempt to give parity of status to all agencies and all child protection workers. On the contrary, it confirms that the social worker is the primary professional in the assessment process, although he or she would have to work together with other professionals from other agencies in reaching decisions. Although this sounds perfectly plausible and unremarkable, in practice a great deal depends on the particular facts of the case and who the social worker consults. If a doctor who has had some experience in dealing with suspected child abuse cases is consulted, his or her diagnosis, if apparently unequivocal and supported by medical evidence, would surely have to be accepted by the social worker, who would not have the prime task of assessment in this case because the matter requires expertise in medical matters. At any subsequent child protection conference, it would be a courageous social worker who suggested that there should be second or third opinions on the matter if a doctor appears to be convinced about the diagnosis. The chairperson would have to be persuasive and tactful about the need for a decision to be reached on an inter-agency consultative basis, rather than predominantly based on one professional's opinion. This is one of the most difficult ideals to realise but no doubt the 'Cleveland factor' may well be sufficient to remind all professionals about the need for a decision to have a multi-agency input.

Thus, although the social worker has the ultimate responsibility for carrying out the assessment and deciding on the best option that should be followed in the particular case, the influence of 'higher-ranked' professionals (at least with regard to what seems to be the perception of the public and many of the judiciary) is ubiquitous and means that medical views, for example, will be accorded a considerable amount of weight.

5.3.12 Guidance for the police

The Home Office Circular No 52/1988 of 6 July 1988, was issued as guidance to the police on the procedures they should adopt in the investigation of child abuse and emphasises that the key to effective action is a 'close working relationship between the agencies concerned, the NSPCC and the health authorities' (at para 2).

The guidance stresses that the primary responsibility for ensuring that all appropriate steps are taken for the protection of the child falls on the social services department (at para 4).

The police have established various joint working arrangements and other strategies, and most police forces throughout the country have appointed child protection officers who specialise in the prevention, detection and investigation of child abuse (see *Fig 2* above). The guidance also states, inter alia, that 'chief officers, through the medium of Area Child Protection Committees, [will wish to consider] whether the arrangements in their area are providing . . . specialist multi-disciplinary assessment' (at para 10). At para 11, it is emphasised that:

> 'where, following a specialist multi-disciplinary assessment or otherwise, an investigation into a criminal offence is initiated, the investigators should work on the principle of interviewing together the source of referral, the victim, and, where appropriate, members of his or her family, the lead in the interview being taken to ensure that information . . . is fully shared between both agencies, subject to any statutory requirements on confidentiality. This information should be made available to both the police officer and social work investigators so that they are in a position to discuss openly each case together and reach an agreed view on how to take the investigation forward.'

This must now be read subject to the *MoGP* which gives detailed advice on joint interviewing of children who may be witnesses in criminal proceedings.

Another Home Office circular, No 59/1990, 'The Cautioning of Offenders', emphasises the importance of inter-agency participation with regard to the cautioning of offenders. A caution is intended to be a speedy method of dealing with a minor offender, in order to divert such a person from the court and to lessen the chances of re-offending. The circular advises that in cases where the cautioned person has particular problems, it is useful for him or her to be referred, on a voluntary basis, to other agencies which can provide guidance, support and involvement in the community.

The role of the police must now predominantly be viewed in the light of *Working Together*, which enunciates the nature of police involvement in child abuse cases 'as stemming from their primary responsibilities to protect the community and to bring offenders to justice' (at para 4.11). This paragraph goes on to say, echoing the 1989 Act and a philosophy more closely associated with civil law that:

'Their overriding consideration is the welfare of the child. In the spirit of *Working Together*, the police focus will be to determine whether a criminal offence has been committed, to identify the person or persons responsible and to secure the best possible evidence in order that appropriate consideration can be given as to whether criminal proceedings should be instituted.'

Further paragraphs describe the criteria for deciding whether or not to initiate criminal proceedings, the standard and burden of proof and their emergency powers under the 1989 Act. They also highlight the different methods of working between social services and the police, the latter concentrating on investigation of alleged offences, the former on child welfare (see paras 4.11 to 4.17).

On the issue of inter-agency co-operation, *Working Together* states, almost in anticipation of problems, that:

'Difficulties will be encountered in joint inter-agency investigations but these can be minimised by the selection of specialist staff who undergo appropriate inter-agency training.'

It stresses (at para 4.17) that:

'it is essential that methods of joint working are established between the two agencies over and above the joint interviewing of child victims . . . It is important that those engaged in child abuse investigation and their supervisors fully understand the responsibilities of both agencies, the powers available to them and the different standards of proof that exist in relation to criminal and civil proceedings.'

5.4 Problem areas in inter-agency practice

Child abuse inquiries over the past two decades have exposed failures in inter-agency co-operation with regard to both planned and ad hoc co-operation. In Scotland, a study of inter-agency practice revealed poor levels of communication and mutual suspicion to be 'regular and recurrent features of case management' (see Taylor and Tilley (1990) *Adoption and Fostering* 13). In England, in the pre-1989 Act era, two further attitudes were identified by Peter Riches (in 'Working Together for whose benefit?' in *Responses to Cleveland* (1989, NCH)) as tending to hamper comprehensive and effective inter-agency and inter-disciplinary co-operation, which were: (1) the notion that policy-makers, managers and practitioners get on very well, but that the other levels still need to learn to co-operate more effectively; and (2) to be quite complacent about a system that has good co-operation at one level, so as deliberately to fail to consider improving co-operation at the other level.

5.4.1 Areas of conflict

Three main areas in which professionals from the different agencies have come into conflict with each other are as follows. First, there has been conflict concerning the *diagnosis* of child abuse. The main questions here are: Do the cases merit referral or intervention? What base-line of normality is being used by various professionals? If medical professionals differ from social workers, will it be acceptable for the social worker's view ever to prevail if it happens to be a marginal case and the assessment is based not purely on medical grounds? Secondly, *prescriptive disagreements* have occurred. Here the professionals may differ on the appropriate course of action to be taken once a case has been referred to them. Thirdly, there have been *management disputes/disagreements*. This has been known to happen both within agencies and between agencies where the more 'senior' figure with the higher public profile tends to have the greater weight placed on his or her opinion and there have also been disputes over the allocation of responsibilities.

Indeed, in recognition of past and potential problems, *Protecting Children: A Guide for Social Workers Undertaking a Comprehensive Assessment* (1988, DOH) highlights 'inter-agency dangerousness' (at para 4.6). This concept has been discussed above (see **5.3.11**). It explains, using the concept of 'dangerousness' that relationships between agencies can reflect dangerous patterns. Examples are: (1) undefined boundaries of roles and responsibilities; (2) absence of clear, written procedures to guide intervention; (3) the existence of hidden agendas that affect formal activity; (4) the presence of competition and hostility among professionals; and (5) the avoidance of overt disagreement about the management of cases. The implication from point (5) is that a particular agency which does not agree with another on the management of the case presumably might still prefer to give the impression that it does agree, possibly for the sake of inter-agency harmony. As the guide points out, such indications, frequently noticed at a case conference, must be understood and carefully handled by the person chairing the conference.

5.4.2 Dangers of superficial inter-agency co-operation

There are problems which are not easily eradicated when agencies interact. First, there may well be a few dominant or so-called 'leading' professionals who have such high profiles and are so familiar with each other's style of management that they might unwittingly exclude the co-operation and participation of others in the field. Secondly, inter-disciplinary working may well create an environment in which individual errors are shielded or even condoned, but no amount of professional co-operation can replace the need for essential skills, knowledge and experience with which to cope with a multitude of pressurised tasks. Further, there is a vast number of agencies and organisations which, in a practical sense, makes it difficult to have a unified form of co-operation.

5.5 Barriers to communication

Peter Riches (see 'Working Together for whose benefit?' in *Responses to Cleveland* (1989, NCH)) identified the following areas as potential barriers to effective inter-agency and inter-disciplinary co-operation: (1) legal powers; (2) duties; (3) aims; (4) traditional ways of working; and (5) structure. Riches argues that because of inherent differences in fundamental characteristics such as their structures and legal powers, it is very difficult for the various agencies to see each other's point of view.

Sadly, despite many years of co-existence and working together more by accident or through necessity than by design, the child abuse cases and inquiry reports (see Chapter 2) illustrate graphically the lack of co-ordination between the different agencies. Thus, despite a detailed allocation of responsibilities for each agency, undoubted commitment to inter-agency (or more accurately, multi-agency) co-operation in child protection work, an impressive array of guidances and a comprehensive Act such as the 1989 Act, the differences in duties, aims and traditional methods of operation within each agency has militated against effective multi-agency co-operation in many instances. For example, even *Working Together* points out (at para 4.16) that

'although in cases of child abuse both the police and social services have as their foremost objective the welfare of the child, their primary functions, powers and methods of working are different. Whilst the police will focus on the investigation of alleged offences, the social services are concerned with the welfare of the child and other members of the family.'

As far as hierarchical structures are concerned, whilst even the newly qualified doctor will enjoy a considerable amount of autonomy in decision-making, as well as status, the social worker and health professional would have to be high up the career ladder, experienced and senior before being able to enjoy equal autonomy or status. Hence, the baseline of different professions makes it difficult for their opinions on what is 'in the child's best interests' in any child protection case to be accorded equal weight.

5.5.1 *Differences in professional perspectives*

Riches (above) also identifies areas of conflict which arise in relation to:
(1) objectives; (2) value systems; (3) work styles; (4) attitudes to confidentiality; and (5) priorities.

In other words, there are clearly different professional perspectives which are adopted at different levels of day-to-day operations. Feedback from inter-agency training conferences, it would appear, revealed that what usually surfaces is a strong adherence to one's individual professional perspective. The police will often approach a suspected child abuse case with the prime aim of securing a conviction and 'putting the abuser where he belongs' (ie in prison). The health professional will be anxious to explore the psychological and psychiatric make-up of the alleged abuser with a view to treating this positively. The social worker will decide which role he or she needs to be assuming for each particular case – investigator, counsellor or post-investigative rehabilitator.

The consultative approach is, therefore, sound in theory but not always easy to implement in practice. Since it is inevitable that not all agencies will have the power to put their views into practice, and because of the different status accorded to different professions, there is often no consensus regarding the 'best way forward' in any child abuse investigation. What usually happens, it appears, is that one of the agencies will assume the initiative and 'take charge' of the situation, either by virtue of their legal powers and responsibilities or because of their high professional profile. Fortunately, the commitment to the child's interest and welfare is an area of common concern and serves to unite different agencies, at least at the practical level. Perhaps more focused training in multi-disciplinary co-operation methods, which forces the different agencies to pool their resources and really work together, supplemented by support for release of the particular professional from his duties once a week in order to attend training courses, will eventually succeed in establishing a more effective inter-disciplinary network for child protection.

5.6 Overview

The implementation of the 1989 Act has had an important impact on the inter-agency network in the field of child protection. There are clearly difficulties involved in realising the ideals of the 1989 Act, but the multi-agency consultative approach at least forces each agency to think about the input of other agencies in making their assessments in the course of child protection work. Each agency now has a sharper perception of its role and its interactive dynamic. However, many of the ongoing problems will not be solved overnight. These include: difficulties in adducing evidence; a reluctance to invoke procedures; a general lack of resources and facilities; bureaucratic structures;

and, ironically, an even larger 'paper mountain' as a result of the many volumes of guidance and regulations which have been issued to supplement the 1989 Act.

It is to be hoped that the child's perspective is kept in the forefront of all this multi-disciplinary activity so that the child will be the ultimate beneficiary. Firm foundations for a co-ordinated child protection system have now been laid with the many volumes of guidance which have been issued and the 1989 Act itself. Even firmer commitment to the welfare of the child will now be required from all child protection professionals.

CHAPTER SIX

Civil Proceedings: Care and Supervision Order Proceedings in the Family Proceedings Court, the County Court and the High Court

6.1 Persons who may initiate care or supervision order proceedings

A local authority or an authorised person may initiate care proceedings under s 31 of the Children Act 1989 ('the 1989 Act'). The only 'person' who has received specific authorisation so far has been the NSPCC (s 31(9)(a)). The provisions in the 1989 Act mark a change from previous law in that the police are no longer allowed to initiate care proceedings for any reason. In nearly all cases involving an application for a care or supervision order it will be the local authority who is the applicant. Where an application is being made for a care or supervision order, such proceedings are generally referred to in Orders directing the arrangement of court business issued by the Lord Chancellor's Department as Public Law Applications.

6.2 Commencing proceedings

6.2.1 Which court?

Generally all Public Law Applications concerning children are commenced in the family proceedings courts (see Children (Allocation of Proceedings) Order 1991, SI 1991/1667 ('C(AP)O 1991'), art 3).

(a) Criteria for transferring cases

Subject to a considerable number of restrictions (see art 7(2), (3) and (4) and arts 15 to 18), a magistrates' court may, upon application by a party or of its own motion, transfer to a county court, proceedings of any of the kinds mentioned in art 3(1) of C(AP)O 1991, where it considers it is in the interests of the child to do so having regard to a number of issues. Thus, the court must consider whether: any delay in determining the question raised in the proceedings is likely to prejudice the child's welfare; the proceedings are exceptionally grave, important or complex; it would be appropriate for those proceedings to be heard together with other family proceedings which are pending in another court; whether transfer is likely significantly to accelerate the determination of the proceedings, and no other method of doing so, including transfer to another magistrates' court, is appropriate and delay would seriously prejudice the interests of the child who is the subject of the proceedings (see C(AP)O 1991, art 7(1) generally).

(b) Restrictions on transfers

There are some restrictions on transfers. Thus, applications for emergency protection orders for child protection, a range of private law matters, and proceedings to give a police constable powers to assist in the removal of children under s 102 (see Chapter 4) can only be transferred from a magistrates' court to a county court in order to be heard together with other family proceedings which arise out of the same circumstances as gave rise to the proceedings to be transferred, and which are pending in another court (see C(AP)O 1991, art 7(3) and art 8).

(c) Requirement to transfer

A magistrates' court *must* transfer proceedings to another magistrates' court where, having regard to the principle that any delay in determining the question is likely to prejudice the welfare of the child, the transferring court considers that the transfer is in the interests of the child. The transferring court may consider this to be the case because it is likely to accelerate significantly the determination of the proceedings, or because it would be appropriate for those proceedings to be heard together with other family proceedings which are pending in the receiving court, or for some other reason (see art 6 generally). The receiving court must, through its justices' clerk, also consent to the case being transferred (C(AP)O 1991, art 6(1)(b)).

(d) Procedure on receipt of request for transfer

Where the justices' clerk or a family proceedings court receives a written request from a party to transfer proceedings, he or the court must issue a certificate in Form CHA 64 granting, or in Form CHA 65 refusing, the request in accordance with the relevant criteria. A copy of the certificate granting the request must be sent to the parties, any guardian ad litem and to the receiving court (see C(AP)O 1991, art 6(2)).

As to which county court a case may be transferred, if it is decided that a vertical rather than a horizontal transfer is in the best interests of the child, this is governed by special rules concerning the allocation of proceedings to particular levels of county courts. In the case of public law proceedings (ie care and associated proceedings) these will have to be transferred to the relevant county court care centre (C(AP)O 1991, arts 14 to 20).

Where the justices' clerk or a family proceedings court has received a written request from a party for a transfer of proceedings to the county court, the procedure to be followed is exactly the same as that following a request to transfer proceedings from one magistrates' court to another. (See above.)

(e) Judicial attitudes to transfer of cases

In addition, when magistrates are presented with potentially complex or lengthy cases, there is now a considerable body of High Court opinion which suggests that they should immediately consider whether or not it is in the best interests of the child to transfer the case to the district judge for his determination as to the appropriate level for the case to be heard. In *L v Berkshire County Council* [1992] 1 FCR 481, the High Court stated that it was a matter of some concern that a lengthy hearing which was to go on before magistrates was going to be heard over a number of separate days because of the difficulty of reconvening the bench on consecutive days. (See, on a very similar issue, *Re L* [1993] 1 FCR 689.) As Thorpe J commented in *Re H (A Minor) (Care Proceedings: Child's Wishes)* [1993] 1 FLR 440 (at p 445) '. . . it is vital for the success of the family justice system that has been introduced to accompany the Children Act 1989, that the allocation of cases to the appropriate level of court within the three-tier system operates effectively'. Thorpe J, in that case, stated that as a matter of course where the estimate of the length of hearing was in excess of two or three days, magistrates should consider transferring the case to a district judge for consideration as to whether it should be heard by a circuit judge or a High Court judge. It was his view that a complex case should always be transferred upwards. He went on to state that a case which seemed to bristle with complexity at the outset and was transferred upward under the Children (Allocation of Proceedings) Order 1991 might nevertheless simplify as it progressed and might then justify a transfer back to the magistrates' court. A case might not manifest any of the criteria set out in art 7 initially, but if any of these factors subsequently developed, the case should be swiftly transferred to a district judge.

He stated that in the case with which he was dealing, 'it was manifest from the outset that it was an acutely difficult case where an able, intelligent adolescent was demonstrating the capacity to blight his prospects of achievement as a consequence of grossly disturbed behaviour'. It was, he said, a class of case more appropriately dealt with by a judge at the Family Division who would have the advantages of the services of the Official Solicitor. The view that care proceedings which are likely to run for more than two or at most three days constituted, in itself, a reason for transferring the case to a county court was reiterated by Thorpe J in *Re A (A Minor) (Care Proceedings)* [1993] 1 FCR 824. In that case, however, he went on to emphasise that it was important that if an application for transfer on the grounds of duration was to succeed, it should be advanced at the earliest possible stage. It was further stressed by Connell J, in *S v Oxfordshire County Council* [1993] 1 FLR 452, that cases involving non-accidental injury and assessment of risk should, generally, be transferred to a higher court.

(f) Refusal of magistrates' court to transfer

Where, however, a magistrates' court refuses to transfer proceedings to the county court care centre, any party may apply to the appropriate county court care centre for an order to transfer the proceedings to that centre (C(AP)O 1991, art 9). In determining whether or not to transfer the proceedings to itself, or for consideration as to whether it should be transferred to the High Court, the court must consider the same criteria which the magistrates' court had to consider when deciding whether or not to grant the request for a transfer (C(AP)O 1991, art 9(2)). In so doing, the county court may reach the decision that the proceedings are more appropriate for determination in the High Court and that such determination would be in the interests of the child (C(AP)O 1991, art 9(3)).

(g) Right to apply for transfer after magistrates' refusal

It is important that those representing children, parents or the local authority in care proceedings appreciate their rights to apply to the county court for a transfer. This was illustrated by the case of *Essex County Council v L* [1993] Fam Law 458, where the local authority had sought to transfer care proceedings to a higher court but the justices had refused their application. By the commencement of the hearing it was apparent that there was conflicting medical evidence and the hearing then took place on non-consecutive days over the course of several weeks. Bracewell J held that the magistrates' courts' practices were contrary to the best interests of children. She stated that 'where justices were told that a hearing was estimated for more than two or at the most three days, or where there was conflicting medical evidence, they should transfer the matter immediately to the nearest care centre'.

(h) Procedural steps on application to county court for transfer

The Family Proceedings Rules 1991, SI 1991/1247 ('FPR 1991') provide for the steps to be taken and the time within which they should be taken where an application for transfer from a magistrates' court is made to a county court (FPR 1991, r 4.6(1)). The applicant is required to file the application for transfer together with the magistrates' certificate of refusal, and to serve a copy of the application and of the certificate personally on all parties to the proceedings which it is sought to transfer within two days after receipt of the certificate by the applicant (FPR 1991, r 4.6(2)). The court must consider the application not before the fourth day after the filing of the application unless the parties consent to an earlier consideration, and either grant the application or direct that a date be fixed for the hearing of the application (FPR 1991, r 4.6(3)). If the latter, the proper officer fixes the date and gives not less than one day's notice of the date to the parties (FPR 1991, r 4.6(3)(b)). Somewhat peculiarly, the rules do not provide for a copy of the original application which it is sought to transfer to be lodged with the county court but it would clearly assist the district judge if this was done.

Where the county court is considering whether to transfer proceedings on to the High Court it may, before deciding whether to make or refuse an order for transfer or whether to fix a date for the hearing or whether such an order should be made, invite the parties to make written representations within a specified period as to whether such an order should be made (FPR 1991, r 4.6(4)). After consideration of the written representations the court may make an order for transfer, determine that such an order should not be made or set a date for the hearing of the issue, but as Thorpe J commented in *Re H (A Minor) (Care Proceedings: Child's Wishes)* [1993] 1 FLR 440 (at p 445) that where it becomes apparent in family proceedings that a case was more complex than it had originally appeared, it was essential that action be taken swiftly to transfer it to the appropriate level of court within the three-tier system.

(i) Horizontal transfer of cases

There is provision for a county court care centre to transfer cases horizontally where, having regard to the avoidance of delay, it considers the transfer to be in the child's interests, and the receiving court is of the same class or classes as the transferring court, or is to be presided over by a judge who is specified in the Family Proceedings (Allocation to Judiciary) Directions 1991 and 1993 (6 September 1993) for the same purposes as the judge presiding over the transferring court (see C(AP)O 1991, art 10 and see the *Children Act Advisory Committee Annual Report* (1992, Lord Chancellor's Department), at Chapter 4).

(j) Transfer of cases to the High Court

A county court may transfer proceedings to the High Court where, having regard to the principle of the avoidance of delay, it considers that the proceedings are appropriate for determination in the High Court, and that such determination would be in the child's interest. (See C(AP)O 1991, art 12.) It should also be pointed out that following the case of *Re AD (A Minor) (Child's Wishes)* [1993] Fam Law 405, the President of the Family Division has issued a practice direction that where children issue applications for s 8 orders (contact, prohibited steps, residence and specific issues orders), such applications raise issues which are more appropriate for determination in the High Court and should be transferred there for hearing. (See *Practice Direction* [1993] 1 FLR 668.) It should be noted that, of course, this may be relevant where a child, following concerns over significant harm, is offered accommodation by the local authority and then exercises his right to apply for s 8 orders under the terms of the 1989 Act.

(k) Transferring a case downwards

Brief mention was made earlier of the ability of the courts to transfer cases downwards and it should be noted that the High Court may transfer a care case back for hearing in the county court where, having regard to the avoidance of delay, it considers that the proceedings are appropriate for determination in such a court and that such determination would be in the interests of the child (see C(AP)O 1991, art 13). It is further provided under the C(AP)O 1991 that a county court may transfer back to a magistrates' court, before trial, proceedings transferred to it by a magistrates' court, having regard to the avoidance of delay principle and the interests of the child and, where the criteria for transfer cited by the magistrates' court or the district judge as the reasons for transfer either did not at the time or no longer apply (C(AP)O 1991, art 11).

(l) Selecting the most appropriate court for a case

The various provisions of the Orders and Rules of Court thus allow, for the first time in public law cases, a certain element of 'forum shopping'. Whilst the general rule, therefore, is that an application for a care or supervision order must initially be made to the family proceedings court, it should be noted that where such an application arises from a direction to conduct an investigation made by the High Court or county court under s 37 of the 1989 Act, provided that court is a county court care centre, the application could be made there, or in such care centre as the court, which directed the investigation, may order (C(AP)O 1991, art 3(2)). Mention has also been made (see (a) and (c) above) of the ability of a person seeking to make an application for a care or supervision order to do so in a court where proceedings are already pending in respect of the child, provided this court is able to hear such an application.

6.2.2 Lodging an application

An application for a care or supervision order may have been preceded by the granting of a child assessment order (s 43), or an emergency protection order (s 44), or by the exercise of police powers of protection (s 46), or as a result of a court-directed investigation under s 37 (see *Fig 4*). Equally, the

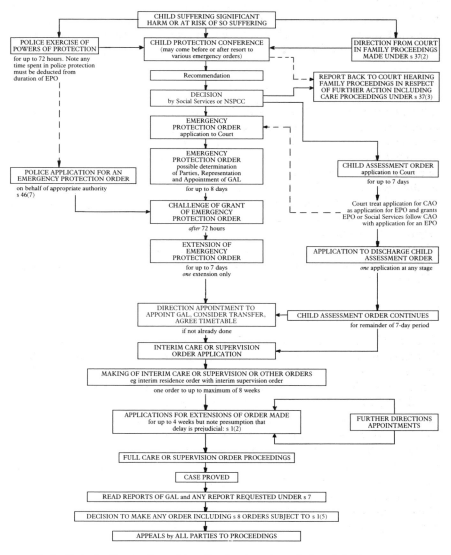

Fig 4: Steps leading to the making of orders in respect of abused children under the Children Act 1989

applicant may be applying to court for an order where no previous action has been taken in respect of the child.

An applicant proposing to bring proceedings for a care or supervision order must file an application in respect of each child in the appropriate form laid down in the rules (see Family Proceedings Courts (Children Act 1989) Rules 1991, SI 1991/1395 ('FPC(CA 1989)R 1991'), r 4(1)(a) and see Form CHA 19), together with sufficient copies for one to be served on each respondent and anyone else to whom notice must be given (see FPC(CA 1989)R 1991, r 4(3)). The notice for service which is part of the form must notify each respondent and anyone else to whom notice is required to be given of the date, time and place fixed for the hearing and give three full days' notice of the hearing (FPC(CA 1989)R 1991, Sch 2, col (ii)). Those persons who are respondents are the child, and anyone with parental responsibility for the child and the local authority if it is not the applicant, and the persons to whom notice must be given are the persons caring for the child at the time proceedings were commenced, every person whom the applicant believes to be a parent without parental responsibility, a refuge provider if the child is staying in a refuge and every person whom the applicant believes to be a party to pending relevant proceedings in respect of the same child (FPC (CA 1989)R 1991, Sch 2, cols (iii) and (iv)).

6.2.3 Directions appointments or first hearings

Upon receipt of the application, the justices' clerk in the family proceedings court, or the clerk in the Higher Court will fix the date, time and place for the hearing or a directions appointment, allowing sufficient time for the applicant to comply with the rules as to service of notice, endorse the date, time and place so fixed upon the copies of the application filed by the applicant and return the copies to the applicant for service (FPC(CA 1989)R 1991, r 4(2)). In most cases where there has been no preceding legal action, the justices' clerk or the court may feel it appropriate to deal with a number of matters at a directions appointment prior to a first full hearing of an application.

In the case of an application for a care or supervision order, no provision is made in the rules for filing of an answer by the respondents to the proceedings.

Where a directions hearing is held the justices' clerk or the magistrates in the family proceedings court or the relevant court in the county or High Court, if a case has been transferred or consolidated, may consider giving, varying or revoking directions for the conduct of the proceedings including: the timetable for the proceedings; the attendance of a child; the appointment of a guardian ad litem under s 41 of the 1989 Act or of a solicitor under s 41(3) of that Act; the submission of evidence including expert reports; the possibility of transferring proceedings to another court and the consolidation with other proceedings (FPC(CA 1989)R 1991, r 14(2)).

It should be noted that at any stage in the proceedings any party may apply for, or the court may, of its own volition, hold, directions appointments and issue the directions referred to earlier (FPC(CA 1989)R 1991, r 14(3)). Any party seeking directions must do so by written request specifying the directions sought, which must be filed and served on the other parties, or to which the other parties have consented and they or their representative have agreed in writing. Where the directions sought are not agreed, all parties having been served must be given the opportunity to attend and be heard or to make written representations. Experience of the first 12 months' operation of the 1989 Act seems to be showing that the presumptive 12-week timetable, felt to be desirable in care cases, is not working in practice. Considerable reservations have been expressed about directions appointments which seem to offer greater opportunity for delaying tactics, and magistrates' clerks report cases taking longer than under the old law. Solicitors and guardians acting for children should be aware of their duty to attempt to speed up proceedings in accordance with s 1(2) of the 1989 Act and, thus, where delays are occurring, directions should be sought for an order that in appropriate cases there be no further directions appointments unless it can be shown to be in the child's best interests.

Thus, one of the most important matters which the court will have to address early on, and probably in the first directions hearing, is the issue of the timetabling of the case. Guidance was issued to the courts that in public law proceedings, 12 weeks is the approximate period after which the full hearing should take place. Clearly, such guidance ties in with the delay principle but the presumption should be capable of rebuttal on the basis of the paramountcy of the child's welfare. It is, of course, possible to argue, using the welfare principle, that a case should take longer than 12 weeks. Thus, where the child is undergoing assessment for the purpose of a psychiatric report, it may not be possible for a specialist's assessment to be done within what may be left of a 12-week period. Where any party realises that there may be problems about the submission of expert evidence due to the nature of the assessment, they should return to court and seek directions on re-timetabling at the earliest opportunity. As the first *Children Act Advisory Committee Annual Report* (1992, Lord Chancellor's Department) reveals, in fact, most public law cases have been averaging 18 weeks before a final order has been made.

6.2.4 Party status

The applicant, who will be either the NSPCC or, more usually, the local authority, is a party to proceedings for a care or supervision order, as is every person who has parental responsibility for the child and, in the case of care or supervision order proceedings, the child himself (FPC(CA 1989)R 1991, Sch 2, col (iii) and r 7(1)). Whereas previous legislation provided specifically for the grandparents of a child to be able to apply for party status in certain circumstances, they are not now specifically mentioned in the rules. The rules provide, however, that any person may file a request in writing that he or someone else be joined as a party to the proceedings (FPC(CA 1989)R 1991, r 7(2)). The court, on considering a request that a person be joined as a party, may: grant such a request without a hearing or representation, whereupon the justices' clerk must inform the parties and the person making the request of that decision; order that a date be fixed for considering such a request and serve notice on the applicant and the parties; or invite the parties or any of them to make written representations as to whether a request should be granted and, after the expiry of a certain period, the court may then either grant such a request or, again, order a hearing of such a request.

As to the principles to be applied when an application is made by another party for leave to be joined as a party to the proceedings, this was considered in *G v Kirklees Metropolitan Borough Council* [1993] 1 FLR 805. In this case, care proceedings were ongoing in respect of a child when the mother's sister (the child's aunt) sought to be joined to the care proceedings. It was, however, implicit in her application that she wished to apply for a s 8 order and the court held, therefore, that the criteria set out in s 10(9) of the 1989 Act were applicable. This meant, therefore, that she had to show: her connection with the child; the nature of the proposed application for the s 8 order; any risk there might be of the proposed application disrupting the child's life to such an extent that he would be harmed by it; where, as was the case here, the child was being looked after by a local authority, the local authority's plans for the child's future; and finally the wishes and feelings of the child's parents. In addition, the court stated that a person seeking leave must establish that he had a case that was reasonably likely to succeed. In this, the High Court was following the reasoning laid down by the Court of Appeal in *Re A and W (Minors) (Residence Order: Leave to Apply)* [1992] 2 FLR 154. Booth J stated that:

'Many a case may be arguable but in reality have little or no chance of success. I consider that the appellant must go further than this and must establish a case that is reasonably likely to succeed if she is to be joined as a party in order to seek relief.'

In the circumstances of the case, Booth J held that there was no purpose in joining the aunt as a party to the proceedings since she would have no reasonable prospect of success in gaining the relief she had sought.

The Court of Appeal has also made it known, in the case of *Re M (Minors) (Sexual Abuse: Evidence)* [1993] 1 FLR 822, that additional parties should not be joined to proceedings as parties unless they have a separate view to put forward in the proceedings. In the particular circumstances of that case, grandparents had been given leave to intervene and appeared, by counsel and solicitors, throughout the 20 days of the first instance hearing. The grandparents had offered an alternative home for the children in the event that the mother was not considered suitable by the court to have their care but the court felt that their interests were identical with those of the mother. The Court of Appeal emphasised that there was no purpose in their being separately represented when they should have been called as witnesses for the mother and their offer could have been presented to the court both by the mother and the children's guardian ad litem. The court emphasised that grandparents, and others, should not intervene unless they could be seen to have a separate view to put forward.

6.2.5 Legal aid

The Legal Aid Act 1988 (as amended) provides that civil legal aid is available to all parties in care and supervision order proceedings. Different rules have, however, been specifically introduced to cover the legal aid position of children, parents and those with parental responsibility involved in care and supervision proceedings, and secure accommodation proceedings, as well as in emergency protection order proceedings. For children, parents and those with parental responsibility the normal legal aid means and merits test will be waived so that legal representation will be available as of right for parents and children, and there is no possibility of delay in providing legal aid in these cases since solicitors are able to act immediately on a self-certifying basis where they are satisfied that a child or parent falls into the relevant category (see the Legal Aid Act 1988 (CA 1989) Order 1991, SI 1991/1924). The solicitor must, however, forward the certificate notifying the local legal aid area office that he is acting (using Form CLA 5A) so as to allow the legal aid office to issue a legal aid certificate. In respect of an emergency legal aid application, cover will be given for necessary work done by a solicitor where proceedings begin over a weekend or at night, provided that the solicitor submits a legal aid form setting out the full details of the case within three working days (which is known as the special procedure) or, in the case of an emergency application, the legal aid area office approves an emergency application on the next available working day. The waiving of the means and merits test in respect of children, parents and those with parental responsibility continues until the proceedings are at an end and will cover all directly related issues, for example the making of interim care orders or the making of s 8 orders in care proceedings. Where an appeal is lodged, however, although the waiver of the means test will continue to be applied, the legal aid board will insist on an application of a merits test with regard to the appeal.

Where the solicitor is applying for legal aid for an adult, only one application and one certificate is needed for family proceedings, but where the solicitor is applying for legal aid for the children in the proceedings, separate applications and certificates are needed for each child.

As far as other parties are concerned, such as grandparents or other relatives who may seek to be joined as parties, provided they have a sufficiently separate view to be put forward, there will be no legal aid merits test but the usual rules concerning financial eligibility for legal aid will have to be applied to such persons (Legal Aid Act 1988, s 15).

6.3 Separate representation of the child

6.3.1 Appointing a guardian ad litem

As has already been noted in relation to proceedings for emergency protection and child assessment orders, the 1989 Act and the relevant rules of court make specific provision for the much earlier appointment of the guardian ad litem (see Chapters 3 and 4). Where a guardian has been appointed earlier, this may have been done by the clerk or by the court in proceedings for an emergency protection order or a child assessment order and the name of the guardian will have been drawn from a list provided by the local guardian ad litem panel manager (see Chapter 4). Each local authority is required by the Guardians Ad Litem and Reporting Officers (Panels) Regulations 1991, SI 1991/2051, to establish a panel of guardians ad litem and reporting officers in respect of their area. Whilst the responsibility for forming such a panel cannot be discharged by other agencies, the day-to-day tasks of running the panel can be delegated and, in a number of areas around the country, this has taken place. Different types of panels exist, including reciprocal arrangements between, usually, two neighbouring authorities, consortia arrangements involving groups of authorities linked together, single authority panels and 'contractual' arrangements with voluntary child care organisations. Guardian ad litem panel managers must ensure that they have a service which is equipped to provide for the court dealing with applications about children in the area covered by the operation of the panel. Further guidance on the management of panels of guardians ad litem and reporting officers and the functions of the panel managers can be gleaned from the *Manual of Practice Guidance for GALRO Panel Managers* (1992, DOH).

Whereas it is the task of the panel manager to organise the panel in order to ensure that there are sufficient guardians on the ground to respond to court requests for their services, appointments of guardians to the panel are actually the formal responsibility of the local authority in whose area the panel is established (GALRO (Panels) Regulations 1991, SI 1991/2051, reg 4(1)). DOH guidance suggests that panel membership should, wherever possible, comprise individuals drawn from the categories of self-employed social workers, employees of a local authority, employees of a voluntary organisation and probation officers (see *The Children Act 1989 Guidance and Regulations*,

Vol 7 Guardians ad Litem and other Court Related Issues (1991, HMSO) at para 2.43). The court rules provide, however, that guardians ad litem serving in any care or associated proceedings must not be any of the following: a member, officer or servant of a local authority, where that local authority is a party to the proceedings (unless employed solely as a panel member); a member, officer or servant of the NSPCC, where that organisation is bringing proceedings under s 31, or other relevant section, of the 1989 Act; a serving probation officer; or a member, officer or servant of a local authority or voluntary organisation involved with, or which has been involved with, that child (FCP(CA 1989)R 1991, r 10(7)). Further extensive advice is given in the DOH guidance in order to ensure the independence of guardians ad litem, but there is widespread concern, even 18 months after the implementation of these provisions, that the rules permitting the employment of guardians who have had prior involvement with the local authority, albeit more than five years previously, or who may have personal connections with those involved in a case, threaten the truly perceived independence of guardians ad litem.

As to the qualifications to act as a guardian ad litem, the DOH guidance states (at para 2.51) that 'it is expected that most guardians will be qualified in social work and also have several years of relevant expertise working with children. They will need an aptitude for the demands and discipline for the type of work'. Whilst the GALRO (Panels) Regulations 1991, SI 1991/2051, look to local authorities determining the eligibility criteria for guardians by reference to obvious indicators, such as qualifications, it is provided that, exceptionally, they may conclude that an applicant, although not possessing a formal qualification in social work, does have relevant experience and qualifications which make appointment appropriate. Despite widespread concern when the 1989 Act was passed that there might not be sufficient guardians ad litem to respond to the requests which might come in to represent children in specified proceedings as defined in s 41(6), such concern does not seem to have been borne out in practice in the first 12 months of the operation of the 1989 Act. Thus, as was noted in Chapter 4, the *Children Act Advisory Committee Annual Report* (1992, Lord Chancellor's Department), indicates that the rate of appointments of guardians in public law cases has yet to reach 50 per cent in the magistrates' court, 33 per cent in the county court and 14 per cent in the High Court and although, as was pointed out, there the low appointment rate may be a result of misreading of the return forms, a shortage of guardians has not *yet* been shown to have materialised.

It would also appear that few delays have been experienced in appointing guardians under the 1989 Act and panel managers have been seen to be deploying the resources of panels as effectively as possible, having regard to their overall costs and the budgets within which those services operate.

Where the court decides, under s 41(1) of the 1989 Act, that it is necessary, in the interests of the child, to appoint a guardian ad litem, the court will send out the notice of appointment (see Form CHA 30) after having consulted closely with the panel manager. The DOH guidance recommends, and this has generally been followed around the country, that the initial selection of a guardian for the court should be undertaken by the panel manager, which allows the most effective deployment of the panel resources and facilitates, wherever practicable, improved matching between the needs of an individual case and the skills or other attributes of a particular GAL. Despite the fact that guardian ad litem panel managers are having to operate within finite budgets, it was made clear, in relation to previous regulations concerning the provision of guardians, that no attempt must be made by social services financially responsible for panels to limit the number of hours' work which can be done on any particular case (see *R v Cornwall County Council ex parte G* [1992] 1 FLR 270).

In proceedings before the High Court it is provided that directions may be given that the role of the Official Solicitor should include the duty to act as guardian ad litem (s 41(8) of the 1989 Act). The proceedings where the Official Solicitor will be appointed are those which commence, and are completed, in the High Court, or which are allocated to the High Court from a lower court and, in either case, no guardian ad litem has been appointed and there are exceptional circumstances which call for the Official Solicitor's involvement rather than a panel guardian. When acting as a guardian ad litem, the Official Solicitor's duties will be those required for guardians ad litem as set out in r 11 of the Rules of Court (see **6.4** below). It should be noted, however, that the Official Solicitor will not be included in the membership of any particular panel of guardians ad litem. The DOH guidance takes great pains to point out that the Official Solicitor and his staff have considerable experience in regard to High Court procedures in child care cases where wider issues of public policy and complexity are present (*The Children Act 1989 Guidance and Regulations, Vol 7 Guardians ad Litem and other Court Related Issues* (1991, HMSO)). The guidance goes on to point out that the frequent use of experts such as paediatricians and child psychiatrists in High Court proceedings has also afforded the Official Solicitor an opportunity to have access to such specialists nationwide and their knowledge will be of value to guardians ad litem. The guidance further advises that panel managers should establish liaison links between their panel and the Official Solicitor so that panel guardians ad litem may have access to such specialists if the need arises in a particular case (*ibid*, para 2.7.3).

In determining the overall membership of an individual panel, local authorities should have regard to the number of children in their area who may become the subject of proceedings and to the different racial groups to which they belong. There should, as far as possible, be flexibility in matching the type of proceedings and needs of the child with the characteristics and skills of the guardian. Whilst, in general terms, it should be possible for a guardian to undertake duties in respect of the full range of potential cases, there will be certain situations, says the DOH guidance, where it is particularly important that the guardian selected be of the same sex, race, language, culture or religion of the child and the family. In cases involving children with disabilities, the guidance also advises that the guardian may have to call on additional specialist assistance. Similarly, it goes on to point out that 'where it is not possible to appoint a guardian who speaks the same language as the child or the child's family, an interpreter will be necessary' (*ibid*, para 2.50).

6.4 Duties of the guardian ad litem

Where a guardian ad litem is appointed in any care and associated proceedings pursuant to s 41(6) of the 1989 Act, his/her duties are as laid down in FPC (CA 1989)R 1991, r 11. (For the duties of the guardian ad litem in proceedings in the county court and High Court see FPR 1991, r 4.11.) In addition, a guide entitled *A Manual of Practice Guidance for Guardians ad Litem and Reporting Officers* (1992, DOH) has been issued specifically to assist the guardian in the performance of his or her duties. The guardian ad litem is appointed with a view to safeguarding the interests of the relevant child before the court and, thus, the rules direct him or her on a number of issues designed to achieve this end.

6.4.1 Promoting the welfare of the child

The first duty laid upon the guardian is provided for in the statute and is a duty to safeguard the interests of the child in the manner prescribed by the rules. The rules go on to provide (r 11(1)) that in carrying out their duties, the guardians ad litem must have regard to the principle that delay should be avoided in children's cases and that where they are looking to safeguard the child's welfare before the court they must be bound by the principles laid down in the welfare checklist set out in s 1(3)(a) to (f) of the 1989 Act. The welfare checklist should, therefore, be read as applying directly to the guardian and the guardian is, thus, required to ascertain the relevant wishes and feelings of the child and to consider these in the light of the child's age and understanding. This provision safeguards the idea that no matter what the guardian's views are of the child's wishes and feelings (and he must, of course, put these before the court in his report (r 11(7) and separately in evidence on his own behalf (r 21(3)(d))), the guardian must ensure that the court is appraised of the child's own wishes and feelings. Both guardians and the court may need reminding that while a young or disabled child may be incapable of articulating or expressing wishes, even a very young or severely disabled child can give strong indications of his feelings on certain matters.

The guardian would be expected, in representing what is in the child's best interests to the court, to take into the account the child's physical, emotional and educational needs as set out in s 1(3)(b) of the 1989 Act. As was the case with ascertaining the child's wishes and feelings, the consideration of the child's physical, emotional and educational needs will require extensive consultation by the guardian, where relevant with the child, and with other agencies concerned with the protection of the child. Linked with both of the previous items on the welfare checklist, the guardian is also expected to advise the court on the likely effects on the child of any change in the child's circumstances (s 1(3)(c)) and this, again, involves the guardian checking evidence available from schools, foster-parents, staff in children's homes, others who might have observed changes in the child since the commencement of proceedings and other professionals, such as health professionals, who may be able to give advice on anticipated effects of change in circumstances. The welfare checklist further requires the guardian to report to court in respect of the child's age, sex, background and any characteristics of the child which the guardian may consider relevant and this must include the child's race, language, religion and culture (s 1(3)(d)). Considerable guidance on the importance of the guardian considering such factors is provided in the *Manual of Practice Guidance for Guardians ad Litem and Reporting Officers* (1992, DOH), at pp 68 to 69.

In care and associated proceedings the guardian has a special obligation to consider any harm which the child has suffered or is at risk of suffering and, clearly, in seeking to make recommendations to the court as to the best course of action to be followed in particular proceedings, the guardian will want to consider, very carefully, the evidence being put forward by the local authority with regard to the issue of significant harm and the issue of the experience of similar children (s 1(3)(e)).

The guardian must go on to consider how capable each of the child's parents are and any other person, in relation to whom they consider the question to be relevant, is, of meeting the child's needs (s 1(3)(f)). Clearly, when examining the proposed course of action to be taken by the local authority applicant, and the alternative proposals being put forward by parents or others, the guardian will have to look very closely at the capabilities of those persons who are seeking to have the child returned to them and should be satisfied that the child will not be placed at undue risk while in the care of any person seeking an order under the 1989 Act or any person in whose favour an order might be made.

Finally, the guardian in making recommendations to the court in the form of his report is expected to consider the range of powers available to the court in the proceedings in question and to advise accordingly. It should be noted that where magistrates decide not to follow the recommendations of a guardian ad litem, the case of *S v Oxfordshire County Council* [1993] 1 FLR 452 makes it clear that the magistrates must give reasons for not following the guardian's recommendations. In this particular case, the child had sustained non-accidental injury and the magistrates had made a supervision order as requested by the local authority, although the guardian had contended that a care order was more appropriate. The guardian's appeal against the making of a supervision order was allowed and a care order was substituted.

6.4.2 *Instructing a solicitor*

Unless a solicitor has already been appointed by the court under the provisions of s 41(3) of the 1989 Act, the rules provide that the guardian shall appoint a solicitor to represent the child and give such advice to the child as is appropriate, having regard to his understanding. Provided that the guardian ad litem and the child do not diverge in their views as to the conduct of the case, the guardian should instruct the solicitor representing the child on all matters relevant to the child's interest, including the possibilities for appeal, which arise in the course of the proceedings (FPC(CA 1989)R 1991, r 11(2)). Guardians may find that both they and the solicitors were appointed at a preliminary directions appointment and the guardian may be of the view that the court's choice would not have been their choice. Where the guardian feels this is a problem, r 12(4) provides that the guardian may apply to the court for an order terminating the appointment of the solicitor, although the solicitor and, where he is of sufficient understanding, the child, must be given the opportunity to make representations. It should be noted as a matter of general principle that all solicitors appointed to represent children must be on the Law Society's National Child Care Panel of Solicitors, specially qualified to represent children in proceedings under the 1989 Act. This Panel consists of local lists drawn up by the Law Society of those specially qualified persons, and membership of the Panel is only open to those solicitors who can provide evidence of considerable experience in cases conducted on behalf of children, or those who have attended approved training courses. The Law Society has done a great deal to improve the standard of solicitors representing children by administration of this Panel, and it is a matter of some cause for concern that the Bar does not feel that a similar panel should be introduced for barristers.

6.4.3 *The solicitor and guardian ad litem partnership*

Nevertheless, r 11(2) does make it clear that it is the guardian who is to instruct the solicitor and, indeed, solicitors who are not trained to deal with children at all and who may have little or no experience of contact with disturbed or abused children, will often find the guardian's assistance invaluable. The rule, therefore, envisages a close partnership between the guardian and the solicitor, both working together in what they consider to be the child's best interests. The rules do, however, further provide that if the solicitor considers, having taken into account the views of the guardian and any direction given to the guardian by the court under r 11(3), that the child wishes to give instructions which conflict with those of the guardian and that he is able, having regard to his understanding, to give instructions on his own behalf, then the solicitor must take instructions from the child (see r 12(1)(a) and see further on this the comments of the Court of Appeal in *Re S (A Minor) (Independent Representation)* [1993] 2 FLR 437). The guardian is also supposed to inform the court of this matter (r 11(3)(b)). This situation demonstrates the workings of the unique system of dual representation operating within the structure of care proceedings. The child, where he is old enough to express his own views, thus has a representative to put these forward, ie the solicitor, and he also has a representative concerned with his best interests, ie the guardian ad litem. Where the guardian ad litem and the solicitor disagree and the solicitor determines that he must take instructions instead from the child, the guardian has the right to give evidence on his own behalf when all other parties, except the child, have given their evidence, whether or not he has already been called as a witness by either side (FPC(CA 1989)R 1991, r 21(3)(d)). Nevertheless, where this occurs, the guardian is acting completely on his own and without legal advice, unless the Panel have made arrangements to provide legal advice for guardians who can no longer be said to be assisted by the solicitor for the child. The guardian is not, of course, entitled to legal aid, because legal aid follows the child. The guardian must go on as an officer of the court to present his totally independent view of what he considers to be in the child's best interests. In addition, in practice, whether in divergence situations or where still acting in conjunction with the solicitor for the child, some guardians have, in the past, experienced great difficulty in persuading the courts to allow them to exercise their independent right to give evidence, and, thus, both they and the solicitors must be aware of their rights under the rules.

Whilst guardians are able to look to the *Manual of Practice for Guardians ad Litem and Reporting Officers* (1992, DOH) in guiding them as to the relationship which they should have with the solicitor for the child, solicitors representing children now also have the benefit of a similar guidance (see P King and I Young *The Child as Client: A Handbook for Solicitors who represent Children* (1992, Family Law)).

6.4.4 Attending directions appointments and other hearings

The guardian is under a duty, unless excused by the justices' clerk or the court, to attend all directions appointments in, and hearings of, the relevant proceedings. Since the implementation of the 1989 Act, members of the judiciary and others have stressed that guardians should take a more pro-active role in processing cases through the court. This, it is understood, is also the view of the DOH. Thus, the guardian is expected, under the rules, to advise the court on the following matters (see r 11(4)).

(1) Whether the child is of sufficient understanding for any purpose, including the child's refusal to submit to a medical or psychiatric examination

or other assessment that the court has power to require, direct or order.

(2) The wishes of the child, in respect of any matter relevant to the proceedings, including his attendance at court.

(3) The appropriate forum for the proceedings.

(4) The appropriate timing of the proceedings or any part of them.

(5) The options available to it in respect of the child and the suitability of each such option, including what order should be made in determining the application.

(6) Any other matter concerning which the justices' clerk or the court seeks the guardian's advice or concerning which the guardian feels that the justices' clerk or the court should be informed.

Any advice which is given may be given orally or in writing. The view that the guardian should take a more pro-active involvement relates particularly to the appropriate form for proceedings and to the appropriate timing of proceedings. These are both matters on which, given the guardian's experience, he should be able to give much-needed advice to magistrates' courts and their clerks and, more particularly, since the guardian is charged with the task, by virtue of r 11(1), of ensuring that the child's case is not subjected to delays.

6.4.5 *Advice on parties*

The guardian ad litem is also required by the rules to notify any person whom the guardian believes should be a party to the proceedings and who would be likely, in the guardian's opinion, to safeguard the interests of the child, of that person's right to be joined as a party. The guardian must then inform the justices' clerk or the court of any such notification given, of anyone of whom he intended to notify but was unable to contact, and anyone else whom he believes may wish to be joined to the proceedings (r 11(6)).

6.4.6 *Acceptance of service*

It should be noted that when a solicitor has been appointed for the child and there is no one to accept or serve documents on his behalf, the guardian ad litem must do so and advise the child of the contents of such documents where the child is of sufficient understanding (r 11(8)).

6.4.7 *Investigation*

The rules further provide (r 11(9)), generally, that a guardian is under a duty to carry out such investigations as may be necessary for him to perform his duties. A number of duties are then set out and these include contacting or seeking to interview such persons as the guardian thinks appropriate or as the court might direct. Thus, as well as interviewing the child and any parent or persons with parental responsibility, the guardian or the court may feel it appropriate to consider the possibility of making s 8 orders in favour of members of the extended family. Before the guardian would be able to put such a proposal to the court, or before the court would feel happy in making an order in favour of such a relative or other person, the court would require evidence that such a person has been seen and would wish to consider the views of the guardian ad litem with regard to the capabilities of that particular person. The guardian is further directed that where he inspects records belonging to the local authority he should bring to the attention of the court all such records and documents which may, in his opinion, assist in the proper determination of the proceedings. Under the provisions of s 42 of the 1989 Act, local authorities are now required to provide guardians with copies of any records of, or held by, the local authority which were compiled in connection with the making or proposed making of an application under the 1989 Act with respect to the child concerned, or any other records of, or held by, the local authority which were compiled in connection with any functions referred to the social services committee so far as those records relate to that child. These provisions give the guardian ad litem wide scope, particularly when local authorities often have material on their files which are actually reports or letters from other agencies concerned with the protection of the child. There would appear to be nothing to prevent the guardian taking copies of such material held on the local authority's file. One problem experienced by guardians ad litem in relation to records is in those situations where they feel it desirable to check police or other agencies' records, such as those of the health authority, and the police or other agency are reluctant to reveal details to the guardian. In those situations, the guardian's ability to seek the assistance and directions of the court under rr 11(4) and 14, generally, can prove particularly useful, and the court, of course, may give an undertaking that any information disclosed will be treated in strict confidence and used solely for the purposes of the proceedings involving protection of the child. The guardian is also able, in carrying out his duties under r 11(9), to obtain such professional assistance as is available to him, which he thinks is appropriate or which the court directs him to obtain. This provision would seem to make it unnecessary to have to transfer a case involving a child to the High Court and to provide for the child to be represented by the Official Solicitor as being the only person who can obtain the requisite professional reports (see **6.3.1** above), more especially since the Official Solicitor's office has made it clear that it will give advice to guardians as to the best experts to use in any particular locality.

6.4.8 *Reports for court*

The rules impose a duty on the guardian to file a written report advising on the interests of the child not less than seven days before the date fixed for the final hearing of the proceedings, unless the justices' clerk or the court otherwise directs. The purpose of the report is to assist the court in reaching its decision, once the case has been proved, as to whether any order at all should be made and, if so, which one (r 11(7) and see s 1(4) and (5) of the 1989 Act). Many guardians see the provision of a report for court as their primary task, not least because the courts are focusing such attention on the report. The work surrounding the preparation of that report can take anything between 40 to 80 hours to prepare, which is now estimated to be the average time needed for the performance of the guardian's duties.

The guardian ad litem's report should have been filed with the court at least seven days in advance of the final hearing. In order to comply with r 21, the justices who will be dealing with the case should have read, before the hearing, any documents filed under r 17, which will include the guardian ad litem's report. Inevitably, therefore, the guardian ad litem's report can now be seen as part of the overall evidence to be taken into account in care proceedings. It will certainly have a crucial bearing on the issue of whether making an order would be better for the child than not making an order at all, and, further, in assisting the court to exercise its discretion under s 1(4) of the 1989 Act, which allows the court to choose from the range of orders available under that Act. In addition, however, there may be situations in which the guardian has gleaned some piece of crucial evidence which could be of importance in the adjudicative stage and which may have slipped the attention of the solicitors on all sides or, indeed, of the court. Where this is the case, the guardian should make his position known to the applicant or to the child's solicitor so that his evidence may be called. But where this is not done he still has the right to be given an opportunity to give evidence in the proceedings (r 21(3)(d)).

6.4.9 Other duties

The guardian ad litem, further, has general court duties, by reason of r 11(10) which provides that the guardian ad litem shall provide to the justices' clerk and the court such other assistance as may be required.

6.4.10 Appeals

When the court has finally disposed of the case, the guardian ad litem, acting together with the child's solicitor, is under a duty to consider whether it would be in the child's best interests to make an appeal against the making of, or refusal to make, any particular order (s 94 of the 1989 Act). Where the case is heard in the family proceedings court, the appeal will lie to the High Court Family Division, and where the case is heard in the county court or in the High Court, the appeal lies to the Court of Appeal, Civil Division (FPC(CA 1989)R 1991, r 11(2), and see Form CHA 30; and see also *Fig 1*

Court Structure Diagram in Chapter 3). Where the guardian ad litem and the solicitor consider that it will be in the child's best interests to appeal, a notice of appeal can be lodged with the relevant court on behalf of the child. The guardian ad litem, however, may consider that an appeal is inappropriate and yet the solicitor, after consultation with his client, the child, may take the view that such an appeal should be lodged. In this case, the solicitor is able to take the instructions of the child if the solicitor deems the child old enough to give such instructions and an appeal can then be lodged on behalf of the child by the solicitor.

The issue of whether the child is of sufficient understanding to instruct a solicitor and the duty of the solicitor to take instruction exclusively from the child, came up for consideration in *Re H (A Minor) (Care Proceedings: Child's Wishes)* [1993] 1 FLR 440. In this case, Thorpe J ruled (at p 450) that:

'in cases involving intelligent, articulate but disturbed children it is necessary for the court to apply rr 11 and 12 of the rules realistically to ensure that not only is the professional voice of the guardian ad litem heard through an advocate's presentation but that also the wishes and feelings of the child, however limited the horizon, should be similarly presented.'

He pointed out that a child suffering from a mental disability or a psychiatric disorder might not have sufficient understanding to instruct a solicitor but, in this particular case, by the time of the substantive hearing, the evidence was that the child was not suffering from such a disorder, although there was some doubt as to whether the child was actually able to give coherent and consistent instructions. Thorpe J pointed out that 'any question as to the child's ability in this respect, should be the subject of specific expert opinion'. He found, as a matter of fact, that 'the child did in fact in this case give instructions to the solicitor but the solicitor fell into error in not giving proper weight to the terms of r 12 and in failing to take his instructions exclusively from the child'. Thorpe J, therefore, found that the child had not been properly represented at the hearing and this involved a fundamental forfeiture of a right of the child, which required the appellate court to exercise its discretion as to whether or not to order a rehearing. In fact, in the circumstances of this case, Thorpe J found, after examination, that it was inconceivable that the magistrates would have been dissuaded from the course they inevitably took, however ably and persuasively the child's disturbed and distorted views had been presented. In the circumstances of the case, therefore, he dismissed the appeal. As well as the child's right to appeal against the making of a care or supervision order, it should be noted that the persons who are, or who have been, made parties to the proceedings in addition to the child, such as parents and, perhaps, grandparents, will also have a right of appeal against the making of any order (see s 94 of the 1989 Act).

6.4.11 Further action by the guardian ad litem

In certain circumstances where a court refuses to make a care or supervision order, and the applicant is determined that it is not going to pursue the matter by lodging an appeal, the question has to be asked as to whether the guardian ad litem has any locus standi to take the matter any further. It would appear clear now that as a result of the ability of any party to the proceedings to lodge an appeal, the guardian could, acting together with the solicitor, take the view that an appeal should be lodged on behalf of the child (see **6.19** below). Since implementation of the 1989 Act, guardians ad litem have, together with the solicitor for the child, lodged a number of appeals both against the making of and the refusal to make an order (see *S v Oxfordshire County Council* [1993] 1 FLR 452 and *Re B (Minors) (Care: Contact: Local Authority's Plans)* [1993] 1 FLR 543). Where, however, the child is quite happy with the outcome of the proceedings and instructs the solicitor not to consider making an appeal, it is a moot point as to whether the guardian could, of his own volition, lodge an appeal against the refusal to make an order. The 1989 Act itself leaves the matter open, with s 94(1) merely stating that 'an appeal shall lie to the High Court against the making, by a magistrates' court, of any order under this Act; or any refusal by a magistrates' court to make such an order'. The relevant rules of court are also peculiarly silent on the issue of who has the right to lodge an appeal against the making of an order.

The issue of the extent to which guardians could apply for orders under s 8 was discussed in *Re M (Prohibited Steps Order: Application for Leave)* [1993] 1 FLR 275, where the guardian had been appointed to act as such in relation to a teenage girl who had run away from home and who had been made the subject of an emergency protection order. The local authority decided to take no further action in the case and, as a result, the guardian applied to a family proceedings court for leave to apply for a prohibited steps order so as to prevent the girl having contact with her father. Apparently, the local authority had reached its decision not to pursue care proceedings at a child protection conference, which the guardian had not attended. It had been decided, instead, that following the recommendation of the conference, the girl should be accommodated with the foster-parents in whose care she had been placed as a result of the emergency protection order. The guardian, however, wished to challenge the local authority's decision, and to invite the court to prohibit contact between the girl and her father, to make an interim care order and to direct an investigation under s 37 of the 1989 Act. The case raised two important issues. First, how long is a guardian ad litem, once appointed, entitled to act in that capacity? Secondly, what should be the attitude of the court in dealing with applications by persons seeking leave under the 1989 Act, s 10(9) to apply for a s 8 order? Johnson J, in ruling that the guardian had no capacity to have a continuing role in relation to the girl in the absence of continuing care or associated proceedings, followed a long line of pre-1989 Act authority. (See *Re T (Minors) (Care Proceedings: Wardship)* [1989] 1 FLR 313, CA; *A v Berkshire County Council* [1989] 1 FLR 273.) Johnson J's ruling, that the guardian ad litem's role came to an end with the proceedings in respect of which he had been appointed, followed the policy line of the earlier decisions. (This is an important point, of course, because, whereas the guardian, as guardian, will be publicly funded, the same person, applying as a private citizen concerned for the child's welfare, will not be so supported.) In answer to the second question as to how the court should consider an application for leave to apply for s 8 orders, this was not a step which the guardian had to take since the court has power of its own motion in any family proceedings to make s 8 orders without an application having been made (see s 10(1)(b) of the 1989 Act). The issue of the continuing role of the guardian ad litem also came up for consideration in the case of *Kent County Council v C* [1993] 1 FLR 308. In that case, the local authority was seeking a care order with the intention of attempting a rehabilitation of the child with her mother and stepfather. In the light of evidence from an eminent psychiatrist, the guardian ad litem opposed the rehabilitation programme and invited the magistrates to make an order for no contact with the child by her mother or stepfather under s 34(2) of the 1989 Act. The magistrates ruled that although they could have made such an order, they would not do so but instead, because of everyone's concern, they made a direction that the guardian ad litem continue to be involved in the case to assess the progress of rehabilitation. On appeal to the High Court it was confirmed that the justices could have made an order for no contact if it had been proved that such contact was not in the best interests of the child but they had *no* power to add a direction to a care order that the guardian ad litem be allowed to continue with his involvement with the child. The addition of such a direction, said the High Court, was a fetter on the local authority's plans, authority and responsibility. For a different approach to whether the guardian ad litem should be involved, where the court made what was, in effect, an interim contact order so that the guardian would continue to monitor the effects of contact on the child, see *Re B (A Minor) (Care Order: Review)* [1993] 1 FLR 421.

6.5 Other procedural issues

6.5.1 Attendance at directions appointments and hearings

In the same way as the guardian ad litem is expected to attend directions appointments or hearings, other parties are required to attend such hearings, unless the clerk or the court otherwise directs (FPC (CA 1989) 1991, r 16(1)).

It is further provided that proceedings may take place in the absence of any party, including the child (see **6.6** below), where the court considers it in the interests of the child, having regard to the matters to be discussed or the likely evidence to be given, and the party concerned is represented by a guardian ad litem and/or a solicitor in the case of a child, or a solicitor in the case of other parties.

The rules further provide that where the applicant appears for a directions appointment or for a hearing, but one or more of the respondents does not, the clerk may proceed with the hearing or appointment in the absence of that respondent, provided it is proved, to the satisfaction of the court, that the respondent received reasonable notice of the hearing and the court is satisfied that the circumstances of the case justified proceeding with the hearing as happened in the case of *Re SW (A Minor) (Care Proceedings)* [1993] 2 FLR 609. In the first 18 months of the operation of the 1989 Act the non-attendance of certain parties at directions hearings prompted extensive use of this power by the clerks since, in many cases, to do otherwise would lead to delay in the particular child's case. Where one or more of the respondents appear at such hearings but the applicant does not, the court may refuse the application or, if sufficient evidence has previously been received, proceed in the absence of the applicant. If neither applicant nor respondents appear, the court may refuse the application. The court is given the power, when hearing proceedings in relation to children, to determine that, in the interests of the child, the proceedings should go on in private when only the officers of the court, the parties, their legal representatives and such other persons as the court specifies may attend (FPC(CA 1989)1991 R, r 16(7) generally). In the High Court and county court, hearings or directions appointments will take place in chambers unless the court otherwise directs (FPR 1991, r 4.16(7)).

6.5.2 Evidence

There are a number of new provisions dealing with evidence across three tiers of courts concerned with child protection proceedings, which have been introduced by the rules and the 1989 Act. (The burden of proof and the requisite standard of proof, together with the difficult nature of some types of evidence will be considered in detail later under the main discussion on evidence in care proceedings.) Under the new provisions, documentary evidence in the form of affidavits has been replaced in the High Court and county court by written statements of evidence, which are also introduced into the family proceedings courts for the first time (FPR 1991, r 4.17 and FPC(CA 1989)R 1991, r 17). The rules on documentary evidence are, thus, common across all three courts and will again facilitate the process of transfer where this becomes necessary. Under the rules, a party must file and serve on the parties and on any guardian ad litem of whose appointment he has had notice, written statements of the substance of the oral evidence which the party intends to adduce at a hearing or directions appointment (FPC

(CA 1989)R 1991, r 17(1)(a)). Such written statements must be signed and dated by the person and contain a declaration that the maker of the statement believes it to be true and understands that it may be placed before the court. He must further file and serve copies of any documents including expert reports upon which he intends to rely (FPC(CA 1989)R 1991, r 17(1)(b)). Such statements and copies of documents must be filed and served at or by such time as the court directs or, in the absence of a direction, before the hearing or appointment. Subject to the direction of the court about the timing of statements, a party may also file and serve a supplementary statement. Failure to comply with these rules means that the party cannot adduce evidence or seek to rely upon a document in respect of which he has failed to reply, unless the court grants him leave (FPC(CA 1989)R 1991, r 17(3)).

The use of expert evidence arising from examination of the child is very strictly controlled. As discussed in Chapter 4, special directions have to be sought from the court in emergency protection order, child assessment order or interim care order proceedings where it is proposed that the child should be medically or psychiatrically examined or otherwise assessed. The rules of court further reinforce this in providing that no one may, without the leave of the court, cause the child to be assessed in such ways for the purpose of the preparation of expert evidence for use in the proceedings (FPC(CA 1989)R 1991, r 18(1)). An application must, unless the court otherwise directs, be served on all parties to the proceedings and on the guardian ad litem (FPC(CA 1989)R 1991, r 18(2)). Where such leave has not been given, no evidence arising out of an examination or assessment may be adduced without the leave of the court (FPC(CA 1989)R 1991, r 18(3)). It is the clear intention of the provision in the rules, as well as those provisions in the 1989 Act restricting the carrying out of medical, psychiatric or other assessments, to prevent what was referred to after the Cleveland affair as system abuse of the child. Thus, it is well known that where the local authority intends to bring psychiatric evidence to support its case, parents will seek to bring in another expert in order to dispute the expert evidence being produced by the local authority. The court should, therefore, consider very carefully whether assessments might profitably be carried out by an expert independently appointed by the court on the advice of the guardian ad litem or whether both experts being employed to prepare reports could usefully conduct their assessments together.

Another difficulty which arises in this context is that there is always some doubt as to who is an 'expert' in child care matters. Guardians ad litem are generally regarded as such, but that status has also been accorded to child psychologists, paediatricians and child psychiatrists. One of the points to emerge from the Cleveland Inquiry was that the paediatricians involved were not necessarily 'experts' in the field, and their diagnoses were contradicted by other more experienced paediatricians and police surgeons. As experienced professionals will testify, there is no one qualification – other than qualitative experience – which readily serves to demonstrate unusual insight or expertise in the field of diagnosis of child sexual abuse and no single professional should be expected to bear the sole responsibility of diagnosis in such cases (see, further, Chapter 5 above). Hence one should regard the views and opinions of experts not only with an open mind but also with some circum-spection.

As far as the duties and role of the expert are concerned, judicial guidance has been given by Cazalet J in *Re R (A Minor) (Expert's Evidence) (Note)* [1991] 1 FLR 291 at p 292:

> 'Expert witnesses are in a privileged position; indeed, only experts are permitted to give an opinion in evidence. Outside the legal field the court itself has no expertise and for that reason frequently has to rely on the evidence of experts. Such experts must express only *opinions which they genuinely hold and which are not biased in favour of one particular party.* Opinions can, of course, differ and indeed quite frequently experts who have expressed their objective and honest opinions will differ, but such differences are usually within a legitimate area of disagreement. On occasion, and because they are acting on opposing sides, each may give his opinion from different basic facts. This of itself is likely to produce a divergence' (emphasis added).

In the case itself, which was heard over seven days, the court heard 10 experts, in an attempt to determine whether a small child's physical injuries were non-accidental in origin. Cazalet J went on to summarise the following points.

(1) The expert should not mislead by omissions. He should consider all the material facts in reaching his conclusions and must not omit to consider the material facts which could detract from his concluded opinion.

(2) If experts look for a report on factors which tend to support a particular proposition or case, their reports should still:

    (a) provide a straightforward, not a misleading opinion;

    (b) be objective and not omit factors which do not support their opinion; and

    (c) be properly researched.

(3) If the expert's opinion is not properly researched because he considers that insufficient data is available, he must say so and indicate that his opinion is no more than a provisional one.

(4) In certain circumstances an expert may find that he has to give an opinion adverse to his client. Alternatively, if, contrary to the appropriate prac-tice, an expert does provide a report which is other than wholly objective – that is one which seeks to 'promote' a particular case – the report should make this clear. However, such an approach should be avoided, because it would:

    (a) be an abuse of the position of an expert's proper function and privilege; and

    (b) render the report an argument, and not an opinion.

Objectivity of the evidence in its presentation and analysis is clearly another important factor to be borne in mind. In the case itself Cazalet J found that where two experts (a consultant paediatrician and a neuro-radiologist) had not prepared their reports with sufficient diligence, thoroughness or objectivity, this persuaded him that their evidence was unreliable.

In certain circumstances, an expert's opinion may be taken into account as indicative of a child's state of mind (see **6.18.4** below).

The court or the justices' clerk or the proper officer of the court is required, under the rules, to keep a note of the substance of the oral evidence given at a hearing or directions appointment (FPC(CA 1989)R 1991, r 20).

By s 96(2) of the 1989 Act, a court, in civil proceedings, may hear the unsworn evidence of a child if, in its opinion, the child understands that it is his duty to speak the truth and he has sufficient understanding to justify his evidence being heard, even though the court is of the opinion that he would not understand the nature of an oath (s 96(1) of the 1989 Act). These provisions bring civil proceedings into line with criminal proceedings. (See Children and Young Persons Act 1933, s 38 (as amended by the Criminal Justice Act 1988, s 34) and see, further, Chapter 7.)

The 1989 Act further provides the Lord Chancellor with power to make orders for the admissibility of evidence which would otherwise be inadmissible under any rule of law relating to hearsay (s 96(3)). The rule of law being referred to here is the general principle that assertions by persons other than the witness who is testifying on oath are inadmissible as evidence of the facts asserted (see *Cross on Evidence* (Butterworths)). The rationale for this rule is that such evidence is likely to be unreliable as proof of a fact which is best proved by either the *direct* testimony of the person who actually experienced the act, or by the person who actually witnessed the act itself. Otherwise, it was asserted that such statements would amount to someone merely repeating what someone else saw or what someone else experienced. Under the previous law most forms of hearsay were rendered inadmissible in the course of care proceedings although a number of very limited exceptions were allowed in order to get the best evidence before the court (see the Evidence Act 1932 and *Humberside County Council v R* [1977] 1 WLR 1251). Given that the 1989 Act represents a clear attempt on the part of the law to treat care proceedings more as inquisitorial than adversarial, it was not surprising that it should give the Lord Chancellor the power to make orders providing for the admissibility of hearsay evidence. This was done to a very limited degree first of all in 1990, but in 1991 the Lord Chancellor issued the Children (Admissibility of Hearsay Evidence) Order 1991, which provides that in civil proceedings before the High Court, county court or family proceedings courts, evidence given in connection with the upbringing, maintenance or welfare of a child shall be admissible notwithstanding any rule of law relating to hearsay. The basis for challenging hearsay evidence in care proceedings was, thus, removed. Whilst the evidence is now admissible, this will leave open the issue of credibility which will have to be determined by the court, which may decide to ignore the hearsay evidence as being too remote. Particularly, where the hearsay evidence is that of a child not giving evidence in the proceedings directly, the court will wish to satisfy itself as to the circumstances in which the evidence was given, the age of the child and the nature of the questioning used to elicit the evidence. One major advantage in the relaxation with regard to the rules of hearsay evidence, however, is that all those giving evidence no longer feel that they may be tripped up at every turn by lawyers when they are giving evidence about the course of their investigations into circumstances which suggested that a child was suffering, or was at risk of suffering, significant harm.

The relaxation of the rules governing hearsay represented by the Children (Admissibility of Hearsay Evidence) Order 1991 was extensive, encompassing evidence given in any family proceedings concerning the upbringing, maintenance or welfare of a child under the 1989 Act. Since the 1989 Act has two provisions designating proceedings as family proceedings, one of which is restrictive (s 8(3) and (4)) and the other all-inclusive (s 92(2)), there was some confusion initially as to whether hearsay evidence would be freely admissible in all proceedings under the 1989 Act – most particularly of concern being applications for child assessment orders in the magistrates' courts and in secure accommodation proceedings. This was, however, clarified in the case of *R v Oxfordshire County Council* [1992] 1 FLR 648, where Douglas Brown J stated that s 92(2) of the 1989 Act took pre-eminence over s 8(3) and, since it provided that proceedings under the 1989 Act should be treated as family proceedings in relation to magistrates' courts, the Children (Admissibility of Hearsay Evidence) Order 1991 would apply and, thus, hearsay evidence could be put before the court in child assessment order proceedings. The 1991 Order has now been superseded and revoked by the Children (Admissibility of Hearsay Evidence) Order 1993, SI 1993/621. This order extends the scope of the 1991 Order even further to include all civil proceedings, thus clearly covering proceedings for child assessment orders and secure accommodation proceedings, and all other civil proceedings involving courts making decisions which will affect a child's upbringing, maintenance or welfare (see, further, **6.18.2** below).

The 1989 Act goes on to provide that the privilege against self-incrimination does not apply to proceedings concerning care or supervision orders under Part IV of that Act or to proceedings under Part V (s 98(1)). In such proceedings, no person will be excused from giving evidence on any matter or answering any question put to him in the course of his giving evidence on the ground that to do so might incriminate him or his spouse of an offence. This provision is designed to ensure that the court in this child's case has the best evidence before it. To the frustration of individual police officers, the 1989 Act goes on to provide that where a statement or admission is made in civil proceedings it cannot, however, be used against the witness or his spouse other than in perjury proceedings (s 98(2)). The justification behind this approach is to ensure that at least children in individual cases are protected if parents or other carers or perpetrators of abuse are encouraged to give evidence without fear of the evidence being used in criminal proceedings. Nevertheless, its actual reception in the care proceedings should ensure that the court is able to make a finding that the child has suffered or is likely to suffer significant harm.

6.6 Attendance of the child at hearings

In contrast with the old law relating to care proceedings, where children were required to be brought before the court, the 1989 Act provides that the court has a discretion as to whether to order that the child be present in court at any stage of the proceedings. The relevant rules of court provide that proceedings may take place in the absence of the child if the court considers it in the interests of the child having regard to matters to be discussed or the evidence likely to be given, and the child is represented by a guardian or solicitor. Before making any such direction the rules require that the court should give the guardian ad litem, the solicitor for the child and, if he is of sufficient understanding, the child, an opportunity to make representations. Many would now accept that where a child is represented by both a solicitor and guardian it may constitute an unnecessary trauma for the child to be present in court during a hearing for care or supervision orders. In some cases, however, the child may wish to be present and it is clear that not all judges are entirely happy with the presence of children in court. This was evidently so in the case of *Re C (A Minor) (Care: Child's Wishes)* [1993] 1 FLR 832 where a 13-year-old girl had been present throughout the proceedings and was further present on a subsequent appeal to the High Court. The guardian ad litem had followed the provisions in the court rules but the girl had indicated a clear desire to be present and the magistrates had exercised their discretion under s 95(1) to allow the child to be present in court at their hearing. The child was present in court throughout the hearing before the justices, save for brief intervals when evidence was being given which the child's guardian thought it better for her not to hear. None of the other parties had raised any objections at this stage nor in the appeal. Notwithstanding this, Waite J ruled that the presence of children should not be encouraged to develop into settled practice. He further directed that guardians ad litem who arranged for children to be present at hearings should consider their reasons for doing so carefully and be prepared to give them in court if asked. Given that the philosophy which underpinned the 1989 Act was that of according increasing recognition and respect for the ascertainable wishes and feelings of children, this seems quite an extraordinary direction and one which suggests that it is the judges rather than the child who find the child's presence during court proceedings uncomfortable. No one would suggest that a child should ever be forced to be present in court but where the young person has indicated to the guardian ad litem a very clear desire to be in court during the proceedings or a wish to see the judge privately, such a request should be very carefully considered by the court. In the latter situation it must, however, be made clear to the child that even though he may see the judge in private, the confidentiality of such discussions cannot be guaranteed.

6.7 Withdrawal of an application for a care or supervision order

The leave of the court is required before any application for a care or supervision order may be withdrawn (FPR 1991, r 4.5(1) and FPC(CA 1989) R 1991, r 5(1)). The person seeking leave to withdraw an application must file and serve on the parties a written request for leave setting out the reasons for the request, unless the request is being made orally in court and the parties and guardian ad litem or welfare officer are present. Where this is the case, if the parties consent and if the guardian ad litem (if he is involved in the case) has had an opportunity to make written representations, the court can grant the request if it thinks fit. It is clear from the case of *Re F (A Minor) (Care Order: Withdrawal of Application)* [1993] 2 FLR 9 that under this rule the guardian ad litem must be present personally and cannot be deemed to be present solely because the child's legal representative was present. In *Re F* the family proceedings court had failed to give proper notice to the guardian ad litem of the local authority's application to withdraw the proceedings. The High Court found that the magistrates were in error and should not have given leave for the application to be withdrawn on the material before them. Hollings J further gave guidance on how courts should consider an application to withdraw. He emphasised that an application for withdrawal of care or supervision order proceedings had to be considered *as carefully* by the court as any other application for an order in respect of a child under the Act. He stated that there was a statutory duty upon the court to have regard to the welfare of the child, and this included the duty to hear expert evidence from the guardian ad litem prepared in accordance with the guardian ad litem's statutory duty, before the court could allow proceedings to be withdrawn. In addition, in this case, the magistrates had failed to comply with FPC(CA 1989)R 1991, r 21, which requires the court to give adequate reasons for their decision. Hollings J held that the reasons given in this particular case were totally inadequate and did not set out the magistrates' findings of fact as required nor did they set out the basis of the magistrates' decision by referring to those facts. Hollings J directed that the matter should be remitted for rehearing by another court and that, in the circumstances of the case, the right court to rehear the matter was the county court. It was also noted that upon hearing of the appeal, the justices' clerk, on behalf of the magistrates, had attempted to communicate with the High Court to

explain their decision or otherwise to amplify their reasons. The judge emphasised that it would be quite wrong to allow magistrates to supplement reasons
already given by further correspondence with the court.

Where the court does grant an application to withdraw, the justices' clerk
or the proper officer as appropriate, must inform the parties and the guardian
ad litem or the welfare officer accordingly. The court may, instead of granting
the request, determine that there be a hearing of the request. In the case of
the High Court or the county court, the court can direct the date to be fixed
for the hearing and the proper officer must then give at least seven days'
notice of the date fixed to the parties, the guardian ad litem and the welfare
officer, where relevant. Where the request was made to the family proceedings court, the justices' clerk can decide upon and fix a date for a hearing,
giving the same notice (see, generally, FPR 1991, r 4.5 and FPC(CA 1989)
R 1991, r 5).

6.8 The various stages in proceedings for a care or supervision order

Whilst the various stages in proceedings for a care or supervision order may
have been rehearsed in outline when applying for interim orders (see Chapter
4) once the final hearing is underway, the applicant must prove on the balance
of probabilities that:

(1) the child concerned is suffering or is likely to suffer significant harm;
    (often referred to as the first limb of the care grounds);

(2) that the harm or likelihood of harm, is attributable to:

    (a) the care given to the child, or likely to be given to him if the order
        were not made, not being what it would be reasonable to expect a
        parent to give to him; or

    (b) the child being beyond parental control (this is often referred to
        as the second limb of the care grounds).

In addition to the court being satisfied that these two conditions are being
met, it must further be satisfied that:

(3) making an order in respect of the child will be better for the child than
    making no order at all (s 1(5) the 'positive advantage' principle). The
    court must satisfy itself that such is the case by applying the welfare
    principle as informed by the welfare checklist.

Where the court is satisfied that making an order will be better for the
child than making no order at all, it must then consider the range of options
open to it under the 1989 Act (s 1(4) and see also *Humberside County Council
v B* [1993] 1 FLR 257). The court will no doubt have been considering
throughout the course of the presentation of evidence on both sides, whether
the making of a care or supervision order would be appropriate or whether

the making of orders under s 8 would be more likely to achieve what is in the best interests of the child, as, for example, in *C v Solihull Metropolitan Borough Council* [1993] 1 FLR 290. The court will have a range of evidence before it including, possibly, experts' reports, the views of the parents or other carers of the child, the views of the child as represented by the child's solicitor, and the views of the guardian ad litem as expressed in his/her report, which may have been amplified in the course of cross-examination. In many cases the courts may find the guardian ad litem's report to be persuasive, but in others it will be prepared to overrule the guardian ad litem's recommendations.

It should be noted that the court may find both the two limbs of s 31 to be proved but may decide that making an order is not in the child's best interests. This may be because in child protection cases, as *Working Together* points out, the process of negotiation and working in partnership together should be ongoing, even while proceedings are underway and, by the time the proceedings get to a final hearing it may be that that process has resulted in an entirely satisfactory voluntary arrangement between the child's family and social services, such that it is not necessary to obtain a court order. The applicant will have to be convinced that the child will be better protected under this sort of arrangement and to argue his case before the court, since the court may have legitimate concerns for the safety of the child under voluntary arrangements and it is the court which has to be satisfied that it is right not to make an order.

6.8.1 Significant harm

The condition as to significant harm laid down in the first limb of s 31(2) is drawn with reference to the child concerned in the particular case so that the court in care or supervision order proceedings must look at the position, characteristics and needs of each particular child. This is reflected in the requirement that separate forms of application must be completed for each child, and the criteria met, before an order would be made in respect of each individual child (s 32(1)(a) and (b)).

The first limb of s 31(2) covers situations both where the child *is* suffering or *is likely to* suffer significant harm. The use of the term 'is suffering' is intended to concentrate attention on present or continuing conditions but problems which have been temporarily ameliorated since the commencement of proceedings or even since the involvement of the local authority with the family, could still found an application. Such was the case in *Northamptonshire County Council v S and Others* [1993] 1 FLR 554 where the children of the family had suffered minor non-accidental injuries early in 1991 while living with their mother and the father of one of the children. In June 1991 the children had been placed in voluntary care and, following an assessment indicating that the children were at risk with the mother, in December 1991 the local authority applied for a care order under s 31. The father and the paternal grandmother then each applied for a residence order but the family proceedings court made a care order in respect of the child. The father appealed, submitting that it had not been shown that the children were suffering significant harm at the time of the hearing and, he asserted, that the court should not have found that harm was attributable to the care being given to the children, because the grandmother would provide care which would not cause harm. Ewbank J, in dismissing the appeal, stated that 'the use of the present tense in s 31(2) could relate to the period immediately before the process of protecting the child was put into motion. That meant that the court had to consider the position immediately before a protection order, if there was one; or an interim care order, if that was the initiation of the protection; or when a child went into voluntary care'. It should be noted that following the implementation of the 1989 Act in such a situation the children would now be described as being accommodated by the local authority under s 20 and, thus, when giving effect to the phrase 'is suffering significant harm' this could apply, inter alia, to the position immediately before the child was accommodated under s 20. Applications relating solely to past events could, therefore, not found an application unless linked in some way to the present evidence by some harm continuing or being likely to continue (as was the case in *Re B (A Minor) (Care Order: Criteria)* [1993] 1 FLR 815).

As to relying on the future possibility of harm as indicated by 'likely to suffer significant harm' the court in *Newham London Borough v AG* [1993] 1 FLR 281 indicated that it would be wrong to equate the phrase 'likely to suffer' with 'on the balance of probabilities'. The Court of Appeal emphasised in this case that the court, in such circumstances, was not applying a test to events which had happened in the past, and deciding on the evidence, on the balance of probabilities, whether an event had in fact happened. Rather, in considering the phrase 'likely to suffer' the court was looking to the future and had to assess the risk. When looking to the future, all the court could do was to evaluate the risk. The Court of Appeal found that in the present case the judge had to make an assessment of the future risk to the child in the light of the evidence before him. He had found that there was a real significant risk of the child suffering significant harm if he did not make a care order and his conclusion was amply supported by the evidence given by the mother's psychiatrist as to the mother's unstable and unpredictably violent psychiatric condition. Thus, in compliance with the correct procedure, when relying on the future possibility of harm as indicated by the phrase 'likely to suffer significant harm', the applicant must seek to show that there would be a greater risk to the child in leaving him with his family than by seeking his removal. As was seen in the *Newham* case, when balancing these risks, the court will have to decide, on all the evidence, including experts' reports and guardian ad litem reports, which constitutes the greater risk. A case involving difficult issues of risk assessment was that of *Re D (A Minor) (Care or Supervision Order)* [1993] 2 FLR 423, where the father of a baby had previously been imprisoned for offences relating to cruelty to children some nine years earlier when he was living with his first wife. One child, a two-month-old baby, had suffered a fractured skull and many other injuries for which the father was thought to be responsible. The father had returned to his first wife after serving his sentence of imprisonment but then left and, in due course, started living with the another woman. It was their baby, born in January 1992, who was the subject of the present proceedings. All the expert professional opinion in the case recognised the risks for the baby posed by the father but he, his partner and her family denied that he constituted a risk to the child as he had denied responsibility for the other baby's death. Despite the views of the local authority that a supervision order would allow for proper monitoring, the court held that the baby's protection was *decisive* in deciding that there should be a care order.

Whilst the view had been expressed by the *Review of Child Care Law* (1985, DHSS) that in cases of emotional or psychological harm the approach which would be taken would be that which would prevent an unwarranted intervention (at para 15.18), the courts seem to have taken a much more robust view regardless of the species of the apprehended harm. Thus, Scott-Baker J, in *Re H (A Minor) (Section 37 Direction)* [1993] 2 FLR 541, stated that 'the likelihood of the harm is not confined to present or near future but applies to the ability of a parent or carer to meet the emotional needs of a child for years ahead'.

The harm suffered or apprehended must be 'significant' and where this turns on the child's health or development, they should be compared with the health or development which could be expected of a similar child (s 31(10)). As far as the word 'significant' is concerned, the *Review of Child Care Law* (1985, DHSS) stated that minor shortcomings in the health care provided, or minor deficits in physical, psychological or social development, should not give rise to compulsory intervention unless they are having, or are likely to have, serious and lasting effects upon the child (at para 15.15). The Lord Chancellor has also said that 'unless there is evidence that a child is being, or is likely to be, positively harmed because of a failure in the family, the State, whether in the guise of a local authority or court should not interfere' (Joseph Jackson Memorial Lecture (139) NLJ 505 at p 508). In the early days of the operation of the 1989 Act, however, there were widespread signs that both local authorities and the courts were placing an over-emphasis on the words 'significant' and were failing to make a care or supervision order in situations in which they were obviously required. In the *Newham* case (above) it is noteworthy that Sir Stephen Brown, the President of the Family Division, in response to concerns about failures of social services to take proceedings and of courts to make orders, stated that 'it was to be hoped that in approaching cases under the Children Act 1989, courts would not be invited to perform in every case a strict legalistic analysis of the statutory meaning of s 31'. He stated that the words of the statute must be considered, but they were not intended to be unduly restrictive when the evidence clearly indicated that a certain course of action should be taken in order to protect a child.

6.8.2 Comparison with a similar child

When looking at whether harm suffered by a child is significant, comparisons have to be made with a similar child (s 31(10)). The comparison to be made with a similar child is not a problem-free one, since it is required that a comparison is made between this subjective child with that hypothetically similar child. This issue came up for consideration by the courts in the case of *Re O (A Minor) (Care Order: Education: Procedure)* [1992] 2 FLR 7, which concerned a girl aged 15 years and 4 months old, who had persistently truanted from school for over three years. Ewbank J had supported magistrates who had made a care order on the basis that the girl's intellectual and social development was suffering and was likely to suffer, and that the harm which she was suffering from or was likely to suffer from was significant. It was further urged on behalf of the girl that, in determining whether the harm was significant, the comparison which had to be made was with a 'similar child', and there was no evidence that she had suffered harm compared with a similar child. Ewbank J took a very robust view of what constituted a similar child in such circumstances. He stated that in his view 'similar child' meant 'a child of equivalent intellectual and social development, who has gone to school, and not merely an average child who may or may not be at school' (at p 12). Clearly if the child is disabled in some way, and that has affected his health and development, the court must ask itself what state of health and development could be expected of a child with a similar disability. As to whether 'similar' commits any consideration being given to the child's background, this is doubtful since, according to the Lord Chancellor, 'the care that a parent gives to his child must relate to the circumstances attributable to that child in the sense of physical, mental and emotional characteristics' (*Hansard* (HL) Deb Committee, Vol 503, col 355). The child's background, however, may be considered relevant once the care conditions are satisfied when the court is considering whether or not to make an order (s 1(3)(d)).

6.8.3 Proof that the harm or likelihood of harm is attributable to an absence of reasonable care being offered to the child or likely to be offered to the child

When looking at whether the care given to the child, or likely to be given to him if an order were not made, is not what it would be reasonable to expect the parent to give, the type of care is not further defined in the 1989 Act.

Clearly, if harm can encompass, as it does, the impairment of mental, physical, emotional, intellectual and social development (s 31(9)), 'care' can then be defined in the same way and may include the lack of emotional care demonstrated by a complete disregard for the child's feelings. This was indeed a point made by Douglas Brown J in *Re B (A Minor) (Care Order: Criteria)* [1993] 1 FLR 815, where he stated that care for these purposes goes 'beyond physical care and includes emotional care which a reasonable parent would give a child'. He went on to state that 'in the case of a child who has been sexually abused, that reasonable emotional care includes listening to the child and being able to monitor the child's words and actions so that a professional assessment can be carried out'. In *Re B* the child had been placed with foster-parents who had been specially trained to deal with children who had been victims of sexual abuse and the judge felt it important that she remained with those foster-parents who were giving her the right degree of emotional care such as one would reasonably expect from a parent.

Again, in *Re C* [1992] 2 FCR 65, Thorpe J found that while there were doubts as to whether the father had sexually abused the first five children in the family, there was undoubtedly evidence that they had been sexually abused and whilst it would be wrong to make a specific finding that the father had abused the children, it would be equally wrong to ignore the risk the father might pose to the sixth child. He also found that there was a catalogue of inadequate parenting of the elder children, that there was evidence of physical abuse and of emotional abuse and that the totality of the evidence established the local authority's case on both the first and second limb in relation to the first five children. The issue which he then had to consider was whether the parents' performance in respect of the five eldest children was so inadequate that it would be inappropriate to expose the sixth child to the risk of repetition. As he pointed out, this involved a balancing exercise and the balance was a fine one. Thorpe J indicated that expert evidence of experienced child psychiatrists and developmental paediatricians would have been particularly valuable. He felt that in this case the decision was not so plain that the past record outweighed the mitigating circumstances that could be urged for the parents in that they had been very young when they embarked on family life, and the accepted failures were almost inevitable given the size of the family with which they had burdened themselves. In the circumstances, the chances for natural parenting, although slender, deserved further investigation by an independent expert and the case was adjourned for this to take place.

As was pointed out earlier, this condition also has a prospective element so that even where the child is being provided with accommodation at the time any proceedings are instituted, the court can look to a previous lack of care and of the likelihood of this being repeated if the child is returned to the parents' care (see *Northamptonshire County Council v S* (above)). Furthermore, if other children have remained in the family setting and there are now concerns about them, the care of the child dealt with in earlier proceedings may become relevant when considering the likelihood of harm to them and the standard of care which they may have received. It is, however, important to remember that each child's case must be considered individually.

Whilst the test is subjective in looking at the child, it is clearly objective in looking at the standard of care offered by the parents. Thus, it must be an objectively reasonable standard of care offered by the hypothetical reasonable parent. The parent cannot rely on his or her personal inadequacies to argue that he or she could not provide a better standard of care because parents are expected to seek assistance from the local authority to provide the requisite degree of care (see Chapter 3, and Part III of the 1989 Act, generally). Where the parent has failed to avail himself or herself of such services and the child has suffered significant harm, the local authority would be justified in intervening through care or supervision order proceedings.

6.8.4 The child being beyond parental control

The second limb in s 31(2)(b) refers to the child being beyond parental control, which is a matter of fact on which evidence can be presented (much as it was under the old law). Whilst roughly 10 per cent of all care orders made under the old law were based on the child being beyond parental control, a local authority will be reluctant to take action on this ground unless the breakdown is so serious that court intervention is warranted, and parents will not easily be able to avoid responsibility for their troublesome teenagers. Where a parent has done all in his or her power to offer good quality care and advice to a child, but the child has rejected this by opting at an early age for a life of crime, or of sexual exploitation, the child will be deemed to be beyond parental control and the quality of care limb will not be an issue.

The case of *Re O (A Minor) (Care Order: Education: Procedure)* [1992] 2 FLR 7 is again of relevance when considering the second part of the second limb and is further interesting in its reference back to the law applicable under the Children and Young Persons Act 1969. Ewbank J held that in his judgment 'where a child is suffering harm in not going to school and is living at home, it will follow that either the child is beyond her parents' control or that they are not giving the child the care that it would be reasonable to expect a parent to give'. He then quoted, with approval, the judgment of Lord Denning MR in *Re S (A Minor) (Care Order: Education)* [1978] QB 120 at 140F to the effect that 'if a child was not being sent to school or receiving a proper education then he was in need of care'.

6.8.5 *Making an order is better for the child than making no order at all*

Once the court is satisfied that the threshold care conditions are met, it must go on to satisfy itself that making an order is better for the child than making no order at all. In considering this the court will regard the child's welfare as its paramount consideration and must be bound by the welfare checklist. An important item on the checklist for these purposes is the range of orders available in the proceedings (s 14 of the 1989 Act) which can include, for the first time, the mixing of private law with public law orders. Thus, whilst the court could determine on making a care or supervision order alone, it can equally determine on making a residence order in favour of some member of the child's family other than a parent and, in a large number of cases, relatives have put themselves forward in this way.

Clearly, before making any private law orders in proceedings the court must consider the evidence of the local authority, any experts and the recommendation suggested by the guardian ad litem to the court. If, having taken all this evidence into account, the court decides to make a residence order in favour of a member of the family, subject to certain conditions in favour of the parents, the residence order may be combined with, for example, a supervision order. This was the solution adopted in *C v Solihull Metropolitan Borough Council* [1993] 1 FLR 290 by Ward J. In this case, there had been an application for a care order but the magistrates had made a supervision order. Neither order was appropriate in Ward J's view, since, in the absence of a final assessment, it would be better to make a residence order in favour of the parents subject to conditions, and an interim supervision order also subject to conditions. The conditions to be attached to the residence order were that the parents would undertake a programme of assessment and access to the child and the condition attaching to the interim supervision order was that the child be subject to various medical assessments. Although the effect of s 9(5) of the 1989 Act is to prevent the local authorities applying for prohibited steps orders or specific issues orders where the result of such applications would achieve the result of a residence or contact order by the back door (see *Nottinghamshire County Council v P* [1993] 2 FLR 134), this does not prevent the court from making such orders in family proceedings of its own motion (see s 10(1)(b)) where the local authority has correctly applied under Part IV of the 1989 Act for a care or supervision order and where the court considers such action is appropriate. Precisely which orders, if any, are to be made will depend upon the court's view of what is in the paramount interests of the child, having received experts' reports and the report of the guardian ad litem.

6.9 The conduct of proceedings for a care or supervision order

The Court Rules provide that the court may give directions as to the order of speeches and evidence at a hearing but, in the hearing of such directions, the Rules provide that the parties and guardian ad litem should adduce their evidence in the following order (r 21):

(1) the applicant;
(2) any party with parental responsibility for the child;
(3) other respondents;
(4) the guardian ad litem;
(5) the child, if he is a party to the proceedings and there is no guardian ad litem.

The justices' clerk or a proper officer of the court or the court itself must keep a note of the substance of the oral evidence given during the course of the proceedings in relation to a care or supervision order.

Generally, the applicant local authority would seek in its opening speech to lay the evidence before the court upon which it has based an application for a care or supervision order. The local authority will then call witnesses in any order which facilitates the presentation of the case to the court as clearly as possible. Witnesses are usually called in the chronological order in which signs of significant harm to the child might have been noted. This may be followed by calling for social workers' testimony regarding family circumstances which may indicate that the child is not receiving the requisite degree of care or that the child is beyond parental control. There will first be the 'examination-in-chief' of these witnesses, wherein the applicant will endeavour to elicit testimony from the witnesses he has called, in support of the particular interpretation of the facts which he seeks to establish.

Any of the other parties may, at the completion of the evidence of any particular witness, request a right to question the witness concerned and this process is called 'cross-examination'.

At the completion of the applicant's case any party with parental responsibility for the child or any other respondent may seek to present their side of the case and cross-examination may be undertaken by the applicant and the child's solicitor. Once the other respondents have completed their evidence the guardian ad litem can be called upon to give evidence on behalf of the child, in particular where the guardian ad litem has a contribution to make with regard to the main substantive issues in the hearing. Much of the work which guardians now do is intended to elicit whether the child has suffered or is likely to suffer significant harm and the degree to which this is attributable to the absence of reasonable parental control. Where there is no guardian ad litem, the child, through his solicitor, can make any points which he wishes to make. Given the fact that the child will rarely be in court, there is, however, no opportunity to cross-examine him in respect of any evidence given on his behalf. This is felt by some to be unduly prejudicial to parents and those with parental responsibility where evidence is sought to be produced to the court by means of videorecorded interviews with the child. The courts will be extremely cautious in attaching weight to such video evidence (see, further, 'Evidence in Civil Proceedings' at **6.13** below).

It has already been noted that the reports of experts and the guardian ad litem will have had to be circulated to all parties and will have been lodged with the court in advance of the hearing. Indeed, the court dealing with the case must have read in advance any documents which have been filed under r 17 of the Court Rules in respect of the hearing. This should enable courts better to follow the evidence of expert witnesses when they are called by any party to the proceedings.

Finally, after hearing all the evidence, the court must make its decision as soon as practicable (r 20(4)). When making any order or refusing any application the court must state any findings of fact and reasons for any decision. A series of cases decided by the High Court have emphasised the fact that justices must give full reasons for their decisions (see *Oxfordshire County Council v R* [1992] 1 FLR 648; *Hillingdon London Borough Council v H* [1992] 2 FLR 372; *Re B* (1992) *The Times*, July 16; *W v Hertfordshire County Council* [1993] 1 FLR 118).

Where the courts decide not to follow the recommendations of a guardian ad litem they must equally give reasons setting out why those recommendations were not followed (*S v Oxfordshire County Council* [1993] 1 FLR 452).

Any order which is made must be recorded by the court or proper officer either in the appropriate form laid down in the Rules or, where there is no such form, in writing and the order must be served on all the parties (s 91(3) of the 1989 Act).

It is clear that following on from the old law (see LCD Circular JC (86)) the courts are reluctant to attach conditions to care orders in order to provide for the review of the local authority's care plan (see *Re B (A Minor (Care Order: Review)* [1993] 1 FLR 421), nevertheless, the decision of the Court of Appeal in *Re B (Minors) (Care: Contact: Local Authority's Plans)* [1993] 1 FLR 543 would seem to indicate that the making of a care order together with an interim contact order might be an appropriate way of reviewing a family's progress in working towards rehabilitation of the children within the family. A further case illustrative of the view under the new law that courts should retain oversight of difficult cases and not make final orders prematurely can be seen in the case of *C v Solihull Metropolitan Borough Council* [1993] 1 FLR 290, in which Ward J gave useful guidance on how a difficult case might be handled under the 1989 Act. The case involved an apparently non-accidental injury which had not been adequately explained and a mother whose past unhappy experiences of social services when she herself was a child had made her wary of the local authority. It was clear that an assessment was needed but the mother would probably not co-operate if the child was taken away from her, making future rehabilitation difficult. The justices, accordingly, had decided to return the child to the mother, subject to an unconditional supervision order. Ward J found that this did not give the child sufficient protection. He stated that it would have been better for the court to have maintained a supervisory role and, in order to achieve this, he made, on an interim basis, a residence order which was conditional upon the parents undertaking a programme of assessment and co-operating with the local authority, including allowing the local authority access to their home at any reasonable time, even without notice. He further made an interim supervision order with conditions attached to ensure that medical assessments on the child were carried out (1989 Act, Sch 3, para 4).

Nevertheless, where the court has finally determined on the order which it is going to make, various requirements are then imposed as to the steps which the court should make to record its orders in writing (r 21(5) to (8)). Although the court rules do not now require that the court engages in an oral explanation to the parties involved, it is suggested that good practice would dictate that the court should engage in such an oral explanation.

An example for the format of this explanation was given in *A Child in Trust; Jasmine Beckford* (1985, DHSS) ('the *Jasmine Beckford Report*') at pp 169 to 170. It was suggested that the explanation should contain the following.

(1) A statement that upon the court's decision to make a care order, the particular local authority, through its appropriate committee and officers in the social services department, will be responsible for the child until he is 18. (Where a supervision order is being made instead, the court should explain that the child is being placed under the supervision of the local authority social services and that this supervision will continue for at least one year.)

(2) A statement that it will be for the local authority to decide, under a care order, where the child will live; and that the local authority has the right to decide whether the child would be allowed to go home. (Similarly for supervision orders, a statement should be made that it will be for the supervising officer to give directions as to where the child should live, what activities the child might engage in and whether the court has decided to make any directions for psychiatric or medical treatment of the child.)

(3) An explanation that where a care order has been made and the local authority decides to allow the child home, it will be for social workers to visit him at home in pursuance of the exercise of their parental responsibilities under s 33, in order to ensure that the child is being properly looked after.

(4) A statement that if at any time it is thought that the child is not likely to be treated properly he may be removed from home by the local authority, as the local authority is still holding a care order which gives it parental responsibility under s 33.

(5) A statement to the parents and the child (where the child is in court) that each has a separate and independent right at any time to apply to the court to put an end to the care order; and that if they decided to take this step they could apply for legal aid in their application. No promises would be given by the court that the order would be discharged. The local authority itself may also ask the court at any time to discharge the order. In that event it was more likely that the court would agree to do so, because the social services generally know when it is no longer necessary for the child to be away from his parents' home. (In addition, under the Review of Children's Cases Regulations 1991, local authorities, when conducting reviews of children subject to care orders, must actively consider in the review, together with the child, whether it is appropriate either for the authority or the child to apply for the discharge of any orders in respect of the child.)

(6) A question directed to the parties asking if they understood and whether they wished to say anything more.

It was further stressed in the *Jasmine Beckford Report* that in making a care order the court had no power then to make any recommendations or to endorse the expectations of the local authority.

6.10 Consideration of contact

It should be noted that before making a care order with respect to any child, the court must consider the arrangements which the authority has made or proposes to make for affording any personal contact with a child to be made the subject of an order; and invite the parties to the proceedings to comment on those arrangements (see Chapter 8 below).

6.11 Orders which may be made when the case is proved

In addition to the range of private law orders which may now be made in proceedings brought under s 31 (see **6.8.5** above), the court also has the power to choose to make either a care order or a supervision order (s 31(1)(a) and (b)).

6.11.1 The effects of making a care order

Where the court decides to make a care order, the local authority designated in a care order must be the authority within whose area the child is ordinarily resident or, where the child does not reside in a local authority area, the authority within whose area any circumstances arose in consequence of which the order has been made (s 31(8)(a) and (b)). The care order places the designated authority under a duty to receive the child into its care and to continue to keep him in its care whilst the order remains in force (s 33(1) and (2)), and it further gives the authority parental responsibility for the child (s 33(3), (4), (5), (6) and (7)). It was noted by the courts, in *R v Kirklees Metropolitan Borough Council ex parte C* [1992] 2 FLR 117, that the care order, in conferring parental responsibility, confers on the local authority the power to consent to a child being admitted to a hospital for the mentally ill in order to be assessed. It was stated in that case that it is not necessary to go through the procedures of compulsory admission under the Mental Health Act 1983. Thus, the local authority exercises parental power to consent to health care acquired by virtue of the care order. Under a care order the parents·also retain considerably attenuated parental responsibility and it is the local authority which has the power to determine the extent to which a parent or guardian of the child may meet his responsibility for him (s 33(3)(b)). Where a parent wishes to challenge the exercise of the local authority's discretion he or she will have to do so by means of judicial review unless, perhaps, the parents can bring themselves within the operations of the representations procedure provided by the local authorities pursuant to s 26(3) of the 1989 Act (see Chapter 9 below).

The making of a care order will operate to extinguish a residence order or any s 8 order, and any wardship order also ceases to be of effect. The making of a care order will also bring to an end a supervision order under s 35 and a school attendance order. The care order will continue in force until the child reaches the age of 18, unless brought to an end earlier. It should be noted that no care or supervision order can be made with respect to a child who has reached the age of 17 (or 16 in the case of a child who is married) (s 31(3)). Where the court makes a care order it has no power to add any direction as the responsibility for the child is firmly with the local authority. It was emphasised, in *Kent County Council v C* [1993] 1 FLR 308, that the court cannot, as happened in that case, direct that a guardian ad litem be allowed to have continuing involvement in order to investigate the rehabilitation process and apply to have contact terminated if appropriate. The question was left open in that case as to whether a guardian had power under s 34(2) to apply for an order that the child be allowed or denied contact to particular individuals.

6.11.2 *The effects of making a supervision order*

It may be thought appropriate in some cases involving issues of child protection to continue to involve the local authority in some way without using the measure of a care order. This can be done by the making of a supervision order under s 35. The new supervision order which is governed both by s 35 and Sch 3, Parts I and II to the 1989 Act has a great deal more teeth than the old supervision order provided under the Children and Young Persons Act 1969. While the supervision order is in force, it is the duty of the supervisor to advise, assist and befriend the supervised child, to take such steps as are reasonably necessary to give effect to the order and, where the order has not been fully complied with, or the supervisor considers that the order may no longer be necessary, to consider whether or not to apply for the discharge of the order. While the order is in force the supervisor can direct that the child participate in certain activities, undergo medical or psychiatric assessment or can ask the court to direct that the child undergo medical or psychiatric treatment (Sch 3, paras 2 to 5). The supervisor can now direct, with the consent of any responsible person, that he takes all reasonable steps to ensure that the supervised child complies with any direction for activities, medical and psychiatric examinations or with any directions as to medical and psychiatric treatment, and that the responsible person participates in certain activities. This particular provision may be extremely useful in dealing with cases where there are real concerns as to the continuing possibility of significant harm, because the supervisor can require the parent to participate in such activities as attending a family centre for assessment. This option was considered but ultimately rejected by the court in favour of a care order in *Re D (A Minor)(Care or Supervision Order)* [1993] 2 FLR 423.

A supervision order has a limited life, ending one year from the date on which it was made, and the prescribed number of days in respect of which, for example, a residence condition might be included is now without limitation, following an amendment effected by the Courts and Legal Services Act 1990, Sch 3, para 7(1)). The supervision order can be extended or further extended for such a period as the court thinks fit, except that it cannot be extended to run beyond the end of three years beginning with the date on which it was made (Sch 3, para 6(4)).

One of the factors which might influence either a guardian ad litem in making a report to the court, or the court itself in considering a supervision order, is the availability to the court of the range of private law orders in s 8 and s 16 of the 1989 Act to complement the supervision order. Thus, the court might wish to make a residence order to a grandparent whilst recognising the risk to the child, and may decide to make a supervision order alongside the residence order. It should, perhaps, be made clear at this stage that a residence order will settle the arrangements as to whom the child should live with and will further give that person parental responsibility (see s 8(1) and s 12(1) of the 1989 Act). Contact with the child's parents might be controlled, if necessary, so that an order might be made allowing contact with the mother in the grandparents' home but a prohibited steps order also made forbidding the father from having contact with the child.

6.12 Variation, discharge and termination of care and supervision orders

Under the Children Act 1989 the court does not possess any power to vary a care order, but can, on the application of any person entitled to apply for the discharge of the care order, substitute a supervision order for a care order (s 39(4)). Before the court can order such a substitution it must be able to satisfy itself that the welfare principles have been adhered to, and that, in making a substitution, it does not have to be satisfied again that the threshold conditions are met (s 39(5)). The rationale for this must be that the conditions were obviously met at the time the original order was made and, rather than re-directing the court to go over conditions which have already been satisfied, it is better to focus on whether the substituted order will be in the child's paramount interests (s 1(1) and (3)) and will be better for the child than not ordering such a substitution (s 1(5)).

A care order, including an interim care order, can be discharged by the court on the application of the child himself, the local authority designated in the care order or any person with parental responsibility for the child (s 39(1)). It should be noted that this will include parents, since the making of a care order does not operate to terminate their responsibility, but it would exclude grandparents or former foster-parents with whom the child had lived under a residence order and who had previously held parental responsibility in consequence of that order, because the making of a care order will have discharged the residence order (s 91(2)). This will mean, therefore, that such persons will be unable to apply for the discharge of the care order.

The conditions which must be satisfied before the court can grant an order discharging the care order are contained within s 1 of the 1989 Act. Thus, the court must determine that a discharge will be in the paramount interest of the child and, since the order is an order under Part IV of the 1989 Act, the welfare checklist comes into operation and the court must, therefore, consider the likelihood of harm occurring to the child. Finally, the court has to consider whether granting an order for discharge will be better for the child than not so doing (s 1(5)). A phased return home may be achieved by substituting a supervision order with residence requirements. In such situations, an application would have to be made by the local authority for such a variation, so that the court may be dealing with an application by a parent for discharge of a care order which is then being countered by the local authority applying for a substituted supervision order in order to achieve a phased return of the child to his home.

In those circumstances where the court refuses an application for the discharge of a care order or the substitution of a supervision order for a care order, the 1989 Act provides that no further application can be made within six months of the determination of such application, unless the court grants leave (s 91(15)(a)).

A care order will terminate when the child reaches the age of 18, unless it is brought to an end earlier (s 91(12)). It will also be terminated by the making of a residence order (s 91(1)), since an application can be made for such an order even though the child is the subject of a care order (s 9(1)). The child can also make an application for a residence order to be made in favour of a particular person if, for some reason, that person is unable or unwilling to make an application himself, and provided that the child is of sufficient understanding. This may certainly be the case where such persons would be ineligible for legal aid, whereas the child would generally be eligible for legal aid subject to the means and merits test in respect of an application for a s 8 order. It is further provided in the Act that a care order will also terminate where the child is taken to live in Northern Ireland, the Isle of Man or any of the Channel Islands, provided the court's prior permission of such removal has been obtained and the relevant authorities in those jurisdictions have indicated their willingness to take over the care of any such child, and the court has since been notified of their willingness (s 101(4) and, for the conditions, see the Children (Prescribed Orders (Northern Ireland, Guernsey and Isle of Man) Regulations 1991, SI 1991/2032).

As far as supervision orders are concerned, these can be varied or discharged on an application being made by the child, supervisor or any person who has parental responsibility for the child (s 39(2)). The conditions which must be satisfied before the court can order variation or discharge of the terms of the supervision order are once more those provided by s 1 of the 1989 Act. Where the variation sought is the substitution of the supervision order by a care order, the requirement of s 31(2) would again have to be met, since s 39(5) only applies to the substitution of a care order by a supervision order and not vice versa. Where such an application is made the court must consider whether it is necessary to appoint a guardian ad litem (s 41(6)(d)). This will more especially be the case where concern had previously been focused around issues of the risks to the child and the child is now felt to be at great risk whilst on a supervision order. The supervisor may seek variation of the terms of the supervision order where the earlier order is not being complied with, which may include a requirement that the child live in a specified place for a period or periods so specified, participate in certain activities, undergo a medical examination or psychiatric examination or psychiatric or medical treatment (Sch 3, Pt I, paras 2 to 5). No court should include a requirement that the child undergo such assessment or treatment unless it is satisfied that where the child has sufficient understanding to make an informed decision, he consents to its inclusion (Sch 3, Pt I, para 5(5)(a)). This provision must now be read subject to the decision of Douglas Brown J in *South Glamorgan County Council v W and B* [1993] 1 FLR 574. In that case, where a 15-year-old girl had exercised the power of veto over a court-ordered assessment issued pursuant to similar provisions in s 38(6) of the 1989 Act, it was held that the High Court, under its inherent jurisdiction, could override, in a proper case, the wishes of a child and give consent for medical assessment or treatment. Where a supervision order has imposed requirements on a 'responsible person', not being a person with parental responsibility, that person can also apply for variation of the order as it relates to him (s 39(3)). No further application can be made for the discharge of a supervision order within six months of the previous application, except with the leave of the court (s 91(15)(b)).

Finally it should be noted that a supervision order will terminate when the child reaches the age of 18 (s 91(13)), or when a care order is made (s 91(3)), or when an adoption order is made, or when the court takes action in respect of the child by making orders under the Child Abduction and Custody Act 1985 (Sch 3, Pt II, para 6(2)).

EVIDENCE IN CIVIL PROCEEDINGS

> 'The law of evidence determines how facts may be proved in a court of law and what facts may not be proved there' (Cross and Wilkins *Outline of Evidence* (1975, Butterworths)).

6.13 General

There is now greater awareness in various common law jurisdictions of the potential evidential contribution of young children, particularly in cases involving child abuse. In the last 10 years, an increasing body of research on children as witnesses has been rapidly accumulating (see Spencer and Flin *The Evidence of Children* (1990, Blackstone) and Dent and Flin *Children as Witnesses* (1992, Wiley)), despite an historical bias against accepting the child as either a competent or credible witness in such cases. The reason for this change in attitudes in English and other common law jurisdictions has not yet been definitively established. As far as young children are concerned, Pigot noted this change but could not say whether this was due to changed perceptions about the truthfulness of children or to growing international concern about the extent of the problem of child abuse (see Pigot *Report of the Advisory Group on Video Evidence* (1989, Home Office) at para 1.11). Nevertheless, it has taken the implementation of the 1989 Act and the Criminal Justice Act 1991 ('the 1991 Act') to delineate, more clearly, the dividing line between the civil and criminal jurisdiction regulating the treatment of child witnesses.

Children have certainly appeared in different capacities in court both 'as alleged perpetrators and as victims of abuse within the family, direct or indirect victims of crimes by strangers, or as witnesses of crimes' (see Morgan and Williams 'Child Witnesses and the Legal Process' (1992) *Journal of Social Welfare and Family Law* 484). We shall see in Chapter 7 how the Home

Office Code of Practice for videorecording of children's evidence (the *Memorandum of Good Practice on Videorecorded Interviews with Child Witnesses for Criminal Proceedings* (1992, DOH) ('the *MoGP*')) operates with particular reference to procuring evidence from child witnesses in criminal proceedings. However, the videorecording reforms wrought by the Criminal Justice Act 1991 and the *MoGP* will also affect the conduct of civil proceedings since many of the families affected by the criminal prosecution of alleged abuse will frequently also face concurrent civil proceedings. We, therefore, consider the application of the *MoGP* in the civil law context as well (see below).

It is first worth noting, however, some other general considerations relating to evidence in civil proceedings. In the context of child sexual abuse, especially alleged abuse within the family, the rules of evidence can only serve as procedural guidelines. In effect, two competing principles have to be balanced and resolved. These have been described by Waite J in *Re W (Minors) (Child Abuse: Evidence)* [1987] 1 FLR 297, as follows:

'[Cases of] Alleged child abuse within the family . . . [pose] exceptional difficulty, because they . . . contrast two principles . . . fundamental to our society. One is the basic requirement of justice that nobody should have to face a finding by any court of serious parental misconduct without the opportunity of having the allegations . . . clearly specified and cogently proved. The other is the public interest in the detection and prevention of parental child abuse which is liable, if persisted in, to do serious damage to the emotional development of the victim.'

In sexual abuse cases which are unaccompanied by any signs of physical injury, there will be greater difficulties in adducing enough cogent evidence to convince the judge of the truth or falsehood of the allegations. In such cases, no witnesses will usually have been present, the child will be under pressure not to reveal all that transpired, and may have inhibitions, fears and confusions, the perpetrator will probably not wish to face the fact that he is an abuser, and the child's mother will frequently either not believe the allegation or even collude with the perpetrator. Thus, rather than presenting one or two key pieces of evidence, assorted fragments of evidence may have to be brought to the court's attention until a coherent scenario may be presented to the court.

Unlike criminal proceedings, however, civil proceedings seek to safeguard and promote the welfare of the child and to decide what is best for the child's future. The court, therefore, considers whether the child has been abused, but not by whom, and, if so, what should be done for his welfare. It does not, as in criminal proceedings, seek to determine the guilt or innocence of anyone who may have been accused in criminal proceedings but in care proceedings seeks to establish a sequence of events or an incident or course of behaviour which has resulted in the child suffering significant harm. It must then be shown on the balance of probabilities that such harm is attributable to a lack of reasonable parental care or that the child is beyond parental control. In other associated areas the judicial task is, therefore, one of assessing or balancing the potential risk to the child of, for example, allowing his father to continue to have contact with him. Under the 1989 Act, if a child is taken into care, such parental contact can only be refused where the authority is satisfied that this refusal is a matter of urgency and is necessary to safeguard or promote a child's welfare and, in any event, must not last longer than seven days before it is put before a court (see s 34(6) of the 1989 Act and Chapter 8 below).

6.14 Evidence of, and concerning, children in civil proceedings

Issues concerning the unsworn evidence of children, the attendance of the child in court, documentary and expert evidence about the child and the privilege against self-incrimination have been considered earlier (see **6.5.2** to **6.6** above).

6.15 Proof in care proceedings

Since care proceedings are essentially civil proceedings, they are conducted in accordance with the civil rules of evidence. There are three main issues which must be addressed with regard to the question of proof in civil proceedings.

(1) The *burden of proof* – the responsibility which a party has to prove its allegations.
(2) The *onus of proof* – the responsibility which a party bears at any given stage of the proceedings.
(3) The *standard of proof* – the degree of probability which the evidence must reach in order to satisfy a court that the facts in issue have been established.

The standard of proof in civil proceedings is based on the balance of probabilities.

In general terms, the burden of proof would be discharged if the judge could say that it is 'more probable than not' that a particular fact has been established (*Miller v Minister of Pensions* [1974] 2 All ER 372 at p 373).

Within this concept of burden of proof there are three discernible aspects:

(1) the 'evidential burden' – the burden of adducing enough evidence to justify proceeding with the particular issue;
(2) the burden of establishing the admissibility of the evidence; and
(3) the legal burden – the burden of satisfying the court with regard to a particular issue.

In fact, there is some difficulty in differentiating between the second and third of these aspects and the only real difference between the two is that the legal burden remains with the party initiating the proceedings, whereas the evidential burden might lie initially with the party bringing the proceedings but then shift to the other party according to the way the case proceeds and the evidence is tendered. The evidential burden is in the nature of a first hurdle that must be overcome before anything else can proceed.

6.15.1 Applicant bears burden of proof throughout hearing

In care proceedings, the applicant bears the legal burden throughout the hearing, which means that the court has to be satisfied that a prima facie case must be made for establishing the dual conditions of 'significant harm' *and* its attribution to the lack of adequate parental care or control under s 31(2) of the 1989 Act. However, although the applicant will bear the evidential burden at the commencement of the proceedings, once the applicant has adduced sufficient evidence to satisfy the court that the conditions do exist, the evidential burden then shifts to the child or other representative acting on the child's behalf or to the parent to counter the applicant's case.

6.15.2 Standard of proof

In civil cases, the likelihood of the facts having taken place as alleged must carry a reasonable degree of probability. Thus, the applicant in care proceedings must prove to the court that it is more likely than not that the facts as alleged occurred and that these facts satisfy the prerequisites of the 1989 Act. With special reference to cases of child abuse, there appears to be some degree of difference in the standard of proof required to satisfy a court that sexual abuse had taken place, depending on whether it was a father who was the alleged abuser, rather than some other person, or, indeed, depending on the particular facts of the case and the need to protect the child. The judicial view in cases of suspicion against a father appears to be that a higher degree of probability might be required to satisfy the court of his culpability (see *Re G (No 2) (A Minor) (Child Abuse: Evidence)* [1988] 1 FLR 314 discussed at **6.17.1** below). On the other hand, in child protection cases initiated by the local authority, the Court of Appeal has held that the standard of proof might be lower than the normal civil standard where the courts were looking to the likelihood of harm within the meaning of s 31 of the 1989 Act (see *Newham London Borough Council v AG* [1993] 1 FLR 281 discussed at **6.17** below).

The Court of Appeal has also intimated that where the court is concerned with what has happened in the past, this must usually be established on a balance of probability. Nevertheless, where serious allegations amounting to criminal or grossly immoral conduct are made, the degree of probability must be commensurate with the occasion and proportionate to the subject matter (see *Re H (A Minor); Re K (Minors) (Child Abuse: Evidence)* [1989] 2 FLR 313, discussed at **6.17.2** below).

6.16 Court's evaluation of evidence

6.16.1 Some key concepts

(1) **Weight of evidence** The probative value which a court places on a given piece of evidence is known as the weight of evidence and this is a question of fact, not law, to be decided on the basis of the case's circumstances and the court's appraisal of the reliability and credibility of the witnesses.

(2) **Prima facie evidence** This is evidence which, unless contradicted by other evidence which is called by the opposing side, will be sufficient to establish a particular contention. The party which tendered the prima facie evidence and finds it unchallenged or uncontradicted must, therefore, succeed in its case.

(3) **Relevance** Only those facts which are relevant to the issue and facts in issue (those facts necessary to prove or disprove a case) are admissible in evidence. Facts relevant to the issue are those facts which tend to prove or disprove the facts in issue. Thus, any evidence which is not sufficiently related to the facts in issue will be deemed irrelevant and excluded.

(4) **Admissible evidence** Evidence which may be presented to the court, such as facts in issue (see, further, **6.18** below).

(5) **Hearsay evidence** Evidence given by a witness of a statement made by some other person as proof of the truth of that statement (see, further, **6.5** above and **6.18.1** below).

6.17 Standard of proof in child abuse cases in the civil courts

Despite the general principle that the standard in civil proceedings is for the court to be satisfied 'on a balance of probabilities' that the case has been proved, several cases have suggested that the standard of proof in such proceedings may vary depending on the gravity of the issue to be resolved, the consequences which may ensue if it is proved and the particular facts of a given case (see, eg: *R v Secretary of State for the Home Department ex parte Khawaja* [1984] AC 74; *Re G (No 2) (A Minor) (Child Abuse: Evidence)* [1988] 1 FLR 314; *Re F (Minors) (Wardship: Jurisdiction)* [1988] 2 FLR 123; *Re JS (A Minor) (Declaration of Paternity)* (1981) FLR 146; *W v K (Proof of Paternity)* [1988] 1 FLR 86; *Re H (A Minor); Re K (Minors) (Child Abuse: Evidence)* [1989] 2 FLR 313; *R v Waltham Forest Justices ex parte B* [1989] Fam Law 348; *Bradford Metropolitan District Council v K and K* [1989] 2 FLR 507; *Newham London Borough Council v AG* [1993] 1 FLR 281).

The standardisation of the courts' procedures and the Children (Admissibility of Hearsay Evidence) Order 1993, SI 1993/621, and the Children (Admissibility of Hearsay Evidence) Order 1991, SI 1991/1115, have made the effect of some of the pre-1989 Act cases less significant, since all courts now tend to allow hearsay in most cases involving suspected child abuse.

Nevertheless, it is still instructive to consider judicial remarks made in some of these cases.

6.17.1 *Some illustrative cases*

Re G (No 2) (A Minor) (Child Abuse: Evidence) [1988] 1 FLR 314, a pre-1989 Act case, contained authoritative guidance on civil proceedings generally. In this case, a child's mother and grandmother alleged that the child had been sexually abused by the father, and a place of safety order, followed by an interim care order, had been made by a juvenile court. The local authority initiated wardship proceedings and the father applied therein for care and control of the child. Sheldon J considered the evidence in detail and said:

'I should make plain that there is no evidence that would justify the prosecution of Mr G for any form of sexual abuse or improper behaviour with his daughter: the available evidence falls far short of the standard of proof beyond reasonable doubt that would be needed to lead to a conviction in criminal proceedings, as those would be. In the present context, however, this is not an end of the matter. In wardship proceedings, as these proceedings are, although alleged wrongdoing by an individual may be in issue, *the predominant consideration is the welfare of the child and not the behaviour of any particular adult.* They are also civil proceedings.
   I therefore agree with Waite J in *Re W (Minors) (Child Abuse: Evidence)* [1987] 1 FLR 297, . . . that in general terms the standard of proof to be applied in such proceedings as these is based on the balance of probabilities. On the other hand, having regard to the diversity of issues that might be raised in such proceedings, I also take the view, as was expressed by Denning LJ . . . in *Bater v Bater* [1951] P 35, that the "degree of probability" required in any particular context may vary and must be "commensurate with the occasion" or "proportionate to the subject matter". Thus, in my opinion, in such proceedings as the present, a higher degree of probability is required to satisfy the court that the father has been guilty of some sexual misconduct with his daughter than would be needed to justify the conclusion that the child has been the victim of some such behaviour of whatever nature and whoever may have been its perpetrator.' (Authors' emphasis.)

He went on to say:

'In the latter context . . . I am of the opinion that the gravity of the matter is such that from the child's point of view *any tilt in the balance suggesting that she had been the victim of sexual abuse would justify a finding to that effect.* In my view, indeed, there may also be circumstances in which the application of a "standard of proof" as that phrase is commonly understood, is inapt to describe the method by which the court should approach the particular problem; as, for example, where the suspicion of sexual abuse or other wrong-doing, although incapable of formal proof, is such as to lead to the conclusion that it would be an unacceptable risk to the child's welfare to leave him in his previous environment; or (more likely in the case of older children) where, although the court may be satisfied that no sexual abuse had taken place, the very fact that it had been alleged by a child against a parent suggests that, in the child's interests, some change in, or control over the existing regime is required'. (Authors' emphasis.)

In the present case, this 'unacceptable risk' was found to exist and the court found that even applying a more stringent test than a mere 'balance of probabilities', the father had been guilty of an 'over-familiar and sexually inappropriate' relationship with his daughter, which bode ill for the future and which created a 'particularly vulnerable' little girl. A care order was, therefore, made under s 7(2) of the Family Law Reform Act 1969, on the basis that the child should remain with foster-parents with monthly supervised access by the father.

In *Re F (Minors) (Wardship: Jurisdiction)* [1988] 2 FLR 123, one of the Cleveland cases tried by the High Court, Purchas LJ referred to Hollis J in the court below, who in considering the approach to be taken by a wardship case in relation to the standard of proof required in sexual abuse cases, was quoted as saying:

> 'it must be remembered that judgments are to some extent tailored to suit the facts of the case for decision. It seems, therefore, that if the risk of the child having been sexually abused while in his or her family environment is a real, reasonable or distinct possibility, action should be taken. I think that this is really consistent with what Sheldon J is saying [in *Re G* (above)]. I do not consider that a probability has to be shown but a real possibility. In that way, the interests of the child will be safeguarded.'

It should be noted that even though the two-stage hearing has now been abolished with the repeal of the old care grounds under the Children and Young Persons Act 1969, the two-stage decision-making process as laid down in cases such as *Re H; Re K* (see below) will probably become more explicit. Hence, even though the issues on admissibility of hearsay evidence have been superseded by the 1991 and 1993 Hearsay Orders (above) (see **6.13** and **6.18.2** below), *Re H; Re K* remains instructive on the standard of proof required in civil cases where child abuse has been alleged.

6.17.2 *Re H; Re K*

In two separate pre-1989 Act cases, *Re H; Re K* [1989] 2 FLR 313, one of the issues that arose concerned the standard of proof which was required when allegations of sexual abuse were made against a parent in access proceedings. In both cases, the circuit judge had refused access to a father on the grounds that allegations of sexual abuse against the father had been established, based partly on the evidence of interviews between the child and the social worker. The father appealed in both cases and the Court of Appeal considered the cases together. The respondents submitted that to prove abuse, only a real possibility needed to be shown and not proof on a balance of probabilities. Butler-Sloss LJ gave her opinion regarding the standard of proof required in child cases, before considering the facts of each appeal. She held first that, in child cases, including those where there was an allegation of abuse of children, the standard of proof was that required in civil proceedings generally, namely proof on a balance of probabilities. However, where serious allegations were made, amounting to criminal or grossly immoral conduct, the standard of proof remained the balance of probabilities, but the degree of probability must be commensurate with the occasion and proportionate to the subject matter (referring to *Bater v Bater* [1951] P 35). In cases of allegations of sexual abuse, the result may be, as Sheldon J suggested in *Re G* (above), that there is sufficient evidence to make a finding that the child has been the victim of unacceptable behaviour, but insufficient to make a finding as to the perpetrator. In *Re F (Minors) (Wardship: Jurisdiction)* [1988] 2 FLR 123, Nourse LJ had suggested that 'a real, reasonable or distinct possibility of a child having been abused', would have to be shown and that 'a real possibility has to be contrasted with an unreal or fanciful possibility, and the latter is something on which a court does not act'.

Secondly, Butler-Sloss LJ then clarified that there were two stages in the decision-making process where a judge exercises his discretion in child cases. At the first stage, the judge 'evaluates the evidence adduced both as to facts already in evidence and frequently expert opinion as to the future advantages and risks of possible decisions as to the child's future'. At the second stage 'upon the evidence provided to the court, the judge exercises his discretion with the test of the welfare of the child paramount, and weighs in the balance of all the relevant factors and assesses the relevant weight of advantages and risks to the child of possible courses of action'. She noted that the judge may have found individual facts, such as 'inappropriate knowledge or behaviour, which constitute a high degree of concern about the child without being able to say on the test that they amount to actual abuse'. These facts would be relevant to the exercise of the discretion. On the other hand, the judge may have found 'sufficient evidence of concern about past care for the child to be satisfied that the child was in a potentially abusive situation without having sufficient evidence to be satisfied as to the extent of the abuse in the past, or the identity of the abuser. He has to assess the risks and, if there is a real possibility that the child will be at risk, he will take steps to safeguard that child'.

A key point made by Butler-Sloss LJ is that the 'court can only act on evidence' wherein she agrees with Nourse LJ in *Re F* (above). The view of Butler-Sloss LJ suggests that when the court is considering acts of the past as a means of assessing the future likelihood of events, the standard used must be the normal standard of proof, which is on a balance of probabilities. However, in considering the future risks that might be involved, the court has merely to be satisfied that there is a real possibility of risk in order to exercise its discretion, which suggests that it need not be satisfied on a balance of probabilities that such future risks exist.

In the cases themselves, the appeal was allowed in *Re H* but in *Re K*, the case was remitted for rehearing in the Family Division.

6.17.3 *Newham London Borough Council v AG*

The recent Court of Appeal case, *Newham London Borough Council v AG* [1993] 1 FLR 281, was considered in detail earlier (see **6.8.1** above) but it should be noted at this point that it not only gives guidance on the threshold conditions of s 31 of the 1989 Act but in so doing, confirms the Butler-Sloss approach in *Re H; Re K* (above) in the context of the standard of proof required in assessing future risks. Since s 31(2) now governs the decision whether or not orders will be made to place a child into care or to make any other child protection orders, it is worth noting that the phrase 'likely to suffer' is not to be equated with 'on the balance of probabilities' nor does it suggest a requirement that 'a very strong degree of significant harm was a real likelihood'. On a technical point, since this was a pending wardship case (within the meaning of Sch 14 to the 1989 Act), the 1989 Act was not strictly relevant and s 31 was only invoked by common consent of the parties and the court. Hence, comments on s 31 could, in strict theory, be treated as *obiter*. In any event, from 14 October 1992, there should no longer be pending wardship cases in which the child has been placed into care (see the Children Act 1989 (Commencement No 2 – Amendment and Transitional Provisions) Order 1991, SI 1991/1990). On the other hand, it is highly likely that future Benches of the Court of Appeal might adopt this approach, particularly since it follows previous appellate authority.

6.17.4 A two-stage decision-making process

It is clear from these cases, therefore, that although there is no longer any two-stage hearing in care and related civil proceedings, courts will still have to undertake a two-stage decision-making process as outlined in *Re H; Re K* (above). The recent case of *Humberside County Council v B* [1993] 1 FLR 257 confirms this (see Chapter 4).

The following points may, therefore, be noted about these two stages. First, with regard to the first stage, case-law indicates that in family proceedings involving allegations of abuse of children the judge must exercise his discretion at stage one by determining: (1) whether abuse did take place; and (2) if it did, the abuser's identity. Here, the standard of proof would be the balance of probabilities but if there are serious allegations relating to criminal or grossly immoral conduct, the degree of probability may vary according to the particular occasion and proportionate to the subject matter (see Stuart-Smith LJ in *Re H; Re K* (above) at p 342). On the question of the abuser's identity, a higher degree of probability may be required to identify the alleged abuser. For example, if a parent has been accused of sexually abusing his child this may require a higher degree of proof than if the allegation were levelled against some other person (see *Re G (No 2) (A Minor) (Child Abuse: Evidence)* [1988] 1 FLR 314).

Secondly, at stage two, the judge will need to keep the child's welfare as the paramount consideration in deciding what should be his appropriate course of action. It had been suggested by Sheldon J in *Re G (No 2) (A Minor)* (above) that the very fact that an allegation had been made against a child suggested that the child's interests required some change in or control over the child's existing arrangements. Here, the balance of appellate judicial opinion suggests that Sheldon J was wrong (see Croom-Johnson LJ in *Re H; Re K* (above) at p 316). Thus, mere concern, suspicion, or unsubstantiated allegations would not be sufficient to satisfy the degree of risk necessary for significant harm to be established. Evidence of a real or distinct possibility would have to be established. In every case, the judge would have to balance the risk of abuse against the risk that to take a child away from the only home he has known and from parents, however inadequate, to whom he is attached, might cause him greater harm (see *Re H (Minors) (Wardship: Sexual Abuse)* [1991] 2 FLR 416). The Cleveland cases indicated that serious difficulties were encountered at the proof stage (see eg *Cleveland County Council v B* [1988] FCR 593; *Cleveland County Council v C* [1988] FCR 607; *Cleveland County Council v D* [1988] FCR 615). In the process of evaluating evidence of child sexual abuse, it is now recommended that recourse be made to the different inter-agency and other guidances which are currently available (eg *Working Together*; *Diagnosis of Child Sexual Abuse: Guidance for Doctors* (1988) and the *Report of the Royal College of Physicians of London: Physical Signs of Abuse in Children* (1991)). It bears repeating that the general principles of the 1989 Act are also ever-present and, as such, bestride the whole pre-interview stage in child abuse investigations. Hence, the protective philosophy of the 1989 Act, melding with the centrality of the child's welfare has to be reconciled with notions of parental responsibility, partnership with parents, and support of the child. It should, therefore, be noted that professionals must keep a sharp weather-eye on how the child's paramount interests must continue to be promoted in the midst of procuring evidence according to a multiplicity of guidelines and different objectives.

6.18 The admissibility of evidence

6.18.1 The hearsay rule

Cross on Evidence (6th edn) at p 454, states the rule against hearsay:

'Evidence of a statement made to a witness by a person who is not himself called as a witness may or may not be hearsay. It is hearsay and inadmissible when the object of the evidence is to establish the truth of what is contained in the statement. It is not hearsay and admissible when it is proposed to establish by the evidence, not the truth of the statement, but the fact that it was made.'

Thus, assertions by persons other than the witness who is testifying on oath may or may not be admissible depending on the purpose for which they have been introduced as evidence. The rationale for this rule is that such evidence is likely to be unreliable as proof of a fact which is best proved by either the direct testimony of the person who actually experienced the act, or by the person who actually witnessed the act itself. Otherwise it would amount to someone merely repeating what someone else saw or what someone else experienced.

6.18.2 *Admissibility of hearsay evidence: the Orders*

Under the Children (Admissibility of Hearsay Evidence) Order 1991, SI 1991/1115 ('the 1991 Order'), which came into force on 14 October 1991, it was stated that in civil proceedings before the High Court, a county court or magistrates' court, evidence given in connection with the upbringing, maintenance or welfare of a child 'shall be admissible notwithstanding any rule of law relating to hearsay' (art 2).

This was the second Order (the first being the Children (Admissibility of Hearsay Evidence) Order 1990, SI 1990/143 ('the 1990 Order')), made by the Lord Chancellor pursuant to the powers given him under s 96(3) of the 1989 Act, namely to make provision for the admissibility of evidence which would otherwise be inadmissible under any rule of law relating to hearsay. A third Order has now been made (see below).

The 1990 Order (see first edition of this book), was unfortunately problematic in that different rules applied between county courts and the High Court, and magistrates' courts.

The explanatory note to the 1991 Order, attached to the instrument provided:

> 'the only real difference between this order and the previous order, which it revokes, is that, for magistrates' courts, the rule precluding hearsay evidence is now abolished completely in family proceedings (within the meaning of s 8(3) of the Children Act 1989) as had already been achieved for all civil proceedings in the High Court and the county courts; the previous order made admissible only certain hearsay statements in certain magistrates' courts'.

The effect of the 1991 Order was far-reaching and any ground for challenging the admissibility of hearsay was thereby removed. Under the 1991 Order, hearsay evidence (see **6.16.1** above) was permitted in civil proceedings where given *in connection with the upbringing, maintenance and welfare of children* in all family proceedings in the magistrates' courts. Hence, magistrates were given the power to receive second-hand hearsay in all 1989 Act proceedings, including applications for secure accommodation orders (see *R v A Local Authority* (1992) *The Independent*, March 9), but they will, of course, continue to have a discretion to ascribe such weight to it as they deem appropriate.

In the county courts and in the High Court, admissibility of hearsay evidence, in connection with the upbringing, maintenance and welfare of children, was also governed by the 1991 Order. This was in addition to the relaxation of the rules of evidence in applications for emergency protection orders (s 45(7) the 1989 Act) and the fact that hearsay evidence can also be put forward in child assessment proceedings (*Oxfordshire County Council v R* [1992] 1 FLR 648). The Court of Appeal has also ruled that, in principle, there is no good reason for excluding the operation of the 1991 Order in relation to hearsay in contempt proceedings, but it would depend on the judge, in each case, to decide whether the 1991 Order should also apply to such proceedings (see *C v C (Contempt: Children's Evidence)* [1992] Fam Law 570).

Hence, the judge may decide to disregard the hearsay evidence altogether, as Butler-Sloss LJ remarks in *Re W (Minors) (Wardship: Evidence)* [1990] 1 FLR 203:

> 'The weight which [a judge] might place on the information received was a matter for the exercise of [the judge's] discretion. He might totally disregard it; he might wish to rely on some or all of it. Unless uncontroversial it had to be regarded with great caution . . . The age of the child, the context in which the statement was made, the surrounding circumstances, previous behaviour of the child, opportunities for the child to have knowledge from other sources, any knowledge . . . of a child's pre-disposition to tell untruths or to fantasise were among the relevant considerations.'

The weight to be attributed to hearsay evidence is obviously critical, since it applies to evidence given in connection with the upbringing, maintenance or welfare of a child, and the scope of the 1991 Order has been steadily widened (see above).

A third such Order has been made, namely the Children (Admissibility of Hearsay Evidence) Order 1993, SI 1993/621 ('the 1993 Order'), which supersedes and revokes the 1991 Order (above) such that it extends the scope of the previous Order to include all civil proceedings including those under the Child Support Act 1991. Hence, these issues may arise not just in family proceedings as defined by the 1989 Act, and the various proceedings mentioned above but also in proceedings under the Child Support Act 1991 and the Child Abduction and Custody Act 1985. In principle, there also appears no reason why the 1993 Order should not be extended further to disputes over ownership of the home arising outside the context of matrimonial proceedings (such as s 30 proceedings under the Law of Property Act 1925), if the court's eventual decision will affect a child's upbringing, maintenance or welfare. These sorts of proceedings would have important consequences for the child as far as unmarried parents are concerned. The 1993 Order may arguably also be extended to cases involving fatal accident or personal injury claims or claims under a will or trust in which the child's maintenance is involved (see Hershman and McFarlane 'Admissibility of Hearsay Evidence' [1990] Fam Law 164).

On the other hand, it might be argued that following the reasoning in *Richards v Richards* [1984] FLR 11, hearsay may be excluded in applications for orders under the Domestic Proceedings and Magistrates' Courts Act 1978, if the view taken is that the children's interests are merely peripheral to the main issue before the court or that they are being used as pawns by the parents to gain the court's sympathy. It is submitted that provided the case does involve, to an appreciable extent, a child's upbringing, maintenance or welfare, there should be no reason in principle why the 1993 Order should not apply to such proceedings as well.

If we assume that the 1993 Order is intended to broaden the scope of hearsay in the context of children's welfare, then it should still allow for the admissibility of hearsay in respect of statements by children, statements against interest by those with control, or concerned with the control, of the child, and statements contained in reports submitted by a guardian ad litem or a local authority. It is also important to note that hearsay may also be allowed in wardship proceedings, infrequent though such proceedings may become (see *Re W (Minors)* (1989) *The Times*, November 10). It is also clear that the 1993 Order applies to appeals from care proceedings, secure accommodation orders, and contributions for maintenance of a child in care and similar appeals. In *B v X County Council* [1993] Fam Law 118, a case heard in December 1991, Rattee J held that a Crown Court, hearing an appeal against the making of a child care order by a juvenile court, could receive hearsay evidence under the 1990 Order. In a case dealing with an appeal from a secure accommodation order, *Oxfordshire County Council v R* [1992] 1 FLR 648, Douglas Brown J gave a very clear indication that hearsay evidence contained in reports and statements was admissible, since proceedings commenced under s 25 of the 1989 Act by a local authority in a magistrates' court must be treated as family proceedings in accordance with s 92(2) of the 1989 Act. It would be ironic if the repeal of the 1990 Order, which was seen as insufficiently wide, then resulted in a narrower interpretation of the 1993 Order! Secure accommodation proceedings were covered by the 1990 Order until 14 October 1991, after which the 1991 Order applied (and, presumably, they are now covered by the 1993 Order). The explanatory note to the 1991 Order only referred to s 8 of the 1989 Act, but case-law has been rapidly establishing these Orders' clear intention which is to broaden the admissibility of hearsay evidence in the promotion and protection of children's welfare.

The 1991 Order used the term 'evidence' rather than 'statement' as in the 1990 Order, which was wide enough to cover statements and actions. Thus, the 1993 Order must include: (1) children's statements recorded on videotapes or sound recordings; (2) the actions of a child, such as a gesture or gesticulation which, in theory, should also be included if observed in a diagnostic interview. The doctrine of *res gestae*, which admits statements made contemporaneously with the occurrence of some act or event which the court is considering and is, therefore, part of the overall scenario, should be unaffected by the 1993 Order.

6.18.3 *Further points on hearsay*

Another exception to the hearsay rule exists under the common law which allows the court to admit an admission or confession by a party to the proceedings. This was extended, in the *Humberside* case (*Humberside County Council v DPR* [1977] 1 WLR 249), to admissions by 'someone who has control of the child or who is concerned with the control of the child'. A parent or guardian who is a party to care proceedings would come within this exception.

Under the Evidence Act 1938, a document containing the statement of someone who had personal knowledge of the incidents and events or someone under a duty to record information supplied by another person who possessed such knowledge (eg a medical record compiled by hospital staff or by a health visitor) may be admissible even if the maker of the statement is not called as a witness. However, it cannot include a statement 'made by a person interested at a time when proceedings were pending or anticipated' (s 1(3) of the 1989 Act). Hence, the evidence of a social worker involved in a particular case tended to be excluded as proof of abuse, but if it related to a particular statement, this was often admitted as proof that it was in fact made, rather than as proof of the truth of the allegation.

6.18.4 *Expert's opinion is evidence of child's state of mind*

It is clear that s 96 of the 1989 Act and the 1993 Order now seek to cover as many possible situations as may arise in relation to the evidence available in a child law case. The main objection to admitting hearsay is, of course, the inability to cross-examine the person who is supposed to have witnessed the relevant incident. Nevertheless, as Lord Moulton put it in *Lloyd v Powell Duffryn Steam Coal Ltd* [1914] AC 733 at p 751: 'It is well established in English jurisprudence that, in accordance with the dictates of common sense, the words and acts of a person are admissible as evidence of his state of mind'. It is significant to see that the Court of Appeal recently placed evidence of a child's state of mind in the same category: *Re H; Re K* (above). In the words of Stuart-Smith LJ:

'What a child says not in the witness box is only inadmissible to prove the truth of the fact stated. It is admissible to show the state of the child's mind. Thus it may be the case that a suitably qualified expert may be able to say as a matter of opinion from what the child has said or the way in which he said it that the child has been sexually abused.'

However, the House of Lords appear to have had problems with this issue. In *R v Blastland* [1986] 1 AC 41, Lord Bridge said:

'The principle that statements made to a witness by a third party were not excluded by the hearsay rule when they were put in evidence solely to prove the state of mind of the maker of the statement or the person to whom it was made applied only where the state of mind evidenced by the statement was directly in issue or of direct and immediate relevance to an issue.'

Thus, if the issue was whether it was proved that the accused committed an act of child abuse, mere knowledge of the incident was neither in issue nor of relevance to the issue.

As McEwan points out ((1989) *Journal of Child Law* at p 106), evidence of a child's knowledge would be relevant if the actions and terms employed by the child indicate knowledge incompatible with that child's age and are difficult to explain in the absence of abuse. Hence, a witness is quite permitted to testify that he heard the child use a word or phrase unexpected in someone of that age, but would not be permitted to testify that upon being shown an anatomically correct doll, for instance, the child started committing acts of abuse if that were then presented as an implied assertion of abuse by his parent. The assertion would be a fact of which the interviewer would have no direct knowledge and would, therefore, be hearsay. Such evidence (ie of inappropriate knowledge or distress) is acceptable whatever the age of the child, since his reliability and potential competence as a witness himself would not be in issue.

6.18.5 *Interviewing children: videos in civil proceedings*

Both *Working Together* and the *Memorandum of Good Practice on Videorecorded Interviews with Child Witnesses for Criminal Proceedings* (1992, DOH) ('the *MoGP*') suggest that a 'substantive' interview be conducted if the investigation indicates that this is warranted. However, it is by no means clear what criteria should be used in deciding when or whether to conduct videorecorded interviews. Such interviews may at least satisfy a civil standard of proof in civil proceedings since the whole thrust of the various joint interviewing procedures, guidances and the *MoGP*, in particular, has been to improve the quality of such interviews, primarily so that they satisfy evidential requirements in *criminal justice proceedings*. The *MoGP* states that a videotaped interview could be for either civil or criminal proceedings, but fears have already been expressed by a researcher in the field that this shift in focus, wrought by the *MoGP*, could mean that, in practice, the child's immediate needs may take a secondary place to evidentiary requirements; and cases in the civil courts could possibly be weakened (Wattam *Making a Case in Child Protection* (1993, Longmans) at p 107). This may result precisely because of the joint inter-agency approach adopted in *Working Together* and followed up in the *MoGP*. The *MoGP* appears to place greater emphasis on police expertise in evidential interviewing, so that the social worker perspective may be unintentionally sidelined in such matters. If social workers have spoken to the child before the 'substantive' interview in a less formalistic atmosphere, there immediately arises the question of whether 'leading questions' might have been put to the child which, if proven, would already begin to undermine the child's credibility as a witness. On the other hand, if compliance with the *MoGP* is required for an interview that could satisfy criminal standards of proof, this might result in an exceedingly artificial and restrictive interview which might not achieve any free-flowing narrative for any purpose, civil or criminal. This is a dilemma for which there appears to be no straightforward solution since different aims and objectives appear to be pulling in different directions in this particular matter.

It needs to be clarified, therefore, what the status of a particular interview is, the roles of various professionals in the light of joint interviewing and the priorities of each professional in that interview and in the overall investigation (see **6.18.6** below for the designated phases in the *MoGP*, and Chapter 5 above).

As far as the general process of interviewing children who are suspected of having been abused is concerned, the advice given in the *Cleveland Report* (at para 12) has now acquired the status of authoritative guidance which even the judiciary have acknowledged (see, eg *Re E (A Minor) (Child Abuse: Evidence)* [1991] 1 FLR 420). A strong body of opinion believes that, wherever possible, children should be spared the trauma of a court appearance as well as having to face the persons who have abused them with all the conflicting emotions and pressures that this might entail. A partial solution has been for child protection officers and professionals to record the interviews with such children on videotape, a recording of which could then replace the child's actual appearance in court, or to set up live television links with such child witnesses who would be situated outside the courtroom.

Since 1 October 1992, videorecordings of children's statements have been allowed in criminal proceedings by virtue of s 32A of the Criminal Justice Act 1991. This new provision is the focus of the *MoGP*. Such videorecordings will clearly have an impact on decisions taken in the context of the 1989 Act and civil proceedings. Indeed, a new era of technology has been ushered in, wherein a great deal more expertise and skill will be expected of all child care professionals who are involved in child protection. A detailed analysis of the child as witness in criminal proceedings, the application of the *MoGP* and the evidential value of videos is undertaken in Chapter 7 below. We consider here, however, some of the implications of the new guidance on videotaped interviews with children with special reference to civil proceedings.

Even where a video has been made primarily for criminal proceedings, it will also be admissible in civil proceedings where rules of evidence apply less strictly. Indeed, there is nothing in the *MoGP* to prevent video interviews being broken up into different segments so that one part could be used for possible criminal proceedings and another for civil proceedings. The *MoGP* is voluntary and not legally binding so that any videorecording which does not strictly comply with the *MoGP* will not automatically be ruled inadmissible (see *MoGP* at p 1). The *MoGP* also states that an important reason for videorecording interviews with children is to reduce the number of times they are called upon to repeat their accounts during the investigation of the case. As the *MoGP* points out, although it concentrates on the evidential implications for criminal proceedings at the time the interview is planned, it may not be known whether criminal proceedings will follow and, even if they do, civil proceedings concerned with the welfare of the child, which would also benefit from a videorecorded interview, may come first. At an early stage of the investigation, if the probative value of the early stages of the recorded interview with the child is considered insufficiently convincing for a criminal

prosecution, the need to have recourse to other interviewing techniques, or
aids such as anatomically correct dolls, may arise. In that event, the general
antipathy of the courts towards such devices must be borne in mind (see
Chapter 7 below).

Thus, the interview might need to serve objectives which are additional
to, and no less important than, those with which the *MoGP* is primarily
concerned. For example, under the 1989 Act the child's wishes and feelings
should usually be ascertained pursuant to s 1(3) and this part of the interview
might not be suited to a fact-based or event-based method of approach which
a criminal proceeding would usually require.

Another point to be noted with regard to videorecorded interviews is that
as a consequence of the 'no-delay' principle under the 1989 Act (s 1(2)), it
is quite probable that the evidence concerning the allegations of sexual abuse
will be heard in civil proceedings before being heard in criminal proceedings.
Consequently, defendants who were parties in the civil action, will have heard
the substance of the evidence prior to the criminal proceedings and be better
prepared for defending the case in the criminal court.

The *MoGP* even suggests that 'it may not be necessary or even appropriate'
to adopt the *MoGP*'s event-oriented approach when only particular civil
proceedings such as matrimonial proceedings are involved. Hence, although
adhering to the standards and form of questioning recommended in the
MoGP will not prejudice the quality of the videorecorded interview in any
way, it suggests that a more relaxed approach might be followed in the case
of recordings intended for civil proceedings. The *MoGP* also emphasises that
interviews carried out under the *MoGP* should not be called either disclosure
or therapeutic interviews because the main purpose is 'to listen with an open
mind to what the child has to say, if anything, about the alleged event'.

The *MoGP* considers when and where to make a videorecording and what
equipment to use. It also covers various matters which are connected with
planning for the interview, including whether the child will be able to give
a reasonably coherent account of the events under investigation; the duration
and pace of the interview; who should conduct the interview; who else should
be present during the interview; and whether the child's consent to the
videorecording is required. However, the *MoGP* does not address the potential difficulties involved in this area of informed consent. Although expecting
a sufficiently mature and intelligent child to be given an explanation of the
video so as to give his consent 'freely', written consent is not required (at
para 2.29) although it states that 'it is unlikely to be practicable or desirable
to videorecord an interview with a reluctant or distressed child'.

In other words, the *MoGP* says nothing about a 'mature' child's right to
refuse consent to an interview, only that he should be given an explanation
of the purpose of the interview commensurate with his age and understanding
and implies that his consent should normally be obtained as a matter of
practicality.

Further, the *MoGP* also points out that a child needs to be advised that 'whether a videorecording is made or not, he or she may be required to attend court to answer questions directly'. However, even though the child might not have to testify in court, other professionals will be allowed to look at the videotaped interview, for example in family proceedings in the civil court, even if the case does not proceed to the Crown Court.

The actual way in which the interview should be conducted is then discussed in the next section of the *MoGP*, with the declaration that 'the basic aim of the interview is to obtain a truthful account from the child, in a way which is fair and in the child's interest and acceptable to the courts'.

6.18.6 *The MoGP: the four phases*

The *MoGP* suggests that interviews follow a 'step-wise' style of interviewing which involves proceeding through four prescribed phases, which are: (1) rapport; (2) free narrative; (3) questioning which might be carried out in four stages; and (4) closing the interview and thanking the child.

(1) **Phase one** – establishing rapport with the child. The problem with this is that it assumes that children will spontaneously narrate their experiences of sexual abuse, if this has taken place, to highly sensitive and well-trained interviewers. As Smith explains: 'There is little empirical evidence to support this' (G Smith 'Good practice or yet another hurdle: Videorecording children's statements' (1993) *Journal of Child Law* 21). Indeed, Smith goes on to relate that 'many primary investigations demonstrate quite the opposite, which is that children who are highly likely to have been sexually abused do not make allegations during formal interview'.

The need for a clear demarcation between the beginning and end of investigative interviews is recognised by the *MoGP*, which indicates that interviews with children should follow a set regime, last approximately 60 minutes and only in exceptional circumstances should the child be interviewed on more than one occasion. In the light of the many repeated interviews in cases such as the Orkney Islands affair, this clearly bears reiterating.

(2) **Phase two**, the 'free narrative account' stage, is supposed to be conducted at the child's own pace and the interviewer is supposed to act 'as a facilitator not an interrogator'.

(3) **Phase three** involves more questioning, using first, open-ended, then specific, questions. This phase may, therefore, consist of a number of stages, commencing with open-ended questions and, depending on the child's responses, then more focused and specific questions, followed by 'closed' and leading questions. Closed questions are those which would give the child a limited number of responses, whereas leading questions are those which imply a particular answer or assume facts which are likely to be disputed.

The *MoGP* is careful to stress that it will not always be necessary to work through all these phases, since it will depend on how the interview has progressed, and the interviewer should not ask closed and leading questions in the first instance. Further, it is careful to point out that leading questions would not normally be allowed if the child were giving its evidence-in-chief live during criminal proceedings and would be excluded by the court in such proceedings. Responses to such leading questions would, therefore, be of very limited evidential value in criminal proceedings. However, in civil proceedings, it is certainly conceivable that, given the availability of video equipment and the encouragement of videorecordings, families of defendants could make rival videotaped interviews which showed the child in question denying any occurrence of untoward behaviour by the alleged perpetrator, or retracting statements recorded earlier (see P Smith 'Child Witnesses: Implications for Civil Proceedings' [1993] Fam Law 110 at 112). A conflicting videotaped interview could then be played to the relevant authorities as a means of exerting pressure on them to drop the case, perhaps even using the argument that the child should not be required to undergo yet another potentially traumatic and emotionally draining interview.

(4) **Phase four** deals with closing the interview and thanking the child. The *MoGP* reiterates here that 'it may be appropriate to terminate an interview before sufficient information has been obtained from the child for criminal proceedings'. Certainly, within the one hour that is allocated for this type of interview, this may be the situation in many cases. This does not necessarily mean that the interview might have been sufficient for child protection professionals to have decided what was in the child's best interests in the context of civil proceedings. For a variety of reasons, the *MoGP*'s one-hour maximum may well be unattainable. For example it has been argued that the 'rules of conversation' which apply in such interviews with children who are suspected abuse victims might result in the use of leading questions. Within such a short space of time, the amount of detail required by such interviews under the *MoGP* might well confuse the child who will be used to a more conventional or succinct style of description (see Wattam *Disclosure: The Child's Perspective* (1990, NSPCC) and see, further, Chapter 7).

Similarly, McEwan has pointed out that most witness statements are composites, having been taken over different periods of time, so that the experience of the nature of disclosure (when it does take place) is not consonant with the child providing all relevant information 'at one fell swoop' (McEwan 'Where the Prosecution Witness is a Child: the Memorandum of Good Practice' (1993) *Journal of Child Law* 17).

6.18.7 Comments on the MoGP

Several other reservations about the *MoGP* may also be noted. First, there is considerable concern about the shortage of necessary interviewing skills.

Social workers' training, for example, does not prepare them adequately for skilled interviewing even with, or perhaps particularly with, the *MoGP* guidance. Secondly, satisfying evidential requirements in order to facilitate the prosecution of an offender while still trying to promote the paramountcy of the child's welfare may often cause a considerable amount of confusion, not least because civil proceedings serve different functions to criminal ones. Can interviewers meet the requirements of the criminal justice system and still manage to protect the children they are interviewing?

Thirdly, early indications and responses to the *MoGP* in the social work field have not been encouraging (see, eg Ward 'Interviewing Child Witnesses' [1992] NLJ 1547).

Another potential problem with the *MoGP* appears to be the lack of guidance or criteria that will determine whether an investigative or facilitative interview should be carried out. Smith argues that there are risks involved in interviewing the child before he is ready to speak freely about having been abused, and suggests that 'the weight of the available evidence should define the purpose of the interview itself' (see G Smith 'Good practice or yet another hurdle: Videorecording children's statements' (1993) *Journal of Child Law* 22). Hence, interviews purely for civil proceedings may be conducted without as many legal constraints as criminal proceedings would require. However, it is submitted that in many cases, even if the nature of the evidence appears to be reasonably clear, open-ended interviews conducted within the broad structure of the *MoGP*, particularly in the light of the Cleveland guidelines and the paramount welfare of the child, may not be sufficient to enable a child to speak freely about having been abused.

Other special problems that a child might face in communicating his views and experiences might be the result of mental disability or extreme youth causing him to have little or no language. A child who needs an interpreter throughout the interview will require a considerably longer period. A child's emotional trauma might have to be overcome before he will be able to communicate in any coherent way (G Smith *ibid*, at p 23).

Thus, although the *MoGP* is a positive step towards enhanced interviewing, it would seem that the new era of technology has already succeeded in creating more problems than it has currently solved. Videorecorded interview guidance must not be allowed to dictate the only way in which children are to be interviewed, or the way in which suspected child victims are to be treated or, indeed, counselled but rather be merely one of the useful tools which may be used in child protection. Ultimately, the situation where, in seeking to be fair to all parties concerned in a child abuse investigation, we lose sight of the child's paramount welfare and immediate needs, must be avoided. In certain cases, the desire to convict a particular perpetrator and to satisfy criminal standards of proof may have to be secondary to the need to protect the child forthwith through the use of civil proceedings.

APPEALS

6.19 Appeals

6.19.1 Introduction

The 1989 Act provides that any party to proceedings for a care or supervision order (including interim orders) has a right of appeal (s 94(1)). The appeal lies to the High Court Family Division against the making of or refusal to make any such order by a magistrates' court. An appeal against the making of or refusal to make any such orders by a judge in the county court or in the High Court lies to the Court of Appeal, Civil Division. In contrast with the old law, this means that children, parents, local authorities and anyone else who attains party status in the proceedings, have equal rights to appeal against decisions made by the courts with which they are dissatisfied. This right of appeal has been exercised extensively in the first 18 months of the operation of the 1989 Act. Whereas local authorities used to have to seek to use wardship as a means of remedying their lack of a right of appeal under the old law where a court had refused to make an order, there has been no shortage of cases brought by local authorities under the 1989 Act disputing the courts' refusal to make orders (see, eg *Croydon London Borough Council v A (No 1)* [1992] 2 FLR 34; *W v Hertfordshire County Council* [1993] 1 FLR 118, and *Gateshead Metropolitan Borough Council v N* [1993] 1 FLR 811).

6.19.2 Procedure

An appeal against the making, varying or discharging of or the refusal to make, vary or discharge any care or supervision orders (including interim orders) is lodged by filing in the court in which the appeal is to be heard, and serving on the parties to the proceedings and any guardian ad litem, a notice of appeal in writing setting out the grounds upon which the appellant relies (FPR 1991, r 4.22(2)(a)). Accompanying this, there must be filed a certified copy of the summons or application and of the order appealed against and of any order staying its execution, a copy of the notes of evidence, and a copy of any reasons given for the decision. It has been emphasised by the President of the Family Division, in a direction issued by him, that these documents must be filed in the registry (which is also a care centre) nearest to the court in which the order appealed from was made (see *President's Direction* [1992] 1 FLR 463). The notice of appeal must be filed and served within 14 days after the determination against which an appeal is brought (FPR 1991, r 4.22(3)(a)), unless it is an appeal against an interim care or supervision order, in which case it must be within seven days (r 4.22(3)(c)) or with the leave of the court to which, or judge to whom, the appeal is to be brought, within such other time as that court or judge may direct (r 4.22(3)(c)).

Where the appeal is being brought in the Divisional Court of the Family Division by a party other than the child, but the child was a party to the proceedings in a lower court and is affected by the appeal, the procedure to be followed is laid down in *Practice Direction* [1986] 1 All ER 896. The notice of motion should be served on the guardian ad litem of the child appointed in the court below, and no order is required appointing him guardian ad litem in the Divisional Court proceedings providing his consent to act and his solicitor's certificate, referred to in the Rules of Court, are filed in the Principal Registry by that solicitor as soon as practicable after the service of motion (FPR 1991, r 9.2(7)).

Where any parties who were respondents in the earlier proceedings wish to contend, on appeal, that the decision of the lower court should be varied, either in any event or in the event of the appeal being allowed in whole or in part, or that the decision of the lower court should be affirmed in whole or in part, or by way of cross-appeal that the decision of the lower court was wrong in whole or in part, then they must, within 14 days of receipt of the notice of appeal, file and serve on all other parties to the appeal a notice in writing, setting out the grounds upon which they rely (r 4.22(5)). No such right exists, however, in respect of an appeal against an interim care or supervision order made under s 38.

An appeal to the High Court will be heard and determined by a single judge who will normally sit in open court, and an application to that court to withdraw the appeal and have it dismissed with the consent of all the parties to amend the grounds of appeal may be heard by a district judge.

Where it is sought to bring fresh evidence before the appeal court, the case of *Croydon London Borough Council v A (No 3)* [1992] 2 FLR 350 provides guidance as to how such fresh evidence should be dealt with. In that case the court ruled that the proper approach for the appellant court to take was to consider, first, what view to take of the judge's decision below on the material that was before him, ignoring, at that stage, any fresh evidence which might have been adduced before the appellate court. If the judge below was plainly wrong, or had misdirected himself by taking into account some matter he should not have done or by failing to take into account some matter he should have done, the appeal should be allowed, unless the fresh evidence led to a different conclusion. Where the appellate court was minded to dismiss the appeal, it would be necessary to look at the fresh evidence, having regard to the disadvantages of having to decide on statement evidence only. It has been emphasised in *Croydon London Borough Council v A (No 1)* [1992] 2 FLR 341, that on an appeal from the magistrates' court under the 1989 Act, the appeal court has wide-ranging powers to consider and deal with the way in which the court below reached its decision, but it is not empowered to hear evidence save in *exceptional* circumstances.

6.19.3 Powers of the appellate court

It should be noted that the power of the appellate courts in children's cases may be exercised in any one of three ways.

(1) *Remit the case with directions* – where the appellate court is satisfied that the order was wrong but is uncertain, on the basis of the evidence before it, as to what order should be made, it may remit the case with such directions for the care of the child in the interim period as are consistent with the paramountcy of the child's welfare. (This was done, for example, in *Humberside County Council v B* [1993] 1 FLR 257, where Booth J discharged an interim care order on appeal and remitted the matter back to the magistrates to consider what order to make.

(2) *Substitution of orders* – where the appellate court is satisfied that the lower court's order was plainly wrong in law and it has before it all the relevant evidence, the court may substitute its own order where it reaches a different conclusion. (See *West Glamorgan County Council v P (No 2)* [1993] 1 FLR 407; and also *Nottinghamshire County Council v P* [1993] 2 FLR 134.)

(3) *Hearing the evidence* – in very exceptional circumstances, as has already been noted, the appellate court may hear evidence, although where it is the case that either or both of the parties are seeking to put fresh evidence before the court, then, again, as has been noted, great care will be exercised by the court in such circumstances in accordance with guidance issued by the Court of Appeal in both the pre-1989 Act case of *M v M (Transfer of Custody: Appeal)* [1987] 2 FLR 146, and in the post-1989 Act case of *Hounslow London Borough Council v A* [1993] 1 FLR 702. The appellate court may then either allow the appeal and substitute its own orders or dismiss the appeal. In cases where new evidence suggests the lower court reached its decision without being aware of some crucial factors, the appellate court may remit the case for reconsideration in the wake of such evidence (see *A v A (Custody Appeal: Role of Appellate Court)* [1988] 1 FLR 193; and *Re B (Minors) (Custody)* [1991] 1 FLR 137).

When drafting a notice of appeal in all these situations, it is vital that the document reports fully the reasons upon which the lower courts' decision was based and, where the sequence of events in the case is very complex, it is further helpful to the appellate court to have before it a chronology of events (see *Re B* (1992) *The Times*, July 16). The court rules require magistrates, as well as judges, to provide written reasons for their decisions which must be announced at the time of the decision (see *Hillingdon London Borough v H* [1992] 2 FLR 372 and *W v Hertfordshire County Council* [1993] 1 FLR 118) and these reasons must be sufficiently detailed for an appellate court to be able to scrutinise them and must be set down in the manner prescribed by the Court of Appeal (see *Re B* (1992) *The Times*, July 16).

6.19.4 Orders pending appeals

It is provided for the first time by the 1989 Act that the court has power to make orders pending appeals in care or supervision order proceedings (s 40). It was clearly the intention of Parliament to provide some continuity in the child's life by reason of the powers which have been given and, since such orders come within Part IV of the 1989 Act, they are again subject to the application of the three limbs of the welfare principle (s 1). The criteria which must be met are that there must have been some intervention already in the child's life in the proceedings represented by the making of a care or supervision order or an interim order (s 40). There is, however, a lacuna if the intention is to appeal against a refusal to make a first interim order since an earlier emergency protection order would not seem to qualify as an order being made pending such an appeal in order to provide for the child to remain in the care of the local authority (s 40(1)(b) and (2)(b)). Where the court dismisses an application for a care order and the child is, at that time, subject to an interim care order, the court may make a care order pending the appeal (s 40(1)). Where a court dismisses an application for a care order or supervision order and the child is, at the time, subject to an interim supervision order, the court may make a supervision order pending the appeal (s 40(2)). The court, further, has the power in each case to include directions in the order on any matter to do with the child's welfare as it sees fit. Where the court grants an application to discharge a care or supervision order, it can order that, pending the appeal, the decision is not to have effect (s 40(3)(a)), or that the order should remain in force subject to any directions it gives (s 40(3)(b)). Where an appeal is lodged against a decision of another court with respect to an order pending appeal, the appellate court may extend these orders (s 40(5)). Those orders which are made pursuant to this provision can only have effect until the date upon which the appeal is determined (s 40(6)(a)) or, where no appeal is made, the period during which an appeal could have been made (s 40(6)(b)). Where the court has made a residence order, together with any other s 8 orders in care or supervision proceedings, it further has the power to postpone the coming into effect of the order or to impose temporary requirements pending an appeal (s 11(7)). It should be stressed that under no circumstances should the power to make these orders pending the outcome of the appeals lead to unnecessary delay or contribute to adverse effects on the child's welfare as a result of lingering uncertainty. Appeals should generally be heard by the High Court Family Division within 28 days, and the Court of Appeal is equally bound in children's cases by the 'no delay' principle to be found in s 1(2) of the 1989 Act.

SUPPLEMENTARY PROCEDURES TO PROTECT CHILDREN

6.20 Wardship

Prior to the enactment of the 1989 Act the ability of local authorities to make a child a ward of the High Court was exercised extensively in order to circumvent the difficulties posed by obtaining care orders under the old law or to provide a right of appeal against the making, or refusal to make, care or supervision orders where such right was not given by the existing legislation. As a result of the 1989 Act, the ability of local authorities to use wardship as a means of protecting the child by obtaining an order committing the child into the care of the local authority has now been abolished through the repeal of various statutory provisions, and a clear message has gone out to local authorities that if their desire is to get the child committed into their care in order to gain the requisite degree of protection, they can only do this by using care proceedings under the 1989 Act (ss 100 and 31). The provisions of the 1989 Act further make it clear that it will not be possible for local authorities even to seek to invoke the inherent jurisdiction of the High Court (s 100) unless the remedy being sought is not available elsewhere, and the court deems it to be necessary, in the interests of protecting children, to exercise the inherent jurisdiction in favour of granting a local authority an order as, for example, in *South Glamorgan County Council v W and B* [1993] 1 FLR 574. As far as child protection matters are concerned, therefore, the avenue of wardship is clearly closed to local authorities. Where child protection is a matter of concern to other third parties they should clearly make an approach to the local authority either for the local authority to initiate action, or where the individual has taken the step of applying for an emergency protection order (see Chapter 4), steps should be taken quickly to ensure that the case is handed over to the local authority for investigation under s 47 and the consideration of the possibility of further proceedings under s 31. Where an interested relative or third party believes that the only course of action in which he can engage is to commence wardship proceedings, legal advice should be sought as to whether, in the current climate, this is really the most appropriate course of action. Given, therefore, the extremely attenuated possibility of anyone seeking to use wardship specifically to deal with concerns about child protection issues, it has not been felt worthwhile to go into the detail of a procedure which would be so little used. For those wishing to consider the many various other features of wardship, reference should be made to a specialist work such as Lowe and White *Wards of Court* (2nd edn) (1992, Butterworths).

6.21 Inherent jurisdiction

Whilst wardship is no longer available to be used by local authorities when the intention is to get a child committed into care as a result of concerns about child protection issues, it may, however, be possible for local authorities to seek to invoke the inherent jurisdiction of the High Court, provided the remedy they seek is not available elsewhere and the court deems it to be necessary in the interests of protecting children to exercise the inherent jurisdiction in favour of granting a local authority an order (see s 100 of the 1989 Act). It is not, therefore, possible to seek to invoke the inherent jurisdiction of the High Court to get a child committed into the care of a local authority but it is possible to invoke the inherent jurisdiction of the High Court to override a child's refusal to undergo a court-ordered medical assessment under s 38(b) of the 1989 Act even where the child is deemed to be competent to give such refusal (see *South Glamorgan County Council v W and B* [1993] 1 FLR 574). The full implications of this decision are discussed in detail in Chapter 10 below. The inherent jurisdiction of the High Court over children is exercised by the Family Division of the High Court (Administration of Justice Act 1970, s 1(2) and Sch 1) and is, thus, accessible in the provinces through the district registries, as well as in London through the Principal Registry. It is also possible, once the main issues in a case have been decided by the High Court, to transfer cases to the county court (Matrimonial and Family Proceedings Act 1984, s 38(2)(b)). Although the rules make no provision for a procedure to be followed when making an application to invoke the inherent jurisdiction of the High Court, it is submitted that an application could be begun by an originating summons which should be filed at the relevant court office together with an affidavit (see FPR 1991, r 5.1(1)). Whilst individuals seeking to invoke the inherent jurisdiction of the High Court do not need to seek leave, local authorities are required, under the provisions of s 100, to obtain the leave of the court before they can invoke the jurisdiction (s 100(2) and (3) of the 1989 Act).

6.21.1 Steps to invoke the inherent jurisdiction

There may well be situations in which local authorities have obtained a care order and where the issue of child protection demands further additional orders which cannot be made by the court in the course of care or supervision order proceedings. Thus, once a care order has been made, the provision of s 9(1) of the 1989 Act prevents a court making any s 8 order with respect to a child who is in the care of a local authority. Where it is felt necessary, therefore, to provide further protection for the child, by means of an injunction, to prevent particular persons going near or in the vicinity of the child, this will have to be done by invoking the inherent jurisdiction of the High Court under the terms of s 100. Such an application would not be defeated by the provisions of s 100 of the 1989 Act, since the child is already in local authority care, thus overcoming the restriction that the court cannot exercise its jurisdiction so as to require a child to be placed in care (see s 100(2)) and the order is not being made for the purpose of conferring on the local authority power to determine any particular question in connection with any aspect of parental responsibility for a child (s 100(2)(d)). Since, before it seeks to invoke the inherent jurisdiction of the High Court, the local authority must seek leave of the High Court, the provisions of s 100(4) make it clear that the court will only grant such leave where it is satisfied that the result which the authority wishes to achieve could not be achieved through the making of any other order and that there is reasonable cause to believe that if the court's inherent jurisdiction is not exercised with respect to the child he is likely to suffer significant harm (s 100(4) and see *Nottinghamshire County Council v P* [1993] 2 FLR 134).

Since, in the circumstances envisaged, it is not possible for a local authority to obtain a prohibited steps order to prevent unwarranted interference with or undesirable contact with any particular child, particularly by third parties who would not be covered by the terms of a no contact order under s 34 of the 1989 Act, it is anticipated that the High Court would be prepared to grant leave for an application to be made.

Where the High Court is prepared to exercise its inherent jurisdiction, the court has the power to make any orders which may be deemed necessary in order to prevent the child suffering significant harm, although it would have to be shown that making an order is in the best interests of the child (s 1(1) of the 1989 Act).

There have been a few cases where the High Court's inherent jurisdiction has been exercised with respect to a child in response to a local authority's concern that the child would be likely to suffer significant harm. This was the case in *Re W (A Minor) (Consent to Medical Treatment)* [1993] 1 FLR 1. The case involved a girl of 16 who was in the care of the local authority and, thus, could not be made a ward of court. Authority was therefore sought from the High Court exercising its inherent jurisdiction to authorise treatment of a 16-year-old girl with anorexia where she was refusing treatment. The Court of Appeal stressed that the inherent jurisdiction of the court was exercisable in this case and, indeed, commented that it would have been equally exercisable had the child been a ward of court. The court's powers, it was stated, were theoretically limitless but there were far-reaching limitations in principle on the exercise of the inherent jurisdiction. The child's welfare was, however, the court's paramount consideration and, whilst the court would have regard to the views of a child of sufficient understanding to make an informed decision, where the child's welfare was threatened by a serious risk to his life or irreparable damage to his health, then the court should intervene and override the child's refusal of treatment.

Local authorities have, in the past, been successful in invoking the inherent jurisdiction of the High Court where it has been necessary to determine whether or not operations should take place in respect of a child who is in the care of the local authority and the parents are not agreeing to the operation being performed (see, for example, *Re C (A Minor) (Wardship: Medical Treat-*

ment) [1990] Fam 26). The ability to seek the exercise of the High Court's inherent jurisdiction will clearly continue to be of value to local authorities in those situations in which there may be a conflict over the issue of consent to medical treatment or operations. The court will, again, consider the matters by reference to whether an order is necessary to prevent the child suffering significant harm but it would appear clear from all the recent cases that if a child is refusing to give consent to treatment, and those with parental responsibility under a care order, *viz* the parents and the local authority, cannot agree, then the courts will make such orders as they deem best in the interests of the child. (See for an illustration of the principle, although it involved a wardship case, *Re E (A Minor) (Wardship: Medical Treatment)* [1993] 1 FLR 386.) Note also the stance taken by Thorpe J in *Re K, W and H (Minors) (Medical Treatment)* [1993] 1 FLR 854 and see also *South Glamorgan County Council v W and B* [1993] 1 FLR 574 discussed above and in Chapter 10).

By contrast with the position of local authorities, individuals do not need to seek the court's leave in order to be able to make an application to invoke the inherent jurisdiction of the High Court. Given the stance previously taken by the High Court in relation to its reluctance to interfere in children's cases where the children are the subject of care orders, it is unlikely that individual parents would meet with much success in seeking to invoke the inherent jurisdiction in order to challenge the care being given to a child by a local authority (see *A v Liverpool City Council* [1981] 2 All ER 385) unless they can employ some other provisions of the 1989 Act (see *Re B (Minors) (Care: Contact: Local Authority's Plans)* [1993] 1 FLR 543). It is suggested that the only situation in which the court may consider exercising its inherent jurisdiction will be where there is some allegation that the local authority is acting in some way in breach or disregard of its statutory duties (per Lord Wilberforce in *A v Liverpool City Council* (above) at p 395). Even in those situations, however, it has been pointed out, in a number of cases, that the more appropriate step for the parent to take is to look to the use of the process of judicial review as the proper means by which the court can exercise supervisory control over statutory bodies. (See *Re DM (A Minor) (Wardship: Jurisdiction)* [1986] 2 FLR 122; *Re RM and LM (Minors) (Wardship: Jurisdiction)* [1986] 2 FLR 205; *R v Bedfordshire County Council ex parte C, R v Hertfordshire County Council ex parte B* [1987] 1 FLR 239, and see generally Chapter 9.)

CHAPTER SEVEN

Criminal Proceedings

7.1 Deciding whether to institute proceedings

Several crucial matters need to be considered before criminal proceedings are instituted, for example the sufficiency of evidence, the possibility of care proceedings (where a lesser burden of proof is required) instead of criminal proceedings and the status of the witnesses. For example, a young child's evidence, despite the reforms effected by the Criminal Justice Act 1991, will still be regarded with some circumspection particularly where the complaint is the commission of a sexual offence (see Chapter 3). Police may, instead of bringing criminal proceedings, caution a young offender (see below).

7.1.1 Persons who may initiate proceedings

The Crown Prosecution Service ('CPS') usually initiates proceedings under s 1 of the Children and Young Persons Act 1933 ('CYPA 1933'), and, occasionally, the NSPCC will also initiate proceedings. However, a local authority may do so, either as the local education authority or through its social services committee (CYPA 1933, s 98). Local authorities are also required to take reasonable steps to reduce the need to bring criminal proceedings against children in their area and may provide schemes of activities in which the person cautioned may voluntarily participate.

7.1.2 Terminology

As far as the criminal law is concerned, persons under 18 are generally referred to as juveniles. However, the terminology in the relevant statutes such as CYPA 1933, CYPA 1963 and CYPA 1969 and age-limits contained therein are different from those used in civil law (see s 105 of the Children Act 1989 ('the 1989 Act') where all persons under 18 are 'children'). Under CYPA 1933 and CYPA 1969, 'child' means a person under 14 while 'young person' refers to anyone who has attained the age of 14 but is under 18. Children and young persons as a group are known as 'juveniles'. For pre-trial procedures such as the investigation of offences and detention under the Police and Criminal Evidence Act 1984, juveniles who have attained the age of 17 are treated in the same way as adult offenders.

7.2 Grounds for criminal liability

Under s 1 of CYPA 1933 (as amended by the 1989 Act) any person who is at least 16 years old, and has responsibility for any child or young person under that age, who wilfully causes or procures that child to suffer assault, ill-treatment, neglect, abandonment, or exposure in a manner likely to cause the child unnecessary suffering or injury to health, will be liable to criminal prosecution.

7.2.1 Persons liable under this section

CYPA 1933, s 1 describes the kinds of persons who may be held liable for committing the prohibited types of conduct stipulated in the section. Under s 17 of CYPA 1933 (as amended by the 1989 Act):

(1) any person who has parental responsibility for the child or young person; or is otherwise legally liable to maintain him; and any person who has care of him shall be presumed to have responsibility for that child or young person.

(2) A person who is presumed to be responsible for a child or young person by virtue of the above section shall not be taken to have ceased to be responsible for him by reason only that he does not have care of him.

7.2.2 Types of prohibited conduct

CYPA 1933, s 1(1) lists five types of cruel conduct, although these may overlap with each other. This appears from *R v Hayles* [1969] 1 QB 364, wherein the Court of Appeal indicated that a defendant's conduct could fall within more than one statutory category, eg neglect may, in certain circumstances, also be described as ill-treatment.

The types of ill-treatment mentioned are:

(1) assault;
(2) ill-treatment;
(3) neglect;
(4) abandonment or exposure;
(5) unnecessary suffering or injury to health.

The leading case on s 1 is *R v Sheppard* [1981] AC 394, wherein the House of Lords considerably modified the strict liability principle laid down by *R v Senior* [1899] 1 QB 283, which had previously decided that the particular state of mind of the parent was irrelevant once it was established that the 'reasonable parent' would have realised that his child required medical aid. That parent would be liable under s 1 so long as he did not obtain medical treatment for the child, which resulted in the likelihood of the child's unnecessary suffering or health. However, a majority of the Lords in *Sheppard* decided that conviction under the section could only be established if the prosecution could prove that (1) the child needed medical care at the relevant time, and (2) that the parents had deliberately or recklessly failed to provide that care. Hence, a genuine lack of appreciation that the child needed medical care or failure to provide that care through stupidity, ignorance or personal inadequacy were both good defences to a prosecution under s 1. This appears to have shifted the focus from the objective test of a 'reasonable parent' to a more subjective standard, requiring a greater element of conscious, intentional wrongdoing and a reckless disregard for the child's welfare. Nevertheless, it would seem that a parent would have to prove that he genuinely failed to appreciate the need for the child's medical treatment and that no deliberate act of neglect was ever contemplated.

Physical assault involves any unlawful interference with a person's body which causes the apprehension of harm, whether or not there is physical violence. Under s 1, it is necessary to show that the child was treated 'in a manner likely to cause' either actual suffering or injury. Clearly, if the offence involved physical violence, it will usually be difficult to prove unnecessary suffering or injury to health. On the other hand, assault without battery or physical contact of some sort might raise problems of proof of the likelihood of unnecessary suffering, particularly if the fear was too short-lived or trivial to satisfy s 1. Hence, it would appear that something more than common assault is required in order to bring a successful prosecution under this section (*R v Hatton* [1925] 2 KB 322, wherein Lord Hewart LCJ stressed that the section contemplates something more than an ordinary assault, such as is likely to cause the child unnecessary suffering). Merely causing the child astonishment and disgust is not an assault within the meaning of the section. Possible alternatives might be to utilise an alternative charge of common assault under s 42 of the Offences Against the Person Act 1861 or under s 39 (common assault and battery) of the Criminal Justice Act 1988 (see *Clarke, Hall and Morrison on Children* (1988, Butterworths)).

If it is uncertain as to whether a child has unusually brittle bones, the Crown Court may order tests to be carried out to see whether the child who is the subject of charges of causing grievous bodily harm and cruelty, does indeed suffer from brittle bone disease (*R v Cottee* [1984] CLY 603).

Examples of an assault without battery are forms of physical confinement, threats with some instrument, or some form of punishment which exceeds the bounds of reasonable chastisement. An unreasonably long period of unlawful detention or confinement might also constitute false imprisonment, for which a parent might also be criminally liable (see *R v Rahman* [1985] Crim LR 596, CA).

It seems reasonable to assume, in the light of *Sheppard*, that the age of the child and its particular sensibilities would probably be taken into account. Furthermore, if the child is an abnormally sensitive child, the parent must be aware of the child's unusual propensities. Otherwise, the parent could not be said to have possessed the requisite intention to commit the offence if he was unaware of the child's abnormal sensitivity and, for example, carried out a form of punishment which a normal child would not have found injurious to his health.

7.2.3 *Punishment administered by parent, teacher or others (s 1(7))*

It is instructive at this point to refer to CYPA 1933, s 1(7) which stipulates that the section does not affect the right of any parent, teacher or any other person having the lawful control or charge of a child or young person, to administer punishment to him. A schoolteacher's right of correction is now governed by s 47 of the Education Act 1986, which has abolished corporal punishment in all maintained schools, special schools, independent schools which are maintained or assisted by public funds (ie Ministry of Defence schools and direct grant schools), and wherever any education is otherwise provided by a local education authority. It also covers pupils who attend independent schools which are supported by public funds. But CYPA 1933 does not apply to any other private schools.

In a recent European Court of Human Rights judgment, it was confirmed that private schools in Britain retain the right to administer limited corporal punishment such as 'slippering' their pupils, provided the children do not suffer any long-lasting after-effects. The case was *Costello-Roberts v The United Kingdom* (1993) *The Independent*, March 26, and involved a seven-year-old boy at an independent school who had been admonished for talking in the corridor on a number of occasions and had been late to bed on one occasion. Three days after he had been told he would be punished by being beaten, he was hit on his clothed buttocks three times with a rubber-soled gym shoe, by the headteacher of an independent private school. This was held by a majority of the European Court (5:4) not to be severe enough to constitute 'degrading punishment' within the meaning of Art 3 of the European Convention on Human Rights, even though it was imposed automatically as part of the school's disciplinary system. The court emphasised that its judgment was not to be taken as approving corporal punishment in schools but that, on the facts of the case, the punishment meted out did not amount to any human rights' violation. The majority of the court ruled that a 'particular level of severity' had to be reached in order for the punishment to be 'degrading'. However, it was not made clear by the court in which circumstances such a level would be reached. The four dissenting judges (who did not include the British judge) argued that the ritualised character of the corporal punishment was 'striking'. A spanking on the spur of the moment might have been permissible but the official and formalised nature of the punishment meted out, without adequate consent of the mother, was 'degrading' to the child concerned and, therefore, violated Art 3 of the European

Human Rights Convention. The British judge was only prepared to say that the case was 'at or near the borderline' of what was acceptable.

In 1983, a 15-year-old boy, Matthew Prince, had been caned by his head-master at Brighton College, East Sussex. He was left with bruised and swollen buttocks. His case was dropped after the government offered a settlement of more than £20,000. The implication of the *Costello* case is that the *Prince* case (unreported) may have been held to have breached Art 3.

Article 19 of the United Nations Convention on the Rights of the Child (UNCRC) provides that all States must take all appropriate measures to 'protect the child from all forms of abuse, neglect or negligent treatment . . . while in the care of parents'. If corporal punishment is allowed in certain schools, purely because, as some argue, parents should retain the freedom to send their children to such schools, their freedom to make that choice is surely an abuse of their child's right to be protected within the meaning of Art 19 of the UNCRC. Excessive force is clearly child abuse by another name; how does one decide, in marginal cases, what is 'moderate and reason-able' and 'below a certain (undefined) level of severity'?

It is not clear whether the same standards would apply to both parents and teachers but it is certainly arguable that in some circumstances, parents might find themselves in breach of Art 3, which expressly prohibits 'inhuman' and 'degrading' punishment. Independent schools of more than 50 pupils are treated as 'registered children's homes' under the 1989 Act. Thus, such schools are prohibited from inflicting corporal punishment on their pupils. The current position, therefore, remains that some independent schools retain the right to administer corporal punishment where the common law still applies: the punishment would have to be moderate and reasonable or crimi-nal or tortious liability will arise. Under s 47(3) of the Education Act 1986, action taken to avert personal injury or immediate danger to property is permitted.

The Department of Health ('DOH') has also issued guidance on corporal punishment in independent schools, as part of the series of guidances and regulations issued to accompany the 1989 Act. In *The Children Act 1989 Guidance and Regulations, Vol 5 Independent Schools* (1991, HMSO), at paras 3.93 and 3.94 it states:

> 'It should be noted that section 47 of the Education (No. 2) Act 1986 has abolished the use of corporal punishment in LEA maintained schools, non-maintained special schools, prescribed categories of independent schools maintained or assisted by the Government or assisted by LEAs, and for pupils in independent schools whose fees are paid, at least in part, directly by central Government or an LEA . . . The implications of this legislation will need to be carefully considered by proprietors and SSDs . . . If, in exceptional circumstances, it is decided to use corporal punishment, it should not be unreasonable (for trivial offences or applied indiscriminately to whole classes) or excessive.'

Clearly, the principle behind the punishment has not really been addressed by the courts or by the government, only the degree of severity. Are we quite prepared to accept that corporal punishment should be allowed as a matter of principle? If so, on what basis? Apart from physically preventing a very young child from hurting itself, what justifications are there for physically beating a child *except* to humiliate and degrade that child? When people talk of 'disciplining' their child, rather in the manner in which some people 'discipline' an animal that has misbehaved itself, one should be allowed a great deal of scepticism about both the justification and efficacy of such punishment. Even if such actions might appear to stop a child behaving in a particular way, one could also question the long-lasting benefit this actually has on the child and the message he is being given about the use of physical force. It is submitted that the law as it stands is neither clear enough nor fair enough to all children, particularly of school-going age.

A parent may be criminally liable for inflicting upon his child physical injury which exceeds the bounds of reasonable chastisement – it must be moderate and reasonable (*R v Hopley* (1860) 2 F&F 202). Reasonableness will be assessed in the light of all the circumstances, with particular reference to the age, physical condition, intellectual understanding and emotional maturity of the child and the reason for administering the punishment. A person *in loco parentis* has the right to discipline and punish and the criterion used to determine whether a person stands in that particular relationship appears to be whether the care or control (or 'charge') of the child has been entrusted to that person by the parent or, where the parent is absent or there is no parent, is assumed by that person (*Powys v Mansfield* (1837) 2 My & Vr 359; *R v Cheeseman* (1836) 7 C&P 455).

7.2.4 Ill-treatment

Ill-treatment may be established if a course of conduct, which would not in itself be sufficiently serious to warrant criminal proceedings, is repeated over an inordinate length of time. Case-law suggests that one single act may be sufficient (see *R v Holmes* [1978] Crim LR 52, which held that one slap on the face of a mentally ill patient was enough to constitute ill-treatment). It is submitted, however, that on a strict construction, a court may take into account all the circumstances of the case especially since the age of the child and particular reason for the slap may come within the bounds of reasonable chastisement. This once again highlights the uncertainty that might arise in marginal cases.

It should be noted that 'ill-treatment' includes most forms of neglect and that the words 'assaults, ill-treats, neglects, abandons or exposes' are not separate, mutually exclusive offences (*R v Hayles* [1969] 1 QB 364).

Neglect has been the form of conduct on which most charges have been based and is the ground which was specifically considered by the House of Lords in *Sheppard* (see **7.2.4.1** below). The type of conduct covered by this ground is failure to provide medical aid to a child, or even refusing to provide such medical aid, if such refusal is unreasonable in the light of the nature of the operation required, or the reason for such refusal is purely on religious grounds.

7.2.4.1 *Mens rea* and *actus reus* required

The leading House of Lords case, *R v Sheppard* [1981] AC 394, has established that (1) the offence of wilfully neglecting a child, contrary to s 1(1) of CYPA 1933, is not an offence of strict liability to be judged by the objective test of the reasonable parent and the civil law concept of negligence was not to be imported into the offence; and (2) the *actus reus* of the offence was simply the failure, for whatever reason, to provide the child, whenever it was necessary, with the medical care needed, while the *mens rea* is that the parent was aware at that time that the child's health might be at risk if it was not provided with medical aid, or that the parent's unawareness of this fact was due to his not caring whether or not his child's health was at risk. Hence, the parent must have deliberately or recklessly failed to provide that care.

7.2.4.2 Failure or refusal to maintain the child

A parent is also liable under s 26 of the Social Security Act 1986, if social security benefits have to be provided for his child because of persistent refusal to maintain or neglect in maintenance of that child. The criminal penalties under this Act are not as severe as those under CYPA 1933.

Under common law, it is wilful neglect to fail to pay part of one's earnings towards the support of one's child (*Cole v Pendleton* (1896) 60 JP 359), but the reasoning in *Sheppard* suggests that it will have to be proved that the parent knew that the child needed support. Furthermore, the case of *Bernstein v O'Neill* [1989] 2 FLR 1, suggests that there can probably be no wilful refusal or culpable neglect by a person who simply has not the means to pay.

7.2.4.3 Suffocation while lying in bed

Under s 1(2)(b) of CYPA 1933, where a child under three years of age dies as a result of suffocation (not being suffocation caused by disease or the presence of any foreign body in the child's throat) while he is lying in bed with a person over the age of 16, this will amount to neglect, provided it is shown that the person was under the influence of alcohol when he went to bed.

7.2.5 *Parents jointly charged*

If the parents are jointly charged, although only one of them committed the act of neglect, the other is equally guilty if he had seen what was going on (*R v Bubb, R v Hook* (1850) 14 JP 562).

7.2.6 *Refusal of one parent to allow operation on child*

It has been held that a refusal by a parent to allow an operation on a child who requires it may be an offence under s 1 if the circumstances are such as to make the refusal unreasonable. Thus, the nature of the operation and the reasonableness of the refusal to have it performed must be considered by the court (*Oakey v Jackson* [1914] 1 KB 216).

7.2.7 *Abandonment or exposure*

It would appear that to constitute an offence under this category of offence, the exposure need not necessarily consist of the physical placing of the child somewhere with intent to injure it (*R v Williams* (1910) 4 Cr App R 89). 'Abandon' means to leave a child to its fate (*R v Boulden* (1957) 41 Cr App R 105).

Two illustrative cases are *R v Whibley* [1938] 3 All ER 777 and *R v Boulden* (above). In *Whibley*, five children had been left abandoned at a juvenile court. It was held that this action was unlikely to cause them unnecessary suffering or injury to health, since this was not a place which would expose them to injury.

In *Boulden*, after the children had been abandoned by first their mother and then their father, the court held that the criterion to be employed is: did the parent take all reasonable steps to ensure that the child had been received into care? The fact that the father had left them alone and unattended with only a small quantity of food was sufficient to constitute abandonment and neglect of the children.

7.2.8 *Exposure to risk not covered*

It has been held that wilful exposure under s 1(1) does not extend to exposure to risk (*R v Gibbins* [1977] Crim LR 741), where a father took his eight-year-old son and five other boys on to a baulk of timber on a disused section of the London docks and punted them into deep water; in fact, none suffered harm. Thus, it is submitted, that if some injury had in fact been suffered, the father would have been liable. It must surely depend on whether the risk actually materialised.

7.2.9 *Prosecution under Offences Against the Person Act 1861*

As far as infants under two years are concerned, the possibility of prosecution under s 27 of the Offences Against the Person Act 1861 should be noted. The offence can still be made out even if the parent did not have actual custody, but merely by having knowledge and allowing the child to be left on his doorstep for six hours on an October night (*R v White* (1871) 36 JP

134). In addition, if a person carefully wraps a five-week-old child and sends it by train on a short journey to the child's other parent's house and has it delivered at that other parent's lodgings, he would still be guilty of abandonment within the meaning of the 1861 Act, even though the child suffered no actual injury (*R v Falkingham* (1870) 34 JP 149).

7.3 Penalties

Offences under s 1 of CYPA 1933 are triable on indictment or summarily. On conviction on indictment the defendant will be liable to a term of imprisonment not exceeding 10 years. On conviction in a magistrates' court, he will be liable to a fine not exceeding a prescribed sum on Level 5 on the standard scale or a term of imprisonment not exceeding six months or both (s 1(1)). The courts will take account of the degree of neglect involved (*R v Burcher* (1988) *The Times*, March 4) and whether the injury was inflicted in a fit of temper, where there was a momentary loss of self-control (*R v Durkin* (1989) *The Times*, June 20) (see 'Sentencing Guidelines', at **7.22** below). Cases of common assault are now covered by s 39 of the Criminal Justice Act 1988, under which they are classified as summary offences. This would cover the cases of assault which are not serious enough to produce the unnecessary suffering or injury that s 1 requires. More serious cases would come under ss 18, 20 and 47 of the 1861 Act, in cases of unlawfully and maliciously wounding, or causing grievous bodily harm to the child with the intention of doing him some harm. An additional charge under s 1 of CYPA 1933 may be brought even where any of these offences are brought.

CRIMINAL LIABILITY OF JUVENILE OFFENDERS

7.4 Persons who may initiate proceedings

There are no restrictions on persons who wish to lay an information (a formal accusation) against a juvenile but, if someone wishes to do so, he must give notice of his decision to the appropriate local authority, unless that authority is itself laying the information (CYPA 1969, s 5(8)). The appropriate authority is that for the area in which the juvenile appears to reside or, if he appears not to reside in a local authority's area, that within whose area the offence was allegedly committed (CYPA 1969, s 5(9)). If the juvenile is 13 or over, the prosecutor must give notice to a probation officer before any proceedings may be commenced (CYPA 1969, s 34(2)). Either the police or the CPS may notify the probation officer once a decision has been made to prosecute the juvenile offender.

7.4.1 Arrest

If a juvenile is accused of a criminal offence, he may be brought before a court by being arrested, with or without warrant, or by summons. Where a juvenile is arrested, the arresting officer has an obligation to try to notify the person responsible for that juvenile's welfare (CYPA 1933, s 34(2)) (as substituted by s 57 of the Police and Criminal Evidence Act 1984 ('PACEA 1984')). The effect of the section is that where a child or young person is in police detention, the police are required to take all practicable steps to ascertain the identity of the person responsible for his welfare. Once such a person is identified, he should be informed that the juvenile has been arrested, the reason for the arrest, and where he is being detained, as soon as practicable. The Police and Criminal Evidence Code of Practice ('the PACE Code') makes it clear (at para 3.6) that the appropriate person shall be asked to come to the police station to see the child or young person. It states further (at para 13.1) that a juvenile, whether suspected of a crime or not, must not be interviewed or asked to provide or sign a written statement in the absence of the appropriate adult, although 'in exceptional cases of need' this may be done.

Under s 34(5) of CYPA 1933 (as amended) the persons who are responsible for the welfare of a child or young person are: (1) his parent or guardian; or (2) any other person who has, for the time being, assumed responsibility for his welfare. If a juvenile is illegitimate, his father will not, prima facie, be a parent, nor a guardian unless he has custody (*Re M* [1955] 2 QB 479). However, an unmarried father who has parental responsibility (under s 4 of the 1989 Act or via a parental responsibility agreement) will certainly qualify as a parent for these purposes.

The PACE Code states (at para 13A) that where parents or guardians of a person at risk are themselves suspected of involvement in the offence concerned, or are victims of it, it 'may be desirable' for the appropriate adult to be some other person. If the child is in care but is living with his parent or guardian, that parent or guardian should be informed, in addition to the local authority or voluntary organisation.

Where the juvenile is subject to a supervision order, his social worker or the probation officer supervising him is also to be informed as soon as practicable. If the juvenile is in the care of a local authority, 'parent or guardian' includes the local authority. However, if a child is in the care of a voluntary organisation which does not have parental responsibility, the appropriate adult will be the parent or guardian.

Under s 34(9) of CYPA 1933, it is stated that the rights conferred under that section in ss 2 to 7 are in addition to those conferred under s 56 of PACEA 1984. It may transpire that older children may want someone other than a parent or 'appropriate adult' informed. They have the right to make such a request under s 56 of PACEA 1984 which gives a right (under s 56(1)) to have one friend, relative or other person who is known to them or who is likely to take an interest in their welfare to be told, as soon as is practicable. Under s 56, however, the police have the right to delay the exercise of that right in circumstances outlined in s 56(5). However, the rights under s 34(2) of CYPA 1933 (as amended) may not be suspended.

7.4.2 *Cautioning juveniles as an alternative to prosecution*

According to the Home Office Circular No 52/1988, when a case of child sexual abuse has been investigated and it is established that there is sufficient evidence to justify prosecution, the police should consider whether there is an acceptable alternative to the prosecution in the interests of the child and the family, such as a caution. In the most recent Home Office Circular No 59/1990, intended to provide chief constables with guidance on the cautioning of offenders, which has been agreed with the Association of Chief Police Officers and the CPS, it is stated that 'there should be a presumption in favour of not prosecuting juveniles' and that 'Cautioning is recognised as an increasingly important way of keeping offenders out of the courts and in many circumstances reducing the risk that they will re-offend'. The purpose of a formal caution is:

(1) to deal quickly and simply with less serious offenders;
(2) to divert them from the criminal courts; and
(3) to reduce the chances of their re-offending.

There is no statutory provision for the police cautioning of offenders but the Home Office has encouraged the use of cautioning for juveniles. The appendix to the Circular enunciates the guidelines for the administering of a caution and these are essentially as follows.

(1) A caution may only be administered where there is either an admission of guilt or evidence of guilt sufficient to give a realistic prospect of conviction.
(2) The juvenile must admit the offence.
(3) The juvenile and his parents/guardian must understand the significance of a caution and give informed consent to the caution.

Where the evidence does not meet the required standard, a caution cannot be administered. Neither will it be appropriate to give a caution to a person who does not make a clear and reliable admission of the offence. With regard to a juvenile under the age of 14, it is necessary to establish that he knew that what he did was wrong and, where applicable, that he had the necessary intent. The next thing to consider is whether a caution is in the public interest. Facts that should be taken into account are: (1) the nature of the offence; (2) the likely penalty if the offender was convicted by a court;

(3) the offender's age and state of health; (4) the previous criminal history; and (5) his attitude towards the offence.

It is desirable, before a caution is given, that the victim should be contacted to establish his or her views about the offence. But the victim's consent to a caution is not essential.

In reaching a decision on prosecution, the police will wish to take full account of the views of other agencies concerned with the case, especially the social services departments, on how a prosecution might affect the victim and others in the family. The CPS will be ready to offer advice on the sufficiency of evidence in any case and the balance of the public interest in deciding whether or not to initiate criminal proceedings.

If the police do decide on prosecution, the discretion of the CPS to continue or discontinue criminal proceedings is open to challenge by judicial review but only where it is patently demonstrable that the decision was made regardless of, or contrary to, a settled policy of the Department of Public Prosecutions ('DPP') which is in the public interest, for example the policy of administering a caution to juveniles. However, according to *R v Chief Constable of Kent ex parte L* (1991) *The Times*, April 17, it would only be in the rare case where the defendant could show that a discretion had been fatally flawed to the extent that a decision was made which was so contradictory to such a policy and it was a policy that the CPS was bound to apply.

7.5 Treatment of juveniles by the courts

Recent reports and studies have indicated that there is a growing number of children and young persons who abuse other children physically and sexually. A recent report on sexually abused children indicated that nearly a third of such abusers were in fact under 18. (See *The Report of the Committee of Enquiry into Children and Young People who Sexually Abuse Other Children* (1992, NCH) ('the *NCH Report*'). One of the key issues that was raised during the consultative process which preceded the NCH investigation was whether there was a need for a legal mandate to work with young perpetrators of sexual abuse.

The following general principles may be noted.

(1) A child under the age of 10 is presumed conclusively in law not to be capable of committing a criminal offence (CYPA 1933, s 50).
(2) Criminal matters involving children aged 10 to 17 will be dealt with by magistrates in the youth court, formerly known as the juvenile court.
(3) Certain restrictions are imposed on the interrogation of juveniles as well as special provisions relating to bail which do not apply to adults.
(4) A greater degree of flexibility exists about the decision to take court action, and alternatives such as cautioning the juvenile who admits the offence may be used (see above).

(5) Since 1985, it has been official policy to reduce the use of prosecution for juvenile offenders. The rationale appears to be that if a young person manages to avoid entry into the criminal justice system at an early age, it will be possible to avoid the system altogether. Although the 1990 Home Office Circular explicitly declares that there should be a presumption in favour of not prosecuting juveniles, in certain cases the seriousness of the crime or absence of other options may necessitate prosecution as the only suitable alternative.

(6) The power in s 22 of the Powers of Criminal Courts Act 1973, to suspend custodial sentences, has been repealed in relation to people under 21. The intention appears to be to emphasise to the mind of the sentencer the unique character of custody.

(7) Apart from a custodial sentence, the only sentence available for those aged between 18 to 20 which is not also available for adults, is an attendance centre order, not exceeding 36 hours. This is the same for offenders aged 16 to 20.

(8) Persons under 21 cannot be committed to the Crown Court for sentencing under the 'protection of the public' limb of s 38 of the Magistrates' Courts Act 1980, but may be so committed under the new 'seriousness' limb of s 38 of the Criminal Justice Act 1988.

7.6 Presumption for child aged between 10 and 14

A child aged between 10 and 14 is in law presumed not to know right from wrong, but this presumption may be rebutted upon proof that at the time of the act, he knew it was wrong. It is sufficient that he knew the act was morally wrong (Smith and Hogan *Criminal Law* (5th edn) (1983, Sweet and Maxwell) at p 163), or that the officer who saw the defendant asked him if he appreciated that what he was doing was seriously wrong, to which he received an affirmative answer (*IPH v Chief Constable of South Wales* [1987] Crim LR 43). In addition to proof of such knowledge, the usual proof of *mens rea*, or a guilty mind, would have to be shown.

In *McC v Runeckles* (1984) *The Times*, May 5, it was suggested that proof of *mens rea* and *actus reas* of an offence would not suffice unless the prosecution could also show that the child was aware that his act went beyond mere mischievousness. In those circumstances, Goff LJ posited four elements:

(1) there is the presumption;
(2) the prosecution have to rebut it;
(3) the ordinary criminal burden of proof applies to the prosecution's rebuttal;
(4) the prosecution has to show that the child appreciated that what he was doing was seriously wrong.

As the child gets older, the presumption gets progressively weaker until it disappears on the child's fourteenth birthday (*X v X* [1958] Crim LR 805).

The court may hear evidence of the child's background in order to ascertain the child's ability to determine right from wrong (*F v Padwick* [1959] Crim LR 439) and not rely on his demeanour in court (*Ex parte N* [1959] Crim LR 523).

Evidence that is prejudicial to the child may also be relevant and may be admitted; this includes evidence of a boy's previous convictions (*R v B; R v A* [1979] 3 All ER 460). A case may be dismissed if no evidence is called to rebut the presumption.

A boy under 14 cannot be found guilty of rape and allied sex offences, and any evidence that proves the particular boy has reached puberty and that the alleged act took place will be inadmissible. The boy may still be convicted of indecent assault or common assault. Although the sentences for each of these offences are significantly different, in practice they will have very little significance to a boy under 14. If the juvenile is over 14 there are no restrictions – he will be treated in accordance with the normal procedures.

7.6.1 Taking the pleas of a juvenile

Taking the pleas of a juvenile means that the juvenile will be asked whether he pleads guilty or not guilty to the charge. There is a duty to explain to the juvenile that he may give evidence or address the court as well as call witnesses, but this duty only applies if he is not legally represented.

CRIMINAL PROCEDURE: JUVENILES

7.7 Plea of not guilty

If the juvenile pleads not guilty at the commencement of the hearing, the normal order of trial proceeds. The prosecution will make its opening statement, and the court will then hear the evidence of the witnesses for the prosecution and each of them may be cross-examined by or on behalf of the juvenile. The juvenile may wish to change his plea just before the court makes its final order. In this case, the court has a discretion to allow him exceptionally to do so, in the interests of justice (*Re S (An Infant) v Manchester City Recorder* [1971] AC 481).

7.7.1 The welfare criterion

Every court dealing with a juvenile who is brought before it as an offender must have regard to his welfare and must, in a proper case, take steps to remove him from undesirable surroundings and see that proper provision is made for his education and training (CYPA 1933, s 44). This is intended to ensure that in criminal proceedings the juvenile's welfare is one of the factors that will be considered by the court. Of course, in a criminal case, the protection of the public is a relevant and very important consideration (see also discussion, below, on the Criminal Justice Act 1991).

7.7.2 Proper judicial forum for juvenile

As far as criminal proceedings for a juvenile are concerned, there is an initial choice of whether the proceedings should be in the youth or the adult magistrates' court. The general rule is that a charge against a juvenile is to be heard by a youth court but this is subject to six exceptions:

(1) where the juvenile is jointly charged with an adult;
(2) where the juvenile is charged with an offence arising out of circumstances which are the same as, or connected with those giving rise to an offence with which a person who has attained the age of 17 is charged at the same time;
(3) where the adult is charged with aiding, abetting, causing, procuring, allowing or permitting the offence by the juvenile; or
(4) where the juvenile is charged with aiding and abetting, causing, procuring, allowing or permitting the offence by the adult;
(5) where proceedings against the juvenile are started in the adult court and it only becomes apparent later that the defendant is a juvenile;
(6) where the court is conducting remand proceedings.

As far as the first exception is concerned, the case must be heard in the adult magistrates' court, but in cases (2) to (4) the court has a discretion. In the case of (6), an adult court, where necessary, may hear a remand of a juvenile.

Under the Code for Crown Prosecutors, various factors are listed to assist the CPS to decide, where a discretion is allowed, which court should hear a particular case involving a juvenile. Among the factors mentioned are the respective ages of the adult and the juvenile; the seriousness of the offence, the likely plea, the presence or absence of charges against the juvenile before the youth court and the need to deal with the interests of justice.

7.7.3 Summary trial of juvenile

A juvenile does not enjoy the adult's rights of trial by jury. Hence, a juvenile charged with an indictable offence must be tried summarily in the youth court, unless one of the exceptions applies so that it is either necessary (where there is a joint charge with an adult) or discretionary for the case to be heard in the adult magistrates' court. The cases in which a juvenile must be committed for trial from the adult or youth court to the Crown Court are:

(1) where he is charged with homicide; or (2) where he is a young person (aged between 14 and 17) and the court considers it ought to be possible for him to be detained for the longer periods suitable under s 53 of the CYPA 1933; or (3) where he is jointly charged with an adult and the court considers it necessary, in the interests of justice, to commit them both for trial (s 24 of the Magistrates' Courts Act 1980 ('MCA 1980')).

7.7.4 *Conduct of trial in the youth court*

The procedure for the conduct of a trial in a youth court is the same as for a magistrates' court (see MCA 1980 and the Magistrates' Courts Rules, SI 1981/552 ('MCR 1981')), save to the extent that it is excluded. The rules of procedure which apply specifically to youth courts are mainly contained in the Children and Young Persons Acts and the Magistrates' Courts (Children and Young Persons) Rules 1992, SI 1992/207 ('MC(CYP)R 1992'). (For the order of speeches and procedure see Chapter 6.)

The trial in the youth court will begin with the substance of the charge being explained to the juvenile in simple language. Unless the juvenile is legally represented, his parents or guardian must be allowed to assist in conducting his case, including the cross-examination of witnesses. If the juvenile is not legally represented or being assisted in this manner, the court must convert any assertions he may make into questions, for the purposes of cross-examination (MC(CYP)R 1992, r 6). Otherwise, the evidence is called and the case proceeds in the same order as in the adult court.

Where a juvenile is found guilty of any offence other than homicide by any court other than a youth court, he must be remitted to a youth court unless the court is satisfied that it would be undesirable to do so (CYPA 1933, s 56(1)).

7.8 Plea of guilty

If the juvenile pleads guilty the prosecutor relates the facts of the case, and the magistrate will ask the juvenile whether he has anything to say about the events. This enables the court to ascertain whether the juvenile has, in fact, understood the nature of the charge and the truth or otherwise of the juvenile's statement. The statement will also assist the court in assessing the character and background of the juvenile.

A person who has reached the age of 16 may enter a plea of guilty in writing in the youth court in cases where the procedure envisaged in s 12 of MCA 1980 has been adopted by the prosecutor (Criminal Justice Act 1991 ('CJA 1991'), Sch 11).

As mentioned above, the court is required to have regard to the welfare of the juvenile when dealing with him (CYPA 1933, s 44).

7.8.1 *Finding of guilt*

If a juvenile is found guilty, the court must make copies of any written report before it to be made available to the child's legal representative, if any, and to any parent or guardian of the juvenile present at the hearing. The reports must be made available to the juvenile unless the court finds it impracticable to do so because of the child's age and level of understanding or because it is undesirable to do so having regard to the serious harm which might thereby be suffered by the child.

Where a juvenile is found guilty, but it subsequently appears that it would be in the interests of justice that the case be heard again, a court constituted in the same manner may, within 28 days, beginning with the finding of guilt, give a direction to this effect (MCA 1980, s 142).

If a juvenile is found guilty in the courts, he may be remitted to a local youth court acting for the area where the juvenile normally resides (CYPA 1933, s 56(1)).

7.8.2 *Orders which the court can make in criminal proceedings*

The following orders can be made by the court in criminal proceedings.

(1) Committal to Crown Court for trial.
(2) Committal to Crown Court with a view to restriction order.
(3) Detention centre order in young offender institution.
(4) Remand to local authority accommodation.
(5) Attendance at attendance centre.
(6) Community sentences (includes supervision/probation orders/curfew/ combination/community service) (see below).
(7) Hospital or guardianship order.
(8) Binding over parent/guardian.
(9) Binding over juvenile.
(10) Fine.
(11) Absolute discharge.
(12) Conditional discharge.

A youth court may not impose detention under CYPA 1933, s 53(1) and (2), since this may only be imposed following conviction on indictment. The youth court is also precluded from imposing a restriction on discharge from hospital where a hospital order is made.

7.8.3 *Secure accommodation*

Applications for secure accommodation are now made under s 25 of the 1989 Act and the Children (Secure Accommodation) Regulations 1991, SI 1991/

1505. These may be made to the family proceedings court, youth court, magistrates' court or Crown Court (in criminal proceedings).

Under s 25 of the 1989 Act, upon the application of a local authority, a court may make a secure accommodation order in respect of the child if it appears that:

(1) (a) the child has a history of absconding and is likely to abscond from any other description of accommodation; and
    (b) if he absconds, he is likely to suffer significant harm; or
(2) if he is kept in any other description of accommodation he is likely to injure himself or other persons.

The Children Act 1989 Guidance and Regulations, Vol 4 Residential Care (1991, HMSO) makes it clear that it is expected that secure accommodation will be used as a 'last resort'. Secure accommodation, or a secure placement of a child, may be the 'most appropriate and only, way of responding to the likelihood of a child suffering significant harm or injuring himself or others' (at para 8.5). The child should not continue to be kept in secure accommodation if the criteria cease to apply.

The maximum periods which a court may order for placement in secure accommodation are three months for the first application and up to six months for any subsequent application (see Children (Secure Accommodation) Regulations 1991, SI 1991/1501 ('C(SA)R 1991')). Regulation 4 has been amended by the Children (Secure Accommodation) (Amendment) Regulations 1992, SI 1992/2117 ('C(SA)(A)R 1992'), so that the approval required by the Secretary of State for the placement of children under 13 years of age in the secure accommodation of a community home is subject to terms and conditions.

Defendants under 17 who are refused bail will usually be remanded 'to local authority accommodation'. As such, they will become children 'looked after by a local authority' within the meaning of s 22 of the 1989 Act. The accommodation into which a juvenile is remanded will not usually be secure accommodation. However, the local authority may place a juvenile in secure accommodation for up to 72 hours within any 28-day period. If they wish to detain the young person in secure accommodation for longer than this, they must apply to a youth court or other magistrates' court for authorisation (C(SA)R 1991, reg 10; and CJA 1991, s 60(3)). The maximum period of authorisation is normally the period of the remand. However, there are variations depending on different circumstances.

Four further points should be noted: (1) s 1(5) of the 1989 Act should always be kept in mind, so that it should still be shown that it is better to make an order for the child; (2) the child's welfare should be a paramount consideration; (3) the welfare checklist under s 1(3) of the 1989 Act is not of particular relevance to s 25 proceedings but is not irrelevant; (4) delay was likely to prejudice the welfare of the child (see also *Hereford and Worcester County Council v S* [1993] 2 FLR 360). Proceedings under the 1989 Act have been designated under the Rules of Court as requiring the appointment of a guardian ad litem except where the court does not consider this necessary to protect the welfare of the child (see Family Proceedings (Amendment) Rules 1991, SI 1991/2113)).

In *Hereford and Worcester County Council v S* (above), Connell J held that s 25 of the 1989 Act was only one of a number of provisions enabling the liberty of a child to be curtailed. Others included: s 2 of the Mental Health Act 1983; s 53 of CYPA 1933; and ss 20(5) and 43 of the 1989 Act. The fact that the criteria under any of those provisions had been satisfied did not preclude the court from considering whether an order under s 25 of the 1989 Act should be made. The learned judge also made it plain that a court should authorise a secure placement only for as long as was necessary and unavoidable. This was an 'important factor'. Placing a child in secure accommodation was not within the province of the local authority. It could not do so unless it could satisfy a court of the relevant statutory criteria, especially those in s 25(1).

7.8.4 *Remanded juvenile committed to Crown Court*

If the remanded juvenile is committed for trial in the Crown Court, the order may be for a maximum of 28 days. Further: 'When a juvenile is remanded to appear before the Crown Court for trial or sentence it will be necessary for applications for orders under s 25 to continue to be made to a youth court or a magistrates' court other than a youth court' (*The Children Act 1989 Guidance and Regulations, Vol 7 Guardians ad Litem and other Court Related Issues* (1991, HMSO), at para 5.5).

7.8.5 *Remanded juvenile charged with certain offences*

Where a remanded juvenile is detained under s 38(6) of PACEA 1984 or is remanded in local authority accommodation and is charged with or convicted of an offence punishable with 14 years' imprisonment, or more in the case of an adult or a violent offence, or has previously been convicted of a violent offence, different criteria are laid down by C(SA)R 1991, reg 6. These criteria are that: (1) the child is likely to abscond from non-secure accommodation; or (2) the child is likely to injure himself or other people if he is kept in non-secure accommodation (see C(SA)R 1991, reg 6(2) as amended by C(SA)(A)R 1992). Such children would, therefore, be exempted from the criteria in s 25(1)(a) and (b) of the 1989 Act and subject to those under reg 6. Regulation 6 also exempts children remanded to local authority accommodation under s 23 of the CYPA 1969 from s 25 of the 1989 Act and they would be governed by the criteria under reg 6 instead.

A 'violent offence' is defined in s 31 of CJA 1991 as an offence which '. . . leads, or is intended to lead, to a person's death or to physical injury to a person' including offences of arson (ie criminal damage by fire (Criminal Damage Act 1971, s 1(3)). 'Sexual offences' are defined in CJA 1991, s 31 to include most statutory sexual offences with the exception of those concerned with prostitution and certain consenting acts between homosexuals.

✳ 7.8.6 *Guidance on secure accommodation under the 1989 Act*

The Children Act 1989 Guidance and Regulations, Vol 1 Court Orders (1991, HMSO), para 5.7 states that:

> 'it is the role of the court to safeguard the child's welfare from inappropriate or unnecessary use of secure accommodation, by both satisfying itself that those making the application have demonstrated that the statutory criteria in section 25(1) or Regulation 6, as appropriate, have been met and by having regard to the provisions and principles of section 1 of the Act. The court must therefore also be satisfied that the order will positively contribute to the child's welfare and must not make an order unless it considers that doing so would be better for the child than making no order at all.'

The Children Act 1989 Guidance and Regulations, Vol 4 Residential Care (1991, HMSO), at para 8.24 advises that a local authority wishing to restrict the liberty of a child under 13 should first discuss the case with the Social Services Inspectorate. There are two classes of people who may not have their liberty restricted in any circumstances: (1) people aged 16 or over, but under 21, who are provided with accommodation in a community home under s 20(4) of the 1989 Act; and (2) children subject to a child assessment order under s 43 of the 1989 Act.

Local authorities who have children placed in secure accommodation are required to review each case within one month of the start of the placement and, thereafter, at intervals not exceeding three months. Each authority must appoint at least three persons to undertake such reviews, one of whom must not be employed by the local authority looking after the child or by the local authority managing the secure accommodation in which he or she is accommodated (C(SA)R 1991, reg 15). Such appointed persons are required to satisfy themselves that the criteria for keeping the children in secure accommodation continue to apply and such a placement continues to be necessary and whether or not any other description of accommodation would be appropriate (C(SA)R 1991, reg 16). Regulation 16(2), thereof, requires that in undertaking the review referred to in reg 15, the persons appointed shall, if practicable, ascertain and take into account the wishes and feelings of the child, any parent, any person with parental responsibility, and any other person who has had the care of the child, the child's independent visitor if there is one, and the local authority managing the secure accommodation in which the child is placed if that authority is not the authority which is looking after the child.

7.8.7 *Legal representation*

It is important to note that a court *cannot* make a secure accommodation order *unless* the child is legally represented, or has been offered legal aid but has refused or failed to apply for it. The unruly certification process has been abolished by CJA 1991.

If a boy aged 15 or 16 who has been charged with, or convicted of, (1) a violent or sexual offence, or (2) an offence punishable in the case of an adult with imprisonment for 14 years or more, or (3) who has a history of absconding while remanded to local authority accommodation, and is charged with or has been convicted of an imprisonable offence alleged or found to have been committed while he was so remanded, and the court is of the opinion that only remanding him to a remand centre or prison would be adequate to protect the public from serious harm from him, it may remand him to a remand centre or prison but only if he is legally represented, or has been offered legal representation but has refused or failed to apply for it. Consultation between the court and a probation officer or a local authority social worker must also have taken place.

7.8.8 *Wards of court*

If a child is a ward of court and subject to directions made in exercise of the inherent jurisdiction, the directions cease to have effect in three or six months.

7.8.9 *Other points on remands*

Section 60 of CJA 1991 contains provisions which, when fully in force, will effect the abolition of the practice of remanding 15- and 16-year-old males to prison department establishments. This will be a two-stage process. In the interim stage, s 62, which came into force on October 1992, contains 'transitory provisions' whereby the provisions of s 60 will initially be implemented in a modified form. Thus, 'the option of a penal remand will remain open to the court in defined circumstances. The court will have a new power, after consultation with the local authority, to require any person remanded to local authority accommodation to comply with such conditions as it could impose under s 3(6) of the Bail Act 1976 if he were then granted bail . . . Subject to consultation with the local authority, the court may impose requirements on that authority to secure compliance with any such conditions the court may have imposed on the child' (*The Children Act 1989 Guidance and Regulations, Vol 7 Guardians ad Litem and other Court Related Issues* (1991, HMSO) at para 7.5).

In the longer term 'once there is general agreement that adequate alternative arrangements exist, juvenile penal remands will be abolished. Courts will then have the new power to direct that certain remanded juveniles must be placed in local authority secure accommodation' (at para 7.6).

7.8.10 *Permissible forms of control of children in residential care*

A current issue which has been highlighted by some recent cases reported in the media, is the extent to which it is permissible to restrain or restrict the liberty of children in residential care (see also Chapter 2, at **2.18.2** on the discussion of *The Pindown Experience and the Protection of Children: The Report of the Staffordshire Child Care Inquiry* (1991, Staffordshire Social Services) ('the *Pindown Report*'). In the latest DOH guidance (*Guidance on Permissible Forms of Control in Children's Residential Care* (1993, DOH)) on permissible forms of control of residential care children (see, further, below), there is a warning that the common law position on unlawful restriction of liberty and the criminal law relating to assault will be relevant. It also suggests that staff in such establishments take account of the nature and seriousness of the offence that has led to the refusal of bail in considering the kind of intervention and level of physical restraint that is necessary to prevent the child causing injury or serious damage. Clearly, there may well be occasions where staff will have to decide how best to react to a situation which might lead to either another public inquiry, or at least a complaint or even criminal proceedings, if their methods of physical restraint are seen as unreasonable and illegal. On the other hand, the 1993 DOH guidance (above) points out that the recent Court of Appeal decision of *Re W (A Minor) (Consent to Medical Treatment)* [1993] 1 FLR 1, suggests that parents or others with parental responsibility, which would include a local authority which was currently holding a care order, or the courts, may override the withholding of consent to medical treatment of even a 16- or 17-year-old child. The implication, it would appear, is that, in certain circumstances, the local authority or the courts would have the power to override the child's wishes, on the basis that it was in the child's best interests to do so.

This recent judicial approach has been questioned by a variety of commentators and it is submitted that the unique nature of the situations to which it has given rise were the only justifications for it. In both *Re R (A Minor) (Wardship: Medical Treatment)* [1992] 1 FLR 190 and *Re W* (above), the child involved was suffering from a mental malfunction which was potentially life-threatening. Unless this sort of mental disorder or illness can be shown, it is debatable whether the principle could be extended to 'normal' children. On the other hand, in the case of disruptive or violent children, the courts may have very little option but to agree that, subject to the latest guidelines, the local authority must do as it sees fit, and act in what it perceives to be the best interests of the children.

In *Re K, W and H (Minors) (Medical Treatment)* [1993] 1 FLR 854, a hospital had two secure units specialising in cases of highly disturbed adolescents. Among those admitted to the unit were three female adolescents, all aged 15 who were in the care of the local authority. Before admitting a patient to treatment, the units required written consent from parents or local authority, or both, to the unit's regime which included the emergency use of medication. A committee constituted to investigate complaints from the adolescents advised the local authority to apply for a s 8 order under the 1989 Act, for authorisation of treatment in respect of the adolescents. Thorpe J followed *Re R* (above) and held that the applications were misconceived and unnecessary. If a child were *Gillick*-competent he could consent to treatment but if he or she declined to consent, consent could be given by someone else who had parental responsibility. In the present case, he found that none of the children was *Gillick*-competent but, even if they were, their refusal of consent could be overridden by someone who had parental responsibility, or the court. The fact that the children were subject to secure accommodation orders did not affect the disposition of the case, since such orders bear no relevance to parental responsibility. Under s 25(9) of the 1989 Act, a parent, in the absence of a care order, may still remove a child from accommodation provided by the local authority under s 20, even though a secure accommodation order has been made.

The Children Act 1989 Guidance and Regulations, Vol 4 Residential Care (above) states: 'The placement of children in secure accommodation, should, wherever practicable, arise as part of the local authority's overall plan for the child's welfare'. It stresses the need to 'have regard' to the local authority's 'general duties' under s 22 of the 1989 Act, including the duty to safeguard and promote the child's welfare (s 22(3)(a)) and 'so far as is reasonably practicable, ascertain the wishes and feelings regarding the matter of the child, his parents, any other person who has parental responsibility for him and any other person whose wishes and feelings they consider relevant' (s 22(4) of the 1989 Act). It must be said that, comprehensive as this list is, in the context of secure accommodation, it is obvious that the key phrase to the whole section is '*so far as is reasonably practicable*'. It is submitted that in the case of children who have absconded and are likely to do so again, the potential danger to themselves and others overrides the guidance's rather idealistic aspirations, precisely on the basis that such accommodation is part of the duty to safeguard and promote a child's welfare.

The guidance reiterates the statutory framework for the restriction of liberty. This must be met before a child, who is being looked after by a local authority, can be placed and, if placed, kept in secure accommodation. The main statutory criteria are enunciated in s 25 of the 1989 Act (see **7.8.3** above at point (1)), and the associated regulations are C(SA)R 1991 (which replace the Secure Accommodation (No 2) Regulations 1983, SI 1983/1808 and the Secure Accommodation (No 2) (Amendment) Regulations 1986) and the C(SA)(A)R 1992.

Further, s 1(5) of the 1989 Act requires that the court should not make an order unless this would be better for the child than making no order; and s 1(1) of the 1989 Act requires that the child's welfare must be the court's paramount consideration.

The concept of 'restriction of liberty' is discussed in para 8.10 of the guidance (above), which states: 'any practice or measure which prevents a child from leaving a room or building of his own free will may be deemed by the court to constitute "restriction of liberty".' It points out that whilst the locking of a child in a room or part of a building to prevent him leaving voluntarily will be prohibited by the statutory definition, other practices which place restrictions on freedom of mobility (for example, creating a human barrier) are not so clear cut. In the latter case, the views of the authority's legal department should be sought in the first instance as to the legality of the practice or measure.

It clarifies that in the community homes system, the liberty of children may be restricted only in secure accommodation approved by the Secretary of State for such use. The guidance (above) also discusses the extent to which restriction of liberty may be permissible within a variety of contexts but the point which has emerged from staff in these residential establishments is that there is uncertainty as to how best to deal with situations in which they need to assert control, particularly in the context of children in residential homes who display disruptive or violent behaviour. To a certain extent, this uncertainty has been a reaction to the latest 'scandal' of abuse of children in residential homes by staff, eg under the 'Pindown' regime in Staffordshire (which led to an inquiry, which was critical of social workers). This was followed by several other residential homes' scandals such as the 'Frank Beck' affair. (See Chapter 2 for a discussion on 'Pindown' and other cases dealing with residential care.) Staff from the various children's homes in England complained to the DOH, stating, inter alia, that the 'Pindown' scandal has left them unclear as to the limits of reasonable control.

In response to the representations made by individuals and organisations to the DOH regarding this uncertainty, the DOH circulated first a Draft Guidance, followed by a guidance issued on 28 April 1993. Another, presumably more extensive, guidance is to follow, since the April 1993 guidance states that 'in implementing this guidance, staff may find it helpful to refer to the forthcoming Departmental guide *Safe and Sound* which will deal with a range of management and practice issues, including control and discipline, which apply specifically to secure accommodation'.

The key points of the April 1993 guidance are as follows.

(1) The guidance is derived from and builds upon the relevant parts of *The Children Act 1989 Guidance and Regulations, Vol 4 Residential Care* (above). It applies to all those establishments covered by *Vol 4* but does not extend to foster care, psychiatric wards and schools (except those schools that are registered children's homes).

(2) It covers children up to 18, who are referred to as children, in accordance with the 1989 Act.

(3) *Physical restraint* is defined as 'the positive application of force with the intention of overpowering the child'. It continues:

> 'That is, in order to protect a child from harming himself or others or seriously damaging property. The proper use of physical restraint requires skill and judgment, as well as knowledge of non-harmful methods of restraint.'

It stresses that:

> 'the onus is on the care worker to determine the degree of restraint appropriate and when it should be used. In particular, staff must be careful that they do not overreact.'

We would comment that this assumes that the particular social worker will be specially trained to cope with situations requiring forms of physical restraint with 'skill and judgment and knowledge of non-harmful methods of restraint'. There are no such requirements in recruitment of care staff to work in residential homes and the guidance states, in Section XI ('Training') that 'It is not usually helpful for staff to receive in-service training in self-defence in isolation from training in positive means of control'. Earlier in Section XI, it states that 'methods of restraint are routinely taught in some sectors of care work' and cites the psychiatric sector as one example. Further, it states: 'Above all, managers should satisfy themselves that any training sought is relevant to a Social Services setting and appropriate for use with children and young people'.

However, there are, at present, serious shortages of any sort of staff, and particularly specially trained ones, in residential care. Accordingly, until this fundamental resource is addressed, and greater clarity is given as to the degree of restraint which is appropriate, the guidance will be extremely difficult to operate in practice. Nevertheless, the fact that there is scope for interpretation must mean that regional variations will, inevitably, occur and this is surely what this document was intending to prevent.

The points on *physical restraint* are summarised in para 5.6 of the guidance as follows.

(a) Staff should have good grounds for believing that immediate action is necessary to prevent a child from significantly injuring himself or others, or causing serious damage to property.

(b) Staff should take steps, in advance, to avoid the need for physical restraint, eg through dialogue and diversion; and the child should be warned orally that physical restraint will be used unless he desists.

(c) Only the minimum force necessary to prevent injury or damage should be applied.

(d) Every effort should be made to secure the presence of other staff before applying restraint. These staff can act as assistants and witnesses.

(e) As soon as it is safe, restraint should be gradually relaxed to allow the child to regain self-control.
(f) Restraint should be an act of care and control, not punishment.
(g) Physical restraint should not be used purely to force compliance with staff instructions when there is no immediate risk to people or property.

Guideline (b) may not always be feasible. If, as is often the case, a child who is placed in secure accommodation has been refused bail because he is seen as disruptive and or violent, oral warnings may exacerbate the situation or be regarded with contempt and derision by the child. On point (f), the guidance reminds us (at para 5.1), that s 8 of the Children's Homes Regulations 1991, SI 1991/1506, which deals with control and discipline, lists disciplinary measures which are prohibited in children's homes and includes corporal punishment. Thus, treating physical restraint as an act of care and control, *not* punishment, is certainly laudable and must be the way forward. One difficulty, however, is that such an attitude must be internalised by social workers working at the 'coal-face', so that despite the inevitable stresses and strains of the moment, they have to bear this guiding principle in mind. The other problem is the need to find a way of getting the message across to the children that despite their being physically restrained, this is not to be interpreted as a form of punishment.

(4) *Children remanded or detained within local authority accommodation.* As far as children remanded or detained under CYPA 1969, s 23, PACEA 1984, s 38 or CYPA 1933, s 53, are concerned, Section III of the April 1993 Guidance states that: 'the fact that a child is detained under a court order is in itself a proper basis for imposing requirements on the child which do not apply to all children in an open home'. It continues: 'Staff should intervene positively if a child, subject to one of these orders, indicates (*sic*) [presumably: indicates an intention] or attempts to leave the home without authority.'
     It states that when the child is within the confines of the secure unit, the criteria for physical restraint should be the same as for a child living in an open setting. However, subject to its guidance on preventing a detained child from running away from such units, it declares that 'staff *should* intervene physically, including restraining the child in accordance with the following principles:

(a) the staff member must have reason to believe that the attempt to escape has a realistic chance of success unless some sort of intervention is made;
(b) physical restraint should be attempted only where there are sufficient staff at hand to ensure that it can be achieved safely;
(c) physical intervention should not be substituted for waiting patiently when, for example, a child has got onto a roof and, although in some

danger, is unlikely to escape further; physical intervention could create greater danger'.

(5) *Guidance on physical intervention to prevent a detained child from running away while being escorted outside a secure care unit.* Paragraphs 3.4 to 3.5 deal with preventing a detained child from running away while being escorted outside a secure accommodation care unit. It stresses that before the child is escorted outside such a unit, there should be an explicit and witnessed understanding between the child and the escort on how close the child should stay to the escort and how he should indicate what he wants to do and where he wants to go. The escort should carry official identification (see para 3.4). Managers and staff 'must take special precautions' which may include the provision of more than a single escort, all trained in methods of control and restraint'. The comments made above on the lack of trained personnel are equally applicable here. The guidance distinguishes between children who have committed a grave crime and those who have not. In the case of children who have committed a grave crime, the guidance emphasises that if such a child has to be escorted outside the unit for, for example, hospital treatment, he or she 'cannot be allowed to escape'. Thus, the guidance states: 'the escorts should be under instruction to ensure that he is given no opportunity to escape. They should employ *vigorously physical restraint techniques* of a force necessary to prevent that happening'. It is explicit in saying that 'managers and staff should understand that in all escape attempts involving the detained child the escort(s) *must be prepared to stop him by the use of physical restraint*' (authors' emphasis).

It is submitted that there will certainly be occasions where 'vigorous physical restraint techniques' may be necessary, if not essential, to prevent a child from escaping in these circumstances. However, it will need more than an ordinary amount of skill and tact, if the child puts up a fierce struggle and almost certainly more than one escort, to ensure that matters do not get out of hand and that restraint is kept within reasonable bounds.

For the child whose offences are far less serious, the implication is that a single escort may be all that is available or, indeed, assigned and although physical restraint must be exercised to prevent his escape, in these cases 'there will be limits to what a single escort can do'.

This section of the guidance ends by stating that if physical restraint has failed to prevent an escape so that the child successfully absconds, the escort must then inform the secure unit and the police immediately.

(6) *Responding to a young person who intends to leave without permission.* The guidance states that if a young person indicates his intention to leave without permission, or run away, the staff member who has reason to be concerned about this 'should take vigorous action'. He should warn the

youngster with clear instructions about the consequences if he does not comply and 'the staff member may use his physical presence to obstruct an exit and thereby create an opportunity to express concern and remonstrate with the child'. The guidance states that this is subject to the principles in para 9.3. This must be a misprint since there is no para 9.3 in the guidance. It must be a reference to para 10.3, which lists the following principles in relation to the use of an adult's physical presence. It states that the physical presence:

(a) must be likely to be effective by virtue of the overall authority carried by the staff member, and not simply his physical presence;

(b) must be used in the context of trying to engage the child in discussion about the significance and implications of his behaviour;

(c) should not be persisted in if the child physically resists. In this case a decision will need to be made about whether another form of intervention is justified.

The guidance makes it clear, in the general section on 'Physical Restraint', that if the young person were to leave the unit and there was a strong likelihood of injury to himself and others, 'it would be reasonable to use physical restraint to prevent him from leaving'. However, it stresses that this will only deal with the immediate problems and careful follow-up work will be needed, probably with additional professional advice, to bring about longer-term stability and prevent repeated use of physical restraint.

(7) *Age and competence of the child is a relevant factor.* It is worth noting that under Section IV, 'The Restriction of Liberty', the guidance again distinguishes between a young child who escapes from a home, who would be extremely vulnerable to dangers, and an adolescent 'whose absence from the home is judged unlikely to lead to serious damage'. In the latter case, it declares that physical restraint would be 'inappropriate'. Further, 'staff should recognise that there are practical limitations on their ability to prevent young people running away from an open children's home if they are determined to do so'. The practice of 'gating' or 'grounding' is common and acceptable provided the child is not prevented from leaving by being locked in or physically restrained and the Children's Homes Regulations, SI 1991/1506, reg 8(2)(c) (restrictions on visits or communications) is observed.

If, however, staff 'require a child to remain in a building or part of a building for an unreasonable length of time without relief, then this may constitute the use of accommodation to restrict liberty, even though no actual locking up is involved. This will depend upon circumstances including the space available to the child within which he is restricted, his age, competence and physical and emotional well-being'. The guidance then refers to 'unacceptable' practices revealed by the Pindown

Inquiry (see Chapter 2).

In the case of children with an impaired ability to recognise and understand danger or children with serious learning disabilities, autism or severe emotional disorder, there may be a need to take action, such as physically restraining them, and 'the need for physical intervention may be more frequent' (at para 8.3).

(8) *Child should never be locked up in bedroom at night.* The guidance is very clear that no child, irrespective of age or competence, should be locked into his bedroom at night although, in some circumstances, close night-time supervision may be required (para 8.6). It concedes that youngsters may, however, be barred from going out as a form of punishment (see para 4.5 and see point (6) above).

(9) *Holding and touching children.* Staff may express 'parental' affection towards children in care by holding and touching them in certain acceptable ways which are described by the guidance. Holding would be acceptable if, for example, it would divert a child from destructive or disruptive behaviour, it would separate and guide the child away after he or she had been in a fight or argument or if it was used as a form of discouragement, and especially for younger children for whom mere verbal influence may be insufficiently effective. The guidance suggests 'acceptable limits' using the physical presence of the care worker, such as standing in the way of a child who is ignoring instructions or losing control which may be reinforced by, for instance, placing a hand on the child's arm. This, it suggests, may have the effect of restricting a child's movements 'without the use of (forceful) physical restraint' but is acceptable only if it does not extend for hours. The guidance acknowledges that it may even be counter-productive if the child's anger or distress increases, so that its effectiveness may depend upon the respect that the child has for the particular staff member.

Staff should, of course, be careful *where* they hold children, being careful to avoid contact with a child or young person's breasts or genitals (para 10.5).

Touching is permissible but staff must be careful that since a high proportion of children in residential care have experienced sexual and physical abuse, physical contact must not be misinterpreted as sexual. A goodnight kiss or hug would be acceptable (para 10.6) 'provided this was done in a way that was parental and not sexual'. As if to make this extremely sensitive area even clearer, it states that 'physical contact should not be in response to or intended to arouse sexual expectations or feelings' and that 'age and gender are appropriate considerations in deciding proper physical contact'.

Cultural factors may also be significant in determining the degree of physical contact that may be acceptable (para 10.6) and the guidance also emphasises that 'the issue of touching, in general, should be raised in induction training for staff, and discussed in supervision'. The problem of sexual attraction between staff and young people in their care is also acknowledged in the guidance with a suggestion that this should also be addressed in any induction programme.

It is submitted that while the April 1993 guidance does make a positive attempt to provide general principles as guidelines, with an emphasis on the constructive nature of any sort of physical restraint and restriction of liberty, any training that is given will have to be highly specialist and thorough, particularly in a residential setting where the atmosphere can become highly charged and claustrophobic. Care workers will also have to be highly skilled at self-defence so as not to cause any unnecessary injury to any child, as well as highly skilled at making decisions on how to cope with each situation as it arises, and these requirements may be too demanding of care workers. A recurrent practical problem that arises is deciding whether to exercise physical restraint in the case of children who have not committed serious crimes but who, if they manage to abscond, may begin to do so. This will no doubt continue to be an ongoing problem, with which only the most experienced and empathetic care worker will best be able to cope. Perhaps one of the best measures the government can continue to implement is to issue up-to-date guidance as and when the need arises, and to consult widely and regularly, on a multi-agency basis.

7.8.11 *Criminal Justice Act 1991: General changes*

The Criminal Justice Act 1991 ('CJA 1991') has made a number of changes with regard to juvenile offenders which are as follows.

(1) The juvenile court is renamed the *youth court* and extends its jurisdiction to include 17-year-olds for the purpose of trial and sentence. Thus, the maximum youth custody sentence for 17-year-olds is now 12 months and all those below the age of majority will now come within a jurisdiction which has a statutory duty to have regard to the welfare of the child when reaching its decisions. The youth court, therefore, deals with young people above the age of 10 and below the age of 18.

Courts' powers to remand 17-year-olds will continue to be those which they have in remanding adults. However, remand hearings involving 17-year-olds should normally take place in a youth court rather than an 'adult' magistrates' court.

(2) Exceptions to this general rule are:

(a) where a 17-year-old is required to be brought before a court within a set period and no youth court is sitting during that period;

(b) where a 17-year-old is charged jointly with a person aged 18 or over.

In these cases, the remand hearing may take place in any magistrates' court which is not a youth court.

(3) Youth court magistrates were given new sentences powers (see CJA 1991, Pt III) which were supposed to be exercised within the new sentencing framework along with a new scheme of post-custody supervision. However, on 14 May 1993, the Home Secretary announced that amending legislation would be brought in by the end of the summer to repeal the Act's provisions which deal with unit fines and with the principle of not taking into account the offender's past record.

(4) The principle that sentencing of young people should be governed by individual maturity is retained.

(5) The concept of parental responsibility is reinforced.

(6) Custodial sentences for 14-year-olds are abolished (except under s 53(2) of CYPA 1933, which provides for any offender under 18 convicted of an offence which is punishable in the case of an adult by 14 years' imprisonment or more, to be sentenced to custody for any period up to the adult maximum sentence).

(7) The criteria for the use of custodial sentences will now apply to offenders of all ages.

(8) There is a statutory requirement that community penalties should fit the seriousness of the offence. A distinction is now drawn between 10- to 15-year-olds and those of 16 or 17 years, for whom the whole range of adult community-based penalties is made available.

(9) Young offenders serving sentences of detention in a young offender institution or determinate sentences of detention under s 53 of CYPA 1933 will, if their sentence is four years or more, come under the same powers of early release as adults. This means that the Secretary of State may, if recommended by the Parole Board, release the prisoner on licence.

Once a young offender serving under four years has served half of his sentence, the Secretary of State shall release him if the sentence is for a term of less than 12 months and, on licence, if it is for over 12 months.

(10) Upon release from a custodial sentence, young offenders will be subject to three months' supervision by a probation officer or social worker.

(11) 'Community sentences' may involve one or more of the following orders: (a) a probation order; (b) a community service order; (c) a combination order; (d) a curfew order; (e) a supervision order; (f) an attendance centre order (see below for explanation of these orders).

A court should not pass a community sentence unless it is of the opinion that the offence, or a combination of the offence and one other associated with it, is serious enough to warrant the sentence and the order is the most appropriate for the offender and the restrictions on liberty imposed will be in proportion to the seriousness of the offence or other offences associated with it.

All changes which have been brought in are generally subject to the welfare principle in s 44 of CYPA 1933. Further, the joint Home Office, Department of Health and Welsh Office Circular, *Criminal Justice Act 1991: Young People and the Youth Court*, sets out detailed guidance for the relevant agencies on the steps that need to be taken to implement CJA 1991. It emphasises the need for new inter-agency arrangements for dealing with young offenders in the community.

7.8.12 Community sentences

The following orders are now collectively known as community orders:

(1) probation order;
(2) supervision order;
(3) community service order;
(4) combination order;
(5) curfew order;
(6) supervision order; and
(7) attendance centre order.

7.8.12.1 Probation and supervision orders

CJA 1991 enables probation orders to be made where a person is over 16 years of age. A requirement may be added to the order, in the interests of securing the rehabilitation of the offender, which should enable treatment to be given. The first stage in the enforcement of an order will be a warning or administrative sanction by the supervising officer. The second stage will be to return the offender to court for breach proceedings. The third stage will be a matter for the court to decide.

According to *R v Ipswich Justices ex parte Best* (1993) *The Times*, February 23, justices have no power to deal with breaches of a probation order made before CJA 1991 came into force unless invited to do so by the offender or his supervising counsel.

The Criminal Justice Act 1988 made it possible for requirements to be attached to a supervision order so that, for example, an offender could be made to take part in a programme of intermediate treatment. A supervision order may be made with regard to all offenders who appear before a youth court.

7.8.12.2 Community service order

This will continue to be available as before for 16- and 17-year-olds in the youth court as it is for adults. The minimum length is 40 hours and the maximum for 16-year-olds is increased to 240 hours (as it is for adult offenders). The offender must consent to the order and, before making the order, the court, if it considers it necessary, must consider a report from a probation officer or social worker and must satisfy itself that the offender is a suitable person to perform community service.

7.8.12.3 Combination order

The combination order, introduced by s 11 of CJA 1991, consists of community service, performing unpaid work for up to 100 hours, combined with a probation order of one to three years. It is available for 16- and 17-year-olds.

7.8.12.4 Curfew order

The new curfew order has also been introduced for 16- and 17-year-olds as well as adults. Electronic monitoring of curfews is also made possible under CJA 1991.

7.8.12.5 Attendance centre order

Children aged 16 and 17 can be ordered to attend an attendance centre for up to 36 hours. This will have a maximum length of sentence for 16-year-olds of 36 hours and is also available for all young offenders.

7.8.13 *Parental responsibility*

Under Part III of CJA 1991, courts may require the parents or guardians of 16- and 17-year-olds to attend court or to pay any financial penalties imposed. Similarly, the court may bind over the parents or guardians of offenders aged 16 and 17 to take proper care of, and to exercise proper control over, the offender. However, the court is not under a duty to consider exercising these powers in relation to this age group, in contrast to offenders under the age of 16. With younger offenders, the court must exercise its powers to require parents or guardians to attend court or to pay any financial penalty imposed unless the parents or guardians cannot be found or it would be unreasonable. It must also bind over the parent or guardian if it is satisfied that this would be desirable in the interests of the prevention of further offending. Furthermore, under the new system of unit fines, parents or guardians who are ordered to pay the fines of their children will be assessed on the basis of their own disposable income and not that of the child.

7.8.14 The Children Act 1989: Changes

The 1989 Act makes two major changes with regard to young offenders: (1) the power to make a care order in criminal proceedings is abolished; and (2) the transfer of care proceedings to the magistrates' family proceedings court alters the forum in which nearly all criminal proceedings against juveniles are heard.

Thus, the former indeterminate sentence of a care order made under s 7(7) of CYPA 1969 is abolished, and is replaced by the power, in certain circumstances, and provided certain criteria are satisfied, to add a requirement to a supervision order that a child or young person shall live in local authority accommodation for up to six months (see now CYPA 1969, s 12AA; and see also **7.8.3** above). The 1989 Act has also introduced a new power to attach a residence requirement to such an order. The pre-requisites for such a requirement to be imposed are: (1) that a previous supervision order must have been made with respect to the child; (2) the original order must have imposed a requirement under s 12(a)(3) of CYPA 1933, or alternatively, a residence requirement; (3) the offence must have been committed while that order was in force; (4) the offence must be punishable with imprisonment in the case of a person over 21; and (5) where there is no previous residence requirement, the court must be satisfied that behaviour which constituted the offence was due, to a significant extent, to the circumstances in which the child was living (see the 1989 Act, Sch 12, para 23).

7.8.15 Maturity of the offender

All 16-year-olds become eligible for community penalties or maximum penalties previously restricted to those aged 17 or over, that is, in relation to probation, community service and attendance centre orders. These changes are intended to allow courts to select the most suitable sentence according to the maturity and circumstances of the offender.

7.8.16 Detention of arrested and detained juveniles

Paragraph 7.4 of *The Children Act 1989 Guidance and Regulations, Vol 7 Guardians ad Litem and other Court Related Issues* (1991, HMSO) states the general changes wrought by CJA 1991, which have sought to clarify the limited circumstances in which an arrested and detained juvenile might not otherwise be moved to local authority accommodation while awaiting appearance in court. It states that:

> 'The revised arrangements require such a juvenile to be moved to local authority accommodation unless the custody officer certifies either it is impracticable to do so, or, in the case of an arrested juvenile aged 15 or more, that no secure accommodation is available and that

keeping him in other local authority accommodation would not be adequate to protect the public from serious harm (as defined in the Act) from him.'

As it explains:

'The intention underlying the amended wording of section 38(6) [of PACEA 1984] is to ensure that, apart from cases where the juvenile is aged 15 years or over and protection of the public is an issue, how an arrested juvenile is to be accommodated by a local authority is not a relevant matter to be considered by the custody officer in determining whether or not it is practicable to move that juvenile to local authority accommodation.'

EVIDENCE IN CRIMINAL PROCEEDINGS

7.9 The child as witness in the criminal courts

Since 1 October 1992, the law on the admissibility and competence of a child's evidence has been changed as a result of reforms implemented by the CJA 1991. Section 52 of CJA 1991 inserts a new s 33A into the Criminal Justice Act 1988 ('CJA 1988') which reads:

'(1) A child's evidence in criminal proceedings shall be given unsworn.
(2) A deposition of a child's unsworn evidence may be taken for the purpose of criminal proceedings as if that evidence had been given on oath.
(3) In this section "child" means a person under 14 years of age.'

Section 52(2) has also repealed s 38 of CYPA 1933 (which required children of tender years to give unsworn evidence provided they were of sufficient intelligence and understood the duty of telling the truth). Thus, the power of the court in any criminal proceedings to determine whether a particular person is not competent to give evidence shall apply to a child of 'tender years' as it applies to any other person. In other words, any presumption of incompetence that applied to a child of tender years has been removed. It remains for the court to decide when a child may be said to be of 'tender years' (*R v Campbell* [1976] 2 All ER 272).

An important point to note is that although any child who is assumed to be competent as a witness is also compellable to appear in court as a witness, this does not mean that where a child is a witness for the prosecution the CPS will insist on calling that child as a witness or will include the evidence of that child in every case. Apart from deciding whether it is in the public interest whether a case should be brought to trial at all, the CPS will consider the interests and wishes of the child. Thus, reports to the CPS should always include clear information about the wishes of the child, and his or her parents and carers, about going to court.

Under CJA 1991 reforms, a child under 14 who gives evidence will, therefore, give it unsworn and a child above 14 will give sworn evidence. Thus, the common law rules on competence of witnesses will apply to all persons, irrespective of what age group they fall into. The court will no longer be under a duty, in the case of children under 14, to question the child to decide whether that child is or is not capable of giving sworn evidence or, alternatively, is possessed of sufficient intelligence or understands the duty of telling the truth. Of course, the rule that unsworn evidence of children needed to be corroborated had been abolished earlier by CJA 1988, s 34. The judge is no longer obliged to warn the jury about the dangers of convicting the accused on the uncorroborated evidence of a child (CJA 1988, s 34(2)). It is, therefore, possible for a defendant to be convicted purely on the basis of the unsworn evidence of a child, provided the child's evidence has not been deemed incompetent under normal common law rules, and it will be weighted and evaluated in accordance with the usual rules of evidence, including the standard of proof required for a criminal case to be proved.

Section 33A provides that a deposition of a child's unsworn evidence may be taken for the purposes of criminal proceedings as if that evidence had been given on oath.

Section 52(2) of CJA 1991, having repealed CJA 1988, s 38, goes on to say: 'and accordingly the power of the court in any criminal proceedings to determine that a particular person is not competent to give evidence shall apply to persons of tender years as it applies to other persons'. This rider has been criticised by commentators such as John Spencer who has argued that the reference to 'other persons' is potentially misleading since it suggests that when the competence of a young witness is in issue, the court should revert to its established practice in dealing with over 14-year-olds (see Spencer 'Children's Evidence and the Criminal Justice Bill' (1990) NLJ 1750 at p 1751). However, Birch has argued (see D Birch 'Children's Evidence' (1992) Crim LR at pp 267 to 268) that this cannot be what the rider means since: (1) in the exceptional case where it arises, the dominant consideration with older witnesses concerns their understanding of the oath; and the question of competence, even of adult witnesses, is not to be judged merely on their ability to take an oath; (2) the background to CJA 1991 suggests there was no intention to remove the rational element of competence; and (3) the Pigot Committee, whose recommendations formed the basis of most of the reforms of CJA 1991, took the view that courts should not refuse to consider any 'relevant understandable evidence': if a child's account is available it should be heard (Pigot *Report of the Advisory Group on Video Evidence* (1989, Home Office), at para 5.12) and if the child became incoherent or was unable to testify in an intelligible way after he had begun to testify, this could be dealt with under the judge's existing common law powers to rule incompetent any witness who was unable to communicate sufficiently clearly or rationally to a court because of any mental or other defect. Birch, therefore, submits that the position under CJA 1991, s 52 is that the court no longer has a duty to inquire into the competence of child witnesses as a class but may still decide that an individual child is incompetent under the normal common law rules.

Of course, the court also has the inherent power to decide on the competency of any witness at any stage of his evidence and upon proof of facts affecting the capacity of the witness and may direct the jury to consider the case upon other evidence (see *Whitehead* (1866) LR 1 CCR 33).

It is also possible, under a new s 32A inserted into CJA 1988, to substitute a pre-recorded interview with a child witness to replace the child's evidence-in-chief in cases involving certain sexual offences and offences of violence and cruelty. However, the child must still be available for live cross-examination at the trial, using the 'live link' (ie communicating through television) where appropriate. In such cases, committal proceedings in the magistrates' court may also be bypassed, subject to schedules and procedures set out in CJA 1991, Sch 6.

Where a person has been charged with a sexual offence or offences of violence or cruelty and the DPP is of the opinion (1) that the evidence is sufficient to commit for trial, (2) that a child who is alleged to have been the victim of the crime or to have witnessed its commission will be called as a witness at the trial and (3) that for the purpose of avoiding any prejudice to the welfare of the child, the case should be taken over and proceeded with without delay by the Crown Court, a 'notice of transfer' may be served by the DPP before the relevant magistrates' court has begun committal proceedings.

The decision to serve this notice is not open to appeal or to question in court but, under CJA 1991, Sch 6, para 5, a person to whom the notice relates may apply directly to the Crown Court for dismissal of any charge against him on the ground that there is insufficient evidence for a jury to convict. Under Sch 6, para 5(5), however, the court is prevented from hearing oral evidence from the child in support of the application for dismissal.

A number of other amendments have also been made to reduce face-to-face confrontation between child and accused. The circumstances in which video-recordings of children's testimony may be admitted are stated in s 54 of CJA 1991 and restrictions have been imposed on the extent to which child witnesses shall be examined-in-chief in respect of matters already covered by the video evidence (see CJA 1988, s 34A as amended by CJA 1991, s 55(7)). For instance, the child may still be cross-examined but not by the accused acting in person (s 55(7)) where the court is trying an offence which falls within CJA 1988, s 32(2) and the witness is alleged to be the victim or a witness of the offence and is either: (1) a child; or (2) a witness who is to be cross-examined following the reception by that court of his or her evidence in videorecorded form. This is intended to protect the child witness from defendants who may subject him to a cross-examination which breaches rules of evidence and procedure and which might be difficult for a judge to stop or control, as well as protecting the child from being subject to such an ordeal.

In addition, the *categories of persons* eligible to use the live link have been enlarged, by raising the age limit in sexual cases to 17 (CJA 1991, s 55(6)) and by providing for cross-examination to be by live television link if pre-recorded evidence is used instead of evidence-in-chief (CJA 1991, s 55(2)(b)). Section 55(4) makes it easier to move proceedings before a youth court to a venue where live link equipment is available.

7.9.1 *Issue of a witness summons by another common law country*

If a witness summons is issued by another common law country, as in a case involving a three-year-old child who had been made a ward of court, the English courts have no power to set aside such a summons, even though they believed that it was contrary to the child's best interests to appear in court. This rule was affirmed in a case where an American court-martial issued such a witness summons to an American child who was then residing and being fostered in Britain by English foster-parents (*Re G (A Minor) (Witness Summons)* [1988] 2 FLR 396). The child would, however, be interviewed in the presence of the guardian ad litem (see, further, D Jones 'The Evidence of a Three-year-old Child' (1987) Crim LR 677, which chronicles the American case of a three-year-old child providing an accurate and convincing account on video of her traumatic kidnap and sexual assault; the laws of Colorado allow for a pre-recorded videotaped interview (17 days after the event) and a 'live' one (17 months after the incident) to be admitted into evidence).

7.10 Magistrates' courts: the current position

Under s 103 of MCA 1980 (as amended by s 33 of CJA 1988 and in force since 12 October 1988), there was an enlargement of the category of offences for which a child should not normally be called as a witness for the prosecution, but for which any statement made in writing by that child should be admissible in relation to any matter of which his oral testimony would be admissible. While this maintains the basic position, s 103(2) now applies the section to:

(1) an offence which involves assault or injury or threat of injury to a person;
(2) an offence under CYPA 1933, s 1 (cruelty to persons under 16);
(3) an offence under the Sexual Offences Act 1956, the Indecency with Children Act 1960, the Sexual Offences Act 1967, the Criminal Law Act 1977, s 54 or the Protection of Children Act 1978;
(4) an offence which consists of attempting or conspiring to commit or aiding and abetting, counselling, procuring or inciting the commission of an offence falling within (1), (2) or (3) above.

However, under s 103(3) of MCA 1980, s 103(1) is excluded:

(1) where the prosecution requires the attendance of the child for the purpose of establishing the identity of any person; or
(2) where the court is satisfied that it has not been possible to obtain from

the child a statement that may be given in evidence under s 103 (1); or
(3) where inquiry into the offence takes place after the court has discontinued
     to try it summarily and the child has given evidence in the summary
     trial.

It is not relevant to the operation of s 103 whether or not the witness was
the alleged victim of the offence. However, other reforms have been introduced under CJA 1991 (see **7.20**). Depositions by a child victim instead of
an appearance in court may be obtained where there is concern that a court
appearance may seriously damage a child's health and will be admissible in
evidence in certain circumstances.

The right of the defence to require live evidence from the child at committal
proceedings in the magistrates' court has been removed by CJA 1991, s 55(1),
which repeals the former s 103(3)(a) of MCA 1980, whereunder the defence
could compel a child to testify at committal proceedings by objecting to his
written statement. The age limits applicable to s 103 have also been increased
in line with those applicable to CJA 1991, s 53.

7.11 Privilege

Privilege refers to the right to withhold information or inspection of certain
documents from the parties to the action and the court, and exists in limited
situations in civil and criminal proceedings. The application of this principle
involves a balancing of the interests of justice that the court has all available
information before it and the notion that to force disclosure in certain cases
might lead to public loss of confidence, trust and co-operation with the disclosing party (in police forces or social work departments). It should be noted
that under PACEA 1984, confidential material in the possession of social
workers, doctors and psychologists can only be seized by order of court.

7.12 The child as witness in video or tape recordings

English courts are now using video and tape-recorded evidence with increasing frequency, particularly since CJA 1988 provided for the reception of
evidence by television link in certain cases in order to reduce the stressful
effects of a court appearance upon child witnesses in alleged child abuse
cases.

Since 5 January 1989, under CJA 1988, s 32, evidence may be given in
the normal way, but witnesses may be allowed to testify from a room outside
the actual courtroom. Section 32(1) also allowed evidence to be given by
satellite link where a witness (of any age and in any type of case) is outside
the UK.

7.12.1 *CJA 1991: Video testimony*

CJA 1991 has taken CJA 1988 reforms further in the realm of video or live television links and has made admissible (in most cases) pre-recorded interviews with child witnesses in place of live evidence-in-chief. A new s 32A has been inserted into CJA 1988. A videorecording is admissible only where: (1) the child is not the accused; (2) the child is available for cross-examination (assuming the proceedings get that far); and (3) rules of court, requiring disclosure of the circumstances in which the recording was made, have been properly complied with.

Under s 32A(10), a videorecorded interview is admissible at *all* stages of the proceedings in trials at the Crown Court and in the youth courts for those sexual offences and offences of violence and cruelty to which the live link provisions of CJA 1988, s 32 apply. The offences specified under CJA 1988, s 32(2) are identical to those specified in the magistrates' courts' legislation (see **7.10** above).

If the particular court does not possess live link facilities, CJA 1991 provides for the hearing to be moved to a court which does, even if that involves going outside the petty sessions area for which the court acts (CJA 1988, s 32(3)(a) and (b), as amended). Section 32 of CJA 1988 is also extended so that it now also applies to (1) a child under the age of 17 at the time of the hearing where the offence is covered by s 32(2)(c) and (d) (sexual offence) and (2) a witness who is to be cross-examined following the admission under s 32A of a videorecording of his or her evidence-in-chief.

Live television links are available to any young person who must be cross-examined following the admission of videorecorded evidence. A videorecording of an interview between an adult and a child who is not the accused or one of the accused ('the child witness') is admissible if it relates to any matter in issue in the proceedings (CJA 1988, s 32A(2)). For the purposes of s 32A a 'child' is a person who, at the time when the videorecording was made, is under the age of 14 where the offence is violent or cruel in nature (or, if under 14 when the videorecording was made, is under 15 (s 32A(7))) and under the age of 17 where it is a sexual offence (or, if under 17 when the videorecording was made, is under 18 (s 32A(7))).

In the live television link, the child is allowed to testify from a room adjacent to the court, so that he is able to see whoever is speaking. A picture of the child 'on-screen' is simultaneously relayed back to the court. The defendant may observe the child witness but judicious deployment of the cameras should ensure that the defendant should never be observable by the child.

The recording of an earlier investigative interview with a child victim/witness is not admissible as a matter of course. It has first to be shown to a judge who has the power to declare it inadmissible in certain designated circumstances and if it is felt that it should be excluded in the interests of justice. Thus, before the recording may be given in evidence, leave of court must be obtained and, under s 32A(3)(a), this will not be granted if (1) the child witness will not be available for cross-examination, (2) any rule of court requiring disclosure of the circumstances in which the recording was made has not been complied with to the court's satisfaction or (3) the court is of the opinion, having regard to all the circumstances of the case, that, in the interests of justice, the recording ought not to be admitted. The court is allowed to exclude only that part of a statement which it is not in the interests of justice to admit, but, under s 32A(4), the court is asked to consider whether any prejudice to the accused, or one of the accused, might result by showing the whole or most of the whole of the recorded interview. The construction of the provisions suggests that all three conditions must be satisfied before leave can be given.

Once such a recording has been admitted, the child should not be examined-in-chief on any matters covered in the recording, although cross-examination of the child on other matters not covered in the recording is permitted, and this may be done through a live video link (s 32A(5)). Any statement (which may include drawings and models since 'statement' includes 'any representation of fact, whether made in words or otherwise' (s 32A(9))) disclosed in such a recording shall be treated as if given by the child in oral testimony in the witness box. Thus, it shall not be regarded as hearsay simply because it is a recording. However, under s 32A(6)(b), any statement made in a recording by a witness will not corroborate any other evidence given by that witness.

Under the third condition in s 32A(3)(a), the videorecording may be ruled out if it is not in the interests of justice to view it. The tape would, therefore, need to be of sufficient clarity in sound and picture quality in order for the court to consider it prima facie viewable (see also the *MoGP*, discussed below). The most obvious cases warranting exclusion might be where there are inadequacies in testimony amounting to evidence insufficient to satisfy a criminal prosecution, or the inclusion of inadmissible material such as hearsay narrated by the child, or allegations of similar offences which have not been the subject of charges and which would not be admissible under the similar fact rule (see Birch 'Children's Evidence' (1992) Crim LR 267, at p 271).

Section 32A applies to the trial of offences covered by CJA 1988, s 32 in the Crown Court or youth court and in appeals therefrom, including a reference by the Attorney-General.

Therefore, in certain cases, the child may still be called as a witness and might have to undergo the trauma and ordeal of cross-examination in open court. Amendments moved in the House of Lords (on the basis of recommendations by the *Pigot Report* (above)) to allow the prosecution to have the right to apply for a child witness to be examined and cross-examined at a pre-trial out-of-court hearing which would be videorecorded and shown to the court, did not survive. Two main objections to this form of 'pre-trial examination' may be stated: (1) it would be impractical, unrealistic, and logistically difficult to prepare cross-examination, particularly if it was supposed to be carried out long before the trial and especially if it meant that the child would not be recalled even if new material were discovered; (2) if the child could be recalled for cross-examination at any time during the trial, this may prove to be even more stressful to the child and may prolong the agony and distress of the whole occasion for the child.

If a child is over 14, and is covered by s 32A, he will have to be on oath when testifying and, if the complaint is of a sexual offence, the question of corroboration will arise. This remains a continuing problem in these types of cases. It should, perhaps, be noted that CJA 1988 does not cover all crimes where children are witnesses, only violent and sexual offences. Annex D to the *MoGP* (see further below) contains a listing of the legal elements of the main sexual and violent offences.

7.13 Corroboration warning for other reasons

It should be noted that the judge may still need to give a corroboration warning if this is required for some other reason, for example, if the alleged offence is a sexual offence which requires such a warning by law (eg under the Sexual Offences Act 1956, ss 2, 3, 4 and 22) or by practice (*R v Marks* [1963] Crim LR 370) or (which is more unlikely) if the child is an accomplice to the offence (*Davies v DPP* [1954] AC 378). Thus, in certain cases, children's evidence will still be regarded with caution (*DPP v Hester* [1973] AC 296 is still good law on this point). If, however, a witness testifies that he has seen a child in a distressed condition immediately before the occurrence of the alleged incident, this might constitute corroboration if the child is not, in fact, making a complaint of abuse and was unaware of being observed at the time (*R v Redpath* (1962) 49 Cr App R 319). In sexual offences, although the warning must be given, this does not prevent the jury from convicting upon the uncorroborated evidence of the child, provided it is convinced that the child's evidence should be believed.

7.14 Evidence before trial: disclosure of evidence to police

The police and/or the CPS may wish to view videotaped interviews or to examine evidence contained in local authority files relating to a child, in order to decide whether to prefer criminal charges against the suspected perpetrators of child abuse. Such evidence will often have been obtained by interviews, conducted by others, of the children suspected of having been abused. These interviews will, of course, now have to be conducted, as far as possible, in accordance with the *MoGP*. Once a child has been made a ward of court, the court's consent will always be required before the police may view this evidence. In making a decision whether or not to allow such a viewing, the court will balance the public need to give protection against offenders, against the needs of the individual ward and the effects of the ward being involved in criminal proceedings (*Re S (Minors) (Wardship: Disclosure of Material)* [1988] 1 FLR 1). In *Re S*, the police had begun an investigation into whether criminal proceedings should be brought against the cohabitant of the wards' mother following the Great Ormond Street clinic's finding that some of the four wards suspected of being sexually abused had, in fact, been abused. The Commissioner of Police sought the court's permission to permit disclosure to the police of the records and videorecordings made by the clinic of interviews with the wards. It also wished to interview the wards further and to inspect the records of the local authority.

The court held:

(1) despite the fact that the wards had been committed to the care and control of the local authority, the court retained a duty to protect the wards until the wardship was discharged;

(2) it is for the judge exercising wardship jurisdiction to decide whether the police should see medical records, videorecordings, etc, for the purpose of a criminal investigation. Directions should, therefore, be sought from the court on this matter;

(3) the court has unfettered discretion to grant leave for disclosure. The court will balance the interests of the wards against the public interest requiring that the police should not be hampered in pursuing a criminal investigation.

In *Re S*, leave was given to disclose the medical records and videorecordings, but not the local authority records and leave was given for the police to interview the wards themselves. The public interests, therefore, prevailed. Indeed, the court also said that it would only be 'in exceptional circumstances' that the interests of the individual ward would prevail.

The reasons why the court did not grant the police access to the local authority records were that (1) they were not prepared for legal proceedings and (2) they were confidential documents which, as a general rule, were privileged from disclosure in court. It was held that it was for the local authority to decide whether to release these records. However, if the police were given access to them and wished to take steps directly affecting the wards, leave of the court would be required.

The wards in *Re S* were of ages ranging from two to eight. However, it would appear that if the ward was aged 17 years, it would not be necessary for the police to obtain court approval to interview him (*In re B* (1989) *The Times*, December 20).

7.15 Consent of wardship court not always required

The court will undertake a similar sort of balancing exercise where the police are applying for disclosure of the evidence submitted at the wardship hearing itself (*Re F and Others (Wards) (Disclosure of Material)* [1989] 1 FLR 39, which involved wardship proceedings).

If criminal charges had been laid in cases of sexual abuse, before the children had been made wards of court, it would be 'constitutionally improper' for the wardship court to intervene in the conduct of the criminal trial (*Re K (Minors) (Wards: Leave to Call as Witnesses)* [1988] 1 FLR 435). Hence, the only way in which children may be spared from a traumatic face-to-face confrontation with the accused would be through the use of the live television link (on which see **7.12.1** above).

7.16 Disclosure of evidence to defence

In *R v Hampson* (1993) *The Guardian*, March 29, the Court of Criminal Appeal ruled that the prosecution must disclose to the defence matters adverse to prosecution witnesses. The facts of the case were that the defendant had been charged with four offences of indecent assault between 1988 and 1989 on boys aged 12, 9 and 7, two offences of indecent assault in mid-1990 on two girls of 13, and an offence of buggery of his nephew aged 10, between September and November 1990.

All the boys were friends or acquaintances of the defendant's son. The evidence of indecent assaults against them was not admissible in support of any other charge in the indictment. H, the oldest boy, had, in 1986 and 1987, made allegations of indecent assault against his grandfather and uncle. The defendant was told of these allegations, but given inaccurate information about their nature. He was not told of other criminal sexual conduct admitted by H nor that B, another of the boys, had displayed disturbed behaviour by starting fires. The jury convicted the defendant of all offences. He appealed.

The Appeal Court (per Mr Justice Henry) said that sexual acts usually occur in private so the defence is, to that extent, disadvantaged. Hence, disclosure of matters adverse to prosecution witnesses of the kind the law required was particularly important to the interests of justice. The defence wished for, and was entitled to receive, convictions of prosecution witnesses and the gist of any other sexual complaints made by the victims. The trial would have been different if these matters had been known to defence counsel. The court accordingly held that the non-disclosure was indefensible and capable of being a material irregularity in the trial or rendering the verdicts unsafe and unsatisfactory.

The court could not discount the possibility that, had the jury had the undisclosed information about the boy, H, they might have thought differently of the uncorroborated evidence and have reached different verdicts. The court was less sure about the potential effect on the jury of knowledge of B's fire-raising. There might have been a knock-on effect on the charges relating to the other boys.

However, the charges relating to the girls were in a separate category. Each girl supported the other's account, and there were two other witnesses. Mr Justice Henry said that there was no reason to suppose that any doubts raised in the jury's minds about H and B would, or might, have shaken their faith in the girls' evidence.

The prosecution's failure to give full and accurate information to a defendant about boys who made allegations of indecent assault against him led to the quashing of his convictions. However, the convictions of offences against the girls were upheld.

7.17 Use of screen to shield child not unlawful

The use of a screen to shield the child witness in court has been held by the Court of Criminal Appeal to be not unfairly prejudicial or unfair to the defendants where the purpose of the screen was to prevent the children from seeing, and being seen, from the dock. Counsel were able to see the child. This occurred in the case of *R v X; R v Y; R v Z* (1989) *The Times*, November 3.

The appellants were each convicted of serious criminal offences falling under the heading of child sexual abuse. It became apparent that the children were extremely reluctant to give evidence. The principal ground of complaint was that it was an unfair and prejudicial act to erect the screen and that the jury might think that the screen meant that the persons in the dock had already intimidated the child who was going to give evidence.

The Lord Chief Justice, Lord Lane, ruled that the necessity of trying to ensure that the children would be able to give evidence outweighed any possible prejudice to the defendants by the erection of the screen.

7.18 Compensation to victims of child abuse

The Criminal Injuries Compensation Board ('the Board') offers payment of compensation to victims of child abuse, upon the fulfilment of certain conditions, under the Criminal Injuries Compensation Scheme ('the scheme'). This scheme came into force on 1 August 1964 but since then there have been a number of amendments. The current scheme is known as 'the 1990 scheme', which governs all applications received by the Board on or after 1 February 1990. Under para 4 of the scheme, the Board 'will entertain applications for *ex gratia* payments of compensation in any case where the applicant . . . sustained in Great Britain . . . personal injury directly attributable (1) to a crime of violence'. It is further provided, in para 23, that 'Every application [for compensation] will be made to the Board in writing as soon as possible after the event on a form obtainable from the Board's offices'.

A preliminary point that should be noted is that the making of a claim under the scheme is not a right but a privilege (see *R v Criminal Injuries*

Compensation Board ex parte P (1993) *The Guardian*, May 3 (and see, further, below).

Various conditions have to be fulfilled in order to make a claim.

(1) An applicant must have sustained personal injury caused by a crime of violence and para 10 of the scheme expressly provides that the Board will consider applications for compensation arising out of acts of rape and other sexual offences. Buggery, indecent assault and incest are included among 'other sexual offences' in the guide to compensation claims by child abuse victims (INF 14). But no definition is provided as to what constitutes a crime of violence. In *R v Criminal Injuries Compensation Board ex parte Clowes* (1977) 120 Sol Jo 856, it was held that a crime of violence is one where there is an element of potential danger to personal safety.

(2) The injury has to be of a physical or mental nature, and includes shock or psychological disturbance which is directly attributable to the crime of violence. However, two points should be noted: (1) trivial injuries are excluded from the scheme – para 5 (as amended in January 1992) states that compensation will not be payable unless the Board is satisfied that the injury was one for which (after deductions) the total amount of compensation payable would not be less than the minimum amount which is £1,000; (2) compensation will be awarded on the basis of common law damages.

(3) A time-limit is stipulated, namely, within three years of the incident giving rise to the injury. However, the Board may, in exceptional circumstances, waive this requirement. A decision by the chairman of the Board not to do so will be final. Criteria for the waiving of time-limits are not spelt out in the scheme. In the guide to the scheme (INF 2), para 44 states that the Board will give sympathetic consideration to late applications from or on behalf of victims whose ability to help themselves is or was impaired and to those who were under the age of 18 at the time of the incident. The guide to compensation for child abuse victims (INF 14) declares that the Board has always adopted a 'sympathetic attitude' towards claims made on behalf of children, or by children themselves when made within a reasonable time of reaching full age.

(4) It appears that if the Board chooses to give reasons for a refusal to extend the time-limit, for example, and these are manifestly inadequate, the decision will be amenable to judicial review (*R v Criminal Injuries Compensation Board ex parte Cummins* (1992) *The Times*, January 21).

(5) Conviction of the offender need not be proved but the Board must be satisfied on a balance of probabilities that the events took place. Informing the police and giving them the opportunity to investigate the case would assist in proving that there is substance in the allegations,

although the Board would be sympathetic in the case of a young child who was too frightened or too young to take appropriate action.

(6) The scheme does not lay down explicit guidelines for applications on behalf of minors. The general principles contained in INF 2 suggest that applications on behalf of a person under the age of 18 must be made by an adult with parental rights over the child and that usually the person to make the application will be one of the child's natural parents. It concedes that this might be impossible if the child has been abused by someone within his own family. If a child is in care, the Board will expect the application to be made by the authority to whom care has been granted. In such cases, the application will be signed by the Director of Social Services, or any other responsible officer, on the authority's behalf. Other cases will normally be expected to be signed by the person having parental rights over the child for the time being. If there is no one legally entitled to act for the child, the Official Solicitor's assistance should be sought.

(7) Children who are wards of court must obtain leave from the wardship court to make the application to the Board (see *Registrar's Directions* [1988] 1 FLR 183). This Practice Direction explains that where a ward has the right to make a claim for compensation to the Board, application must be made by the guardian ad litem of the child for leave to apply and to disclose to the Board such documents in the wardship proceedings as are considered necessary to establish eligibility and quantum. If leave has not been obtained from the judge at the wardship hearing, the application may be made ex parte to a registrar by the child's guardian ad litem or, if no guardian has been appointed, by the Director of Social Services of the local authority having care and control of the child.

In *Re G (A Ward) (Criminal Injuries: Compensation)* [1991] 1 FLR 89, Butler-Sloss LJ declared that in her view:

'it is not for the judge, in making such an application for leave to go to the Criminal Injuries Compensation Board, to try the very issue which is specifically within the remit of the Board. The position is . . . that the court should act as a filter.'

She suggested that various questions should, therefore, be raised, such as whether the application was 'hopeless' or 'arguable' rather than whether it would succeed.

'If the application is hopeless, or not arguable, then it is right for the court to say that it is not a proper case to make an application. If it is arguable, then it is a matter for the Board to decide whether it comes within their criteria and whether they should make an ex gratia payment.'

Butler-Sloss LJ further stated that where the application was made by the Official Solicitor on the child's behalf, it was only in the rarest of circumstances that the court should refuse its consent on the grounds that it would not be in the interests of the child that such an application be made.

(8) Since 1 October 1979, it has been possible for compensation to be payable even if the victim and offender were living as members of the same family provided that the offender has been prosecuted or there are good reasons for there being no prosecution.

All applications received by the Board after 1 February 1990 will be dealt with under the 1990 scheme, regardless of when the injury was sustained (see para 28 of the scheme) *except that* where the abuse occurred before 1 October 1979, the Board cannot make an award because under the scheme in force at the time, no award could be made where the victim and the offender were living together as members of the same family.

A recent case that confirms the Board's stance that the change to the rules in 1979 is not retrospective is *R v Criminal Injuries Compensation Board ex parte P* (1993) *The Guardian*, May 3. In that case, a Divisional Court held that the only legitimate expectation that a victim of crime can have is of recovering an award under the rules which are in force at the time. Hence, an adult who was a victim of child abuse is not entitled to compensation under the current (1990) scheme because victims of family violence were excluded at the time she was abused. The facts of this case are as follows. P, born in 1962, claimed that between 1967 and 1976, she suffered serious injury as a result of sexual abuse by her stepfather. For psychological reasons, she suppressed those recollections until 1988 when she heard that young girls were visiting her stepfather's house. She then made a statement to the police. In 1989, her stepfather was imprisoned for offences against other girls but was not prosecuted for any offences against P. Under the 'same roof' rule, applicable under the previous scheme, which remained in force until October 1979, offences committed against a member of the offender's family living with him at the time were excluded. The Board, therefore, refused P's application because, among other things, the offences occurred while the 'same roof' rule was still in force. P, therefore, applied for judicial review and argued that since the rule no longer applied, the Board's decision was arbitrary, irrational and unfair and the improvements introduced to the scheme should have been there from the outset.

Leggatt LJ (with whom Mr Justice McCullough agreed) held that the reality was that the circumstances had been amended in which public money may be paid out to applicants, none of whom were entitled to it. It was a manifestation of the bounty of the Crown. The 'same roof' rule was no more irrational than the exclusion before the scheme of all victims of crimes of violence, or the continuing exclusion, since then, of those injured other than through crimes of violence. The scheme was not irrational at its inception and it had not been rendered so by subsequent amendments. The making of a claim was not a right but a privilege. The exercise of discretion by the Secretary of State under prerogative power could not, in this instance, be impugned.

Under para 7 of the scheme, the Board must be satisfied that there is no possibility that a person responsible for causing the injury will benefit from an award. The Board would also have to be satisfied that it would not be against the minor's interest to receive a full or reduced award. Thus, if the victim and offender were still living together, or it was a case of sibling abuse, the Board would be unlikely to make an award.

There are many reasons why a prosecution may not have been brought. Denyer (see R Denyer 'The Criminal Injuries Compensation Board: Applications By or on Behalf of Children' [1993] Fam Law 34 at p 36) refers to some of them as being: (1) the age of the child; (2) lack of corroboration (see also **7.13** above) although this is not a fatal flaw; and (3) general weakness of the evidence as far as the criminal standard of proof is concerned. He suggests that in these circumstances, if a family proceedings court has made a finding of abuse where standards of proof are different from those of a criminal court, the Board may find this sufficient to establish that a 'crime of violence' has occurred. But the Board would probably have to make a positive finding that making an award would not be against the child's interests.

The child would probably have to undergo an oral hearing before the Board and the particular family circumstances might have to be taken into account. Would an award wreck the chances of a family reconciliation? Would it, in any event, worsen family tensions and family relationships?

(9) Under para 6(a) of the scheme, the Board may withhold or reduce compensation if it considers that the applicant has not taken, without delay, all reasonable steps to inform the police, or any other 'appropriate authority', of the circumstances of the injury and to co-operate with the police or other authority in bringing the offender to justice. Obviously, the child is limited in what he or she might be able to initiate in these circumstances. The guide to the scheme (INF 2) suggests that the Board will be sympathetic so far as this requirement is concerned to children. Paragraph 23 of INF 2 stresses that every case is treated on its own merits and the Board will take a more sympathetic view if it is clear that any delay was attributable to the youth of the child which made it 'difficult or impossible for the victim to appreciate what to do'. Further, para 24 of INF 2 accepts that an 'appropriate authority' in the case of a child may often be the child's parents and if they failed to inform the

police this should not constitute a bar to the child's claim. Apart from these guidelines, however, there are no specific rules which deal with this particular situation.

(10) Special arrangements can be made for minors, for example to pay the amount of any award to any trustee or trustees to hold on such trusts for the applicant, making provision for his or her maintenance, education and benefit and containing such powers and provisions for the investment and management of the fund and the remuneration of the trustee or trustees as the Board thinks fit. Subject to this, the Board will retain a general discretion to make special arrangements for the administration of the award. According to the 1983 annual report of the Board, these may include paying the sum to the Official Solicitor as guardian of the young person's estate under a High Court order or to a public trustee or to the Board's investment account earmarked in the applicant's name. Awards up to £1,000 are usually released to those having parental control of the applicant. Higher awards are frequently invested and managed by the Board through the National Savings Bank during the child's minority. However, these are sometimes released, forthwith, to the child 'to avoid reminding the child at 18 of an unpleasant experience which might otherwise have been forgotten' (see Denyer (above)). If a child is in care, the Board will expect the local authority to undertake responsibility for investment and administration of the award.

The scheme appears to favour the more extreme cases, which are more easily proved, whereas 'lesser' cases, perpetrated with no violence as such, but sometimes sustained over a long period of years (such as *R v Criminal Injuries Compensation Board ex parte P* (above)) are harder to establish but may be even more traumatising to the child.

(11) The financial awards for earlier cases involving regular abuse of children by their parents, grandparents and other relatives by sexual intercourse, buggery, oral sex, digital penetration and French kissing, seemed to have an upper limit of £17,500 (see, eg *Re E, J, K and D* [1990] CLY 1596), but more recent cases suggest that the upper bracket will now lie between £20,000 to £30,000 (see, eg *Re AP (Female)* [1991] CLY 1363). Where the abuse involved only buggery the awards have tended to be lower (see *Re V* [1991] CLY 1370, where the award for general damages was £12,000). (For a fuller account of these and earlier cases see R Denyer 'The Abused Child and the Quantum of Damages/Compensation' [1993] Fam Law 297.)

7.18.1 *Increase in the number of child abuse compensation claims*

The conflicting philosophies of rehabilitation/reunification of parent and child against deterrence and punishment are certainly highlighted by the scheme.

Problems of proof and evidence remain. Nevertheless, in the *Criminal Injuries Compensation Board's Twenty-Seventh Report* (Cm 1782), covering the year 1 April 1990 to 31 March 1991, it was noted that there was 'again an increase in the number of applications to the Board in respect of children who had suffered abuse. The number of applications received during the year showed an increase of 37 per cent over the previous year'. The total number of complaints (including those of a non-sexual nature) was 5,571. With regard to victims under the age of 18 at the date of the incident for all sexual assaults, there were 1,812 applications, compared with 1,318 complaints in the previous period; for sexual abuse complaints within the family or allegedly perpetrated by a relative, there were 1,011 in the period stated above. The Report also states that child abuse complaints have been afforded 'a degree of priority' by the Board which has also enlisted the help of one local authority to conduct an experiment to gather better information more quickly. As a result of the increased number of inquiries about child abuse, the Board has also revised and refined its information leaflet on the subject.

INTERVIEWING THE CHILD

7.19 Diagnostic interviews as evidence of child sexual abuse

We refer here to recorded interviews with suspected child victims. The courts have had a number of opportunities to consider the potential of recorded interviews as evidence that sexual abuse has been committed on a child. Two main legal problems that such interviews present are: (1) the admissibility of such interviews; and (2) their reliability.

7.19.1 Admissibility of videotaped interviews

Videotaped interviews may be regarded either as original evidence or documentary evidence. In the first form of evidence, the tape is real evidence. The court only wishes to see that an incident took place. It would not be concerned with the truth of the incident recorded. In the second form of evidence, the recorder has been utilised to create information which is adduced as proof of the truth of the words and suggestions which it may contain. It provides original evidence of the fact that certain statements were made. This is because it would be classified as hearsay evidence. The *Cleveland Report* conceded that the use of the 'formal' interview was a necessary step in the investigation of alleged sexual abuse (see para 12.10) and its function would be to listen to the child to establish what it had to say, in a spontaneous and sympathetic environment, which gave the child opportunity for free play, although all persons interviewing children should be experienced and skilled in interviewing them (see para 12.12). The formal interview should, therefore, not contain any leading questions, hypothetical situations or any strongly worded promptings. This could be admitted as either (1) one of the exceptions to the hearsay rule, for example as permitted under the amended CJA 1988 or (2) by agreement of the practitioners. The *Cleveland Report* guidelines (see below) have now been taken forward by the *MoGP* which is discussed in detail at **7.20** *et seq*, below.

7.19.2 *Reliability of videotaped interviews*

Two questions the courts ask here are:

(1) how reliable was the technique of interviewing?; and
(2) how reliable was the particular interview as evidence of a fact in issue?

Under the first heading, vital gaps in the evidence might be overlooked by the interviewer. Under the second, the courts have been somewhat less than impressed by the lack of responsiveness to the reactions of the child and the inability of the courts/lawyers to test the veracity of a witness's statement. The best that some judges have thought of videorecordings is that although they are helpful, they are limited to enabling the court to 'catch the context and flavour of the interview, noting the length of pauses, the attitude of the child, the tone of voice of the interviewer' (see *Re W (Minors) (Child Abuse: Evidence)* [1987] 1 FLR 297).

As the *Cleveland Report* pointed out, not all the judiciary are in favour of videorecordings. The Inquiry team appeared to accept that there was always the possibility of interfering with the relationship with the child or a reduction in the spontaneity of accounts (at para 12.49). All in all, a fairly guarded response to these interviews has been given by the judiciary. The 'facilitative' interview was mentioned by the *Cleveland Report*. This type of interview allows hypothetical questions and would take place as a second stage in the proceedings. The problem is that this type of interview would usually begin with an assumption of abuse and would, therefore, have even less probative value, even if admitted by agreement or under one of the exceptions.

The problem in Cleveland was that there was confusion among some professions as to the true nature and purpose of certain interviews that were being carried out. The *MoGP* is intended to ensure that such objectives are now clarified in every case where child witnesses are interviewed pursuant to possible legal proceedings being instituted (see **7.20** *et seq* below, for some of the problems that the *MoGP* still needs to resolve).

7.19.3 *Conduct of child interviews under the Cleveland guidelines*

The guidelines on the conduct of child interviews, which appear in the Cleveland Report, have been judicially approved (see, eg *Re E (A Minor) (Child*

Abuse: Evidence) [1991] 1 FLR 420 (see **7.20** below) and, although they must now be seen as superseded by the *MoGP*, which takes most of the points on board, are nevertheless worth noting. The guidelines are as follows.

(1) It is undesirable to call interviews with children 'disclosure interviews', which precludes the notion that sexual abuse may not have occurred.

(2) All interviews must be undertaken only by those with some training, experience and aptitude for talking with children.

(3) Each interview should be approached with an open mind.

(4) The style of the interview should be open-ended questions. (Note that the *MoGP* suggests that the open-ended phase should only come after the second, 'free narrative', phase.)

(5) There should be, where possible, only one and not more than two interviews for the purpose of evaluation, and the interview should not be too long. (The *MoGP* suggests that the formal interview should only last a maximum of an hour.)

(6) The interview should go at the pace of the child and not of the adult.

(7) The setting of the interview must be suitable and sympathetic.

(8) It must be accepted that at the end of the interview the child may have given no information to support the suspicion of sexual abuse and the position will remain unclear.

(9) There must be careful recording of the interview and what the child says, whether or not there is a videorecording.

(10) It must be recognised that the use of facilitative techniques may create difficulties in subsequent court proceedings.

(11) There is 'great importance' in 'adequate training' for all those engaged in this work.

(12) In certain circumstances it may be appropriate to use the special skills of a 'facilitated' interview. That type of interview should be treated as a second stage. The interviewer must be conscious of the limitations and strengths of the techniques employed. In such cases, the interview should only be conducted by those with special skills and specific training.

However, despite interviews with the child having received judicial approval in some cases, it would appear that everything turns on the facts of each case, the quality of the evidence and whether the interview was relied upon by the prosecution as evidence. Thus, in *R v H* [1992] Crim LR 516, where these guidelines were breached by repeated interviews with a child victim, the Court of Appeal, nevertheless, upheld the conviction. In that case, the appellant was convicted of four counts of cruelty to a child and two counts of aiding and abetting buggery on a child. One of the grounds of appeal was that the interviewing of the boys concerned did not conform to the Cleveland guidelines. It was shown that the boys had been repeatedly interviewed at length before the trial and this was contrary to the Cleveland guidelines (see point (5), above). However, the Court of Appeal held, inter alia, that no injustice was shown and the jury were not aware of the conditions of interview. No application was made under s 78 of PACEA 1984 to exclude the children's evidence. This section allows the court to exclude prosecution evidence if its admission would have such an adverse effect on the fairness of proceedings that the court ought not to admit it. There was full disclosure of all pre-trial material and ample evidence before the jury to convict.

It would seem that here, the jury were, presumably, totally unaware of the nature and duration of the interviews, as they were not relied upon as prosecution evidence.

The pre-1989 Act case of *Re E (A Minor) (Child Abuse: Evidence)* (above) was one where the central issue was whether any of four children (D and Z, both aged four, R, aged three and E, aged five) had been sexually abused or subjected to other inappropriate behaviour by E's parents. All three children had made statements that E's parents were allegedly sexually abusing E or that E was a witness to sexually inappropriate behaviour by E's parents. The three children had been interviewed by several people, including police officers, a GP, social workers and a child protection officer employed by the NSPCC. Z, one of the four-year-olds, had been interviewed on seven occasions by one Mr W, the NSPCC officer. E had a place of safety order taken out on him, following which he lived with his maternal grandparents and was later made a ward of court. Scott Baker J held that he was satisfied that neither of the accused parents had abused their child or any other children. Indeed, the father had not even been in town on the occasions when the abuse had been allegedly committed. This had been corroborated. The following points were enunciated in this case.

(1) The full *Cleveland Report* should be required reading for all social workers, doctors, police officers and others involved in an investigation of whether small children had been abused. The majority of the points set out in para 12.34 of the *Report* (see above) had been breached during interviews carried out in this case because of ignorance of their existence. Leading questions had been asked, inadequate records had been kept and, from the start, the interviewers had been convinced that the children had been abused. Further, having seen the videotaped interviews, read the transcripts and listened to Mr W in the witness box, his Lordship opined that the repeated interviews carried out by Mr W, who had only read the abridged version of the *Cleveland Report*, were 'regrettable', being carried out on the basis that 'because a young child said things then they must be true'. It might even be that the sessions had positively damaged Z.

(2) The introduction of sexually explicit dolls to the child at an early stage of investigation should be avoided. These dolls had also been used inappropriately in the present case.

(3) The interviewing of young children was a more skilful and sophisticated exercise than either the police or the social workers appreciated in this case. It was an 'exercise fraught with uncertainties' to try and analyse exactly what happened and why each child said the things he did. The line between fact and fantasy in a young child was a fine one and easily blurred.

(4) E was found to be a happy and well-adjusted child who was doing well at school, and had never made a complaint that anything untoward had happened to him and there was no evidence of any offence committed against him. Although his parents were said to be unconventional and open about nudity and sexual matters, it was found that they were careful to ensure that nudity did not impinge on visitors, including visiting children. They were also loving, caring parents and it was in E's best interests that he returned to live with them unsupervised. E was subsequently de-warded.

(5) The idea of E's parents being 'bad people' had been implanted in the minds of the other children from the moment they were first questioned.

(6) Each child's behaviour, at the material times, was inconsistent with the truth of the disclosures.

(7) The guidelines in Chapter 12 of the *Cleveland Report* should be followed. Children of tender years should be listened to, but not every detail of a young child's story should be taken literally.

It should be noted that in the Orkneys, in Scotland, children were once again removed from their homes, inter alia, on the strength of allegations made by a child who claimed *other* children had been abused, although the allegedly abused children did not make any allegations themselves. This was found to be a mistake in judgment by the social workers and the police who were involved (*Report of the Inquiry into the Removal of Children from Orkney in February 1991* (1992, HMSO) ('the *Orkney Report*') and the case itself is discussed in detail in Chapter 2).

In *Re A and Others (Minors) (Child Abuse: Guide-lines)* [1992] 1 FLR 439, Hollis J took a very dim view of the breaches of the Cleveland guidelines, in a case involving 13 children between the ages of three and 13. The learned judge found that untrained and inexperienced interviewers were used and that interviewers seemed obsessed with the belief that they were now investigating a case of group satanic ritual abuse which influenced the direction of their questions. It was also found that leading questions rather than open-ended questions were constantly used so that the child was not encouraged in free recall. There were also often more than two interviews and these had not always been conducted at the pace of the child.

As has been said before, these cases must now be read subject to the *MoGP* and to the changes wrought by the CJA 1991.

7.19.4 *Warning against indiscriminate use of anatomically correct dolls*

The use of anatomically correct dolls has become increasingly common in child sexual abuse investigations. They have been used as a means of evaluating children's statements about their abusive treatment. However, it is now clear that the validity and reliability of such dolls as a first stage diagnostic aid is seen by the courts as extremely limited as evidence of child sexual abuse. In fact, the *Cleveland Report* endorsed the view that such dolls '*should certainly not be used as the first stage method of evaluation*' (authors' emphasis) (at para 12.58). This view has been judicially confirmed in *Re E (A Minor) (Child Abuse: Evidence)* (above). With regard to using anatomically correct dolls at a second stage of an interview with a child, the *Cleveland Report* states: 'There is a great danger . . . that this facilitative second stage may be seen as a routine part of the general interviews, instead of a useful tool to be used sparingly by experts in special cases' (at para 12.19).

7.19.5 *Judicial opinions of video interviews*

Judicial criticisms of recorded interviews stem from the following arguments.

(1) There is a misleading use of hypothetical and leading questions (see *Re N (Minors) (Child Abuse: Evidence)* [1987] 1 FLR 280, where doubts were expressed about the scientific or clinical value of such interviews if abuse had not been admitted). Similar criticism was voiced in *C v C (Child Abuse: Evidence)* [1987] 1 FLR 321 where Hollis J also expressed grave disquiet over the use of anatomically correct dolls as a therapeutic or diagnostic aid to detecting child abuse. Hence, a fairly large body of legal opinion has been sceptical about the 'disclosure interviews' technique. Under the *MoGP*, of course, interviews are not to be called disclosure interviews without explaining why this is the case or offering an alternative label (see discussion of the *MoGP*, below). The *Cleveland Report* suggests that the method of interviewing may not elicit reliable information and the investigative process itself may be 'sexualising and abusive' (at para 12.30). This is still true today even with the *MoGP* and it will be as well that all practitioners involved in child interviews bear it in mind.

(2) There may be different interpretations of the interview. Note the difference of opinion in *Re N (Minors)* (above) over whether the gestures made by the child indicated that masturbation had taken place. The child psychiatrist and the social worker disagreed in their interpretation of the child's gestures. In *Re Z (Minors) (Child Abuse: Evidence)* [1989] 2 FLR 3, there was, again, a conflict of opinion between paediatricians in a case where the interviews had not been videotaped but the judge suggested that they should have been in order to keep a record of any interviews

with the child. Bush J opined that the case illustrated the need for caution in using 'the awesome powers of the local authority following a medical diagnosis of sexual abuse. Such a diagnosis required other evidence before it could be confirmed'. He also went on to say that it was ironic in this field that the cry is 'The child must be believed' but that was only applied by some practitioners when the child said something had happened, but not when the child said that nothing had happened (at p 10).

The *Cleveland Report* also points out that interviews, while a helpful step in the recording and assessment of the child, would require proper consultation and the consent, where appropriate, of the parent, child or other suitable person. The *MoGP* agrees that a videotaped interview should, as with any other interview, proceed only after the child is fully informed to a level appropriate to his or her age and understanding and freely consents to the interview session and the videorecording. However, although it concedes that a videorecorded interview with a reluctant child is likely to be impracticable, where the child is not sufficiently mature 'the team should listen to the views of the parents or carers. However, they should guard against the possibility of anyone who may be implicated in abuse of the child exerting any pressure on the child not to give his or her account' (*MoGP*, at para 2.30).

Under the *MoGP* and Cleveland guidelines, therefore, the use of such interviews must be carefully managed and undertaken with requisite tact, sensitivity and skill in accordance with the *MoGP* requirements and using the best possible expert advice, wherever possible.

7.20 Conducting child interviews under the MoGP

7.20.1 Introduction

In 1992, the Home Office and the DOH issued jointly a guide for professionals making a videorecording of an interview with a child witness, called the *Memorandum of Good Practice on Videorecorded Interviews with Child Witnesses for Criminal Proceedings* (1992) ('the *MoGP*'). This is supposed to complement CJA 1991, the majority of which came into force in October 1992. The *MoGP* makes it clear from the outset that its main purpose is to assist those making a videorecording of an interview with a child witness where it is intended that the recording should be acceptable in criminal proceedings. As the *MoGP* explains, videorecorded interviews with children may be admitted in a criminal trial under s 32A of CJA 1988.

The *MoGP* contains several *provisos*.

(1) It is not meant to provide a guide to everything that needs to be known by those making videorecordings of children, nor can it be fully comprehensive about criminal proceedings.

(2) It is not a universal prescription since 'each child is unique and the effective interview will be one which is tailored to the child's particular needs and circumstances'.

(3) It is voluntary (and is not even called a Code), and any videorecording that does not strictly comply with it 'will not automatically be ruled inadmissible. On the contrary, it was Parliament's clear intention that such videorecordings of children's testimony should be admitted unless, in the opinion of the judge, it would clearly be contrary to the interests of justice to do so'. It, therefore, does not have the binding force of statute.

(4) It emphasises that those conducting interviews under it should have clear, agreed objectives which are consistent with the main purpose, which is 'to listen with an open mind to what the child has to say, if anything, about the alleged event'. Accordingly, interviews carried out under it are not, and should never be, called either 'therapeutic interviews' or 'disclosure interviews'. This is because even if the child confirms details of what is suspected by others, and the interview serves a therapeutic or other objective, 'therapy is not the primary aim of these interviews'.

(5) It warns that at the time the interview is planned, 'it may not be known whether criminal proceedings will follow and, even if it is, civil proceedings concerned with the welfare of the child, and which would also benefit from a videorecorded interview, may well come first'.

The *MoGP* also considers when and where to make a videorecording for criminal proceedings and what equipment to use and matters such as whether the child will be able to give a coherent account of the events in question, the duration and pace of the interview, who should conduct the interview, who else should be present during the interview and the question of whether the child's consent needs to be obtained (see below).

7.20.2 *MoGP builds on Cleveland guidelines and Working Together*

The *MoGP* then explains its basic approach which builds on the Butler-Sloss approach in the *Cleveland Report* (see para 12), and *Working Together*, which was revised in 1991 and which was affirmed in circulars and guidance from the Home Office, Department of Health, Department of Education and Science and Welsh Office. This approach was aimed at preventing the child from having to repeat his story to several different agencies and professionals and 'the major element is joint interviewing by social workers and police' (at p 2).

Accordingly, one interview, broken up into four phases, is seen as the norm. The *MoGP* confidently states that 'there is no reason why . . . [the desired] objectives cannot be met within a single interview, provided it is properly prepared'. Yet, as one commentator points out 'it does not necessarily follow that because the need for repetition is avoided by interested agencies working in concert, one interview will suffice' (McEwan 'Where the Prosecution Witness is a Child: The Memorandum of Good Practice' (1993) *Journal of Child Law* at p 16). Wattam, who was a member of the Steering Committee which was involved in producing the *MoGP*, also points out that there are 'rules' of 'ordinary conversation' (ie turn-taking, question and answer, leading into and out of topics) which could not be followed if the requirements of the *MoGP* are to be satisfied. The kind of interviews which need to be carried out within the structure of the *MoGP*, its flexibility notwithstanding, are 'un-ordinary' and artificial, with evidential constraints, and an unusual amount of detail required to be compressed into a relatively short space of time. Thus, a child who makes short statements which could be understood in a common-sense, everyday manner, as suggestive of inappropriate behaviour, may need to be prompted to expand and specify the exact physical details which would satisfy the evidential requirements of an offence (see Wattam *Disclosure: The Child's Perspective* (1990, NSPCC), and Wattam *Making a Case in Child Protection* (1993, Longmans)). Wattam suggests that the child should be taken through a commonplace example of an everyday activity, such as tooth brushing, so as to understand the nature of the conversation and level of detail required. Unfortunately, this will invariably require far more time than the *MoGP* or, indeed, the *Cleveland Report* guidelines (see **7.19.3** above) will allow.

7.20.3 Guidelines for preliminary discussions with the child

As far as preliminary discussions with the child are concerned, the *MoGP* warns that it is very important for the agencies involved to have an opportunity to consider the child's needs, the legal context, possible civil proceedings, and the various implications of the interview before it takes place, so that clear objectives for the interview can be agreed upon. It then emphasises that 'videorecorded interviews, conducted in advance of this process, are likely to be of very limited value and may well compromise the usefulness of any later interviews'.

The *MoGP* lists the following guidelines as basic principles in any 'early discussions' with the child:

> '(a) listen to the child, rather than directly question him or her; (b) never stop a child who is freely recalling significant events; (c) make a note of the discussion, taking care to record the timing, setting and personnel present as well as what was said; (d) record all subsequent events up to the time of the substantive interview.' (at para 1.8).

A *key point* that must be considered here is: what if there need to be *several* such 'early discussions' to establish rapport with the child and they become protracted discussions? What would the legal status of such discussions be? Would they not count as interviews? At which point would these early discussions (pre-interviews?) end and the formal substantive interview phases begin? The *MoGP* states that the child can be informed about the substantive interview as soon as it is planned and that coaching of the child should be avoided. This suggests that early discussions should be differentiated from the substantive interview. Should only videotaped interviews 'count' as substantive interviews? There seems to be no convincing reason for this, other than for purely criminal justice or evidential purposes. In any event, is it really possible to 'cue' or prepare a child for what must be a highly stressful experience which is not made easier by the presence of video and sound equipment, not to mention the presence of strangers and unfamiliar surroundings, so that the child will 'perform' for the 'substantive' or formal videorecorded interview?

The *MoGP* contains several statements which appear to allow deviations from its general guidelines in the interests of achieving more effective communication with the child but at the same time also contains statements which appear to insist on strict compliance with its requirements so that justice may be achieved.

The *MoGP* declares that an interview should be arranged as soon as it becomes clear that a criminal offence may have been committed, since delay is bad for the child because: (1) his stress should be minimised; (2) the risk of the child forgetting important details must be avoided; (3) he might be influenced by others in the interim; and (4) the accused should be acquainted with the allegations made against him or her at an early stage.

In the event of criminal proceedings being decided upon, the *MoGP* states that notes relating to the preparation and conduct of the videorecorded interview will need to be disclosed to the CPS, together with the records of any, perhaps informal, interviews with the child. In addition, no further interviews should be conducted *unless* the joint investigating team, in consultation with the CPS, is 'fully satisfied' that it is necessary to do so to obtain further information. Supplementary interviews should normally also be videorecorded.

7.20.4 *Is more than one formal interview permissible?*

As it stands, there is no further guidance in the *MoGP* on when it might be justifiable to interview a child formally on more than one occasion. All the *MoGP* states is that 'consideration should always be given as to whether holding such an interview would be in the child's interest'. Presumably, this would have to be determined from case to case, since there will always be scope for disagreement amongst professionals about what is or is not in a child's best interests and in the case of alleged abuse by a parent of the child, whether punishment or rehabilitation should govern the conduct of a particular case. If there is disagreement amongst the professionals, a court would have to resolve a disagreement between, for example, a social worker and some other professional (such as a police child protection officer) about whether a particular child should be re-interviewed. The *MoGP* sees adequate planning as essential to any such interview. The absence of such a plan which fails to draw on the skills and experience of the joint investigating team (comprising social workers and police) will possibly lead to an unsuccessful interview. The *MoGP* also details the range of developmental factors that the interviewing team should consider, ie the child's cognitive, linguistic, emotional, social, sexual, physical and other development. There is also special mention of the need to pay proper regard to the child's cultural and religious background. Hence, the team may need to seek advice in advance about particular ethnic customs and beliefs since 'considerations of race, language, and also gender may influence the choice of interviewer'. As para 2.9, thereof, emphasises: 'A child should be interviewed in his or her first language except in the most exceptional circumstances'.

The *MoGP* then considers if the child will be capable of giving a coherent account of the events under investigation. Despite CJA 1991 reforms, which mean that a child is no longer assumed to be incompetent and that there is no duty on the court to examine a child as to competency before the trial, it may still be the case, as with some adult witnesses, that a particular child will be unable to give an understandable account of the events in question. If that happens, that child's evidence will not be allowed to form part of the case for either the prosecution or the defence (and see **7.9** above).

7.20.5 Pace and duration of the interview

Under the *MoGP*, the pace at which the interview should be conducted is at the child's pace and not that of the adult. As for the duration of the interview 'as a rule of thumb . . . less than an hour'. The person who should interview the child 'should be a person who has, or is likely to be able to establish, rapport with the child, who understands how to communicate effectively with him or her', even in disturbed periods, and who has a 'proper grasp both of the basic rules of evidence and the elements of criminal offences'. The *MoGP* concedes that this is a formidable job specification and agrees that 'some compromise will probably be necessary'.

7.20.6 Other person(s) who may be present at the interview

With regard to other persons who should be present during the interview, the *MoGP* is very explicit that a suspected offender should not be present during the interview, and declares that the presence of other people may also distract or put pressure on the child. However, supportive adults for a very young or distressed child may be present, especially if the child requests it, provided these individuals take no part in the interview.

The *MoGP* suggests that interviews should proceed only when relevant parties are conversant with the *MoGP*, although these should be conducted as soon as practicable, allowing time for inter-agency consultation and planning, as well as for any medical examination which is appropriate.

7.20.7 *The issue of consent*

On the issue of consent, the *MoGP* states that if the child is mature enough to understand the concept, that child should be given an explanation of the purpose of the videorecording. In this way the child is 'fully informed to a level appropriate to her age and understanding'. This is so that the child may 'freely consent' to the interview session and the recording. It declares that the child should be advised that irrespective of whether a videorecording is made, he may be required to attend court and face direct cross-examination and that '*written consent to be videorecorded is not necessary*' (*MoGP*'s emphasis). Nevertheless, 'it is unlikely to be practicable or desirable to videorecord an interview with a reluctant or distressed child'. The *MoGP*, therefore, says nothing explicit about a child's right to refuse consent to a videorecording, merely suggesting that it would usually be 'expected' that a child's consent would be obtained and that a child who was not in a suitably receptive frame of mind to be interviewed would not normally be interviewed as a practical proposition. In other words, the consent issue is not really dealt with adequately by the *MoGP*, except in a rather oblique and, perhaps, presumptuous manner.

7.20.8 *Further practical difficulties*

There are general practical difficulties with the conduct of these interviews despite the so-called voluntary nature of the *MoGP*. To begin with, courts will no doubt ask if there has been reasonably faithful adherence to the *MoGP* guidance, any serious breach of which will, as with the Cleveland guidelines, raise a strong presumption that the information obtained in the interview cannot be given the weight or probative value which is presumably being asked for by the prosecution in criminal proceedings. In addition, under s 32A(3)(c) of CJA 1988, the court has the power to exclude all or part of a videotaped interview if to do so would be in the interests of justice (see **7.19.1** above). Thus, a badly conducted interview may compound the distress suffered by the child witness and still fail to meet the evidential requirements of the law. Even worse, a misleading impression could be given to the child protection officers involved, who may think that there is more to what a child said than what was actually said. The Orkney and Rochdale affairs indicate that it is relatively easy to misunderstand what a child has said (or not said) and to read things into what a child has said (see Chapter 2). The other practical problems with recorded interviews that do not fulfil evidential requirements and have been mismanaged is that defence lawyers will have little difficulty in exposing their limitations, gaps and ambiguities. Although defence lawyers take a great deal of care in how they approach a child witness, it is unavoidable in our current adversarial system that the child caught in the middle of opposing counsel will suffer a great deal of trauma and distress. Other non-legal child protection professionals will also find it disheartening and demoralising if they are expected to carry out such interviews without adequate training in child psychology, evidence and criminal law. Hence these interviews might continually be disallowed when court proceedings are being considered. In cases of minor deviations, where most of the interview represents a strong case for initiating criminal proceedings, the courts might use the fact that the *MoGP* is not a Code (the change in name from its draft form is presumably significant) to argue that the videotape might still be admissible in the interests both of the child and of criminal justice.

7.20.9 *The four interview phases*

The main purpose of the *MoGP* is to provide a guide to practitioners in making videorecordings of child witnesses for criminal proceedings. Evidential requirements appear to take centre stage, and given that joint interviewing by different child protection professionals is strongly recommended, this is potentially problematic, not least because there appears to be a strong emphasis on police personnel and social work personnel interviewing the child.

The interview structure in the *MoGP* is founded on the 'step-wise' approach. The four phases are: (1) rapport building; (2) free narrative account; (3) questioning in four stages (if appropriate); and (4) closing the interview and thanking the child. We have already referred, in Chapter 6, to a fundamental difficulty that arises with this approach: children do not tend to spontaneously narrate their experiences of abuse, particularly in the case of sexual abuse. Empirical evidence tends to suggest that in primary investigations, children are highly unlikely to make allegations of sexual abuse during a formal interview, particularly if they are still living with the alleged perpetrator of the abuse (see **6.18.6** above). It is also likely that children will disclose in stages 'yet the criminal law on sexual offences encourages investigators to look for an episode or single event of criminal activity rather than view the experience as a process involving many incidents over an extended period of time' (G Smith 'Good practice or yet another hurdle: video recording children's statements' (1993) *Journal of Child Law* 21).

As far as the competence of the child is concerned, the *MoGP* is not entirely clear how the courts will treat the question of competence in view of CJA 1991 reforms. However, it suggests that the investigating team 'should assume that the courts will be willing to listen to the evidence of any child who is able to communicate about the alleged offence in a way that the team, as a whole, can understand' (at para 2.14). This suggests that if the team is able to understand the child the court will probably be able to do so as well.

It is submitted that whilst this is probably true of most children, there will always be scope for different interpretations of what a child says, and this applies equally to the courts. Additionally, as far as subnormal or disabled children are concerned, the courts will require expert advice on what the child appears to be saying.

7.20.10 *Interviewing children with disabilities*

In a recent NSPCC report (see Marchant and Page *Bridging the Gap* (1992, NSPCC)), a series of interviews with criminal proceedings in mind were carried out by the authors in connection with the suspected abuse of 15 children with multiple disabilities. The authors describe, in some detail, their experience in interviewing such children in accordance with the Cleveland Inquiry guidelines and judgments from the Family Division of the High Court. They stress that the success of an investigative interview with a child with severe disabilities, particularly a child using an alternative method of communication, depends on *careful and thorough preparation*. Their research prompted six recommendations: (1) the child needs a clear explanation of the interview process from a trusted adult; (2) the adult accompanying the child needs an introduction to the purpose and structure of the interview and some practical information and guidelines; (3) the child protection worker needs accurate details of the child's communication and understanding, daily routine and lifestyle; (4) both sets of adults need to be very clear about their own role during and after the interview, and need access to support; (5) practical issues of location, recording methods and communication also need to be considered; and (6) details of all the preparation and the rationale for it must be carefully recorded in order that events at the preparatory stage cannot be held to invalidate a child's statements in an interview.

The *MoGP* addresses these issues but the NSPCC study exposed additional considerations that need to be taken into account when interviewing children generally and disabled children in particular. Although Marchant and Page's research was directed at severely disabled children, many of their findings could also apply to normal children. Accordingly, their main observations are interposed where appropriate in the following discussion of the step-wise approach.

7.20.11 *The NSPCC study on disabled children: appraisal of the four phases*

First, the *rapport stage* was found to be absolutely vital to establish a suitably receptive atmosphere and 'it may be necessary to return to it after breaks or when there is a need to "repair" communication'. The initial period of communication could establish the child's credibility and reliability. In the case of a child with cerebral palsy and additional learning difficulties, it took

35 minutes to establish the interview rules and establish clearly the importance of telling the truth. An important point that emerged from these interviews was that these disabled children responded very well to interviewers, who did not conceal their struggle to understand the children's communication attempts (see Marchant and Page (above), at p 23).

Secondly, in the *free narrative account stage*, experience at the Clermont Child Protection Unit indicates that only a small minority of children who have previously disclosed abuse will, in fact, be able to give a free narrative account at this stage of the interview, as a result of inhibitors, such as the child's own feelings about what has happened, the fear of threatened or imagined consequences of telling, the anxiety about talking about sexual matters of any kind (see Marchant and Page (above), at p 24). Nevertheless, it seemed that two of the 15 children did disclose spontaneously, and it was suggested that an attempt should at least be made to attempt to encourage the child to narrate events as freely as the child was able.

Thirdly, the *questioning phase* should commence with more open-ended questions and it may, where appropriate, consist of a number of further stages. The second stage in this phase, if thought suitable to move to, involves using specific, yet non-leading questions. Questions which require a 'yes' or 'no' answer or ones which allow only one of two possible responses, should not be asked. Language appropriate to the particular child should be used. If the second stage proves unproductive, closed questions may then be attempted. Closed questions are those which permit a limited number of responses such as asking for the colour of the person's scarf. If this style of question elicits very little information, the interviewer may then proceed to ask leading questions, which imply a particular answer or assume facts that it is sought to establish and are likely to be in dispute.

The *MoGP* stresses that a leading style of questioning may produce replies which are excluded from criminal proceedings, since leading questions would not normally be allowed if the child were testifying 'live' in the examination-in-chief during criminal proceedings.

Marchant and Page (above) submit that there are only two sets of circumstances in which it would not be advisable to proceed to this phase. First, where rapport cannot be achieved and secondly, in situations where it has been decided to conduct a planned series of interviews rather than the conventional single one (at p 24).

The fourth and final phase is the *closing phase* where the interview is terminated and the child is thanked. The *MoGP* emphasises that this may sometimes need to be carried out before sufficient information has been obtained from the child to instigate criminal proceedings. Given the amount of detail and accuracy of recall, not to mention the need to establish rapport with the child, the one hour maximum for the substantive interview (suggested in the *MoGP*, at para 2.17 and clearly derived from the Cleveland Inquiry guidelines: see **7.19.3** above) certainly appears to be unrealistic and possibly even damaging.

7.20.12 Comments on the MoGP time-scale

If the interviewers and child are, in some cases, under pressure to achieve a considerable amount of detail within a short space of time, then a lack of success in eliciting the responses which interviewers will need to satisfy a criminal court, may require the interviewer resorting to leading questions which could have psychologically damaging effects on the child, because of the very nature of such questions, particularly if they become more insistent (as indicated in the Cleveland and Orkney affairs).

The view of commentators (see, eg McEwan 'Where the Prosecution Witness is a Child: The Memorandum of Good Practice' (1993) *Journal of Child Law* 17; Wattam *Disclosure: The Child's Perspective* (1990, NSPCC)) is that the suggestion of a maximum period of an hour for the substantive interview (albeit not strictly binding), which is echoed in the Cleveland guidelines, (which have themselves received judicial approval), is not a practical proposition which would allow a child to disclose in his own time and at his own pace. Perhaps with this in mind, the *MoGP* stresses that every effort should be made to ensure that the child is not made to feel that he or she has failed or disappointed the interviewer in any way, is not distressed and is in a positive frame of mind.

As far as criminal proceedings and evidence for criminal prosecution are concerned, a child with whom it is difficult to establish a rapport and who is unresponsive or uncommunicative generally, would not make a good witness as far as cross-examination is concerned, and would do little to assist or support the case for the prosecution. Interviewing that fell short of the requirements of the *MoGP* may only succeed in producing flawed and, therefore, inadmissible interviews.

7.20.13 Advantages and disadvantages of the videotaped interview

There are clearly advantages and disadvantages, to the child, of the video-taped interview. On the one hand, the child is spared giving evidence-in-chief at the trial, stress may be reduced and the risk of fading memories can be greatly diminished. Davies and Noon's study suggests that another advantage would be that the child will, therefore, avoid being asked 'age-inappropriate' questions which tend to confuse when posed by prosecutors (see Davies and Noon *An evaluation of the live link for child witnesses* (1991, Home Office) at pp 55 to 56). More than 25 per cent of cross-examinations involved prosecution and defence asking questions where up to half were not appropriate to the age of the witness. Lapsing into the highly stylised language of the courtroom frequently occurred (see further below on this study).

On the other hand, it is hoped that on occasions when the strict technical requirements of the *MoGP* are not followed, the powers of the court to exclude the videotaped interview (which it now has under both CJA 1988 and PACEA 1984) will not result in justice being thwarted by exclusion being detrimental to a fair trial. Minor departures from the *MoGP*, resulting in an interview that may not conform to the requirements of criminal proceedings, may still provide valuable insights into the case, provided that the tape is admitted. However, the suggestibility of the interviews may itself create a problem of interpretation.

7.20.14 *Therapy and tainting of interview's evidential value*

McEwan argues (see McEwan 'Where the Prosecution Witness is a Child: The Memorandum of Good Practice' (1993) *Journal of Child Law* 17) that in cases where therapy is given to the child before he or she has given evidence in cross-examination 'therapists may seek to claim privilege and refuse to tell prosecutors exactly what was discussed, making it impossible to alert the defence . . . it is [also] difficult to see how successful the counselling would be if silent or neutral about the offence itself'. McEwan points out further that if such therapy took place, how will the child's evidence be regarded at the trial? The *MoGP* recommends that therapy may take place after the recording. Where a child has done a recorded interview and also gives evidence at the trial, the issue of 'taint' might then arise. Case-law suggests that a child's evidence will be excluded altogether if therapy takes place after the interview. It may be desirable, in the interests of a successful prosecution, to postpone therapy until after the testimony in court, but this will surely not be in the best interests of the child. Unfortunately, the CPS are not given guidance from the *MoGP* on this point and simply have to decide whether to bring a prosecution at all. Thus, the interests of the public, in seeing an abuser prosecuted, may well conflict with the child's immediate needs.

One of the difficulties with videotaped interviews is that they are similar to police witness statements. Although such statements may be consulted before coming up for scrutiny in the court, the videotaped interview is supposed to replace the examination-in-chief, which must be given orally and spontaneously in response to non-leading questions (McEwan (above) at p 18). In trying to relieve the child of having to repeat his or her testimony in court, or at least to have to retell it in front of a video camera and an interviewer, the videotaped interview runs into many difficulties in relation to the rules of evidence and criminal procedure.

7.20.15 *Technical issues*

The low technical standards of the tape might also affect its admissibility. The *MoGP* suggests that the interviewing team should aim at the quality of image the court would get if the child were giving evidence through the live link. The camera must not be fixed too high or low so that the child's head and face may not be seen clearly. Sound quality should be good and there should be two microphones to cater for the possibility of a great deal of movement. The voice of the child should be clearly audible and distinct (Davies and Noon (above), at p 124). However, it is submitted that the actual accent of the child, or (as pointed out above) language difficulties or unfamiliarity with the English language may, in turn, give rise to special requirements, or an interpreter, or as the case may be.

7.20.16 *Child suspects and the memorandum*

The *MoGP* also considers the question of the child who reveals his or her criminal actions during the course of an interview. This is certainly not an uncommon situation at the present time, since the latest report from the NCH reveals that a third of all child abusers are, in fact, under 18 years of age (*The Report of the Committee of Enquiry into Children and Young People who Sexually Abuse Other Children* (1992, NCH)), with its chief executive claiming that the true proportion may be even higher, since many cases were unreported and were not believed.

The *MoGP* states that it is not unusual for victims to become abusers. In any event, if the interviewed child admits to offences, such as indecent assault, a prosecution would not normally be initiated. However, the *MoGP* declares that if the situation is such that it is more important to treat the child as a suspect rather than a victim the interview should be terminated so that the child can be cautioned and questioned under the protection of PACEA 1984. This is perhaps an area where the welfare versus justice objectives appear to meet head on and will require resolving the dilemma of weighing compassion against the need for punishment.

7.21 Evaluation of the live link for child witnesses

7.21.1 *Introduction*

Will the live link prove to be a marked improvement on previous face-to-face interviewing? Is it preferable to traditional interviewing methods? Closed circuit television equipment was installed initially in 14 Crown Court centres throughout England and Wales and was later extended to 30 further courts. During the first eight months of usage, about 115 applications to use the link had been heard by judges, of which all but nine had been approved. Of the 106 successful applications, only 61 went to trial, the remainder being resolved by late guilty pleas (see GM Davies 'Children on trial? Psychology, video-technology and the law' (1991) *The Howard Journal of Criminal Justice* 177). It is, however, too early to say whether the above statistics prove the success of the live link and a comparison of committal rates for courts with and without the live link would be more revealing. In deciding whether or not to use a live link set-up, some knowledge of the current empirical evidence of the efficacy of such links is useful.

7.21.2 *Empirical studies*

The majority of researchers and professionals working in the criminal justice system seem to agree that the live link reduces stress for children, makes them less anxious and prevents their worst fear, which is confrontation with the accused, from materialising. Consequently, they are less self-conscious and more self-confident when giving their evidence.

Davies and Noon (see *An evaluation of the live link for child witnesses* (1991, Home Office)) observed, over a two-year period, 154 children giving evidence in 100 live link cases (100 girls and 54 boys, ranging in age from 4 years 9 months to 13 years 9 months) wherein most cases involved some form of sexual assault (94 per cent) with the most common charge being indecent assault. The children giving evidence in this study were compared with children giving evidence in open court. The study found that the child witnesses using live link technology gave more consistent evidence, were more audible and less unhappy (or at least, less stressed) than children giving evidence in open court. Their testimony was also more fluent as well as more consistent and less confused than the other sample children.

However, the worst defect which they found in the system is *delay* at all levels. On average, the children had to wait 10-and-a-half months after making the original allegations before giving evidence at the trial. Research shows that children, more than adults, suffer greater memory loss of peripheral details over a period of time. Hence, the longer the delay, the less effective the evidence tends to be. In addition, the child is not permitted to receive therapy until the trial is over, for fear that the defence might argue that child has been 'coached'. The use of pre-recorded interviews might just be the most effective method of coping with children's memory loss in these circumstances. Delays also occur through last-minute postponements of the trial, sometimes notified on the day when the child has already arrived to testify. While waiting to give testimony the average wait for a child appears to be two hours and 46 minutes.

On the question of whether the live link enhances the status and effect of the testimony, this is very much open to debate. Some observers have seen cases where the emotional impact of the testimony has been 'flattened' (eg K Macfarlane 'Diagnostic evaluations and the use of videotapes in child sexual abuse cases' (1985) *University of Miami Law Review* 135), while others have found that the judge thought that the child witness 'filled the screen and it was almost as if she was in the witness box' (see Platt 'Video evidence – a response' (1989) *Journal of Child Law* 17).

As far as the impact of live link testimony on jurors is concerned, the type of shot used (close-up/medium shot) did have some effect on credibility but its effect was inconsistent and, therefore, again, inconclusive (see Westcott, Davies and Clifford 'The credibility of child witnesses seen on closed-circuit television' (1991) *Adoption and Fostering* 14).

It seems, therefore, that a great deal will depend on the particular witness, and the quality of the recording, so that the *MoGP* should, as far as possible, be followed.

Davies and Noon (above) also found that there was positive feedback from courtroom personnel. Around 76 per cent of all judges and 83 per cent of all barristers (prosecution and defence) formed a 'favourable' or 'very favourable' impression of the live link scheme.

If there is more than one interview with several children, and it is decided to show them all, the effect on personnel of showing lengthy videotapes then arises. Walker mentions cases where the judge appeared to fall asleep after watching lengthy videotapes (see L Walker 'Psychological assessment of sexually abused children for legal evaluation and expert witness testimony' (1990) *Professional Psychology: Research and Practice* 344). One would hope that this is an infrequent occurrence.

7.21.3 Advantages of live link testimony

The main advantage of the live link system is that the child need never see the accused throughout the child's testimony. Hence, a television link can be one-way so that the child never sees the courtroom and only the image of the child is televised to the main court. Davies and Noon's study (above) also suggests: (1) there was a perceived reduction in the stress levels experienced by the children during their testimony; (2) insulation from the oppressive atmosphere of the courtroom was effected; (3) children appeared to be more forthcoming in their evidence – a point directly supported by the in-court observational data; and (4) it opened up possibilities for the provision of testimony from children markedly younger than those who have traditionally appeared in court.

7.21.4 Disadvantages of live link testimony

Three main problems emerged: (1) an impression shared by some judges and barristers that televised testimony might have less immediacy for the jury when compared to a conventional live appearance; (2) a loss of emotional impact when testimony is given via the live link, since emotional outbursts were less likely and when they did occur, might be hidden from the jury by the exercise of the judge's power to switch off the system. (It is highly questionable whether a witness's vulnerability should ever be exploited for the benefit of securing a conviction yet the prosecution might feel that a jury needs to be convinced); (3) there are problems in establishing and maintaining rapport between child and examiner. Clearly, there is a need for all personnel, including legal officers, to be trained in the skills of interviewing children, particularly with this new technology in mind; and (4) the necessity of assembling the live link equipment itself and ensuring its smooth working causes disruptions and delays in the case of malfunctions. Live links will doubtless continue to be used in many courtrooms which are not structurally designed for it. CJA 1988 allows for transfer of proceedings to a better-equipped venue where necessary.

SENTENCING GUIDELINES

7.22 General considerations

It is widely acknowledged that some of the most difficult sentencing decisions are those involving violence to children, where the violence was wrought in the heat of the moment, as a result of a temporary loss of control. The predominant attitude in judicial sentencing in recent years has been influenced by the concept of 'individualisation of sentence'. The two decisions of the sentencer are:

(1) on which side of the system is the case to be decided? Should an individualised measure be used, or is the case to be dealt with on a tariff basis? Once this initial decision is made:
(2) which individualised measure should be issued, or where on the tariff is the sentence to be located? ('Tariff' here refers to the process by which the length of a sentence of imprisonment is calculated.)

The question that often arises is whether a deterrent sentence is required. As far as the worst cases of spontaneous violence are concerned, a custodial sentence may be warranted. However, the variations and degrees of seriousness are such that the courts have to proceed with circumspection.

7.23 Sentencing for grievous bodily harm to children

R v Durkin (1989) *The Times*, June 20, is a case which involved grievous bodily harm to a child, caused in a fit of temper. The facts of the case were that Durkin, a regular soldier home on sick leave, had been looking after his hyperactive 19-month-old son. He had run a little water into his bath, which, due to a faulty thermostat, was scalding hot. As he picked up his child, the child hit the appellant on the nose with his head. It was not known whether this was done intentionally or not, but the appellant lost control at this point and thrust the child forcibly into the bath. As soon as he realised the appalling nature of what he had done, he immediately took the child to hospital and the boy made a good recovery. Owing to the skill of the doctors, the boy was walking in a little while and had recovered, apart from a scar to the top of one foot. Durkin was sentenced to three-and-a-half-years' imprisonment and appealed against his sentence. On appeal, it was reduced to 18 months. Lord Lane reiterated the four principles behind sentencing:

(1) deterrence of others;
(2) punishment – it was necessary to punish someone who had committed this sort of offence;
(3) the need to provide expiation of the offence for the offender;
(4) the necessity of satisfying the public conscience.

As far as the sudden loss of temper was concerned, the deterrence of others was not relevant. Eighteen months was the minimum sentence required in the circumstances.

7.23.1 Sentences should be appropriate to degree of neglect

The case of *R v Burcher* (1988) *The Times*, March 4, is authority for the proposition that the sentence passed for neglect of one's children (in this case the children had been left alone in their home for some time, and electrocuted themselves by accident) should be commensurate with the degree of neglect involved. The facts of the case were that the father of two children (aged 10 and 5) left them alone in his flat one evening and returned to find them dead in the bath, having been electrocuted by a hairdryer plugged into an extension lead. On two counts of the charge of cruelty to a person under 16, he was sentenced to 18 months' imprisonment by Cardiff Crown Court. The Court of Appeal reduced his sentence to 12 months, opining that the degree of neglect involved could not be said to be 75 per cent of the criminality in the worst cases of that type of offence. Parker LJ said that if it were not for the fact that there was a maximum sentence of two years' imprisonment for that offence, their Lordships would not have regarded the sentence as originally passed as being in any way wrong. What was wrong, if anything, was that the maximum sentence for injury done to a child in these circumstances was two years' imprisonment.

7.24 Sentencing in child sexual abuse cases

The Wolfenden Committee on Homosexual Offences and Prostitution (1957, HMSO) (Cmnd 247) stated that the function of the criminal law in the field of sexual offences is:

> 'to preserve public order and decency, to protect the citizen from what is offensive or injurious, and to provide sufficient safeguards against exploitation and corruption of others, particularly those who are specially vulnerable because they are young, weak in the body or mind, inexperienced, or in a state of special physical, official or economic dependence.'

As far as sentencing young offenders who sexually abuse other young children is concerned, *The Report of the Committee of Enquiry into Children and Young People who Sexually Abuse Other Children* (1992, NCH) submitted (at para 4.13):

> 'Sentencing should take into account what is in the best interests of the child or young person. Some sentences, such as a conditional discharge or a fine would appear to be inappropriate because they would not encourage treatment to take place and may well allow the young person to deny the seriousness of the offence. Social minimisation of sexual offending or sexually abusive behaviour ought not to make professionals lose sight of the dangers which are actually involved; nor should the fear of labelling be over-stated. Clearly, an assessment of the abusive behaviour and the needs of the child or young person must be undertaken prior to sentencing.'

CJA 1991 requires a pre-sentence report from a probation officer or local authority social worker when a custodial sentence is being considered.

7.24.1 Cases of incest

The courts have, however, found it very difficult to reconcile various sentences for the crime of incest in different sets of circumstances. Two leading authorities which shed light on this question are *Attorney-General's Reference No 1 of 1989* [1989] 3 All ER 571 and *Attorney-General's Reference No 4 of 1989* (1989) *The Guardian*, November 15.

In *Attorney-General's Reference No 1 of 1989* (above), guidelines were laid down by the Lord Chief Justice for the Court of Appeal for sentencing in sexual abuse cases. The facts of the case were that when the offender's daughter, S, was 11, he committed acts of incest with her and continued, thereafter, for at least four years. The acts of incest were calculated to intimidate her, bearing in mind that the offender had frequently been drinking and, on at least one occasion, had placed a blanket over her face before having sex with her. During the period of this course of conduct, he was violent towards her and put her in fear, never showing her any affection, sympathy, tolerance or understanding.

The offender pleaded guilty to three counts of incest and one count of indecent assault. He was sentenced to three years' imprisonment on each of the three counts and 18 months' imprisonment on the count of indecent assault.

The Attorney-General referred the case to the Court of Appeal for review under s 36 of CJA 1988 on the ground that the sentences were unduly lenient. Section 36 of CJA 1988 provides that the Attorney-General has the power, with leave of the court, to refer sentences which he believes 'unduly lenient' to the Court of Appeal, which is empowered, in place of such sentences, to pass any sentence which it thinks appropriate for the case. The Court of Appeal has also said that a sentence was unduly lenient if 'it fell outside the range of sentences which the judge, applying his mind to all the relevant factors, could reasonably consider appropriate'. In that connection, regard must be had, it stressed, to reported cases and guidance given by the Court of Appeal in the so-called guideline cases (see *Attorney-General's Reference No 4 of 1989* (1989) *The Guardian*, November 15 (below)).

In the present case, the Court of Appeal declared that the age of the victim would be a relevant factor to consider in sentencing for incest cases. The following guidelines were then enunciated (assuming a not guilty plea).

(1) For girls over 16: three years' imprisonment, down to a nominal penalty depending on the force used, the need to minimise family disruption, the harm to the girl and degree to which she was a willing or instigating party or was corrupted.

(2) For girls between 13 and 16: between three and five years' imprisonment, depending on the same factors. The likelihood of corruption increased in inverse proportion to the age of the girl. Nearly all cases in this and other categories had involved pleas of guilty and the sentences in this category seemed to range between two and four years, credit having been given for the plea.

(3) For girls under 13: the widest range of sentences was likely to be found. The ordinary type of case would be where the sexual relationship between husband and wife had broken down; the father had probably resorted to excessive drinking and the eldest daughter was gradually, by way of familiarities, indecent acts and suggestions made the object of the father's frustrated sexual inclinations. Thus, a term of about six years was appropriate, if there were no special factors, adverse or favourable, and the girl was nearly 13.

Aggravating factors would be the age of the girl (the younger the girl, the more serious the crime); evidence that she had suffered harm (psychologically or physically); if the incest had continued over a long period, at frequent intervals, or was accompanied by perversions (buggery or *fellatio*); if the girl had been threatened or treated violently or was terrified of the father; if the girl had become pregnant by the father failing to take contraceptive measures; or the father had committed similar offences against more than one girl.

Mitigating factors would be a plea of guilty and a degree of contrition; genuine affection for the girl by the defendant; where she had had previous sexual experience; where she had made deliberate attempts at seduction; where, as was sometimes the case, a shorter term of imprisonment might be of benefit to the victim and the family.

In the instant case, their Lordships thought that an appropriate sentence would be six years' imprisonment on two counts, each of which alleged incest with the girl when she was under the age of 13; the three-year sentence on the charge when she was 15 would remain unaltered; these sentences would run concurrently, totalling six years in all. Their Lordships, therefore, granted the Attorney-General's application, quashed the earlier sentences and substituted the new, increased sentences.

Several comments may be made about these judicial guidelines. As far as mitigating factors are concerned, Lord Lane appears to believe that where the girl is over 16, a range going down from three years to a nominal sentence would be appropriate. Thus, cases involving children under 13 would attract the most severe penalties. This sliding scale approach suggests a philosophy that would argue that the younger the child, the greater the likelihood that the child has been corrupted by the father. Contrastingly, the older the girl, the stronger the possibility that the girl might have been a willing or even instigating party to the liaison.

However, clinical research evidence does not really support such an approach. Glaser, a leading child psychiatrist, has suggested that older girls, with their greater degree of awareness of the meaning of an incestuous relationship, may suffer just as much emotional scarring as younger girls, for example in their continued fears of an unwanted pregnancy. It also appears that clinical evidence indicates that the closer the degree of relationship between the victim and perpetrator, the more harmful are the consequences. Indeed, it further suggests that children often learn their precocious sexualised behaviour from their fathers, so Lord Lane's suggestion that the sentence should be reduced if the girl has had other sexual experiences apart from with her father, seems to place the blame on the girl for behaviour which she initially learnt from her father, who may well be the root cause of her behaviour in any event (see Glaser and Frosh *Child Sexual Abuse* (1988, Macmillan)).

In addition, Lord Lane's approach may well deter older girls from reporting the incest and this cannot be a trend to be encouraged (see C Yates 'A Family Affair: Part 1: Sexual Offences, Sentencing and Treatment' (1989/90) 2 *Journal of Child Law* 70).

In any event, this case has been cited as one of the leading authorities in subsequent cases, for example in *Attorney-General's Reference No 4 of 1991 (R v Noble)* [1991] Crim LR 925, a case involving indecent assault and unlawful sexual intercourse with a girl under 13. Here, the offender married the victim's mother when the victim was four years old: she treated him as her father. The offender began to assault her indecently when she was five and continued to do so for about three years. The offender admitted three or four acts of sexual intercourse when she was seven or eight years old. The victim's mother left the offender when the victim was eight-and-a-half, and the incidents came to light some time later when it was suggested that the victim should stay with the offender for a time. The offender was sentenced to two-and-a-half years' imprisonment for unlawful sexual intercourse, 21 months' imprisonment concurrent for indecent assault. The Attorney-General asked the court to review the sentence on the ground that it was unduly lenient. The court reviewed the authorities and said that *Attorney-General's*

Reference No 1 of 1989 was the most useful guide in sentencing cases of this sort, although it related to natural fathers rather than to stepfathers. The present case lacked some of the aggravating factors found in similar cases, such as the use of violence or threats, and the relationship began as one of genuine affection; there was a plea of guilty, which was particularly significant in view of difficulties over corroboration in the particular circumstances of the case, and there was no prospect that the offender and the victim would ever meet again.

The court considered that the sentence was unduly lenient in that it was outside the range of sentences which any judge could consider appropriate in the circumstances. Allowing for the fact that the offender had the added anxiety involved in a reference to the court by the Attorney-General, the court would substitute a sentence of four years' imprisonment.

It is unclear how much guidance may really be derived from this case, since guidelines for incest cases being applied to cases of unlawful intercourse by stepfathers should have resulted in something in the nature of six years' imprisonment rather than four. It is particularly unclear how much allowance should be given to the fact that the case had been referred to the court by the Attorney-General.

In another case, *Attorney-General's Reference No 4 of 1989* (1989) *The Guardian*, November 15, the Court of Appeal again laid down further guidance on sentencing in such cases. The facts here were that the girl, V, was 13 when her father starting touching her indecently and she later began having sex with her father (ie after she was 15). The father pleaded guilty to two counts of indecent assault and two counts of incest. On each count, he was sentenced to concurrent terms of 18 months, suspended for three years. Again, the Attorney-General referred the case to the Court of Appeal on the ground that the sentences meted out were unduly lenient.

The Lord Chief Justice said that the factors which made the case unusual and which persuaded the judge to treat it as exceptional could be grouped under three headings.

(1) *The family relationship.* From a very early age, V's relationship with her mother, who seemed to reject her, had been strained. This led to a corresponding closeness with her father. V turned to him for the performance of those intimate tasks which ordinarily a mother might perform. That led to the first indecent touching which later led to sexual intercourse.

(2) *The child's interests.* After the discovery of the offences, V's mother blamed V for what had occurred and the threatened break-up of the family. The two younger daughters resented being deprived of their father. There was also evidence that the offender himself blamed V. V, who was with foster-parents, wished to rejoin a re-united family.

(3) *Mitigating factors.* The offender had pleaded guilty, was of previous good

character, and his regular earnings as a carpenter supported the family. A repetition of the offences was unlikely. Since the hearing, V had had a supervised meeting with her father on her 16th birthday. Intensive work had been undertaken by the social services with the offender and family.

Lord Lane referred to *Attorney-General's Reference No 1* (above), which had suggested that where the victim was between 13 and 16, a sentence of between three and five years seemed appropriate. However, he stressed that circumstances varied infinitely and sentencing should not involve a rigid arithmetical approach. He explained what was considered an 'unduly lenient sentence' (see above) and went on to say:

> 'sentencing is an art rather than a science; . . . the trial judge was particularly well-placed to assess the weight to be given to various competing considerations; . . . leniency was not in itself a vice. That mercy should season justice was a proposition as soundly based in law as in literature.'

In the present circumstances, the trial judge had taken the wholly exceptional course of suspending the sentence in its entirety, because he had been 'principally motivated' by the interests of the victim and the family as a whole. The Court of Appeal than accepted the social worker's suggestion that a probation order, coupled with a condition that the offender reside where directed and comply with such treatment or counselling as may be advised, was preferable to a suspended sentence.

In *Attorney-General's Reference No 17 of 1990* (1990) *The Times*, December 10, the Court of Appeal was again asked to review a case involving buggery of two girls, both aged 10. The 27-year-old offender had approached one girl and a boy, aged 9, in Cardiff, and asked them if they would like to see a bird's nest. They followed him into a wooded area where he attacked and buggered the girl. The boy ran for help and alerted two adults nearby. The offender ran off but within a few minutes he approached some other children aged 10 to 11 and lured them away by the same trick, and attempted to bugger another 10-year-old girl. The offender was arrested the following day and admitted sniffing glue which had sexually aroused him. He was sentenced to three years' imprisonment for the buggery of the 10-year-old girl and one year consecutive for attempted buggery on the other 10-year-old girl. The Court of Appeal (per Lord Lane) held that in such circumstances their Lordships had to consider: (1) the overall gravity of the offence; (2) the necessity for punishment of the offender, 'something which was sometimes overlooked'; (3) the necessity to protect the public from the activities of someone who was prepared to sniff solvent and then, having his sexual intentions aroused, committed such an offence; (4) the public concern at sexual offences on young children; and (5) what one hoped might be the deterrent effect which a severe sentence might have on other people minded to act in such a manner.

They thought that the sentences were pitched far too low and allowed the Attorney-General's appeal, ruling that the proper sentence for the buggery was six years and for the attempt, one year consecutive.

7.24.2 Other recent sentencing cases

Certain guidelines from the Court of Appeal dealing with recent legislation were published recently in *The Times* (see *R v Cunningham et al* (1992) *The Times*, December 3). In *R v Robinson* (1992) *The Times*, December 3, the appellant was 16 at the time of the offence, which was attempted rape of a woman of 90. The woman had been alone in her home at night and had suffered physical injury as a direct result of the attempted rape. The appellant was sentenced to eight years under s 53(2) of CYPA 1933. The sentence might have been longer if the appellant had been older.

In *R v Okinikan* (1992) *The Times*, December 3, the Court of Appeal opined that 'taken on their own or in combination, good character, youth and an early plea were not exceptional circumstances justifying a suspended sentence. They were common features of many cases. They could amount to mitigation sufficient to persuade the court that a custodial sentence should not be passed or to reduce its length. But each case would depend on its individual circumstances'.

7.25 Sentencing powers under CJA 1991

A number of changes to the court process and the disposals available to the court were introduced by CJA 1991. Many of these have already been referred to (see **7.8.11** above). Among the more significant are: (1) the requirement that there should be a pre-sentence report (from a probation officer or local authority social worker) when a custodial sentence is being considered; (2) modifications to the criteria for custody; (3) the relevance of previous convictions; (4) the introduction of unit fines; (5) the abolition of the custodial sentence for 14-year-old males; (6) the availability of the probation order for 16-year-olds; and (7) the extension of supervision orders to 17-year-olds.

Two general points should be emphasised. First, CJA 1991 sought to reduce the use of custody for less serious and especially young offenders and to be more flexible in their sentencing of young offenders. The rationale for this is explained in the *Home Office Guide to the Criminal Justice Act 1991*:

> 'offenders of this age are at a transitional stage between childhood and adulthood. Some will be more developed and independent than others. Bringing all offenders of this age within the jurisdiction of the youth court, and providing the youth court with a flexible range of disposals for offenders will enable the penalty given in each case to reflect the individual's development and circumstances.'

Secondly, every court that deals with a child or young person shall have regard to the *welfare of the child or young person* (CYPA 1933, s 44). The court may also attach greater importance to the concept of rehabilitation and individualised treatment than it might otherwise do in relation to an adult defendant.

Another concept that has been followed is the *notion of proportionality* (CJA 1991, ss 1(2) and 2(2)). One of the main objectives of CJA 1991 is to ensure that serious offences and offenders are adequately dealt with by the courts. Sentencers are now expected to decide on the nature and scale of sentence primarily according to the *seriousness of the offences committed*, attaching less weight to the number of current charges or previous convictions. Hence, as a general principle, there is an expectation that those committing what are often called grave crimes, such as serious offences against the person, will receive more punitive sentences even though the number of such offences may be few and the offender is only facing his first conviction. Thus, an exception to the proportionality principle will be made in the case of violent or sexual offences (CJA 1991, s 2(2)(b)). Another exception to the court not taking into account an offender's previous record or failure to respond to previous sentences is where aggravating factors of an offence are disclosed by the circumstances of other offences committed by the offender (CJA 1991, s 29(2)).

Although the general rule is that any sentence reflects the seriousness of the offence for which it is imposed, it is permissible, in considering the seriousness of the offence, to aggregate offences in certain cases. This can be used when considering whether offences are: (1) 'so serious' that only a custodial sentence can be justified; or (2) 'serious enough' to merit a community sentence. In aggregating the offences the court may only take into account the offence or the combination of the offence and one other offence associated with it (CJA 1991, s 2(2)(b)).

It should be noted that parts of CJA 1991 will be amended in the near future. The Act focuses on the need for a firm response to serious crime but a great deal of criticism has been made of its structure and the argument has been made by judges and practitioners for the right to impose longer custodial sentences for serious and persistent juvenile offenders. The Act was based on the premise that custodial institutions could themselves have a criminalising effect so that rigorous and demanding community programmes could be just as effective as forms of punishment. In practical terms, critics of CJA 1991 have pointed out that the government could not ignore the ubiquitous problem of overcrowded prisons.

Criticisms have also focused on the new system of fines which, through the application of a means test, resulted in some fines being out of proportion to the seriousness of the offence. In addition, the Act's treatment of previous and related offences, which it is suggested should not generally be taken into account, has also attracted criticism, although the principle that previous convictions should not, *per se*, result in more severe sentences for a new offence, was already the rule in existing case-law.

The Home Secretary announced, on 2 March 1993, his plans to deal with persistent juvenile offenders, with the key proposal being that courts are to be given powers to impose a secure training order, for up to two years, on 12- to 15-year-olds convicted of three imprisonable offences. However, statistics published recently by the Prison Reform Trust actually show a fall in the number of juveniles cautioned or convicted of an indictable offence, from 175,800 in 1980 to 110,900 in 1990. Whilst these figures are certainly open to interpretation, they do not indicate an unequivocal crisis in juvenile crime. On 14 May 1993, the Home Secretary announced that the present CJA 1991 systems of unit fines will be abolished and sections of CJA 1991, which restrict reference to previous convictions when sentencing property offenders, will be repealed. Hence, courts will, again, be entitled to take into account all the offences for which an offender is before the bench, and previous convictions in deciding the sentence. It is submitted that the best way forward might be to redraft some of the provisions in such a way that the flexibility is retained but the rules on unit fines could be modified so as to avoid the anomalous situations which have occurred.

7.25.1 *Sentencing for unlawful intercourse with a girl under 16*

The leading case for sentencing in this type of case is *R v Taylor and Others* [1977] 3 All ER 527, wherein the Court of Appeal (Criminal Division) laid down the following guidelines.

(1) The offence known as having unlawful sexual intercourse with a girl under 16 covers a wide spectrum of guilt, and, accordingly, the penalties appropriate to the offence will vary in different cases.
(2) Where a youth has what starts off as a virtuous friendship and ends with sexual intercourse, it would normally be inappropriate to pass a punitive sentence.
(3) Where a youth seeks out a girl with loose morals and has sexual intercourse with her, a fine would usually be appropriate, but where a man in his 20s or older seeks out such a girl, he may expect a stiffer fine or, if the girl is under 15, a short period of imprisonment.
(4) Where the offender deliberately sets out to seduce a girl under 16, the appropriate sentence would be detention in the case of a young man, or imprisonment in the case of someone older.
(5) A man in a supervisory capacity who abuses his position of trust for sexual gratification merits a sentence of imprisonment somewhere near the maximum term of two years.

The recent, much-publicised case of the 15-year-old Welsh boy, *R v W* (1993) *The Times*, March 16, who was charged with raping a 15-year-old girl who was his schoolmate, provided an opportunity for the Court of Appeal to clarify the scope of the courts' jurisdiction in such cases. The boy pleaded not guilty. The court held that although a person under 18, who was charged with rape, might be tried summarily in some circumstances, rape was an offence triable only on indictment for the purposes of CJA 1988, s 35(3). Lord Taylor LCJ, therefore, stressed that the Attorney-General was entitled to refer the case to the court which, therefore, had jurisdiction to entertain that application. The trial judge had imposed a supervision order for three years, with a condition that the boy attend a specified activities programme and his parents were ordered to pay £500 compensation to the complainant. The court said that it understood the reluctance of the trial judge to impose a custodial sentence, but 'a non-custodial sentence was simply not tenable in this case'. The court opined that the rape in this case had aggravating features. The boy apparently raped the girl as she was returning home from the school where both were pupils. When she refused to give him a birthday kiss, he dragged her into nearby woods and committed the offence.

Lord Taylor said that a psychiatric report showed that the girl suffered from post-traumatic stress disorder, with mental flashbacks, nightmares, acute depression, anxiety and irritability. By pleading not guilty, the boy had put her through the further ordeal of being cross-examined to suggest she had consented. Four aggravating features mentioned by counsel for the Attorney-General were the traumatic effect on the victim, the fact that she was 15, a virgin, and had been subjected to oral sex. Mitigating factors mentioned were the boy's age and previous good character.

The whole of the previous sentence was quashed and substituted by detention for two years, pursuant to CYPA 1933, s 53(2), for the rape. No separate order was made for the indecent assault.

7.26 Concluding comments on sentencing policy

The question of the objectives of sentencing policy for different types of offences and different types of offender has never really been properly addressed. In the realm of incest offenders, a great deal of criticism has been heaped on the inadequacy of existing measures, since custody is often ineffectual in preventing re-offending. In the past few months, the issue of juvenile offenders has also been a burning issue, not least because of the cases involving two 10-year-old boys in Merseyside who have been charged with the murder of a two-year-old boy and the case concerning the Welsh boy (*R v W* (above)).

Unfortunately, despite the announcement by the Home Secretary that various central provisions of CJA 1991 will be repealed as soon as possible, there is still the distinct impression that this is yet another panic reaction to widespread criticism and perceived problems, rather than a more rationally considered measure.

We shall have to wait and see how this extremely complex intermingling of conflicting policies involving children in the criminal justice process –

punishment versus rehabilitation, welfare versus justice – will be tackled in the next few months and, particularly, in the longer term.

CHAPTER EIGHT

Contact

'States Parties shall respect the right of any child . . . to maintain personal and direct contact with both parents on a regular basis . . . ' (Art 9, UN Convention on the Rights of Children, 1989)

8.1 Introduction

It should be noted that the term 'contact' as used in the Children Act 1989 is generally understood to be far wider than the older notion of 'access'. 'Access' was usually taken to connote physical contact with the child, whereas 'contact', which certainly includes physically visiting the child or having the child to visit or to stay for short or long periods (s 8(1)), also encompasses contact by letter or telephone. (See *The Children Act 1989 Guidance and Regulations, Vol 1 Court Orders* (1991, HMSO) at para 2.29.) General guidance on issues of contact with children in care can be found in both *The Children Act 1989 Guidance and Regulations, Vol 3 Family Placements* (1991, HMSO) (at Chapter 6) and *The Children Act 1989 Guidance and Regulations, Vol 4 Residential Care* (1991, HMSO) (at Chapter 4). Attention here, therefore, will focus specifically on provisions relating to contact with children who are deemed to have suffered or who are likely to suffer from significant harm. As discussed in Chapter 4, a decision on contact with a child suffering or likely to suffer significant harm will have to be made early on. Such decisions on contact are no longer the subject of overriding discretion operated by local authorities, but are subject to considerable statutory control and direction, most particularly where the child has been made subject to any of the orders under Parts IV and V of the Children Act 1989 ('the 1989 Act'). Less rigorous statutory control operates in relation to those children who are being offered accommodation as a result of preventive practice by the local authority, or as a result of the decision of a child protection conference that the service of accommodation be offered as part of a child protection package. The reason for this, of course, is that pursuant to the 1989 Act's philosophy of working in partnership with parents it would be anticipated that local authorities and parents and others who might wish to have contact with the child would be able to reach an amicable agreement as to the levels of contact which are deemed appropriate. Where this is not the case, however, resort would clearly have to be made to the provisions of private law orders under the 1989 Act, s 8. Where, pursuant to such partnership arrangements with the parents, a child is accommodated for a considerable length of time, it should be noted that Sch 1 of the Review of Children's Cases Regulations,

SI 1991/895, provides that steps must be taken in the course of the review to explain to the child any action which he may take under the 1989 Act, where appropriate, including his right to apply with leave for a s 8 order, which includes a contact order (at para 5). (See, further, **8.2** below.)

Where, as a result of the recommendation of the child protection conference or in response to an emergency, resort has to be made to the seeking of court orders in respect of the child in need of protection then, at every stage of the legal process, consideration is now given to the issue of contact. The rigorous attention given to contact issues when the court makes orders was, in large part, due to the *Report of the Inquiry into Child Abuse in Cleveland 1987* (1988, HMSO), Cm 412, ('the *Cleveland Report*'), which highlighted gaps in the then existing legislation which gave too much discretion to local authorities to restrict contact, without any recourse to the courts being available (at recommendation 4(d) of the report). Depending on the order being sought, therefore, consideration will have to be given to the issue of contact and decisions made about what directions will be sought from the courts.

Where a local authority, or the NSPCC, is considering making an application for a child assessment order, and the child is to be kept away from home, the order must contain such directions as the court thinks fit with regard to the contact that the child must be allowed to have with persons whilst away from home. (See **8.3** below.) Advance consideration must, therefore, be given to the issue of the nature of the harm from which the child is believed to be suffering, and to the person deemed responsible for that harm. Clearly, however, a child assessment order is a very different statutory creature from the emergency and other orders which are made with regard to the protection of children, since it is intended to be a means by which confirmation may be sought on whether a child is suffering from significant harm or not. It may, therefore, be entirely inappropriate to take such steps to terminate contact for all or any part of the duration of the order, since at the end of the day it may be established that no responsibility lies with the parents or existing carers. Where a child protection conference has been held to discuss the application for a child assessment order, a contact order must be discussed and a recommendation also passed on to the authority making the application.

By contrast, where it is believed necessary to apply for an emergency protection order, the applicant may feel that it is in the best interests of the child to seek a direction that contact not be allowed between the child and any named person, which can include adults and children depending on the age of the abuser or potential abusers (s 44(6)(a)). (See further **8.4** below.) Where no such direction is sought from the court, contact between the child and other persons connected with him shall be presumed to be *reasonable* (s 44(13)). As far as other emergency situations are concerned, where the police exercise their powers of protection under s 46 of the 1989 Act, the designated officer is required to allow a wide range of people to have such contact (if any) with the child as, in the opinion of the designated officer, is both reasonable and in the child's best interests. (See further **8.5** below.) The clear difference between the emergency protection order and the police powers of protection is that whilst issues of contact can be challenged in relation to the emergency protection order there is actually no ability to challenge the exercise by the police of their discretion under s 46(10).

Unlike the position with regard to emergency protection orders and child assessment orders, there is no power simply to give directions on contact where an interim care order is made since, for these purposes, the making of an interim care order is treated like the making of a full order (s 31(11)). (See further **8.6** below.) This, therefore, means that before making an interim order the court is required to consider any proposed contact arrangements and to invite the parties to the proceedings to comment on them (s 34(11) and see Form CHA 20). Where any party is dissatisfied with the proposed contact arrangements under an interim order they can also seek a contact order using s 34, as can the child if he is unhappy about the proposed contact arrangements (s 34(2)). (See *A v M and Walsall Metropolitan Borough Council* at **8.6** below.) The guardian ad litem would be expected to advise the court in such situations, and if necessary, to make a report.

Issues relating to contact with a child are never easy but the interpretation given to the new law on contact, particularly by the Court of Appeal, would appear to indicate that there is a greater possibility now of challenging the local authority's determination on contact with a child than was the case under the previous law (see *Re B (Minors) (Children in Care: Contact: Local Authority's Plans)* [1993] 1 FLR 543, when compared to such decisions as *A v Liverpool City Council* [1982] AC 363 and *Re S (A Minor) (Access Application)* [1991] 1 FLR 161).

8.2 Contact with accommodated children

Where, as part of local authority support for a child in need of protection, a local authority social services department makes an offer to accommodate the child with the agreement of the parents, instead of resorting to compulsory removal, it is expected that the local authority and the child's parents, and anyone else who might be relevant, will reach agreement with the local authority on the appropriate level of contact. By s 23(7) of the 1989 Act, where a local authority provides accommodation for the child it is required to secure that that accommodation is as near to the child's home as possible, and under the 1989 Act, Sch 2, Part II, para 15 the local authority is also under a duty to endeavour to promote contact between the child, his parents, anyone who has parental responsibility and any relative, friend or other person connected with the child. The local authority is also empowered, by reason of Sch 2, Part II, para 16 to make payments to any such persons to enable them to maintain contact with the child. As is pointed out in *The Children Act 1989 Guidance and Regulations, Vol 3 Family Placements* (1991, HMSO), for the majority of children there is no doubt that their interests will be best served by efforts to sustain or create links with their natural families. It is suggested that contact with families by way of personal meetings and visits is generally the most common and, for both families and children, is the most satisfactory way of maintaining their relationship. Other means of keeping family bonds alive are, however, suggested, such as letters, telephone calls and exchange of photographs. The guidance goes on to state that the first few weeks during which a child is looked after by the local authority are likely to be particularly crucial to the success of the relationship between the parent, the social worker and the child's carers and to the level of future contact between parent and child. It is at this time that patterns are set, which may be difficult to change, whether the child is looked after by a voluntary arrangement or as a result of a care order (at para 6.10). (See also *The Children Act 1989 Guidance and Regulations, Vol 4 Residential Care* (1991, HMSO), at para 4.10.)

Before making any decision regarding contact, whether it is in respect of accommodated children or other children looked after by the local authority, the local authority must give due consideration to the child's wishes and feelings, having regard to his age and understanding (s 22(5)(a) of the 1989 Act). The local authority may clearly be concerned about the effect which contact may be having on a child but, should it seek to restrict contact to the child's parent or anyone with parental responsibility, that person has the ultimate sanction against the local authority, which is removal of the child. Clearly, in those situations in which a child who has suffered or is at risk of suffering significant harm, has been accommodated by the local authority, and would be deemed to be at risk if a move to return the child to his home was undertaken by the parents, local authority social services must be prepared to take emergency action, if necessary, to prevent removal, which may well involve the initiation of proceedings in which contact will have to be formally considered.

Where there are no problems concerning contact between the child, his parents and other members of his family, it is unlikely that there will be any need to advise the child of his right to apply for orders under the provisions of s 8 of the 1989 Act. Occasionally, however, parents and the local authority may agree that some particular person is not felt to have a desirable influence on the child and may, thus, determine that contact between the child and that person should be stopped. The child could challenge such a decision by applying himself for contact with that other person or that other person could himself apply to leave to make an application for a contact order with the child concerned (s 10(9)).

8.3 Contact under a child assessment order

Where, upon the making of a child assessment order, the court gives directions that the child may be kept away from home for any length of time, it must also consider giving such directions as it thinks fit concerning contact between the child and other persons during the period of the order. Whilst it is appreciated that a temporary overnight stay cannot be equated with being placed in care, the court may be guided on issues of contact by the circumstances of the case, the age of the child, and the presumption of reasonable contact between a child in care and his family, which is established by other provisions such as ss 34 and 44 of the 1989 Act. When giving a direction with regard to contact with a child who is the subject of a child assessment order, the court is required to regard the child's welfare as its paramount consideration (s 1(1)) but, since a child assessment order is an order under Part V of the 1989 Act, the court is not bound by the welfare checklist (s 1(3)), although, undoubtedly, many courts would seek to apply the principles of the checklist.

8.4 Contact under an emergency protection order

As has been described earlier (see Chapter 4), where the court makes an emergency protection order, the applicant may apply for contact to the court, or the court can exercise its discretion to give such directions as it deems appropriate with regard to contact which is or is not to be allowed between the child and any person (s 44(6)(a)). Any directions given by the court may further impose conditions with regard to the exercise of individuals' rights to contact, thus, where it is felt that any person constitutes a threat to the child but the threat is not of such a nature as to merit a direction for no contact, a direction may be sought as to the supervision of such contact. Where the applicant, local authority, NSPCC, the police or any other person have not sought to obtain any directions from the court, there is a general duty on the applicant to allow the child reasonable contact with a range of persons which includes the child's parents, any person who has parental responsibility who is not a parent, any person with whom the child was living before the order was made, any person in whose favour a s 8 contact order is in force with respect to the child, any person who is allowed contact by virtue of an order under s 34, or anyone acting on behalf of any of these people. Both *The Children Act 1989 Guidance and Regulations, Vol 3 Family Placements* (1991, HMSO), and *Vol 4 Residential Care* (1991, HMSO) indicate that emergency admissions require special care if parents are to be reassured from the outset that they have a continuing role in their child's life and to minimise distress for the child. Early visits and meetings should be encouraged, even though parents may need help to cope with the child's distress and their own. Where contact between a child and any of the persons referred to in s 44 is felt to be causing the child undue distress or, alternatively, where a parent or child is dissatisfied with the levels of contact, an application to the court can be made at any time during the emergency protection order for the court to issue new directions.

8.5 Contact with a child in police protection

Where the police have exercised their powers of protection under s 46 of the 1989 Act, either to remove a child from the care of particular persons or to authorise the child's retention in a particular place, it is for the designated officer to decide on the extent of contact which he feels is both reasonable and in the child's best interests. The police must allow contact between the child and the exact same range of persons who are allowed to have contact under an emergency protection order. It is interesting to note that, especially in those cases where social services and the police are conducting a joint investigation of a serious situation, the police may consider exercising their powers of protection first, which would give them the right to refuse contact between the child and the alleged perpetrators of any abuse, without the need to resort to a court order of any description.

8.6 Interim care orders and contact

As was noted earlier (see Chapter 4), where a child is made the subject of an interim order, the court must treat the issue of contact in the same way as it would if it were making a full care order. It must, therefore, consider any proposed contact arrangements being put forward by the local authority and invite the parties to the proceedings to comment upon them (s 31(11) and s 34(11)). Where a parent, a child or anyone else who desires contact is dissatisfied with any of the proposed contact arrangements put before the court, they are able to seek a contact order under s 34 and, provided a guardian ad litem has been appointed, he would be expected to provide a report for the court in the circumstances.

The way in which a court might deal with the issue of preventing contact between a child and alleged abusers under an interim care order was considered by the court in *Croydon London Borough Council v A (No 1)* [1992] 2 FLR 341. In this case a two-year-old child had been the victim of repeated physical abuse from his father who had been convicted of the offence. The child, who had originally been placed under a place of safety order and on the local authority child protection register, was allowed staying access with his mother who, unbeknown to social services and the guardian, was still seeing the child's father. A number of further incidents followed and a supervision order was made although the child was returned to the mother. Following the birth of another child, a violent incident occurred in the premises below the mother's flat, during which the father received stab wounds. The father and mother were clearly in contact with each other, which constituted a considerable risk to the children. Emergency protection orders were made and the children placed in foster care. An application was then made for an interim care order, under which the children were to be placed with the mother in a charitable home with a view to rehabilitation with her, to assess her with the children and to protect them from their father. The court, instead of making the interim care order requested and dealing with contact via a s 34 order, made a prohibited steps order under s 8 forbidding the parents from having any contact with each other. The justices gave as their reasons the fact that the order was to ensure the bonding of the children with their mother for their long-term benefit. The local authority appealed, contending that the justices were wrong to make the prohibited steps order and should, instead, have dealt with the matter by means of an interim care order together with an order for 'no contact' under s 34, which could be disputed by either of the parents. In allowing the appeal, Hollings J stated that the appellate court would not normally interfere with the discretion of a court below unless it considered that that court was plainly wrong or had erred in principle or had taken into account something it should not have done or failed to take into account something that it should have done. On this occasion, however, he stated that the justices were plainly wrong to refuse to make an interim care order which would give more flexibility to the local authority. He further emphasised that where justices were of a mind to make such an order, rather than the interim care order sought by an applicant, they should give the parties an opportunity to address them on the question as to whether such an order should or could be made. He further emphasised that a failure to allow the applicant such a hearing might constitute a defect in the proceedings. As far as the issue of contact was concerned, the justices were also wrong in making a prohibited steps order since contact between adults was not a step which could be taken by a parent in meeting a parent's responsibility for the child and therefore fell outside the terms of s 8(1) of the 1989 Act. The issue of contact could either be dealt with, as should have been the case here, under the flexibility and discretion afforded to the local authority by the making of an interim care order, or by the local authority seeking an order for no, or restricted, contact under s 34.

The issue of whether a local authority should seek an order under s 34 for no contact before the final hearing in the care proceedings came up for consideration in *A v M and Walsall Metropolitan Borough Council* [1993] 2 FLR 244. In that case an interim care order had been made but before the final care order hearing the local authority successfully applied to the family proceedings court for contact between mother and baby to be terminated and the mother appealed. Ewbank J stated that the justices were plainly wrong in coming to a premature decision and allowed the appeal. This was not a case where matters were so exceptional and the risk so severe that contact should be stopped. The problem was that the justices had come to such a firm decision in their judgement, ie that the mother was unable to provide the baby with the level of care that could reasonably be expected from a parent, that they had precluded a reassessment of the provision at the final hearing. They had made findings of fact and gone into details of evidence which were more appropriate for a final hearing and the order could not be allowed to stand.

8.7 Contact with children subject to care orders

As was noted earlier (see Chapter 4), before a court makes a care order, the 1989 Act requires the court to consider any proposed contact arrangements and to invite the parties to the proceedings to comment upon them (s 34(11)). Since local authorities looking after children subject to care orders are now required actively to promote contact between the child and his family (Sch 2, Part II, para 15), the 1989 Act underlines this by providing that contact between the child and any parent, guardian or any other person in whose favour a residence or contact order under s 8 has been made, must be reasonable (s 34(1)). The 1989 Act does not further define what is meant by 'reasonable' in this context, but detailed and illuminating guidance can be found in *The Children Act 1989 Guidance and Regulations, Vol 3 Family Placements* and *Vol 4 Residential Care* (both 1991, HMSO). Where it is proposed that children are to be swiftly rehabilitated with their parents, it is stated that 'contact should be in the family home at the earliest possible stage. Such visits have the advantage of maintaining links with the neighbourhood to which the child will be returning' (*Vol 3 Family Placements*, at para 6.18). *Volume 3 Family Placements* goes on to state that 'if possible, parents should be encouraged to participate in some way in the child's daily life, by preparing tea, for example, or by shopping for clothes, or putting a young child to bed' (*ibid*). It should be noted that this guidance marks a considerable departure from much previously accepted local authority social services practice in relation to contact with children subject to care orders, and many such orders may now be open to challenge using the procedures laid down under s 34 of the 1989 Act. Clearly, however, where decisions on contact have been made with regard to what is in the best interests of the child who is in need of protection, the courts may be reluctant to accede to any request for new directions on contact using s 34.

Where, however, any party to care proceedings is dissatisfied with the proposed contact arrangements, they can seek a contact order under s 34 of the 1989 Act and this includes the child who is unhappy about contact proposals. Where this occurs the guardian ad litem would be expected to give further advice to the court and, if necessary, furnish a further report or an addendum to the original, which will have dealt with contact issues in the care proceedings (s 41).

Where contact arrangements are agreed at the time of the making of a care order, and a party or some other person becomes dissatisfied with the arrangements for contact, an application can be made for a contact order under the 1989 Act, s 34(3). Where an authority feels that contact with a child will be positively detrimental in the light of the child protection issues involved in the case, an application may also be made by the local authority to terminate or reduce contact with a named individual or individuals (s 34(2) and (4)). Whether or not the application for termination of contact will be successful will depend on a number of issues, such as how the case is presented to the court and whether or not termination is in the paramount interests of the child. In *Devon County Council and Others v S and Others* [1993] 1 FLR 842, the local authority had applied to the family proceedings court for leave to refuse contact to both parents, and the welfare officer who had acted as the guardian ad litem in the care proceedings was appointed in the contact proceedings. Documents which were relevant to the case and which concerned conflicting decisions made by the social services had not been disclosed to the parents' solicitor until the morning of the hearing. The magistrates, despite objections having been made to the appointment of the welfare officer as guardian, and to the late submission of documentary evidence, granted the termination of contact order, although their reasons dealt with the justification for the local authority in having brought the rehabilitation programme to an end and not whether, having regard to the ending of that programme, contact should continue in the best interests of the children. Whilst the Court of Appeal censured the magistrates for their conduct of the case in relation to the first two matters, holding that a full-time serving probation officer acting as a welfare officer could not be appointed as a guardian ad litem, and that last-minute disclosures of documents should not occur, their reason for allowing the appeal was the failure by the magistrates to consider properly whether termination of contact was in the children's paramount interests. This last point came up again in *Birmingham City Council v H (No 2)* [1993] 1 FLR 883, where the local authority decided to apply for contact between a 16-year-old disruptive mother living in secure accommodation and her baby son who was to be placed with long-term foster-parents with a view to adoption. The judge in this case made a finding that contact with the mother would be contrary to the son's best interests as the mother's volatile behaviour pattern could cause unacceptable risks to the son. He took the view that since contact was the right of the child and not the right of the parent, in a case where a conflict arose between a mother and son who were both minors, the son's welfare took priority over that of the mother. Accordingly, he terminated contact between mother and son, save for an exchange of information on a twice-yearly basis. The mother appealed and the Court of Appeal, in allowing her appeal, stressed that in all proceedings under the 1989 Act the child's welfare was the paramount consideration. However, in a case where both mother and child were minors and where a conflict arose between their separate interests and welfare, this question had to be approached without giving one priority over the other. The interests of both minors should receive equal weight in considering what appropriate order to make and a balancing exercise must follow. On the facts and having weighed in the balance the respective interests of mother and son, it was premature for the time being to give leave to the local authority to terminate face-to-face contact between the mother and son. The Court might be positively beneficial to the mother and, provided it was adequately monitored, should not, in the short term at least, be detrimental to the son. The Court of Appeal, therefore, ordered that reasonable and supervised contact would be allowed although the position would have to be reassessed when a suitable long-term placement for the son was found. The order below was discharged but the court made no substitute order for contact as the detail of contact was to be left to the local authority pursuant to its statutory duty to promote contact between the child and his parent (Sch 2, Pt II, para 15) and that such contact is to be reasonable (s 34(1)). For guidance as to how the local authority should interpret its statutory duties, the case of *Re P (Minors) (Contact with Children in Care)* [1993] 2 FLR 156 is, perhaps, illustrative of the courts' interpretation of these provisions. In *Re P* two girls, at the time of the case aged 13 and 9½ years, had been in long-term foster care, pursuant to a care order made in wardship some five years previously. At that stage a direction had been given that the children be placed with long-term foster-parents, with a view to adoption but they had not been so placed. They were about to be placed at this late stage and the authority wished contact to be at its discretion so that it could respond to the changing circumstances. The children, however, had stated that they wished contact to remain unchanged, namely, one hour per month, supervised at their foster home. The father then applied for discharge of the care orders which Ewbank J dismissed, but decided to exercise his powers under s 34 of the 1989 Act to make an order for defined, unsupervised contact. The order for contact was to be for not less than two-and-a-half hours, once per month, away from the foster home, with leave for the father to take the children to his home, and a direction that the length and frequency of contact could be extended if the children so desired. His Lordship directed the local authority to 'promote and encourage' contact between the father and the children but made clear that contact was not with a view to rehabilitation. He emphasised that the local authority had a duty to promote contact under Sch 2 para 15 and stated that:

> 'the previous practice of access at the discretion of the local authority should not be the regular practice. Section 34 provides for reasonable access and this should be the norm rather than access at [the local authority's] discretion [which is not the same].'

Reasonable contact implied agreement with the parents; and if no agreement was possible, contact which was objectively reasonable.

Similarly, where the child is unhappy with contact arrangements, he can also apply to terminate, reduce or increase contact with any person, and the court may make such order as it considers appropriate (s 34(3)). Parents, guardians, the holders of prior residence orders or any person who had prior care of the child as the result of the exercise of the High Court's inherent jurisdiction, may also make an application for a contact order, as may any person who has obtained the leave of the court (s 34(3)). Thus, whilst parents may be excluded, in a case involving serious child abuse, from having contact with the child (which may be either at the instigation of the child or the local authority), grandparents, aunts, uncles, godparents or any other significant person in the child's life, including a brother or sister, could seek the leave of the court to make an application under s 34. The local authority may still seek to oppose such contact where it views with suspicion the ability of the person having the benefit of the contact order to restrain visits by the child's parents when the other person is having contact.

Where the local authority or the child makes an application to the court for an order, the court may make an order authorising the authority to refuse to allow contact between the child, any parent or guardian, any holder of a prior residence order or any person who had care of the child under an order made pursuant to the exercise of the High Court's inherent jurisdiction (s 34(4)).

Where an application for a contact order has been made, the court must appoint a guardian ad litem for the child concerned unless it is satisfied that it is not necessary to do so in order to safeguard the child's interests (s 41(1)). It should be noted that the role of the guardian ad litem in such proceedings came up for consideration by the Court of Appeal in *Re S (A Minor) (Guardian ad Litem/Welfare Officer)* [1993] 1 FLR 110. In the course of a father's application for contact with a child who had been placed for adoption following the making of a care order, the local authority had issued a counter-application for contact to be terminated and the court appointed the guardian ad litem who had acted in the earlier care proceedings. The guardian's report supported the local authority's view and, responding to the father's concern that the guardian might be considered to be partisan because his views coincided with those of the local authority, the judge directed that a welfare officer's report be obtained in order to alleviate the father's anxiety. The guardian appealed against that direction on the grounds that the welfare officer's report was superfluous and unnecessary and the Court of Appeal allowed his appeal. The Court of Appeal stated that since the role of the guardian was to represent the child and to advise as to her best interests, that could not be regarded as being partisan. It was, therefore, not appropriate to accommodate the father's natural but unjustified perception by allowing the introduction of another reporting officer, which would mean a duplication of efforts. The guardian may clearly play a crucial role in contact order proceedings, and in *Kent County Council v C* [1993] 1 FLR 308, the guardian took a very strong line in opposing the local authority's proposals for contact between a mother and child in order to assess the possibilities of rehabilitation. The guardian took the view that, given his view of the case, rehabilitation would be unsuccessful and would merely prolong the child's sense of impermanence, and advised instead that the child be placed with long-term foster-parents. The justices were extremely concerned about the guardian's views and concluded that, although they had power under s 34(2) to order that there be no contact between mother and child, which would effectively prevent the local authority from carrying out the rehabilitation plan, they ought not to exercise that power in the circumstances. Instead, when making the care order, they added a direction that the local authority should allow the guardian to have continued involvement with the child for three months to enable him to investigate the rehabilitation process so that, if appropriate, he could apply on behalf of the child to have contact with the mother terminated under s 34(2). The local authority appealed, querying whether, in an appropriate case, the family proceedings court had power to order that no contact take place and, further, whether the court had power to add a direction as to the involvement of a guardian when making a care order under the 1989 Act. In this particular case, Ewbank J, in the High Court, held that 'whilst it was open to the family proceedings court to make orders under s 34(2) that no contact take place between the child and parent, in most cases it would be ill-advised to do so and the preferable course would simply be to make no order for contact, thus allowing the local authority room to exercise its discretion'. He further held that there was no power under the 1989 Act to make directions in relation to care orders since, once a care order had been made, and subject to any subsequent orders as to contact under s 34, the sole responsibility for the care of the child fell on the local authority, and the addition of a direction of any sort to a care order would be a fetter on the local authority's plans, authority and responsibility. Accordingly, he stated, 'since the pace and success of any rehabilitation programme entered into after the care order was made was a matter which could only be decided by the local authority, the appeal would be allowed and the direction deleted from the order'. A way around the position set out by Ewbank J in the *Kent* case was indicated in *Re B (A Minor) (Care Order: Review)* [1993] 1 FLR 421, where Thorpe J determined that the courts certainly had jurisdiction to make a care order together with an interim contact order with a view to the guardian ad litem keeping the progress of contact and, thus, the possibility of future rehabilitation open to review.

It is not possible to determine from the statistics released in the *Children Act Advisory Committee Annual Report* (1992 Lord Chancellor's Division) whether guardians have been appointed in the majority of applications for contact orders. The duties of the guardian will be the same as those which he performs in proceedings for a care and supervision order (see Chapter 6). The focus of the guardian's work in contact order cases will, however, be on whether there should or should not be contact with a specific named individual, and whether or not this is in the paramount interests of the child.

Where the issue of contact surfaces after a period under a care order, where the parent has neither sought nor exercised contact with a child in care, then, following on from the local authority's ability to refuse contact for seven days using the emergency provisions of s 34(6) of the 1989 Act, an application can be made to the court for an order under s 34(4) authorising interim refusal of contact pending a full hearing of the contact order. This was confirmed in *West Glamorgan County Council v P (No 1)* [1992] 2 FLR 369. The court emphasised in that case that s 34(4) gave the court complete discretion, exercisable within the general principles of the 1989 Act, to authorise such refusal of contact for as short or as long a period as it considered necessary for the child's welfare. In the later substantive hearing, *West Glamorgan County Council v P (No 2)* [1993] 1 FLR 407, the magistrates refused the local authority's application for an order for 'no contact' and made an order that there should be weekly supervised contact. On appeal, the Family Division ruled that the magistrates should not have done this. It was emphasised that once a care order is made, the decision as to the long-term future of the child was entirely a matter for the local authority during the subsistence of the care order. Thus, when considering an application under s 34(4), the court is bound to consider the effects of refusing or making any such order on the long-term plans of the local authority for the child's future. The basis upon which the court approached the matter was that the local authority had reached an 'unimpeachable' decision. This, it was suggested, could only be impeached by demonstrating that there was cogent evidence that the local authority had acted contrary to the interests of the child or capriciously. The reasoning of Rattee J in this case was not unexpected and followed the reasoning of the Court of Appeal in the case of *Re S (A Minor) (Access Application)* [1991] 1 FLR 161, which was a decision given before implementation of the 1989 Act, and, thus, applied the old law. Nevertheless, the decision in *West Glamorgan County Council v P (No 2)* was a source of considerable concern for those who felt that it was time that the principle established in *A v Liverpool City Council* [1981] 2 All ER 385, which effectively prevented any examination of a local authority's long-term plans for the child, should at least be examined if not overruled. It was also felt that it was time, given the changes in the law, that a clear interpretation be given in relation to applications under s 34 and their inter-relationship with, and inter-dependence on, local authority long-term plans for a child.

The Court of Appeal's judgment in the case of *Re B (Minors) (Care: Contact: Local Authority's Plans)* [1993] 1 FLR 543 gives clear guidance on the approach to be taken in applications under s 34 and indicates that the approach taken in the cases of *Re S* and *West Glamorgan County Council v P* (above) *should not* be followed. In *Re B*, two girls, aged four and two, were the subject of care orders and the local authority's plans for adoption of the girls had been approved by the Adoption Panel. The children's mother had had a third child, her parenting skills were much improved and she had had frequent and regular contact with the two older children. Despite these improvements, the local authority applied for an order under s 34(4) to terminate contact and the mother applied instead for the discharge of the care order or an increase in contact, supported by the guardian ad litem, with the ultimate view of rehabilitation of the children with her. The judge at first instance followed the line taken in the *West Glamorgan* case and said it would not be right, directly or indirectly, to force the local authority's hand and put pressure on for rehabilitation because he had to consider the application for contact in the context of the plan for adoption and, thus, determine whether the welfare of the children required that contact be refused. He allowed the authority's application and, on the guardian ad litem's appeal supported by the mother, the authority relied upon the principle established in *A v Liverpool City Council* (above) that courts would not generally interfere with a local authority's decision to refuse access by a parent to a child in its care under a care order where the appeal was based solely on the merits of the decision. On appeal to the Court of Appeal, Butler-Sloss LJ, in her judgment, declared: 'I do not, however, believe that the important principle set out in *A v Liverpool City Council* . . . applies to the intervention of the court in response to an application which is properly made, or fetters the exercise of the judicial discretion in an application under the 1989 Act' (at p 549). She considered her own judgment in *Re S* (above), which Rattee J had followed in the *West Glamorgan* case, even though *Re S* had been decided under the old law, and concluded 'I do not consider that my judgment [in *Re S*] adapts felicitously into the philosophy of the Children Act'. The court, therefore, held that the approach adopted in *Re S* and in the *West Glamorgan* case should not be followed when considering applications under s 34. The Court of Appeal went on to elaborate, in considerable detail, the approach which should be taken now in applications under s 34 and this guidance should be followed carefully. Thus, the court directed, that at the moment an application for contact comes before the court, at whichever tier, the court has a duty to apply s 1 of the 1989 Act, which states that when a court determines any question with respect to the upbringing of a child, the child's welfare shall be the court's paramount consideration. The court must have regard to the prejudicial effect of delay, to the checklist including the range of orders available to the court and to the important issue of whether to make an order. On hearing a s 34 application, therefore, the Court of Appeal emphasised that the court has a duty to consider and apply the welfare provisions.

The Court of Appeal went on to point out that contact applications generally fall into two main categories: those which ask for contact as such; and those which are attempts to set aside the care order itself. In the first category, the court stated that there is no suggestion that the applicant wishes to take over the care of the child and the issue of contact often depends upon whether contact would frustrate long-term plans for the child in a substitute home such as adoption where continuing contact may not be for the long-term welfare of the child. (This was the case in *Cheshire County Council v M* [1993] 1 FLR 463.) The presumption of contact, which has to be for the benefit of the child, has always to be balanced against the long-term welfare of the child and, particularly, where he will live in the future. The court emphasised that contact must not be allowed to destabilise or endanger the arrangements for the child and, in many cases, the plans for the child will be *decisive* for the contact application. The court also stated that there may be cases where the parent is having satisfactory contact with the child and there are no long-term plans or those plans do not appear to the court to preclude some future contact. The proposals of the local authority, based on its appreciation of the best interests of the child, must command the greatest respect and consideration from the court, but Parliament has given to the court, and *not to the local authority*, the duty to decide on contact between the child and those named in s 34(1). Consequently, the court may have the task of requiring the local authority to justify its long-term plans to the extent only that those plans exclude contact between the parent and the child.

The court went on to state that, in the second category, contact applications may be made by parents by way of another attempt to obtain the return of the children. In such a case, stated the Court of Appeal, the court is obviously entitled to take into account the failure to apply to discharge the care order and, in the majority of cases, the court will have little difficulty in coming to the conclusion that the applicant cannot demonstrate that contact, with a view to rehabilitation with the parent, is a viable proposition at that stage, particularly if it had already been rejected at the earlier hearing when the child was placed in care. The Court of Appeal suggested that the task for the parents would be too great and the court would be entitled to assume that the plans of the local authority to terminate contact were for the welfare of the child and were not to be frustrated by inappropriate contact with a view to the remote possibility, at some future date, of rehabilitation. In all cases, however, the Court of Appeal emphasised that the welfare section has to be considered, and the local authority has the task of justifying the cessation of contact to the court. It also opined that there may be unusual cases where either the local authority has not made effective plans or there has been considerable delay in implementing them and a parent, who had previously been found by the court unable or unwilling to care for the child so that a care order had been made, comes back upon the scene as a possible future primary caretaker. If the local authority with a care order decides not to consider that parent on the new facts, it is for the court, with the enhanced jurisdiction of the 1989 Act, to consider whether, even at this late stage, there should be some investigation of the proposals of the parent and the possibility of reconsidering the local authority's plans. The Court of Appeal made it plain, in *Re B* (above) that they totally rejected the argument that the court could not go behind the long-term plans of the local authority unless the local authority could have been shown to be acting capriciously or were otherwise open to scrutiny by way of judicial review. Butler-Sloss LJ, quite uncompromisingly, stated that she 'unhesitatingly rejected the local authority's argument'. She did, however, state that the local authority's plan has to be 'given the greatest possible consideration by the court and it is only in the unusual case that a parent will be able to convince the court, the onus being firmly on the parent, that there has been such a change of circumstances as to require further investigation and reconsideration of the local authority plan'. She went on to state that 'if, however, a court was unable to intervene, it would make a nonsense of the paramountcy of the welfare of the child, which is the bedrock of the Act, and would subordinate it to the administrative decision of the local authority in a situation where the court is seised of the contact issue'. That, she declared, *'could not be right'*. The court went on to allow the mother's appeal.

Butler-Sloss LJ did, however, go on to emphasise, at the end of her deliberations, that she did not wish her judgment to be seen as constituting an open door to courts to review the plans of local authorities. She stated that, generally, where parties choose not to pursue applications they are well-advised not to do so. But, she added, there is now a flexibility in the approach of the court to the problems of the child before it and, occasionally, the court may wish to invoke s 10(1)(b) which provides that a court may, in any family proceedings, which includes care proceedings, make a s 8 order with respect to a child if the court considers that the order should be made, even though no application has been made. A court, she suggested, may also make a contact or an interim contact order and impose such conditions as it considers appropriate (s 34(7)).

The shadow of *A v Liverpool City Council* (above) has, thus, been lifted in respect of contact applications under s 34 and the ability to review a local authority's plans for the child.

An example, however, of the first category of case, in which there was absolutely no hope of rehabilitation, was treated by the courts as robustly as Butler-Sloss LJ herself would have wanted it to have been treated. Thus, in *Cheshire County Council v M* [1993] 1 FLR 463, the application of a father to have contact with two children in care, who had been the subject of an earlier order placing them with long-term foster-parents with a view to adoption, was said to have had so remote a prospect of any positive outcome for the children that it would be quite wrong to allow it to go any further and the application was dismissed without oral evidence or further investigation. Thorpe J stated that the court should act robustly in determining an application brought by a parent fortuitously under the 1989 Act, where that application sought to strike at the root of an earlier order made in wardship. One suspects, however, when considering the terms of the judgment of Butler-Sloss LJ in *Re B* (above), that the exact same stance would be adopted in relation to any similar sort of application made by a parent where an earlier order in any sort of proceedings had been made for no contact.

Where a contact order is made under s 34, a local authority cannot depart from the terms of that order unless it is done by agreement with the person in relation to whom the order was made and in accordance with regulations made by the Secretary of State (s 34(8) and see also the Contact with Children

Regulations 1991, SI 1991/891), or in an emergency, where the situation does not last for more than seven days, (s 34(6)). Before the expiry of seven days, the authority, if it wishes to stop contact permanently or to reduce contact considerably, must make an application to the court to this effect, notice must be given to all the relevant parties and a guardian ad litem will again have to be appointed. It is possibly unlikely that in such circumstances the court would be ready to proceed immediately, but at what will effectively be an interim hearing on contact, the court has complete discretion under s 34(4) to make a temporary order pending the full hearing. This was emphasised by the High Court in *West Glamorgan County Council v P (No 1)* (above). In *Hampshire County Council v S* [1993] 1 FLR 559, the local authority had become concerned as to the effects of staying contact on the child, had refused contact for seven days using s 34(6) and had applied to the court for an order reducing contact between the child and the parents. It had been agreed at a directions hearing that only the issues relating to the reduction of contact would be considered at the interim hearing. At that interim hearing the magistrates made an order substantially reducing the parents' contact on the basis of the parties' submissions only and without reading the statements of the local authority or the guardian ad litem's report. No proper reasons were given by the magistrates prior to the order being made and a final hearing was not to take place for a further five months. In allowing the parents' appeal against the making of the interim order, Cazalet J stressed that magistrates should bear in mind that they are not required to make a final conclusion at any interim hearing. On the particular facts of this case an early hearing date was imperative, the magistrates should have considered transferring laterally to obtain an earlier date, and where the interim order would lead to a substantial change in a child's position they should have permitted limited oral evidence to be led and challenged by cross-examination.

Where the court makes a contact order allowing contact between the child and any named person, the order may impose such conditions as the court considers appropriate (s 34(7)). The court may vary or discharge any order under this section on the application of the authority, the child concerned or the person named in the order (s 34(9)).

Where the court is concerned about repeated or vexatious applications for contact with a child subject to a care order, it may take the step of issuing a direction under s 91(14) that no further application for contact be made with respect to the child by a named person without the leave of the court. In the case of *F v Kent County Council* [1993] 1 FLR 432, the President of the Family Division held that the power under s 91(14) of the 1989 Act should be used sparingly and only after hearing representations. In this case, a father had applied for contact with his children who were in care. The justices made a consent order granting him contact but went on to make an order, under s 91(14), restricting his right to apply again although they acknowledged that his application had been proper. The President upheld the father's appeal, finding that the justices had acted improperly in making such an order against a father who had not been vexatious, frivolous or unreasonable in making his application. The President stated that the power to make such a direction would be desirable where applications were being made too often and the other party and the child were suffering from them. Such an order might appropriately be used, following the reasoning of Butler-Sloss LJ in *Re H (Child Orders: Restricting Applications)* [1991] 2 FCR 896 at 899, where contact had been refused after a full substantive hearing and where a subsequent application for contact would have no prospect of success.

8.8 Communicating decisions about contact

All decisions made by either local authorities or the courts should be carefully explained to parents and children and discussed with them. The guidance to the 1989 Act, issued by the Department of Health, states that local authorities should also confirm in writing to the parents and other relevant persons all decisions and agreements about contact arrangements and any changes to the arrangements, and also the outcome of all formal and informal reviews of contact. Issues concerning contact should be fully discussed at a child's review where the child is being looked after by the local authority and the child should also be informed, where appropriate, of his right to apply for any orders under the 1989 Act. (See the Review of Children's Cases Regulations 1991, SI 1991/895, Sch 1, para 5.) The guidance further suggests that contact arrangements should be monitored to check whether the arrangements are working as intended and this is particularly important in cases which have involved significant harm to the child. Steps should be taken to identify any problems which have arisen and any changes which are needed and difficulties should be discussed openly with the parents and with the child's carers so that solutions can be explored and help given. The guidance further emphasises that: 'it cannot be in the interests of the child and is no service to parents to allow them to drift to the periphery of a child's life, without reminding them of the possible implications of this course to the plan for their child and his/her relationship with them' (*Children Act 1989 Guidance and Regulations, Vol 3 Family Placements*, at para 6.38; and *Vol 4 Residential Care*, at para 4.38 (both 1991, HMSO).

Where there is any disagreement between those desiring to have contact with a child and the local authority, the local authority should ensure that it has clear arrangements to inform parents and others about how to pursue complaints about contact and how to ask for decisions to be reviewed. Responsible authorities should ensure that the representations procedure recognises the need to accept complaints from people, other than parents, who have contact with children who are being looked after (see Chapter 9). As the guidances point out, 'arrangements should be made for parents to discuss their anxieties and dissatisfactions with senior officers if they feel they have reached an impasse with their social worker'. It is further pointed out that those arrangements should not be used to prevent or hinder use of the representations procedure provided by the 1989 Act and that all parents and, where appropriate according to the child's understanding, the child, should be informed of these procedures (see *Vol 3 Family Placements* (above), at para 4.37 and *Vol 4 Residential Care* (above), at para 6.37 and see further Chapter 9).

Finally, it is suggested that when a disagreement persists, parents of a child subject to a care order or, indeed, anyone else who disagrees with the authority's plan for contact between himself and the child, should seek a legal opinion on the most appropriate action open to him under the provisions described in this chapter.

8.9 Appeals

As is obvious from the foregoing discussion there has been no shortage of appeals being taken in relation to orders made for the termination, reduction, or expansion of contact. It should be noted that the same appeals procedure which applies to decisions regarding contact with a child in care applies equally on the making of or refusal to make an order in care or supervision order proceedings. Reference, therefore, should be made back to the description of the appeals process at **6.19** above.

CHAPTER NINE

Representations Procedures and Judicial Review

REPRESENTATIONS PROCEDURES

9.1 Introduction

There is clearly considerable scope for using the representations procedures which now have to be established by local authorities under the Children Act 1989 ('the 1989 Act'), Part III, for making complaints about, or taking up issues relating to, the handling by the local authority of child protection issues. This may come up in a number of different ways and it is also possible that events may give rise to the consideration of the possibility of taking action against the local authority using judicial review.

Whilst it should be noted that the representations procedures are available in relation to the discharge by a local authority of any of its functions under Part III of the 1989 Act in relation to children, nevertheless, as has been seen in Chapters 3 and 4, the duties under that part extend to taking reasonable steps to prevent children suffering ill-treatment and neglect, and taking steps to reduce the need to bring care or supervision orders proceedings in respect of children. In addition, where child protection conferences come to the conclusion that no formal legal action is required under Parts IV and V of the 1989 Act, they may conclude that recommendations be made to social services concerning the delivery of services to a child in need of protection in the family, and this may form part of a child protection plan. Where services are being provided in relation to a family in pursuance of such a child protection plan or, indeed, in situations where a decision has been reached that no services should be provided, the representations procedures give parents, children and others concerned with the child, the ability to make representations about the delivery of services or, indeed, to make representations objecting to the delivery of such services. Other child protection arenas in which the representation procedures have already been employed relate to the treatment of children in children's homes, foster homes and other residential settings, where either the children themselves, independent advocates acting on their behalf or parents have made representations to local authorities using the procedure available under Part III.

Voluntary organisations and private organisations running residential establishments are also now required to provide representations procedures for the parents and others with parental responsibility as well as for children who are actually being looked after in such homes (s 59(4)(b), Sch 6, para 10(2)(l), and Sch 7, para 6).

A number of concerns have been raised about the construction of the representations process both in relation to the framing of the legislation and the consequent regulations, but also in relation to the way in which local authorities have actually conducted the procedures. Nevertheless, it remains important to realise that using the representations procedures established under the 1989 Act may be a much more fruitful and productive way of encouraging local authorities to take their duties seriously. It may also have a more direct political effect in raising the profile of such concerns which may be voiced by children, parents and others, in that elected members become aware of the progress of such cases, and that such action will generally be a much speedier and cheaper process than seeking to resort to using the more complex, lengthier and expensive process of judicial review (see **9.7** below). Both procedures have an important role to play, and there will obviously be occasions when it will be right to resort to court rather than seeking to use the local authority representations procedure. In the course of this chapter, both processes will be examined and concerns will be raised about the possible failure of the processes to respond to the needs of children and others who feel let down by the legal framework of child protection.

9.2 Accessing the representations procedures

The 1989 Act provides, for the first time, a means whereby children, parents, anyone with parental responsibility, any local authority foster-parent and any such person as the authority considers to have sufficient interest in the child's welfare, may exercise the right to make representations (including any complaints) to a local authority about the provision of any services, including the service of accommodation under the 1989 Act, or the failure to provide any such services as are envisaged being provided under Part III of that Act (s 26(3)). In addition, those persons having such an interest may also make representations, where relevant, to a voluntary organisation or to a registered children's home using these procedures (s 59(4) and Sch 6, para 10(2)(l)).

As *The Children Act 1989 Guidance and Regulations, Vol 3 Family Placements* (1991, HMSO) points out, the authority, voluntary organisation or home generally referred to as the *responsible authority* (and hereinafter so called), must consider what type of support and encouragement it can offer to its clients, both to make use of the system and to pursue their representations or complaints through the procedure (at para 10.28). The guidance goes on to suggest that information leaflets and open letters to children and parents being provided with services will help to make clients aware of the procedure, and a large number of authorities now ensure that such information is made available to children and parents as soon as the service has been provided. Children admitted to residential homes run by local authorities, voluntary organisations or private individuals must be given, upon admission, clear information about procedures for making representations. Where child protection procedures are concerned, since many services are being provided pursuant to prevention or protection packages, local authority child protection procedures and area child protection committee ('ACPC') guidelines also point out that families and children should be given information about the representations procedures to enable them to follow through any concerns which they may have which cannot be addressed by any other means. The guidance points out, however, that 'some parents and most children will need advice and confidential support to make their representation or complaint, to pursue it, to understand the administrative process and to cope with the outcome' (at para 10.28).

9.2.1 Informal resolution

Whilst it is appropriate that the responsible authorities should seek to make access to the representations procedures clear and well-understood (including, where necessary, the translation of information documents into other languages), it may be possible to resolve any issues which have arisen before the formal step is taken of referring the matter to the complaints procedures. Especially in child protection matters, efforts should have been made to resolve any issues which may be causing a parent, child or other person to consider using the representations procedures. The aim should be to resolve dissatisfaction as near to the point at which it arises as possible and, since some local authorities have appointed specialist children's rights officers or representations officers, it may be useful to involve such a person in providing independent advice and assistance in solving the problem. This should not be seen as a means of preventing the person who wishes to make a more formal complaint from using the representations procedures. As the guidance (above) points out (at para 10.11):

> 'a well-publicised statement of commitment to the representations procedures should encourage the identification and speedy resolution of representations and complaints as they arise. A secondary benefit of the system will be to illustrate for the responsible authority how policies translate into practice and to highlight areas where the responsible authority should be more responsive to the needs of individual clients and the community.'

The guidance also makes it clear that statutory requirements and the associated guidance seek to achieve an accessible and effective means of making complaints close to the point at which the problem arose, but with an independent element which will inspire confidence in the procedure. The inspiring of confidence is a necessary and desirable end, but not one which everyone involved in the system has necessarily felt will be possible to achieve, even under the new framework (see Utting *Children in the Public Care – a Review of Residential Child Care* (1991, DOH), at paras 3.47 to 3.50; and see also MJ Lindsay 'Complaints Procedures and their limitations in the light of the "Pindown" Enquiry' (1991) JSWFL at pp 432 to 441).

In order to achieve the objectives of accessibility and efficiency, and also to inspire confidence, it is necessary that complaints are acted on in the shortest possible time and an early opportunity to challenge the outcome of the considerations is provided. As has been indicated, it is not intended that all problems which arise in the day-to-day handling of child care services in the child protection area should automatically be elevated to the status of a representation. It is understood that when operating in the child protection arena, everyone will be working under considerable pressure and a matter which is promptly resolved to everyone's satisfaction when drawn to the attention of an officer of the responsible authority should not then require referral to the representations procedures. It is important, therefore, that everyone involved in both the child protection procedures and the provision of services on behalf of the local authority should understand the role and nature of representations processes, and that these are not confused with disciplinary proceedings. In the first 18 months of the operation of the 1989 Act there is still considerable confusion, especially in the residential care sector, as to the role and function of the representations process, and more work needs to be done in clarifying the process across all fields of involvement in the child protection process.

9.3 The representations procedure

Under the provisions of the 1989 Act, ss 26(3) and 59(4) and Sch 6, para 10(2)(l), local authorities, voluntary organisations or registered children's homes must establish a procedure for considering any representations (including any complaints) made to it by children, their carers or other persons with sufficient interest about the discharge of any functions under the 1989 Act, Part III. 'Representations' are said to include enquiries and statements about such matters as the availability, delivery and nature of services and will not necessarily be critical. A complaint is said to be a written or oral expression of dissatisfaction or disquiet in relation to an individual child about the local authority's exercise of its functions under the 1989 Act, and about matters in relation to children accommodated by voluntary organisations in children's homes. The guidance (above) states that 'a complaint may arise as a result of an unwelcome or disputed decision, concern about the quality or appropriateness of services, delay in decision-making about services or about their delivery or non-delivery' (at para 10.5 and repeated in *The Children Act 1989 Guidance and Regulations, Vol 4 Residential Care* (1991, HMSO), at para 5.5). Again, as indicated earlier, in the child protection arena complaints could include those made by children about their treatment in a variety of residential establishments, or complaints made by children, carers or parents in relation to the outcome of recommendations made in the child protection conference or the delivery of any services in respect of the local authority's performance of duties to prevent children in its area suffering ill-treatment or neglect, or to prevent the taking of care or supervision order proceedings in respect of them.

The procedure which must be established by a local authority (and, where relevant, a voluntary organisation or registered children's home) is formally a two-stage process, but three stages can actually be identified within the structure laid down in the Representations Procedure (Children) Regulations 1991, SI 1991/894 (as amended). The three stages are: (1) preliminaries; (2) consideration by local authority together with independent person and notification of decision to complainant; (3) notification of dissatisfaction from complainant and reference on to representations panel. Each of these stages will be briefly discussed.

9.3.1 Preliminaries

Where a local authority receives a representation from any complainant, it must forward, to that complainant, an explanation of the procedures set out in the representations regulations and must offer advice, assistance and guidance on the use of the procedure or, alternatively, provide the complainant with advice as to where he may seek such assistance. Where any representation is made orally, the authority must cause such representations to be recorded in writing and forwarded to the complainant, who is then given an opportunity to agree that they have been properly recorded in writing. Once a representation has been properly received by the local authority, the authority must decide, if it has received a representation from someone who is described as 'having a sufficient interest in the child', whether that person has such an interest and, where he does, must cause the information which would be sent to the child, the child's parents or the child's carer, also to be sent to that person (the Representations Procedure (Children) Regulations 1991, SI 1991/894 ('RP(C)R 1991'), reg 4).

9.3.2 Consideration by authority with independent person

Where an authority receives representations, it must then appoint an independent person, who must not be an employee or officer of the local authority, to join with it in the consideration of the representation being made. The authority, together with the independent person, must then consider the representations and formulate a response within 28 days of their receipt. The independent person must take part in any discussions which are held by the authority about the action (if any) to be taken in relation to the child in the light of the consideration of the representations (RP(C)R 1991, reg 6).

This first stage is very much a paper consideration of the representation and, once this stage has been completed, the local authority must send a written notification of the formal response, determined by the authority with the independent person, to the person making the representation (or, if different, the person on whose behalf the representations were made, unless the authority considers that person is not of sufficient understanding or it would be likely to cause serious harm to his health or emotional condition), to the independent person, and to any other person who the local authority considers has sufficient interest in the case. In addition to notifying such persons of the result of the consideration of the representations, the authority must inform the person making the representation of his right to have the matter referred to a panel. Where such notification is made to the person making the representation, that person then has a right to inform the authority, in writing, within 28 days of the date upon which notice has been given to him, of the response that he is dissatisfied with the proposed result and wishes the matter to be referred to a representations panel appointed by the authority for that purpose (RP(C)R 1991, reg 8(2)).

9.3.3 *Consideration of the representation by the panel*

The representation panel must include at least one independent person and must meet within 28 days of the receipt by the authority of the complainant's request that the matter be referred to a panel (RP(C)R 1991, reg 8(4)). Where the person making the representation before the panel wishes to be accompanied by another person of his or her choice to speak on his or her behalf, then the regulations permit this (RP(C)R 1991, reg 8(6)). It may be that the child cannot face making a complaint about the way he has been treated in a particular children's home without the support of an advocate to act on his behalf. The guidance (above) recognises this at various stages, and many local authorities have provided for children to have access to independent advocates to act on their behalf in the representations process. Many will have had such support at the first stage of the process, and later at the formal stage of the panel procedure. Other authorities have not, however, been quite so generous and some children have been overwhelmed by the reaction of local authorities to the children's efforts to instigate the complaints procedures (see Lyon and James 'Editorial' (1992) JSWFL at pp 273 to 275). Where it is felt necessary that a lawyer accompanies parents, children or others with sufficient interest then, in certain circumstances, by analogy with the decision to allow legal aid to be used to finance a lawyer accompanying parents or children in a child protection conference, the legal aid board may, if an appropriate case is made out by legal representatives, be prepared to allow legal aid to finance the payment of a lawyer to assist the child or parents in the hearing before the panel. It could be argued that providing assistance at this stage could prevent the bringing of possible actions for judicial review or breach of statutory duty, or the possible taking of care linked proceedings.

At the meeting of the panel, it must consider any oral or written submissions the complainant or the local authority wish to make and, where the independent person appointed to the panel is different from the person who considered the original complaint, the panel must also consider any oral or written submissions from the previous independent person (RP(C)R 1991, reg 8(5)). When a panel has heard the representations, it must determine on its own recommendations and record them with its reasons in writing within 24 hours of the end of the meeting (RP(C)R 1991, reg 9(1)). The panel must give notice of its recommendations to the local authority, the complainant, the independent person first involved in its considerations, if different from the independent person on the representations panel and any other person whom a local authority considers has sufficient interest in the case (RP(C)R 1991, reg 9(2)). This may include a guardian ad litem who had been appointed in early stages of child protection proceedings where the child protection conference subsequently determined that no further formal legal action was to be considered for the time being.

Finally, the local authority must, together with the independent person on the panel, consider what action, if any, should be taken in relation to the child in the light of the representation, and the independent person must take part in any discussions about any such actions (RP(C)R 1991, reg 9(3)). Where any person making a representation, including a child, remains dissatisfied with the result of the determination of the panel, that person must consider, perhaps, referring the matter to the Commissioner for Local Administration, or taking an action against the local authority, possibly for breach of statutory duty or for judicial review.

9.4 Representations or complaints outside the 1989 Act, Part III

There will be representations or complaints about child care matters which fall outside the expanded scope of the 1989 Act, Part III, which, of course, includes the rights of children to make complaints about their treatment where they are being looked after by a local authority, and the ability of children and others to make representations about services or the failure to provide such services in the child protection arena. Such concerns which cannot be covered by the representations procedure will fall under the Complaints Procedure Directions. These direct the local authority on the way in which it should establish a procedure for dealing with a whole variety of other representations and complaints made by, or on behalf of, individuals qualifying for services from a local authority under a range of statutory provisions. The guidelines are described in detail in *Community Care in the Next Decade and Beyond: Policy Guidance* (1990, HMSO) at Chapter 6 'Complaints Procedures'. The procedure set out there differs, however, from that laid down under s 26 of the 1989 Act in that there is no involvement of an independent person until the review stage and those working with children may have very real concerns about personnel who administer such procedures having the relevant child care expertise. (See, for example *The Children Act 1989 Guidance and Regulations, Vol 3 Family Placements* (1991, HMSO) at para 10.19.) The 1990 *Policy Guidance*, however, points out that 'dissatisfaction about a local authority's management or handling of a child's case, even where related to a court order, may still be appropriate to the representations procedure'. It goes on to say (at para 10.10) that:

'the inclusion of a child's name on the child protection register is an administrative action not carried out under any statutory provision (even where the decision is linked to a recommendation to seek a court order) but it is part of an inter-agency process for which the local authority is in the lead but does not carry full responsibility. Whilst the requirements of s 26 are confined to the local authority's functions under the Act, it would be good practice to provide, with the agreement of the area Child Protection Committee, an appropriate procedure to handle complaints about inter-agency case conferences and their recommendations.'

9.4.1 Other types of representations procedures

Many Area Child Protection Committees ('ACPCs') all around the country have now established their own procedures, in accordance with the guidance (above), to consider representations made to them about the way in which different agencies have handled the recommendations made by the child protection conferences and the quality of inter-agency working. Enquiries made of a number of ACPCs have, however, revealed that no complaints have been made via such procedures, perhaps because parents and others subject to investigation were not made aware of their ability to make complaints or representations. It was suggested that parents tended to use the local authority procedures because they were better publicised.

9.5 The limitations of representations procedures

Despite the fact that Government ministers have constantly sought to claim that the 1989 Act would require all local authorities to have independent complaints procedures, this is a clear misnomer when describing the provisions of s 26(3). Local authorities are, of course, directly managing their own complaints procedures and the independent persons included in the procedures only have as much influence as the local authority permits and, as Masson points out, 'the independent person need not have any particular power' (see J Masson *The Children Act 1989: Text and Commentary* (1990, Sweet & Maxwell)). There also seems to be a considerable degree of scepticism, even 18 to 24 months after the implementation of the 1989 Act, that children necessarily know how to operate the complaints procedures which are in place, although a great many local authorities have taken some very positive steps to inform children of the existence of the procedures. Whilst complaints procedures which children can invoke when they are in care are not new (see Lewis, Cracknell and Seneviratne *Complaints Procedures in Local Government* (1987, University of Sheffield)), nevertheless, it was hoped that the 1989 Act, in establishing representations procedures on a national basis, would have provided more statutory requirements as to assisting children to understanding *what* they may complain about as well as *how* to do so. This was a matter of some considerable concern to Sir William Utting when he conducted his survey on behalf of the DOH on children in the public care. He stated that he was concerned that 'under the formal procedure in the Children Act a child needs to formulate what has happened as a complaint and to know of the existence of a complaints procedure as well as how to activate it' (Utting *Children in the Public Care* (1991, DOH) at para 3.48). Much, therefore, depends on the staff in the local authority, voluntary organisation or private children's home providing information as to the relevant procedures. The 1989 Act merely provides that authorities should give such publicity to their procedures for considering representations as 'they consider appropriate' (s 26(8)). Despite the concerns that many people still have in relation to whether such procedures have been given proper publicity and children have received sufficient help in activating them, there seems to be some evidence to show that a number of authorities have taken their duties under the 1989 Act very seriously, and children not only have access to information about the procedures but clear information as to the support which they can derive in processing their complaints through to the panel stage.

Even where children and young people are encouraged to access the relevant representations procedures, Lindsay, in particular, remains doubtful that the ability to access complaints procedures achieves the greater protection of children, who are looked after, from being abused and mistreated (MJ Lindsay 'Complaints procedures and their limitations in the light of the Pindown Enquiry' (1991) JSWFL 432 at pp 436 to 439). As Lindsay points out, there has been a tendency for social work managers to rule that 'serious allegations' fall outside the remit of complaints procedures. He goes on to point out that the recent cases of Acorn Grove in Birmingham (1988) and Melanie Kline House in Greenwich (1989) have illustrated how 'active' complaints procedures were permitted no part in the consideration of complaints alleging sexual assaults (among other things) by staff on children in care. Those cases, he asserts, demonstrated the gross inadequacies in the handling of these complaints. Disturbingly, staff who might have been guilty of committing criminal offences against children were either transferred to other duties (including child care) or simply permitted to resign. None of the staff were referred for police investigation or subjected to disciplinary action, and none of the complaints were referred to the ACPC procedures, suggesting, says Lindsay, that the social work managers who handled the allegations were more concerned about protecting their 'right' to manage than about protecting children in their care from being abused. As Lindsay and others have pointed out, that children can be abused and mistreated while in care is incontestable, and recent scandals surfacing in the media now appear to be more prevalent than many would like to accept or admit. It is, nevertheless, unquestionably the case, that all those people working in child protection arenas, including staff going into residential establishments, must be clearly aware of their obligation to inform children of their ability to make representations about treatment and to ensure that the climate which is operating in such establishments is clearly one which will take seriously any representations so received. In the past, as Pindown and Warner have illustrated, children in care have shown extreme reluctance in complaining, doubting, with some justification, that anyone would believe them, and fearing, with equal justification, victimisation and reprisals if they complain against those who exercise so much power and control over their lives. As Lindsay has pointed out (above) at p 438, even if Staffordshire had had a complaints procedure in operation during the Pindown years, it is still likely that it would have needed the injunction to put a stop to it. Few children in care, Lindsay asserts, would have been encouraged to make complaints about Pindown, let alone to have pursued these beyond the first stage. He argues that to be credible and effective, complaints procedures need to be genuinely independent. The spirit of 'independence' is too easily compromised by close or former association or by the appointment of 'independent persons' who might not reasonably be expected to have much understanding of matters relating to the care system. Again, Lindsay points out, it is too easy to see complaints procedures as some sort of panacea, but unless children 'being looked after' are provided with a procedure which enables their unrestricted access and entitlement to receive independent advice and advocacy, and a facility for an independent investigation of unresolved or 'serious' complaints, Pindown will prove to be just another scandal in a series of them. Indeed, even since Pindown, there has been a whole series of complaints from children who have been looked after by local authorities in Leicestershire, Clwyd, Gwynedd, Lancashire, Bradford, and even the Department of Health Youth Treatment Centre at St Charles in Essex. Utting stated, in *Children in the Public Care* (1991, DOH), at para 3.48, that 'the Department of Health should, once the operation of the new complaints procedures under the Act has been evaluated, consider how best to meet this point'.

As can be seen, therefore, there is still much concern about the degree of independent scrutiny to which representations procedures are conducted and the capacity for the involvement of truly independent, properly professionally qualified personnel to process complaints and representations against local authorities. In the child protection arena, however, the other professionals who are acting with social services in trying to improve the lot of abused children, must not feel that they are potentially handing over a child to be subjected to yet more abuse in accommodation provided by or on behalf of the local authority. They must be able to have confidence in the system, so that they believe that where any child is being abused or threatened with abuse while in care, he will have proper access to arrangements to make complaints which will be taken seriously. In the meantime, the Department of Health's own information leaflets for children receiving help from, or being looked after by, local authorities provide the names and addresses of a number of voluntary organisations which can help with specific problems. In relation to providing support for children seeking to make representations or complaints about services, care or treatment, Advice and Advocacy Services for Children ('ASC') would appear to be in the forefront and is the first organisation quoted in the Department of Health leaflets. (The address for ASC is: 1 Sickle Street, Manchester, and the Freephone number for children is: 0800 616 101.)

9.6 Other avenues for complaint

9.6.1 The Commissioner for Local Administration

The guidance (above) emphasises that the existence of a second-stage panel within the complaints procedure to be established under the 1989 Act does not affect any rights which a particular individual might have under Part III of the Local Government Act 1974. This Act provides individuals with the right to make a complaint about local authority maladministration, which includes such maladministration by social services departments or others acting on behalf of social services and the individual's right is not excluded by virtue of the representations process, because the second-stage panel consideration is not a decision-making process. It is, therefore, entirely appropriate that a Commissioner for Local Administration may investigate a complaint where the complainant is not satisfied with the conduct or outcome of the authority's own investigation or complaints or representations processes. Whilst it is outside the scope of this work to consider in detail the work of the Commissioner for Local Administration, where an individual wishes to pursue a complaint in this way, the best sources of advice as to how he should do so would be Citizens' Advice Bureaux, Neighbourhood Law Centres and individual solicitors listed as having an expertise in public law areas. Leaflets on the work of the Commissioner and how to make a complaint to him are available from all local authority offices and from town halls.

9.6.2 Elected members

It should also be pointed out that the complaints procedure should not, in any way, affect the right of an individual, be that a child, parent, carer or any child protection professional or organisation, to approach a local councillor for advice or assistance, or to voice their particular concerns. Indeed, it should be pointed out that where an individual has indicated he is not satisfied with the panel's decision, in many authority areas the complaints procedure may go beyond the second stage to a third, informal stage set up by individual local authorities, and which includes the involvement of elected members.

It is clear from the above discussion that not every child, parent, carer or other person with sufficient interest in a child will necessarily be satisfied with the results of representations which they may wish to make. Wherever there is such dissatisfaction, it should be remembered that consideration can also be given to the possibility of taking an action for breach of statutory duty or lodging an application for judicial review of administrative action.

JUDICIAL REVIEW AND CHILD ABUSE CASES

9.7 Scope and meaning of judicial review

Judicial review is the High Court procedure available to individuals or groups, by which the legality of a decision taken by an inferior court or a public body, such as a local authority, may be challenged on the grounds that it has acted illegally, irrationally or with procedural impropriety. The court may quash the decision taken, or order the respondent to reconsider the matter, but in accordance with the procedure designated by the court. The crucial point about judicial review is that it is primarily a decision based on an assessment of the procedural propriety of the case in question, and not on the merits of the case, because the court's jurisdiction is said to be supervisory and not appellate. The legality of the decision-making process is the only matter under review (*R v Slough Justices and Others ex parte B* [1985] FLR 384).

Hence, the court is only asked to rule on whether the decision-making process of the tribunal/authority was correctly carried out, not on the rightness or wrongness of the case.

9.7.1 Leave from High Court must first be obtained

The person wishing to apply for judicial review must first apply to the High Court for leave to make a judicial review application (RSC, Ord 53, r 3). The High Court will grant leave to apply for judicial review to anyone who has sufficient interest in the subject matter. An application will then lie for judicial review of a decision made by an inferior court or a body charged with a public duty, such as a local authority. Unfortunately, the court may not necessarily grant leave at the preliminary application stage unless it is convinced that there is enough evidence to pursue this remedy. The application must, therefore, contain sufficiently cogent grounds for judicial review of the matter at hand. This may be difficult if the applicant does not possess sufficient information to justify the application for review. Hence, the giving of reasons, and general openness of the local authority will be critical factors in many cases.

9.7.2 *Procedural limitations of judicial review*

It appears that although judicial review in the family law and child law arena has a relatively short history, indications from case-law suggest that the judiciary appear to adopt a different attitude towards judicial review of decisions taken in these areas. Apart from the need to obtain leave, judicial review itself is not as effective as other ordinary actions in private law, for a number of other reasons: (1) the judicial review procedure is not conducive to the determination of factual disputes (discovery and cross-examination, for instance, are not available as a matter of course as in private law proceedings); (2) even if the court decides that, in law, the local authority acted improperly, it cannot substitute its decision for that of the local authority. The authority may, therefore, make the same decision as before, provided the correct procedures are followed the second time around; (3) damages will not be available where applicants have shown that the local authority acted contrary to the principles of fairness, legality or propriety. Litigants would have to prove that there had been a tortious wrong, breach of contract or breach of statutory duty (see, eg *R v Lancashire County Council ex parte M* [1992] 1 FLR 109) before damages may be awarded (s 31(4) of the Supreme Court Act 1981); (4) the High Court also expects persons to exhaust all other available remedies before applying for judicial review and may exercise its discretion to refuse judicial review if this has not been done (*R v Chief Constable of Merseyside ex parte Calvely* [1986] QB 424).

9.8 Other reasons for using judicial review in child abuse cases

In the past, challenging the exercise of local authority decision-making was mainly effected through the use of a wardship application to the High Court. Currently, there are at least three reasons for using judicial review in child abuse cases. First, the use of wardship to review the decisions of local authorities was severely circumscribed and effectively ended by the courts in a series of cases, the most important being the House of Lords' decisions in *A v Liverpool City Council* (1981) FLR 222 and *Re W (A Minor) (Care Proceedings: Wardship)* [1985] FLR 879. Secondly, wardship is also not generally available to individuals whose child is in care because a child in care cannot be made a ward of court (s 100(2) of the 1989 Act). Thus, aggrieved parties cannot

Child Abuse

invoke wardship to review the exercise of local authorities' powers and duties. Thirdly, it will not be any easier to invoke the inherent jurisdiction of the High Court (see s 100 of the 1989 Act) in order to review the merits of any local authority decisions. As Lord Scarman stated in *Re W* (above):

> 'The ground of decision in [the Liverpool case] was an application . . . of the profoundly important rule that where Parliament has by statute entrusted to a public authority an administrative power subject to safeguards which . . . contain no provision that the High Court is to be required to review the merits of decisions taken pursuant to the power, the High Court has no right to intervene. If there is abuse of the power, there can of course be judicial review pursuant to RSC Ord 53 . . .'

9.9 The 1989 Act and judicial review

9.9.1 General

Some commentators have questioned whether there is sufficient 'governmental interest' in child care matters for decisions of local authorities in such matters to qualify as a public law function and, hence, for judicial review (see B Hadfield and R Lavery 'Public and Private Law Controls on Decision-making for Children' (1991) JSWFL 454).

However, their examination of the pre-1989 Act case-law indicated that judicial review will continue to be used and, indeed, supplement, the 1989 Act's procedures in three possible ways: (1) if the complaint is that the decision reached is unreasonable rather than that it is the result of procedural irregularity, judicial review is the only means of challenge. The duty to consult under s 22(4) of the 1989 Act will, therefore, not make judicial review redundant; (2) the duty to consult only applies to a child whom the local authority is looking after, or is proposing to look after, and so would not apply to situations where a case conference never considered a proposal to look after the child concerned, if the child was not in need; and (3) judicial review may continue to provide a means of challenging whether a decision taken by a parent or a local authority paid due regard to the child's welfare (although see the discussion in Chapter 8 above in relation to decisions affecting local authority plans, which can now apparently be challenged using 1989 Act procedures in the family courts).

9.9.2 Judicial review of 1989 Act proceedings

Judicial review is, in theory, available for all decisions of all inferior courts. However, before the High Court will grant leave to apply for judicial review, the applicant is currently expected to have exhausted any other equally appropriate, convenient or effective remedy.

An appeal may be made to the High Court against a magistrates' court's decision or refusal to make an order under the 1989 Act, s 94. This will allow a reappraisal of the merits of a decision. There are two exceptions to this: (1) there is no right of appeal against a refusal by magistrates to exercise jurisdiction because they believe the case could more conveniently be heard elsewhere; and (2) no appeal lies against any interim periodical payments order. Judicial review may lie to challenge an illegal or irrational decision made in relation to those exceptions. The court would probably expect any statutory right of appeal to the High Court to be exhausted before any judicial review application may be made. It would need to be established that there was some advantage in pursuing a judicial review rather than an ordinary appeal.

The 1989 Act has created various powers and duties for local authorities and only some of these will require the intervention of the legal process, since one of the Act's key philosophies is that, as a general principle, the court will need to be convinced that making an order for the child will be better than making no order.

A number of questions may have to be resolved by case-law. Everall poses the following questions. (1) To what extent will cases dealing directly with the protection of children be extended to a wider range of decisions under the 1989 Act, for example the duty under Sch 2, para 4(2)? (2) Will the High Court allow judicial review of a breach of procedure under s 26 of the 1989 Act, as it did to the non-statutory case conference procedure? (See Everall 'Judicial Review of Local Authorities after the Children Act 1989' [1991] Fam Law 212, at p 215.)

It would seem that, despite the representations and complaints procedure under the 1989 Act, which has been discussed in the first section of this chapter, applications for judicial review may, nevertheless, continue to be found to be a useful remedy for the reasons discussed above.

9.10 Grounds for judicial review

The leading case dealing with the grounds for judicial review is *Council of Civil Service Unions v Minister for the Civil Service* [1984] 3 All ER 935, where Lord Diplock classified the grounds as illegality, irrationality and procedural impropriety.

9.10.1 Illegality or error of law

Illegality or error of law covers those situations where the local authority or other public body erred in law when making its decision or simply acted ultra vires. Examples of this might be where a local authority failed to allow a child in care to have contact with his or her parent without legal justification and contrary to the 1989 Act, or kept the child in secure accommodation without having the legal powers to do so. Illegality can also arise if a court

misconstrues its powers or misunderstands the meaning of a statutory provision (see *R v Bolton Metropolitan Borough Council ex parte B* [1985] FLR
343).

The Court of Appeal case of *R v Hampshire County Council ex parte K*
[1990] 1 FLR 330, involved a decision by a local authority to withhold the
production of two medical reports about alleged sexual abuse of a child who
had a significant degree of retardation. A writ of *certiorari* (see **9.12** below)
was granted to quash this decision as well as the local authority's decision to
refuse to allow a medical examination of the child. The parents arrived at an
interim care order hearing without prior knowledge of the detail of the allegations of abuse, or of the medical diagnoses of two police paediatricians, which,
as it happened, reached opposing conclusions about the medical examination
which they had carried out on the child. It was emphasised by Watkins LJ
that it was wrong to regard cases of alleged parental abuse as involving
an automatic confrontation between the conflicting claims of child welfare
represented by the local authority and natural justice championed by the
parents. On the contrary, every child has an interest in his parents being
given a fair chance to test evidence of alleged abuse. A policy of open disclosure, excepting documents covered by public interest immunity, should have
been the general rule followed by the local authority, in order to enable the
parents to rebut the charges of abuse made against them.

Under the current 1989 Act Rules of Court, advance disclosure of written
statements of the substance of oral evidence intended to be adduced by all
the parties, and of all documents on which a party intends to rely, is required
(see Family Proceedings Courts (Children Act 1989) Rules 1991, SI 1991/
1395). In *R v Newham Borough Council ex parte P* [1990] 1 FLR 404, another
pre-1989 Act case, a local authority decision to deny access to parents after
an interim care order had been made was quashed by the court. The authority
had previously allowed staying and holiday access to a child and then changed
its mind on the basis of its interpretation of a set of regulations. The court
held, as a matter of law, that the authority did not transfer care and control
of a child merely by giving the family leave to have the child home for the
weekend. Since the regulations in question did not apply to this sort of
situation, the local authority had no lawful basis on which to renege on its
agreement. Presumably, other regulations and the 1989 Act could be similarly
interpreted using this sort of approach.

9.10.2 *Procedural impropriety*

Procedural impropriety covers those situations where a local authority failed
to follow the proper or appropriate procedure, eg by not giving notice of
pending care proceedings to persons entitled to such notice or breaching the
common law rules of natural justice or procedural fairness. Hence, a local
authority should not deny a foster-parent any opportunity to answer allega-

tions of sexual abuse, nor to see a summary of documents laid before the social services' sub-committee (see *R v London Borough of Wandsworth ex parte P* [1989] 1 FLR 387), nor to have a parent's 'home on trial' experiment cancelled purely on the basis of unsubstantiated allegations made against the parent. So, for example, a local authority had to allow a parent to make representations, to point to evidence and to produce witnesses who might refute these allegations (*R v Bedfordshire County Council ex parte C; R v Hertfordshire County Council ex parte B* [1987] 1 FLR 239).

In this last pair of cases, Ewbank J, giving judgment, made it clear that, in deciding whether or not a local authority had acted contrary to the principles of natural justice, he had to decide in each case not whether the decisions were right or fair, but whether the manner in which the judgments were made was fair. The father in the *Bedfordshire* case (above) was given an opportunity to refute allegations against him and to make representations, since these allegations were the *only* grounds for the local authority reversing its decision to return his child home to him on a trial basis. Yet, the mother in the *Hertfordshire* case (above) was not given an opportunity to meet allegations of drunkenness against her because these allegations did not constitute the sole grounds for the local authority's decision not to return her child on a trial basis.

The Court of Appeal decision of *R v Harrow London Borough ex parte D* [1990] 1 FLR 79 suggests that the courts are not willing to extend the ruling in the above cases to allow judicial review on the basis of a breach of natural justice. With reference to placing of a child's name on a child abuse register, Butler-Sloss LJ stated quite clearly that recourse to judicial review in respect of a decision to place a name on the child abuse register ought to be rare: 'All concerned in this difficult and delicate area should be allowed to perform their task without looking over their shoulder all the time for the possible intervention of the court'.

The latest inter-agency guidance *Working Together under the Children Act 1989* (1991, DOH) ('*Working Together*') also deals with the issues of attendance and representation at case conferences (see Chapter 4 above).

In *R v Berkshire County Council ex parte P* [1991] 1 FLR 470, the Court of Appeal refused judicial review of a local authority decision not to call a 17-year-old girl, who alleged sexual abuse against her step-father, to give evidence. The authority preferred to rely on her written evidence under r 2(2) of the Children (Admissibility of Hearsay Evidence) Order 1990 (now replaced by the 1993 Order). Since the rules allowed for such a decision, the court could find no evidence of unlawfulness or unreasonable behaviour by the local authority. The court also held that a magistrates' clerk, who refused to issue a witness summons, acted unlawfully. This was a case where despite the fact that there was a risk of prejudice to the step-father in his case, and a risk to the three other children of the family if the girl's evidence was not put to the test, the interests of the child were given priority over those of the applicant.

Under current law, this case would be dealt with under the Rules of Court covering the conduct of care proceedings (see the Family Proceedings Rules 1991, SI 1991/1247, and the Family Proceedings Courts (Children Act 1989) Rules 1991, SI 1991/1395). A directions hearing would determine this matter and there would be scope for an appeal under s 94 of the 1989 Act.

On the question of denial of natural justice *R v Pontlottyn Juvenile Court ex parte R* [1991] 2 FLR 86 is instructive. In this case, *certiorari* was granted to the natural mother of two boys to quash a local authority's decision to oppose, without notice, her application for the appointment of a guardian ad litem to act on behalf of the boys in access proceedings. The mother had been separated for over 13 years from her children, having suffered from psychiatric disorders until 1984. The long-term foster-parents of the boys were divorcing, and the natural mother sought to have access restored. She was aware that this might be disruptive to the boys, particularly at the present time, so she applied for a guardian. The authority told her that it would oppose the access application but did not mention the guardian. It was assumed by the court clerk that the appointment would not be opposed and he told the natural mother that her attendance was unnecessary. When the application was opposed at the directions hearing, the clerk failed to raise the question of the absent mother and the reason for the absence.

It was held by the High Court that there was evidence of actual unreasonableness and a denial of natural justice. In particular the court considered that the authority had been irrational in opposing the appointment of a guardian, since one was bound to be appointed in the freeing for adoption procedure which had been brought by the foster-mother as a single parent. Curiously, the court did not direct a rehearing and actually made the order for the appointment of a guardian.

9.10.3 *Irrationality or unreasonableness*

The leading case on what constitutes irrationality or unreasonableness on the part of the local authority is *Associated Provincial Picture Houses Ltd v Wednesbury Corporation* [1948] 1 KB 223 ('the *Wednesbury* case'). There, Lord Greene MR, spoke of a decision 'so absurd that no sensible person could ever dream that it lay within the powers of the authority'. The principles for which this case is usually cited are: (1) that a court will only interfere with or overturn a local authority's decision if it is a decision that no reasonable authority could have come to, if they either took into account factors which were irrelevant to the decision or did not take into account factors which were relevant; and (2) a court will interfere with an administrative body's decision which is plainly wrong or so absurd that no reasonable body would have taken it. In *Council of Civil Service Unions v Minister for the Civil Service* (see **9.10** above) Lord Diplock, having used irrationality as a synonym for *Wednesbury* unreasonableness, said that 'It applies to a decision which is so outrageous in its defiance of logic or of accepted moral standards that no sensible person who had applied his mind to the question to be decided could have arrived at it'.

9.10.3.1 Refusal to state reasons

In care proceedings, if substantial evidence was adduced before juvenile justices who, nevertheless, refused to state their reasons for dismissing an application to discharge a care order, and there was conflict between the parties, judicial review was granted in the form of an order for mandamus (see **9.12** below) requiring justices to state a case, ie give reasons for the consideration of the High Court (see Chapter 6).

9.10.3.2 Child protection registers and child protection conferences

Two leading cases in this area have highlighted the issue of the reasonableness of the actions of a child protection conference in placing a child and suspect's name on a child protection register ('CPR'). The pivotal issue in both cases was: if a child's name is placed on a CPR, what are the legal rights of the person suspected of having abused him? Has such a person the right to be treated 'fairly and reasonably'? The two cases are *R v Harrow London Borough ex parte D* [1989] 2 FLR 51, and *R v Norfolk County Council ex parte X* [1989] 2 FLR 120. Both of these cases were pre-1989 Act cases, but they remain important and are included in *Working Together* (see **9.11** below).

In *Harrow*, a mother of three children whose names had been placed on the CPR, sought judicial review on the grounds that failure to invite her to a case conference concerning the abuse of her children was unfair or unreasonable. She was the alleged abuser of her children, who had suffered bruising. The conference had before it the evidence of two paediatricians who had found physical injuries on all three children and thought they were non-accidental, and the evidence of the social worker who claimed to have heard an account from one of the children accusing the mother of causing bodily harm. The children had been removed under a place of safety order obtained by the social worker but were returned to the mother after 24 hours. She had asked, through her solicitor, to attend the case conference, but was informed that she could not, although she was allowed to make written submissions, which she did. The mother's appeal failed in both the lower court and the Court of Appeal. Anthony Lincoln J said that he could not accept that the failure to invite the mother to the conference was unfair or unreasonable. Two reasons were given. (1) The DOH guidelines in *Working Together* (1988 version) omitted parents from categories of persons to be invited and to make submissions to the conference. (2) The facts of the case failed to establish any unfairness as the case conference had the mother's written submissions before it. Furthermore, the children were not, in fact, removed from the mother's care at the conclusion of the conference. The purpose of the conference was not to reach a verdict on the mother's guilt or innocence; it was simply to decide the next step. This step was to place their names on the CPR. Anthony Lincoln J could not see how the mother's presence and advocacy at the conference could have affected this result. In the Court of Appeal, his decision was upheld. *Working Together* (1988 version) was again looked at, the child protection conference and register were both confirmed as non-statutory in status, but, nevertheless, were part of good social work practice and necessary for the protection of children. In the course of her judgment, Butler-Sloss LJ made several important observations, pointing out that:

> 'Although the contents of the register are confidential, a significant number of people inevitably have to be aware of the information contained in it.'

She concluded that the 'level of fairness . . . was amply met by the procedure followed', since the mother had been allowed to make written representations to the case conference although she had been excluded from it and the council's decision to place the children's names on the register was not unfair, unreasonable nor contrary to natural justice. She further observed that 'recourse to judicial review is likely to be, and undoubtedly ought to be, rare. Local authorities have laid on them by Parliament the specific duty of protection of children in their area'. She went on to make some further important points.

(1) If the decision to register can be shown to be utterly unreasonable, there is no reason in principle why judicial review may not be available.

(2) The child protection conference has a duty to make an assessment as to abuse and the abuser, if sufficient information is available. It is, of its nature, unstructured and informal, and is not a judicial process.

(3) In this field, there is a third component not present in other judicial review cases (which usually involve only the individual who may have been prejudiced and the organisation that might have been criticised) which is the welfare of the child who is the purpose of the entry in the register. In proceedings in which the child is the subject, his or her welfare is paramount. In balancing adequate protection to the child and fairness to the adult, the interest of any adult may have to be placed second to the needs of the child.

Clearly, professional advisers have been given due notice that successful judicial review applications are likely to be rare but it is, nevertheless, true to say that each case will turn on its individual facts and circumstances.

In *R v Norfolk County Council ex parte X* [1989] 2 FLR 120, a 13-year-old girl alleged that the applicant, a plumber working in her parents' house, had indecently assaulted her. The local authority social services department convened two case conferences which heard that the girl had previously been registered twice as an abused child (involving other men), that after the child's allegation against the plumber she had made a complaint against a van driver, that she went to school dressed in tight jeans and high heels, and that she was living an unsettled home life between the mother and other relatives and friends. Without reference to the plumber, the case conference decided that it was persuaded that the applicant had committed sexual abuse of the child and that both the mother's name and his should be entered in the CPR. The applicant was sent a letter informing him of this decision and his solicitors wrote complaining about the registration and the conduct of the case conference. The applicant applied for judicial review and was offered the opportunity to attend a reconvened case conference at which he would be allowed to make representations in person or through his solicitor.

Waite J held that the applicant had every justification for refusing to do so. That was an offer from a body that had already condemned him in his absence. He described the consequences of registration as sufficiently serious to impose on the council a legal duty to act fairly. He opined:

'It is a particularly troubling feature of the present case that the possibility does not appear even to have occurred to either case conference – or, for that matter, to any level of the county council's social services – that [the girl's] accusations might be a fantasy or fabrication proceeding directly from her own very evident emotional problems; and that if there was the slightest possibility that such might be the case, they were at risk of stigmatizing an innocent man as an abuser. That is a risk to which their minds could, of course, have been immediately opened if [the plumber] and his professional advisers had been allowed, before the registration was effected, an opportunity of informed comment on the material considered by the two case conferences.'

Although he acknowledged that registration of suspected abusers was useful, 'a child abuse register, nevertheless, remains (at all events as regards the abusers named on it) in essence a blacklist, and as such it also has dangerous potential as an instrument of injustice and oppression'. Since the council had, without warning, applied a procedure that had denied the applicant the opportunity of prior consultation or objection to its decision to place him on the register, the local authority's conduct was unfair and so unreasonable as to come within the notion of *Wednesbury* unreasonableness and its decision was, accordingly, quashed.

Waite J stated, however, that judicial review would not be granted if the particular procedure followed by a local authority represented a genuine attempt to reconcile the duty of child protection on the one hand and the duty of fairness to the alleged abuser on the other.

Other cases are also instructive. In *R v East Sussex County Council ex parte R* [1991] 2 FLR 358, the mother of a boy aged six hit him on the thigh with a wooden spoon. This was discovered when a teacher saw bruising to the child's leg and informed the social services department. The child was examined by a doctor and the mother told the doctor she had hit the boy because he was naughty. The mother refused to discuss the matter with a social worker. A case conference was held and it was decided to place the boy and his younger sister on the CPR. The mother applied for judicial review claiming that the procedure adopted by the local authority was unfair as she was not given the opportunity to make adequate representations; and the decision was unreasonable because what she had done was within a parent's ordinary capacity to discipline a child. Sir Stephen Brown P stated that the approach of the court on judicial review should be as stated by Butler-Sloss LJ in the *Harrow* case (above). He held that the mother had been given ample opportunity to make such representations as she wished and, therefore, the procedure adopted by the local authority was not unfair. On the reasonableness of the decision, the President declared that this was just a case of an exasperated parent spanking a child but, although the injuries were not serious, they did suggest there was a basis of concern as to the treatment the boy might receive. He found that the decision to place the child on the CPR could not be said to be unreasonable in the *Wednesbury* sense.

In *R v Devon County Council ex parte D* [1992] 2 FCR 766, a case which also came before Sir Stephen Brown P, a 13-year-old girl made a statement to the police in which she made specific and detailed allegations of having been subjected to unlawful sexual intercourse by her father. Two doctors examined the girl and found that there was a probability that she had had sexual intercourse. The local authority was informed and a case conference was convened but the father was not advised of it. This was at the request of the police who were investigating the matter, although criminal proceedings were not instituted against the father. At the case conference it was decided to place the name of the child on the CPR. The local authority informed the father of its decision 11 days after the case conference and sent him a leaflet which told him what steps he could take if he wished to complain. He did not take any of these steps. Soon after, the father became friendly with a woman who had children. The local authority told that woman of its concern for children in a household in which the father resided. The father subsequently consulted solicitors with a view to challenging the decision of the local authority to place the child on the CPR. Six months later, the child's name was removed from the CPR. Three months after that, the father applied for a judicial review.

Sir Stephen Brown P held that, in the light of the girl's complaint, the local authority were under a statutory duty to act to safeguard her welfare, which they did by placing her name on the CPR. The father's name had not been placed on the CPR as an alleged abuser. Although the local authority had not informed the father of the case conference, notification of the decision, accompanied by the explanatory leaflet, was sent to him subsequently. In considering whether to grant *certiorari*, it was a relevant factor whether the father had taken the action open to him to complain to the local authority.

It was also relevant that there had been a delay of over a year before the judicial review application had been made. Further, by that time, the child's name had been removed from the CPR. Over and above that, however, was the quality of the decision made by the local authority. This could not be categorised as unreasonable. It was, therefore, held that judicial review would be refused.

The court also stated, *per curiam*, that the local authority could not be criticised for making contact with the woman in whose household the father was residing after the case conference was held. It was understandable that it considered that it had a duty to do so (see, further, **9.11** below).

In *R v London Borough of Wandsworth ex parte P* [1989] 1 FLR 387, a child aged 14 months had been placed with a foster-mother. Fifteen months later the child was placed with prospective adopters who said that she seemed sexually precocious and had said things which were interpreted as meaning that the foster-mother had sexually abused her. Reports were obtained from a psychiatrist and a psychotherapist. The Director of Social Services, who saw the foster-mother, mentioned the allegations to her but gave her no opportunity to respond to them, merely telling her that he had decided not to place any children with her in future. The mother applied for judicial review. The local authority then informed her that the matter would be reviewed by a sub-committee and she was invited to attend that sub-committee meeting. The local authority's solicitor produced a summary of events which included details of the alleged abuse which were more extensive but not entirely consistent with allegations the Director of Social Services had referred to. The mother attended the meeting, in which her solicitor addressed the sub-committee on the basis of the summary. However, unknown to the mother and her solicitor the committee also took into account reports from a psychiatrist and psychotherapist. The sub-committee confirmed the decision of the Direction of Social Services.

In fact, the psychiatrist had not even seen the child but the foster-mother had been given the impression that he had interviewed the child. The psychiatrist had reported that although the child had made substantial allegations, she could not say whether these were true or not. On the other hand, the psychotherapist had seen the child but had reported that she saw no signs of the sexual interest which were reported to have occurred.

In the subsequent judicial review hearing, with which the mother persisted, Ewbank J held that the documents which the sub-committee had taken into account were privileged but the foster-mother needed to know them in sufficient detail for her to rebut them. In a case of sexual abuse of a child, where evidence comes mainly from a child, he added 'it must be rare indeed that the bare allegations will be sufficient for a foster-mother to meet the case'. Significantly, he also emphasised that the foster-mother needed to know 'the extent to which the allegations are interpretations by other people of remarks made by the child which might have some other interpretation . . . [and]

where there have been reports by a child psychiatrist, the foster-mother ought to have some details of the nature of the interviews by the child psychiatrist and the conclusions drawn'. The decisions of both the sub-committee and Director of Social Services were quashed.

In *R v Lewisham London Borough Council ex parte P* [1991] 2 FLR 185, another case involving foster-parents, the applicant was formerly on the local authority's list of approved foster-parents. A disturbed child, who had once been cared for by the applicant and his wife, alleged that the applicant had sexually abused him and that the foster-father had also treated the foster-mother with violence. It was impossible to question the applicant because, since the time of the alleged event, he had suffered two strokes and was severely mentally impaired. The council informed the carers of all the children who had been fostered by the applicant of the allegations that had been made against him. The applicant's wife sought judicial review on his behalf and submitted that it was not necessary for the alleged abuser to be named. Booth J held that the council was wrong in following a policy of full disclosure and its decision to inform the carers constituted unreasonableness within the *Wednesbury* principle and would be quashed. The duty to give first consideration to the child's welfare did not stand in isolation. Parents and other custodians were entitled to look to the council for a fair procedure to be followed, even though their interests were secondary to those of the child. The social services department should have considered, as a separate question, whether the children's welfare required disclosure of the applicant's name. The local authority must conduct a balancing exercise between the need to protect the children by naming the alleged abuser and the consequences to the individual of such disclosure. It was stressed, further, that:

> 'This balancing exercise can only properly be achieved by the local authority considering all the circumstances of the case, including the credibility of the allegations and the weight to be attached to them as well as the benefit to be derived by the other children concerned by the naming of the alleged perpetrator, always bearing in mind that the allegation is no more than an allegation and is not a proven fact.'

It was found that this balancing exercise had not been carried out properly by the local authority, who had not considered the credibility of the child's allegations. It should have taken into account: (1) the fact that the child was disturbed; (2) there was reason to believe that he had suffered sexual abuse before he had been placed with foster-parents; and (3) in addition to the foster-mother's denial of the allegation that her husband was violent towards her, social workers had seen her on many occasions and at no time was there any suspicion of anything of that nature. Accordingly, the local authority's decision to name the foster-father was unreasonable and was, therefore, quashed.

In *R v Devon County Council ex parte L* [1991] 2 FLR 541, the applicant was an illiterate 41-year-old man who was alleged to have abused a girl when she was four years old. The man cohabited with the girl's mother for some time in 1986 and ceased to do so in August 1987. He continued to contact the girl's mother occasionally, but in 1988 she obtained an injunction against him. The girl subsequently became disturbed at school and when she was referred to a consultant paediatrician stated that the applicant had been touching her in an inappropriate manner. The paediatrician concluded that there was no physical evidence of abuse but there were signs of inflammation in the vaginal area. In January 1988, the child's name was placed on the CPR and it was recorded that there was a 'possibility of sexual abuse by unknown perpetrator'. The child was interviewed in February 1988 and indicated that the applicant had abused her. The applicant was arrested but was never charged. He signed a caution which he apparently did not understand, which gave rise to doubt whether this amounted to an admission of any offence. The applicant later cohabited with another woman and her son, aged four. When the local authority heard of this, it informed the woman of the alleged sexual abuse. Warnings were issued regarding placing the woman's son on the 'at risk register' and that there might be care proceedings. Although the woman was carrying the man's child, she ordered him to leave. The applicant's solicitor wrote to the local authority complaining that the applicant was being branded a child abuser without sufficient evidence, but was told by the local authority solicitor that there was information which could be relied upon, although insufficient for a prosecution.

The applicant subsequently lived with a married couple and their two children, aged 10 and 4, and this couple were again informed of the allegations. They also required the applicant to leave. This happened yet again with another woman and her children, who also asked the applicant to leave.

The local authority wrote in reply to the applicant's solicitor's letter of complaint that as the local authority did not keep a register of abusers, it could not be said that the applicant had been blacklisted (as in the *Norfolk* case (above)). No case conference had ever been convened on this matter and no one from social services had ever interviewed the applicant.

In subsequent judicial proceedings, Eastham J held that the letter from the local authority solicitor did not amount to a 'decision' capable of judicial review and that the local authority had acted in good faith. In addition, he observed that, even if its decision to tell the various women of its belief that the applicant was a child abuser amounted to a reviewable decision, the application would nevertheless be dismissed.

R v Bedfordshire County Council ex parte C (1986) 151 JP 202, was a case involving four children whose parents had separated. Their mother made allegations not connected with care proceedings that the father had committed buggery with a teenage boy whom he had brought to the matrimonial bed, and had forced the mother to have sex with the boy. These allegations were not made known in care proceedings in the course of which care orders were made. The local authority intended to place the children with the father but, before it could do this, the mother repeated her allegations to the police, who informed the local authority. The local authority did not ask the father about these allegations but simply decided not to place the children with the father. The court, at the judicial review hearing initiated by the father, said that if unsubstantiated allegations were made, a local authority should at least allow an opportunity to make representations and to point to evidence and produce witnesses who might refute the allegations. The local authority's decisions were quashed as it had failed to do so and it was also ordered to give the father an opportunity to make such representations before making any new decisions about the children's future.

9.11 *Working Together*: parental involvement in case conferences

The rules of natural justice require both the absence of bias or partiality in the hearing of one's case and the opportunity for both sides to present their views (*audi alteram partem*). *Working Together* contains advice on the involvement of children, parents and carers in child protection case conferences (at para 6.11 and see Chapter 4 above).

On the question of a possible conflict between the interests of parents and children, para 6.12 is very clear: 'in such cases the child's interests should be the priority'.

Since various judicial cases have discussed the fairness or otherwise of excluding a parent from a child protection conference, para 6.15 declares that 'exclusion should be kept to a minimum and needs to be especially justified'. It stresses that the local procedures should lay down criteria for this, including the evidence required. It declares that a strong risk of violence, with supporting evidence, by the parents towards the professionals or the child might be one example of evidence that the conference would be likely to be disrupted.

Nevertheless, it also states that the possibility that one of the parents might be prosecuted for an offence against the child does not, in itself, justify exclusion. The ultimate decision on exclusion should rest with the chair of the conference, who should base his decision on the criteria laid down in the local protection procedures (see, further, Chapter 4 above).

Working Together also caters for the situations which arose in cases such as *Norfolk* case (above). Paragraph 6.17 states that if parents are excluded or are unable or unwilling to attend a child protection conference it is important that they are encouraged to find a method of communicating their views to the conference. This may be done through a letter or tape recording. It also allows for the possibility of the social worker and/or another professional to agree with the parent that they should represent the parent's views and wishes.

Thus, *Working Together* does *not* say that parents may not be excluded from such conferences, but only suggests that individual ACPCs should 'formally agree' the (presumably general?) principle of including parents and children in all conferences and that guidance on their inclusion should be contained in the local ACPC Guidelines and all local child protection procedures (at para 6.14).

9.11.1 Information about abusers

Working Together (at paras 6.52 to 6.54) deals with procedure concerning maintenance of information about abusers (and see also Chapter 4 for further detail on information about abusers).

9.12 Remedies for judicial review

When an application for judicial review succeeds, the High Court has the power to make orders for, inter alia, *certiorari*, *mandamus* and prohibition. The court has a discretion whether or not to grant a remedy. These orders derived from the prerogative writs and were generally issued by individuals against public bodies to challenge the exercise of their power or to enforce the performance of a public duty or, indeed, to require courts to carry out certain functions with judicial propriety. An order of *mandamus* empowers the High Court to order a magistrates' court to state a case, ie give reasons for its decision. *Certiorari* empowers the High Court to quash a decision on the grounds that it was improperly made and by prohibition, the High Court can prevent a court from exceeding its jurisdiction. In these proceedings, of course, the High Court is concerned only with the legality of the decision-making process, not the merits of the case. Moreover, the court can refuse judicial review because: (1) there was an unreasonable lapse of time between the incident and the application; (2) even if the local authority had acted correctly, the decision would have been the same; (3) the particular irregularity is only a technicality; (4) the issue is academic because, for example, the decision has already been carried out and the applicant has not suffered any real detriment; or (5) the paramount welfare of the child overrides all other considerations.

It is worth bearing in mind that although the High Court can no longer ward a child who is in local authority care because of s 100(2) of the 1989 Act, the inherent jurisdiction of the High Court, from which wardship may be distinguished, may still be invoked, and the relatively uncertain scope of this jurisdiction will provide an opportunity for manoeuvre in cases where wardship would previously have been allowed.

9.13 Comment

It is clear that there is a wide variety of cases in which a local authority's decision regarding children in its care has been challenged successfully by judicial review, particularly where there is suspected child abuse. *Working Together* has not made parental attendance or participation a 'right' but has left it to the discretion of the chairperson of each child protection conference, and individual procedures (see Chapter 4). However, it has impliedly created a presumption or general guideline for ACPCs that parents and children would normally be expected to attend child protection conferences, exclusion being the exception, requiring justification. However, under the section in *Working Together* dealing with the list of invited agencies at a child protection conference, it is stated that 'all those who are invited should be informed that the child, the parents and other carers have been invited' (at para 6.25). So the position is something of a compromise. Nevertheless, *Working Together* is non-statutory and a wide discretion is still given to the local authority.

As far as case-law is concerned, in both the *Harrow* and *East Sussex* cases (above) the fact of the abuse did not seem in doubt, which made it easier for the court to decide that the local authority had not acted unfairly. However, in the *Bedfordshire*, *Wandsworth* and *Norfolk* cases (above), the court, in each case, considered the information upon which the local authority had acted to be inadequate as it had excluded representations from the alleged abuser. The *Lewisham* case is particularly poignant for its approach to the relevant factors which ought to be taken into account by a local authority in arriving at its discretion. On the other hand, in the *Devon* case dealing with the illiterate itinerant man (above), the weakness of judicial review was exposed. Thus, if a local authority acts informally by not convening a child protection conference, and makes no formal decision, there is, therefore, no decision which is reviewable. Yet it may act in such a way that a person is effectively disadvantaged and besmirched and in the circumstances of the case, only a private action might have been able to stop the local authority from acting in this way. In other words, the local authority has no need to weigh the need to protect the children against the consequences of relaying its suspicions about the alleged abuser before taking any informal steps. Although the facts of this particular case were extraordinary, it does not seem fair or reasonable that, in principle, an aggrieved person does not appear to have the right to challenge local authority decisions or actions (because they were taken informally) in these circumstances.

Under the 1989 Act, the recourse to judicial review might well depend on how effective the ACPC complaints procedures and s 26 procedures will prove to be in ensuring that decisions made by ACPCs and local authorities, in relation to children suspected of having been abused, are fair, reasonable and maintain the focus on the child as the paramount consideration. Judicial review will probably be most useful in dealing with cases outside ss 22 and 26 of the 1989 Act, for example if the decision does not relate to the child but to a third party, as in the *Norfolk* case. In the case of child care scandals, such as the Pindown affair, Lindsay has argued that the 1989 Act complaints procedure would not have been very effectual, since those children subjected to the regime would have been obliged to complain first to the same staff who themselves implemented the Pindown regime (see **9.3** above and M Lindsay 'Complaints Procedures and their Limitations in the Light of the Pindown Inquiry' (1991) JSWFL 432 at p 438). One of Lindsay's concerns is that an 'independent' person will only have as much influence as the particular local authority allows him to have (see also **9.3** above). In an urgent case, it is perfectly possible that a court may be persuaded that judicial review will be more expeditious and more effective than invoking the s 26 procedure, in ensuring that justice is seen to be done as soon as possible, particularly bearing in mind the avoidance of delay principle under the 1989 Act, so that all interested and affected parties, including the child, will have an opportunity to put their case forward.

CHAPTER TEN

Child Abuse and the New Law

10.1 A review of progress

The impact of the Children Act 1989 ('the 1989 Act'), on the work of everyone concerned with protecting children, has been enormous. The provisions discussed in this book reflect the fact that Parliament took extremely seriously the many criticisms which had been levelled at the old law, and provided a legal framework whose potential for achieving the greater protection of children has not yet been fully explored in practice, due to limitations on resources. In addition to the 1989 Act and consequent rules and regulations, however, the Department of Health ('DOH') produced for the first time in relation to any piece of legislation, a comprehensive and invaluable series of guidance, not only for local authorities to refer to, but also for other agencies involved in working with children. *The Children Act 1989 Guidance and Regulations* documents, which run to 12 volumes, including the *Principles and Practice* document and the *Introduction to the Children Act*, have been extensively referred to throughout this book, and in cases concerning children, throughout the country, since they became available. The DOH has also, over the years, produced two compilation studies looking at the main messages arising from the various child abuse official inquiries (*Studies of Inquiry Reports 1973–1980* and *1980–1989*). As has been stated, they are source books not only for the social work practitioner, but for all those dealing with children. A special *Introductory Guide to the Children Act* was also produced for workers in the National Health Service and, all over the country, educational authorities and other agencies produced their own guides to the 1989 Act with particular reference to their own service needs.

In the field of protecting children, the DOH issued a new version of *Working Together* in 1991 which has formed the framework for additional material produced by local authorities on child protection and also by area child protection committees when producing their guidelines (*Working Together under the Children Act 1989* (1991, DOH)). As was pointed out in Chapter 4, however, the DOH is aiming to produce *Guidelines on Medical Confidentiality in Child Protection* in the autumn of 1993 (see **4.3** above) and, apparently, invitations have been issued to local authority social services and chairs of area child protection committees ('ACPCs') to submit comments, criticisms and suggestions about the current version of *Working Together* to the DOH. This might seem to suggest the possible issuing of a supplement to *Working Together* either appended to, or, perhaps, incorporating, the *Guidelines on Medical Confidentiality in Child Protection*. In addition, the 1989 document *Protecting Children – a Guide for Social Workers Undertaking a Comprehensive Assessment* has achieved much wider circulation than its original targeted group. Other documents produced by the DOH, such as *Patterns and Outcomes in Child Placement* (1991, DOH), have also been seen in the hands of many others apart from social work professionals. Lawyers have not been afraid to use all the source books available and, where arguments have raged about the local authorities' plans for children in care, recourse has been made to the *Patterns and Outcomes* document. The DOH, as part of its wide publicity campaign under the 1989 Act, has also played its part in trying to ensure that a range of leaflets constituting guides for children, young people and their parents, has also been made widely available. These leaflets, which range from a guide for parents entitled *The Children Act and Local Authorities* (CAG1) through to one entitled *Living Away from Home – Your Rights* (CAG7), which is a guide for children and young people, are all available from the Department of Health Stores, Health Publications Unit, Number 2 Site, Manchester Road, Heywood, Lancashire OL10 2PZ.

Even in the 18 to 24 months since the implementation of the 1989 Act, however, various myths have developed about the circumstances in which orders may be sought from the courts and, similarly, about whether the courts will make orders. Some of these myths have given rise to considerable concern, particularly amongst the judiciary, and these have been further discussed in three informative reports which were produced in late 1992 and early 1993. The first of these reports to emerge was the first *Children Act Advisory Committee Annual Report 1991/2* published by the Lord Chancellor's Department in December 1992. Also published in December 1992 was a Social Services Inspectorate study entitled *Court Orders – a Study of Local Authority Decision-making about Public Law Court Applications* which provided important evidence to the DOH about the way in which local authorities were approaching use of the 1989 Act in cases of children in need of protection. Finally, the DOH published its own *Children Act Report 1992*, which the Government was obliged to produce under the provisions of the 1989 Act itself. This report purports to provide a comprehensive review of how the 1989 Act is working out in practice, as well as pointing to some concerns specifically related to the areas of child protection.

The first *Report of the Children Act Advisory Committee* (a Committee consisting of members of the judiciary dealing with family law at all levels and other personnel such as magistrates' clerks) states that its terms of reference were to provide a brief overall view of how the 1989 Act is working throughout the country, and of how the Committee sees the way ahead. As Booth J comments in the preface to the report, 'it would be remarkable if a statute as radical as this one undoubtedly is, did not give rise to difficulties in the early stages of its active life'. She goes on to comment that 'over the first twelve months of the operation of the Act, a few problems, particularly procedural ones, have emerged or have been identified'. In common with many other judges, she also comments that 'there have been and continue to be, some deeply felt concerns which have their origins largely in the resource limitations of local authorities'. The Committee itself, in its report, is, however, rightly cautious about the certainty of any messages emerging from the first year of the 1989 Act's operation. It suggests that there are reasons for thinking that it might be premature to treat such messages definitively, first because the 1989 Act is challenging in its scope and content, requiring a radical change of thinking by the courts, such that a learning curve is unavoidable and, secondly, because at least during the first six months of the operation of the 1989 Act, surprisingly few applications were made to courts in the public law or care sector. This view was supported by evidence from a small-scale survey of some 500 decided cases in five magistrates' courts in South Wales over a six-month period. Out of the sample of 500 cases only 83 involved public law or care applications and the researchers noted that their sample suggested that 'at least for the first six months of the Act's operation, there was a marked downturn in the number of public law applications in the courts'. (See Butler, Noaks, Douglas, Lowe and Pithouse 'The Children Act and the Issue of Delay' [1993] Fam Law 412 at pp 413 to 414.) By the end of the first year, however, the public law case load seemed to be increasing, and reports available in March 1993 from different parts of the country indicated an upturn in activity in child protection cases. As to the factors which might have prompted the initial downturn in child protection cases, this was specifically the remit of the Social Services Inspectorate study on *Court Orders* (see above). The study examined the decision-making processes in relation to decisions about public law court applications in four local authorities. Arising from that study and departmental discussions with a number of local authorities, was a belief that the 'no order' principle of s 1(5) of the 1989 Act required local authorities to demonstrate that working in partnership had broken down or had been exhausted before an order would be made, one of the myths which has grown up in the aftermath of the implementation of the 1989 Act. That such a view is widely held by those working in local authorities was also supported by a report of seminars held in Leicestershire during October and November 1992 to review progress locally in implementing the 1989 Act. (See Martin Shaw 'The Children Act 1989 – one year on in Leicestershire' (1993) *Adoption and Fostering* at pp 41 to 44). In the seminar looking at child protection, court processes were discussed and Shaw notes that 'there was particular concern about delays in taking legal action, because of the need to have a "cast-iron" case in order to overcome the "no order" presumption' (at p 41). The DOH in its *Children Act Report 1992* (1993, DOH) (at para 2.21), emphasises that this was not the intention of the legislation. The DOH clearly sets down in its report its rejection of this myth. It states that:

> 'where a local authority determines that control of the child's circumstances is necessary to promote his welfare, then compulsory intervention, as part of a carefully planned process, will *always* be the appropriate remedy. Local authorities should not feel inhibited by the working in partnership provisions of the Children Act from seeking appropriate court orders. Equally the existence of a court order should not of itself impede a local authority from continuing its efforts at working in partnership with the families of children in need. The two processes are not mutually exclusive. Each has a role to play, often simultaneously, in the case management of a child at risk.'

Figures produced, therefore, in the *Children Act Advisory Committee Annual Report 1991/2*, may show a significant increase in its next report. The figures are also subject to close scrutiny in the DOH's *Children Act Report 1992* (above). Thus, comparisons across all types of protection orders demonstrate the significant, and in the light of the Department's own expressed concerns, potentially very worrying downturn (see Table 2.8 of the report).

There has not just been a downturn in court activity, however. As a follow-up to the issuing of the new version of *Working Together* in 1991, the 1989 Act monitoring survey asked a series of questions around the issue of child protection, designed to complement existing management information returned, and to establish whether the guidance in *Working Together* was being followed. Again, the data returned were extremely interesting from the child protection perspective. The DOH *Children Act Report 1992* comments that as far as the entry of children's names on child protection registers was concerned, there had been a steady upward increase nationally, for numbers on the register, registrations, and deregistrations up to 1991. Numbers on the register, for example, had increased from 41,200 in 1989 to 45,300 in 1991. The publication of *Working Together* in 1991 brought about significant changes with regard to the entry of children's names on the register (see further Chapter 4 above). Whether it was the removal of the 'grave concern' category or simply the combined effect of the emphasis being given to the new philosophy under the 1989 Act supplemented by the guidance given in *Working Together*, the *estimated* numbers on the register at 31 March 1992 have shown a considerable reduction of some 15 per cent and registrations in that period fell by 16 per cent. As the DOH points out, this is the first reduction in either category since national data have been collected (see further the *Children Act Report 1992* (above) at Table 2.9) and it remains to be seen whether this was a real reduction and whether this will be maintained in the second year of the operation of the 1989 Act. Of course, during the first year of the operation of the new *Working Together* guidance, the category of grave concern was still available for use in placing children on the register, but the returns revealed that numbers registered under the grave concern category during the year to 31 March 1992 fell by 37 per cent and numbers on the register under the grave concern category fell by 38 per cent. Whilst the DOH notes that these changes have made virtually no difference to the numbers under the other categories, either for registrations or for numbers on the register, the reduction in the number on the register under 'grave concern' is much less than the DOH had anticipated, although it rightly points out that some authorities were unable to implement changes to review procedures and systems from 14 October 1991. It was indeed the experience in many areas of the country that ACPCs and local authorities generally took three to 12 months to finally make the changes required as a result of the guidance issued in *Working Together*. The DOH points out that it will continue to monitor these figures, but its belief is that the discipline of having to review the reason for registration, the need to re-classify registrations previously categorised under 'grave concern' and the emphasis on 'partnership' under the 1989 Act has had an effect. If this is so, the DOH anticipates that the new pattern of the fall in numbers on the register and the numbers of registrations will continue in future years (see *Children Act Report 1992* (above) at para 2.4(4)).

Despite the optimism expressed by the DOH in relation to registrations, there is still very considerable concern about the numbers of unallocated child protection cases. The report points out that to secure effective intervention, guidance (see *Working Together*, at para 5.15.2) requires that each child on the register must have a named key social worker from either the social services department or the NSPCC. Failure to do so not only prevents progress in carrying out the child protection plan, but reduces opportunities for full parental participation and the views of the child to be taken into account in any decision about his or her future. Where no such key worker has been identified, the child's case was taken to have been unallocated, and questions must be asked about the degree of protection afforded to such children in such circumstances. The DOH notes that at 30 June 1992 the total number of unallocated child protection cases in 104 local authorities was 1,110 or 3.2 per cent of the total on the register. Whilst almost 40 per cent of local authorities were able to allocate all child protection cases to a social worker, 60 per cent could not guarantee total coverage, although those unable to allocate all cases showed considerable variations (see para 2.47 and Figure 2.25). The DOH expresses very grave concern about the non-allocation of cases and emphasises that ACPCs need to receive information about unallocated cases, so that they may take appropriate steps. Perhaps, even more surprisingly, the DOH report identified that there were also unallocated children who were being looked after by local authorities, and that these numbered 2.9 per cent of the total numbers of children being looked after by local authorities. As the DOH report points out, a large number of duties are now laid upon local authorities in respect of children looked after by them, and these essential tasks cannot be achieved without having a social worker allocated to the case. The essential principles enacted by Parliament – parental participation, due regard to issues of race and culture, seeking out the wishes and feelings of the child – are all in jeopardy unless the case is allocated and this must be a particular cause for concern in situations where the child has been abused or has been identified as being at risk.

As far as preventive strategies are concerned, much of the DOH report is taken up with a consideration of local authorities' work in identifying children in need, publishing services in respect of children in need, and monitoring the quality of the provision of such services. As far as determining the groups of children who were to be treated as in need under the provisions of Part III of the 1989 Act, the report indicates that 'it was clear that the highest priority was accorded to children for whom authorities already had some existing responsibility, eg children at risk of significant harm, at risk of neglect, in accommodation or care' (at para 3.8). In the analysis of the provision of present and future services, information revealed that child protection cases were given greater priority in terms of the services which it was possible to offer across the range of local authorities responding. The figures revealed that only respite care for the disabled topped the provision of services to children in need of protection. All of this provides encouraging signs that local authority social services are indeed taking their obligation to take preventive measures, in order to minimise the risk of children in their area already identified as being at risk of suffering ill-treatment and neglect, extremely seriously. The major concern of those working across all agencies, however, is that insufficient resources remain for a more general preventive strategy. (See **4.2** above.)

The report goes on to report the monitoring of work in various other sectors covered by the 1989 Act, including independent schools, residential children's homes, and also looks at the degree to which local authorities have responded to the 'leaving care' provisions of the 1989 Act. The report further considers the provision of the guardian ad litem service and, again, reveals some interesting statistics for involvement of guardians in public law proceedings. Thus, in the period 1 April 1992 to 30 September 1992, there were 7,546 individual applications in public law proceedings in which a guardian was appointed. This suggests, says the DOH, an annual total in excess of 15,000 if the same level of appointment continued throughout the year. The interesting thing about these figures is that they would appear to indicate a vastly higher rate of appointment than that reported in the first Children Act Advisory Committee Report for 1991/92 (see the *Children Act Advisory Committee Annual Report* (above) at Table 4) although a possible reason for this has been discussed in Chapter 3 above. The DOH, in its report, concludes overall that the guardian ad litem service appears to be performing well. It further reports that there are sufficient guardians on panels to undertake work promptly, thus eliminating the delays that had bedevilled the service in some parts of the country before October 1991. It states that the service provided to family proceedings courts and to the higher courts appears to be effective and working well.

The report concludes with surveying a number of issues of concern and also identifying work in progress. Some of these are of specific relevance to the issues of child protection. The DOH reports that two research studies have been commissioned to look at the new provisions concerning child protection. The first study will consider a pre-court stage, in which the child's personal and family circumstances are assessed by the local authority. This will further investigate the process by which cases are handled by the local authority in stages leading up to possible court intervention, focusing on the determination of a child at risk of 'significant harm'. A second study has also been commissioned, entitled 'Statutory Intervention under the Children Act', which will look at compulsory intervention in cases of child protection and its management by the courts. In particular, this study will look at how the new extended menu of orders is used by the courts. In addition, the report identifies other studies, looking at how local authorities are responding to the challenge to extend and improve the provision of family support services to children in need.

The DOH also identifies a need to take specific child care initiatives to respond to specific concerns around a particular child care theme. The report notes (at para 10.22) the child abuse treatment initiative launched in 1990/91. The first stage of the initiative was the National Children's Home survey of existing treatment facilities for abused children and young perpetrators. The DOH, it reports, is currently making grants to support a number of projects by voluntary organisations providing different types and ranges of treatment. In addition, a child abuse training initiative was launched in 1986, and almost £3 million has been awarded since the initiative began.

Whilst the DOH report inevitably concentrates its attention on the performance by local authorities of their duties under the 1989 Act, the first *Children Act Advisory Committee Annual Report 1991/92* (above) concentrates much more specifically on the issues to do with the courts. In addition to the points already noted, it expresses concern about possible delays in the court, and notes that issues to do with the transfer of cases in public law situations have now approached expected levels in some areas. It does, however, note considerable concern about transfers taking place when the appropriate level of judge might not be available within the timetable laid down. It is all very well, as was noted in Chapter 6, for the High Court judges to insist that more difficult cases are transferred to them, but if that transfer then results in further delay to the consideration of the child's case, the basic principles in s 1 of the 1989 Act will be being violated.

The Committee, in its report (above), also expresses a number of concerns about issues relating to guardians ad litem (at paras 11 to 14). The Committee notes concerns about the independence of guardians ad litem, and its fear that guardians' independence may be compromised as paid employees of local authorities. Whilst the Committee acknowledges the substantial safeguards taken to preserve the independence of guardians ad litem, and accepts that funding need not threaten independence, it is equally conscious of the guidance issued in the *Cornwall* case (see Chapter 6) that it is essential that the court and the public should have confidence in the independence of guardians and that guardians themselves should feel confident of their independent status. The Committee states, therefore, that it will continue to monitor the situation and canvass views regionally for evidence of general practical problems and, where necessary, discourage inappropriate pressures. Concern had also surfaced about the fact that legal aid is specifically disallowed for a guardian ad litem who is separately represented from the child (see, further, Chapter 6). The Committee points out that the legal aid system is intended only to provide legal representation for private individuals while the status of the guardian ad litem is part of the public service. In these circumstances, as was pointed out in Chapter 6, the local authority is deemed to be the proper source to pay a guardian ad litem's cost of legal representation, but it has been suggested to the Committee that because the guardian ad litem unquestionably is continuing to represent the child's interests, any distinction in such circumstances is artificial, and that guardians ad litem should be entitled to legal aid when separately represented. The Committee has stated that it will seek to clarify the position and will consider future scope for action.

The Committee report notes the value of family court business committees ('FCBCs') in resolving issues of concern in local areas. Several issues raised as matters of concern for the attention of the Advisory Committee were apparently first identified through FCBCs. The report points out that other problems, such as that of emergency protection orders being granted for very short periods of time in one part of the country, have been resolved by setting up prompt discussions between FCBC chairmen, local justices' clerks and local authorities.

The Committee report goes on to identify issues relating to court forms, and it notes that the requirement to fill in separate forms, even in public law applications, has not proved to be popular. Whilst, however, the Committee is prepared to recommend that there should be only one form per child in private law proceedings, it does not take the same approach in relation to the public law applications, although clearly this will be kept under review by the Committee. Much of the rest of the Committee's report is taken up with issues of private law and is of less concern to those dealing with issues of child protection. Nevertheless, it is worth nothing, as we hope we have illustrated throughout this text, that the 1989 Act has already spawned a considerable body of case-law, demonstrating the very considerable role of the courts in the interpretation of the words of the statutory provisions in individual child protection cases.

When the Children Act 1989 was passed onto the statute book it was variously hailed as a Parents' Charter, a Charter for Children, or as a restructuring of the processes for state intervention in the lives of families and the children living in them. What was inevitable, given that this was a major piece of new legislation, was that the courts would play a very considerable role in interpreting the new provisions and striking a balance between all the various competing claims and interests emerging from the cases. We have chosen to describe the assertions made by all the different parties who might bring actions as 'claims', or 'interests', rather than 'rights' because the 1989 Act itself (see s 3), and the way in which it has been interpreted by the courts (see, for example, *South Glamorgan County Council v W and B* [1993] 1 FLR 574 and *Re CT (A Minor) (Wardship: Representation)* [1993] 2 FLR 278), seem to lean far more heavily in the direction of making adjustments between one person's or body's 'claims' or 'interests' and attempting to determine which may take precedence over another. Whilst the apparent watering down of parental rights in statute law (s 3), was mirrored by the landmark decision in *F v Metropolitan Borough of Wirral DC and Another* [1991] 2 FLR 114, the importance of the sanctity of family life and stricter limits for intervention by the court seemed to receive a countervailing boost in the so-called principle of 'judicial non-interference' or the 'no order' principle (s 1(5)). The enactment of the Child Support Act 1991 and its phased implementation between 1993 and 1996 may also prove to be a very considerable boost to the importance of parental rights, as has been the already very marked retreat from the principles of the *Gillick* decision as exemplified first in *Re R (A Minor) (Wardship: Medical Treatment)* [1992] 1 FLR 190, and subsequently in *Re W (A Minor) (Consent to Medical Treatment)* [1993] 1 FLR 1, and more specifically in relation to the 1989 Act by *Re K, W and H (Minors) (Medical Treatment)* [1993] 1 FLR 854, and *South Glamorgan County Council v W and B* [1993] 1 FLR 574 (see Chapters 3, 4 and 6 above). Whilst judicial non-interference, by reason of s 1(5) of the 1989 Act, might be considered, with other provisions, to be encouraging a resurgence in the precedence to be given to parental claims, interests or responsibilities, judicial paternalism has been perceived as curbing the growth of children's so-called 'rights', and forcing commentators to re-evaluate, in the context of the 1989 Act, whether such 'rights' really exist. As many commentators have pointed out, it makes more sense, and is less misleading, most importantly to children, to describe the rights being asserted by different parties, including the children themselves, as 'claims', 'interests' and 'responsibilities'. (See, for example, MDA Freeman *The Rights and Wrongs of Children* (1983, Frances Pinter); J Eekelaar 'The Emergence of Children's Rights' (1986) *Oxford Journal of Legal Studies* 161; 'The Importance of Thinking that Children have Rights', in Alston, Parker and Seymour (eds) *Children, Rights and the Law* (1992, Clarendon Press).

It is not, perhaps, surprising that if professionals working with children in child protection cases tell the children that they have 'rights', for example to veto a court-ordered medical or psychiatric or other assessment under ss 38(6), 44(7) or 43(8) of the 1989 Act, the children feel cheated and let down when they learn that the High Court, exercising its inherent jurisdiction, can overrule their statute-given 'right' of veto, as happened in *South Glamorgan County Council v W and B* [1993] 1 FLR 574. In that case, Douglas Brown J stated at p 584 that:

> 'In my judgment, the court can in an appropriate case – and they will be rare cases – but in an appropriate case, when other remedies within the Children Act have been used and exhausted and found not to bring about the *desired* result, can resort to other remedies, and the particular remedy here is the remedy of providing authority for doctors to treat this child and authority, if it is needed, for the local authority to take all necessary steps to bring the child to the doctors so that she can be assessed and treated.'

(authors' emphasis added). In this case, the situation was not life-threatening, although the 15-year-old girl's conduct was extremely bizarre and the particular remedy sought was authority for the psychiatrist to treat the child and, if it was needed, for the local authority to take all necessary steps to take the child to the unit so that she could be assessed and/or treated. The court stated that the welfare of the child was its paramount consideration, implicitly asserting, therefore, that the state, through the courts, has a 'claim' or 'interest' in ensuring that a child does not embark on a course of behaviour which might affect the healthy development of the child's mind. This seems to go rather further than what some might perceive as the legitimate 'claim' or 'interest' of the state in not allowing a child to invite his own death, as in *Re E (A Minor) (Wardship: Medical Treatment)* [1993] 1 FLR 386, and *South Glamorgan* (above). It would appear that children, even of the age of 15, cannot be allowed to make decisions which adults, with the support of courts, view as wrong-headed. As Douglas Brown J indicated in the *South Glamorgan* case, it was clear that the child did not wish to go to the unit, but the overwhelming professional views were that the child must be admitted to the unit *in her own interests*. The court would therefore give the local authority the leave which it sought.

It is right to point out here that the judge did emphasise that he had taken into account fully the wishes and feelings of the child, but did not feel that it was in the girl's interests to go along with her wishes. The 'right' of the child to have her wishes and feelings taken fully into consideration, even where it is determined that her welfare takes precedence over her wishes, is perhaps the most important 'right' which professionals should seek to emphasise when working with children, and that what those wishes are, are statements of 'claims' or 'interests' which the child wishes to advance. The court may then be asked to determine whose 'claims' or 'interests' will take precedence, but the crucial point is that the child's view has been heard and accorded due respect and that the child appreciates that this has been done. As J Eekelaar comments:

> 'No social organisation can hope to be built on the rights of its members unless there are mechanisms whereby those members may express themselves and wherein those expressions are taken serioulsy. *Hearing what children say* must therefore lie at the root of any elaboration

of children's rights. No society will have begun to perceive its children as rightholders until adults' attitudes and social structures are seriously adjusted towards making it possible for children to express views and towards addressing them with respect' (J Eekelaar 'The Importance of Thinking that Children have Rights', in Alston, Parker and Seymour (eds) *Children, Rights and the Law* (1993, Clarendon Press)).

The Children Act 1989 goes a little way down the road towards making such adjustments but it is important that we mislead neither ourselves nor the children with whom we are working that it represents, either in its provisions or in its interpretation by the courts, a Charter for Children.

As Booth J comments in her preface to the Committee report, 'the next few years are likely to be busy for all those who are concerned with cases which come before the courts'. She further notes that the job of monitoring the operation of the 1989 Act to ensure that its guiding principles are being achieved, will need to continue until the Advisory Committee can be sure that the way ahead is clear. Booth J's comments in the concluding paragraph of her preface are undoubtedly ones with which most people would agree. She states that:

> 'what can be said with confidence is that the enthusiasm and goodwill that greeted the Act have remained unabated. So, too, has the co-operation of everyone concerned with it. This Report reflects the way in which members of every discipline whose work brings them into contact with the Act have all come together for the first time and have given unstintingly of their time and energy with one object only in mind – to make it work. In these early days we think that they are succeeding and that the guiding principles of the Act are being achieved.'

As we hope we have identified throughout the course of this book, the law now contains a much wider range of powers and responsibilities providing for the protection of children and for the investigation of situations in which children may be said to be at risk than was previously the case. The 1989 Act is still in its infancy and is clearly suffering from a number of teething problems. As this book was going to press, news emerged of the imminent publication of 'One Scandal Too Many – The Case for the Comprehensive Protection of Children in all Settings', a Report of a Working Group convened by the Calouste-Gulbenkian Foundation, (1993, Calouste-Gulbenkian). It was reported that, in the introduction to the Report, the Working Party had stated that 'it is clear that, whatever the intention, the provisions afforded for the protection of children by the law and current policies and practice in all settings are far from adequate'. Considerable scope for improvement remains, therefore, in the field of child protection both by using the legal framework which now exists and by channelling the energies and commitment of all those who are concerned with the protection of children from abuse. Were the aims set by the 1989 Act to be pursued to their logical conclusion using, to their fullest extent, all the various powers and duties set out therein, we would be a considerable way along the road towards eradicating child abuse altogether. The fact that we have yet to fulfil many of the aims of that Act means that much still remains to be done.

As United Nations Secretary-General Javier Pérez de Cuellar stated during the drafting of the UN Convention on the Rights of the Child:

'The way a society treats its children reflects not only its qualities of compassion and protective caring, but also its sense of justice, its commitments to the future and its urge to enhance the human condition for coming generations.'

INDEX